JN049098

瀬戸内国際芸術祭 2022

Setouchi Triennale 2022

瀬戸内国際芸術祭 2022

開催期間	春＝ 2022 年 4 月 14 日（木）～ 5 月 18 日（水） 35 日間 夏＝ 2022 年 8 月 5 日（金）～ 9 月 4 日（日） 31 日間 秋＝ 2022 年 9 月 29 日（木）～ 11 月 6 日（日） 39 日間
会場	直島、豊島、女木島、男木島、小豆島、大島、犬島、沙弥島（春）、本島（秋）、高見島（秋）、粟島（秋）、伊吹島（秋）、高松港周辺、宇野港周辺
テーマ	「海の復権」
参加作家	33 の国と地域から 188 組のアーティストが参加 （作品数 213 点、イベント数 19）※発行日現在
主催	瀬戸内国際芸術祭実行委員会

会長　池田豊人（香川県知事）

名誉会長　真鍋武紀（元香川県知事）

浜田恵造（前香川県知事）

副会長　泉雅文（香川県商工会議所連合会会長）

大西秀人（高松市長）

総合プロデューサー
福武總一郎（公益財団法人 福武財団名誉理事長）

総合ディレクター
北川フラム（アートディレクター）

構成団体＝以下 49 団体
香川県、高松市、丸亀市、坂出市、観音寺市、三豊市、土庄町、小豆島町、直島町、多度津町、玉野市、（公財）福武財団、（公財）福武教育文化振興財団、香川県市長会、香川県町村会、四国経済産業局、四国地方整備局、四国運輸局、中国四国環境事務所四国事務所、国立療養所大島青松園、香川県医師会、四国経済連合会、香川県商工会議所連合会、香川県商工会連合会、（一社）香川経済同友会、香川県農業協同組合、香川県漁業協同組合連合会、香川大学、四国学院大学、徳島文理大学、高松大学、香川県文化協会、（公財）四国民家博物館、（公社）香川県観光協会、（一社）日本旅行業協会中国四国支部香川地区委員会、（公財）高松観光コンベンション・ビューロー、香川県ホテル旅館生活衛生同業組合、四国旅客鉄道（株）、高松琴平電気鉄道（株）、香川県旅客船協会、（一社）香川県バス協会、香川県タクシー協同組合、（公財）香川県老人クラブ連合会、（一社）香川県婦人団体連絡協議会、（公社）日本青年会議所四国地区香川ブロック協議会、香川県青年団体協議会、さぬき瀬戸塾、（株）百十四銀行（監事）、（株）香川銀行（監事）

オブザーバー＝以下 3 団体
岡山市、岡山県商工会議所連合会、岡山大学

SETOUCHI TRIENNALE 2022

Dates: Spring: April 14th – May 18th (35 days)

Summer: August 5th – September 4th (31 days)

Autumn: September 29th – November 6th (39 days)

Location: Naoshima, Teshima, Megijima, Ogijima, Shodoshima, Oshima, Inujima, Shamijima (Spring Only), Honjima (Autumn Only), Takamijima (Autumn Only), Awashima (Autumn Only), Ibukijima (Autumn Only), Takamatsu Port, Uno Port

Theme: Restoration of the Sea

Participating Artists: Featuring 188 artists from 33 countries and regions (213 artworks, 19 events) *To date of publication

Organizer: Setouchi Triennale Executive Committee

President: Toyohito Ikeda (Governor of Kagawa Prefecture)

Honorary President: Takeki Manabe (former Governor of Kagawa Prefecture)

Keizo Hamada (former Governor of Kagawa Prefecture)

Vice President: Masafumi Izumi (President of Kagawa Prefectural Federation of Chambers of Commerce and Industry)

Hideto Onishi (Mayor of Takamatsu City)

General Producer: Soichiro Fukutake (Honorary Chairman, Fukutake Foundation)

General Director: Fram Kitagawa (Art Director)

Affiliated Bodies:
Kagawa Prefecture, Takamatsu City, Marugame City, Sakaide City, Kan-onji City, Mitoyo City, Tonosho Town, Shodoshima Town, Naoshima Town, Tadotsu Town, Tamano City, Fukutake Foundation, Fukutake Education and Culture Foundation, Kagawa Prefectural Association of City Mayors, Kagawa Prefectural Association of Towns and Villages, Shikoku Bureau of Economy, Trade, and Industry, Shikoku Regional Development Bureau, Shikoku Transport and Tourism Bureau, Chugoku-Shikoku Regional Environment Office Shikoku Office, National Sanatorium Oshima Seishoen, Kagawa Medical Association, Shikoku Economic Federation, Kagawa Prefectural Federation of Chambers of Commerce and Industry, Kagawa Prefectural Federation of Societies of Commerce and Industry, Kagawa Association of Corporate Executives, Kagawa Prefectural Agricultural Cooperatives Association, Kagawa Prefectural Federation of Fisheries Associations, Kagawa University, Shikoku Gakuin University, Tokushima Bunri University, Takamatsu University, Kagawa Prefectural Culture Association, Shikokumura Museum Foundation, Kagawa Prefecture Tourism Association, Japan Association of Travel Agents Chugoku-Shikoku chapter Kagawa Branch, Takamatsu Convention and Visitors Bureau, Kagawa Prefectural Hotel and Ryokan Association, Shikoku Railway Company, Takamatsu-Kotohira Electric Railroad Company, Kagawa Prefectural Passenger Boats Association, Kagawa Prefectural Bus Association, Kagawa Prefectural Taxi Cooperatives Society, Kagawa Prefecture Federation of Senior Citizens Clubs, Kagawa Prefecture Women's Organizations Liaison Council, Kagawa Bloc Council of Junior Chamber International Japan, Kagawa Prefecture Council of Youth Societies, Sanuki Seto Juku, 114 Bank, Kagawa Bank

Observers:
Okayama City, Okayama Prefectural Federation of Chambers of Commerce and industry, Okayama University

目次

INDEX

プロジェクト　Projects

記録　Documents

ごあいさつ

池田豊人

瀬戸内国際芸術祭実行委員会会長／香川県知事

瀬戸内国際芸術祭は、「海の復権」をテーマに掲げ、美しい自然と人間が交錯し交響してきた瀬戸内の島々に活力を取り戻し、瀬戸内海が地球上の全ての地域の「希望の海」となることを目指して、2010 年から3年に一度のトリエンナーレ形式で開催してきました。

第5回を迎えた「瀬戸内国際芸術祭 2022」は、前回と同様、瀬戸内海の 12 の島々と2つの港周辺を舞台に、四季折々に変化する瀬戸内の美しい景観を楽しみながら、ゆったりと作品を巡っていただくため、春・夏・秋の3会期に分けて、計 105 日間にわたり開催しました。

今回は、コロナ禍の中での開催となりましたが、「瀬戸内の里海・里山の隠れた資源の発掘と発信」、「国内・世界とのつながりの継続、より質の高い交流への転換」、「瀬戸内の農水産物を活用した『食』の充実・強化」及び「持続可能な社会の実現に向けた取り組みの推進」の4点を重点的な視点として掲げて、さまざまなプロジェクトを展開しました。

特に、アートプロジェクトについては、地元に精通した地域の方々や市町職員をはじめとした関係者の皆様と勉強会や協議を重ね、作品のテーマや設置場所の選定等を行った結果、小豆島の寒霞渓や屋形崎、坂出市の与島、多度津町本通など、これまでの芸術祭で取り上げていなかったエリアでも作品やイベント、アーティストによるワークショップなどを展開し、瀬戸内の魅力ある自然や歴史、文化、生活などとあわせて、多くの来場者に楽しんでいただきました。

開催に当たっては、芸術祭を支えるボランティアサポーター「こえび隊」や「企業・団体ボランティアサポーター」として、作品の制作や受付などに多くの皆様に参加いただき、来場者や地域の方々との交流の輪が広がりました。

また、芸術祭の趣旨に賛同いただける企業・団体に対して協賛を募った結果、262 企業・団体の皆様から過去最多となる現金・現物協賛をいただきました。

さらに、会場の島々では、アーティストとの協働による作品の制作や受付、地域の特色を活かした食の提供やおもてなしのほか、港での島をあげての温かい出迎え、見送りなどに地域の方々が大勢参加し、一緒になって芸術祭を作り上げ、盛り上げ、そして成功に導いていただきました。

会期中の新型コロナウイルス感染症対策については、地域の方々や来場の皆様に安心して芸術祭を楽しんでいただけるよう、飛沫の抑制や手洗い・消毒、換気、密集の回避など基本的な対策はもとより、検温及び体調確認、島での有症状者の発生時の対応など、島ごとの状況に応じた対策を適切に行った結果、芸術祭関係者の間でのクラスターの発生など大きな混乱等はなく、ウィズコロナ時代における大規模イベントの新しいモデルを示すことができたものと考えております。

瀬戸内の島々には、長い歴史の中で培われてきた固有の文化が、美しい景観とともに今も残されています。アートを求めて島々を訪れた人たちは、その作品の素晴らしさのみならず、瀬戸内の島々や、そこに暮らす人々の魅力を存分に感じ取っていただけたのではないでしょうか。島の文化や生活に溶け込んだアートを通じて、国内外の多くの人々に瀬戸内の素晴らしさを体感していただいたことは、この上ない喜びであり、今後も、瀬戸内の魅力を広く積極的に発信するとともに、着実に育ってきた地域の力を、島々をはじめとした瀬戸内地域のよりいっそうの発展につなげてまいりたいと考えています。

芸術祭を盛況のうちに終えることができましたのは、関係者の皆様方の多大なるご尽力の賜物であり、支えていただいた方々や心温かく見守り応援していただいた方々に、心から感謝いたします。

皆様、本当にありがとうございました。

Greetings

Toyohito Ikeda
President, Setouchi Triennale Executive Committee / Governor of Kagawa Prefecture

Under the theme of "Restoration of the Sea", the Setouchi Triennale has been held every three years since 2010. It aims to restore vitality to the islands of the Seto Inland Sea, where beautiful nature and humans have intermingled and resonated with each other for generations, and to make the Seto Inland Sea the "sea of hope" for all regions on earth.

In 2022, the Setouchi Triennale was held for the fifth time over 105 days in three sessions (spring, summer, and autumn) on twelve islands and in two harbors in the Seto Inland Sea. Visitors could enjoy the beautiful scenery as it changed from season to season while leisurely going around to the artworks.

While held amidst the coronavirus pandemic, a variety of projects unfolded. They focused on four key themes: "discovering and highlighting the hidden resources of Setouchi's ocean and mountain forest communities", "maintaining connections with Japan and the world and shifting to higher quality interactions", "enhancing and strengthening food using agricultural and marine products from the Setouchi area", and "promoting efforts to realize a sustainable society".

For the art projects, artwork themes and installation sites were selected after a series of study sessions and discussions with local residents, city and town officials, and other related parties well versed in the local area. This led to artworks, events, and artist workshops also being located in areas that had not been featured in previous years, such as Kankakei and Yakatazaki on Shodoshima Island, Yoshima Island in Sakaide, and Hondori in Tadotsu. Many visitors enjoyed these art projects along with these places' natural environments, history, culture, and daily lives—spheres that are filled with what makes Setouchi a wonderful place.

A great number of people participated in the Triennale as Koebi-tai and corporate/organization volunteer supporters, being involved in artwork production, reception area duties, and more, leading to interactions spanning a wide swath of visitors and local residents.

In addition, after soliciting sponsorship from companies and organizations that would support the objectives of the Triennale, we received a record number of cash and in-kind sponsorships – from 262 companies and organizations.

On the Triennale's islands, many local residents participated by creating artworks in collaboration with the artists, working at reception areas, providing food and hospitality that made the most of local characteristics, and warmly welcoming and sending off visitors in large groups. They worked together to create, enhance, and make the Triennale a success.

Measures were taken to prevent COVID-19 infections. So that local residents and visitors could enjoy themselves with peace of mind, droplet control, hand washing/disinfection, ventilation, anti-crowding, and other basic measures were, of course, in place, as well as measures adopted according to the situation of each island, such as temperature/physical condition checks and addressing symptomatic cases on the islands. As a result, there were no cluster infections amongst people involved in the Triennale or any other major disruptions. We believe that we were able to demonstrate a new model for large-scale events as we live with the coronavirus.

The islands of the Seto Inland Sea still retain their unique culture, nurtured over a long history, along with their beautiful scenery. I believe those who visited the islands in search of art not only enjoyed the artworks' splendor but also fully appreciated what is wonderful about the islands and the people who live on them. It is my greatest pleasure that so many people in Japan and abroad have experienced the splendor of the Seto Inland Sea through art integrated into its islands' culture and daily life. I want to continue actively highlighting the Sea's great characteristics and use the local strength that has steadily developed to further grown its islands and the Setouchi region.

I would like to express my sincere gratitude to all those who supported the Triennale and those who warmly watched and cheered us on. It concluded on a high note thanks to the great efforts of everyone involved.

Thank you.

瀬戸内国際芸術祭2022を終えて

福武總一郎

瀬戸内国際芸術祭 総合プロデューサー／公益財団法人 福武財団 名誉理事長

第5回となった瀬戸内国際芸術祭2022は、春・夏・秋の3会期に渡って、105日間開催されました。新型コロナウイルス感染症の影響下での開催で、準備の段階から、徹底した感染防止対策を講じて、安心安全な芸術祭を第一として、運営を進めてまいりました。多くの方々のご協力のおかげで、大きなトラブルや感染拡大もなく、住民の皆さんにとっては「来られてよし」、来訪者の皆さんにとっては「訪れてよし」の瀬戸芸ができましたことを大変うれしく思います。心より御礼申し上げます。

実行委員会会長である浜田前香川県知事、会長を引き継がれた池田新知事、北川フラム総合ディレクターをはじめ、アーティストの皆さま、県議会および各自治体の市長・町長・議会の皆さま、生活の場を会場としてご提供いただいた住民の皆さま、関連業界団体・関連機関の皆さま、こえび隊の皆さま、さらには、ご協賛やご協力をいただいた企業や個人の皆さまなど、本当に多くの方々に支えていただいて、今回も大変素晴らしい芸術祭になったと思います。重ねて、総合プロデューサーとして、心より感謝申し上げます。

コロナ禍の影響により、来場者数は72万人あまり、前回の瀬戸芸2019に比べて61%にとどまり、特に、前回は24%を占めておりました海外からのお客様は、今回はほとんど来ていただけませんでした。その分、国内のお客様には、じっくりと瀬戸芸を体験していただけたことにつながり、その結果がお客様のアンケートにおいて、満足度および次回の瀬戸芸への期待感のポイントのアップにつながっております。(P.274参照)

特に、この3年間、コロナ禍により、社会も地域も大変閉塞感の強い状況が続いてきました。こうした状況だからこそ、瀬戸芸により、人の行き来、人と人との交流を取り戻し、みんなでいっしょに語らい、感動し、自分自身を見つめ直す。そういう、アートや文化の本来の力を、それぞれのアートが持つメッセージを通して、また、各島の島民の方々との交流を通して、さらには、企業フォーラム、アジアフォーラムなどの各イベントを通して、広く発信できたのではないかと確信しております。特に、気候変動・環境汚染・貧富の格差といった大変大きな社会課題が我々の前に突きつけられている現在、メッセージ性の高い現代アートに向き合い、美しい自然の中に身を置くことによって、本当に持続可能な社会とは何かを、改めて深く考えることは、大変意義があることではないでしょうか。

おかげ様で、瀬戸内国際芸術祭は日本を代表する地域型芸術祭としての評価をいただくまでになりました。しかしながら、瀬戸芸の目的は、決してどこにでもある観光振興ではありません。あくまで、アートの力により、それぞれの地域を元気にしていくことが目的です。すなわち、アーティストが、それぞれの地域の独自の歴史・風土・生活を掘り起こし、自然や食や住民の生活など地域の魅力に光をあて、その場所でしか成立しないアートを住民の方々といっしょに作り上げ、さらには、アートを媒介に住民と来訪者が交流することによって、住民の方々が自分の住んでいる場所の魅力を再発見し、誇りを取り戻していただく。そのプロセスこそがとても大切だと思っています。

その背景には、瀬戸内は国立公園の第1号に選ばれた、世界に誇れる多島美と島ごとに豊かな文化が残っている場所であるにもかかわらず、過度な近代化、都市への一極集中、文化の均質化、経済成長のみを追い求めてきた社会によって、瀬戸内の島々が犠牲になり、負の遺産を負わされてきたという歴史的な経緯に対する強い疑念があります。私は、瀬戸芸をはじめるにあたって、北川さんと、豊島と大島は会場からはずせないと確認しましたが、豊島の産業廃棄物の不法投棄事件と大島のハンセン病の誤った隔離政策は、まさに近代化の負の遺産の象徴として、また二度と起こってならないこととして、これからも後世に受け継いでいかないといけないことだと考えます。

このように、私は、北川さんとともに、瀬戸芸を通して、現代アートを武器に現代社会に対する問題提起をし続けてきました。そして、地方にこそ、経済指標だけでは測れない、本当の豊かさ、本当の幸福があることを、瀬戸芸の活動から来訪者の方々に知っていただきたいと思い、活動してきました。

今回も、瀬戸芸に参加していただくことで、アートから、そうしたメッセージを感じ取っていただき、島々の景観や島民の方々の暮らしから、本当の豊かさとは何かに思いを至らせていただけたのなら、これほどうれしいことはありません。

これからも瀬戸芸の活動を通して、個性と魅力あふれる地域の集合体こそが、これからの日本のあるべき姿であるという文明観を瀬戸内から発信していきたいと思います。

Looking Back on the Setouchi Triennale 2022

Soichiro Fukutake
General Producer, Setouchi Triennale / Honorary Chairman, Fukutake Foundation

The fifth Setouchi Triennale was held in 2022 for 105 days over spring, summer, and autumn sessions. Due to the spread of COVID-19, we took thorough infection prevention measures from the preparation stage and proceeded with peace of mind and safety as our first priority. Thanks to the cooperation of many people, there were no major problems or outbreaks, and I am very glad that locals were happy to have had visitors and visitors were glad to have attended. I would like to offer my sincere gratitude to everyone.

Many people supported us in making this Triennale a great success, including the former governor of Kagawa Prefecture, Mr. Hamada, who served as chairman of the Executive Committee, the new governor, Mr. Ikeda, who succeeded him as chairman, General Director Fram Kitagawa, the artists, the prefectural assembly, the mayors, and council members of each municipality, the residents who let us use their daily life space as venues, related industry groups and organizations, the Koebi-tai, and all the companies and individuals who sponsored and cooperated with the holding of the Triennale. Again, as the general producer, I would like to thank you from the bottom of my heart.

Due to the pandemic, the number of visitors was just over 720,000, 61% of the people who came to the 2019 Triennale. There were particularly few people from abroad, who accounted for 24% of visitors in 2019. This led to domestic visitors being able to experience the Triennale in a more leisurely fashion, which in turn led to an increase in their satisfaction and excitement for the next edition in our visitor survey (see p.274).

In particular, the past three years have been very stagnant in both society and the region due to the pandemic. It is precisely because of this situation that due to the Triennale, with the flow of people and interactions between them being restored, everyone talked together, was moved, and looked at themselves afresh. I am confident that we were able to widely communicate the inherent power of art and culture through the message of each artwork, through interactions with the people on each island, and through events such as the Corporate Forum and the Asia Forum. Especially at a time when we are faced with major social issues like climate change, environmental pollution, and the wealth gap, it is very meaningful to reflect on what a truly sustainable society really means by encountering contemporary art, which has a strong message, and by being in the midst of beautiful natural environments.

Thanks to your support, the Setouchi Triennale has earned a reputation as one of Japan's leading regional art festivals. However, its purpose is by no means under the ubiquitous banner of "tourism promotion". The sole purpose is to energize each community through the power of art. In other words, artists dig up areas' unique histories, customs, and lifestyles, shed light on what makes each place special (including the natural environment, the food, and the local residents' lives), and work with residents to create art that is only possible in particular places. Also, by using art as a medium for interaction between residents and visitors, local people rediscover the charm of their homes and regain pride in it. I believe that process is very important.

Why? Because I am trouble by the history of the Seto Inland Sea – the first national park in Japan and a place of world-class beauty with many islands and rich culture. Its islands were sacrificed and burdened with a negative legacy due to excessive modernization, the concentration of populations in cities, the homogenization of culture, and a society that has pursued only economic growth. When I started the Triennale, I confirmed with Mr. Kitagawa that the islands Teshima and Oshima would not be excluded from the Triennale venue list. The illegal dumping of industrial waste on Teshima and the misguided leprosy patient isolation policy on Oshima must be shared with future generations as symbols of the negative legacy of modernization and as things that must never happen again.

Thus, with Mr. Kitagawa, I have continued raising issues to contemporary society through the Triennale, using contemporary art as a weapon. I have also been working to help visitors sense from the Triennale's activities that true wealth and true happiness, which cannot be measured by economic indicators alone, are to be found in areas outside of major urban centers.

I would be more than happy if participants in this Triennale sensed this message from the art and also felt true richness from the islands' landscapes and the lives of their residents.

Through the activities of the Triennale, I will continue to transmit from Setouchi my view that Japanese civilization should be a collection of regions full of individuality and charm.

瀬戸内国際芸術祭2022を振り返って

浜田恵造

瀬戸内国際芸術祭実行委員会名誉会長／前香川県知事

瀬戸内国際芸術祭2022が、県内外から大勢の来場者をお迎えして成功裡に終了したことを、心からお喜び申し上げます。

私は、第1回目の瀬戸内国際芸術祭2010が開催されていた2010年9月5日に香川県知事に就任し、当時の真鍋武紀知事から、瀬戸内国際芸術祭実行委員会会長の職を受け継ぎました。第5回目の瀬戸内国際芸術祭2022は、私にとっても5度目の芸術祭となりましたが、夏会期の閉幕日である2022年9月4日に香川県知事の任期が満了し、会長の職を池田豊人知事に引き継ぐという巡り合わせになりました。

時代が大きく変化する中、瀬戸内国際芸術祭は当初から『海の復権』を掲げ、現代アートと瀬戸内の美しい自然や文化、歴史を同時に体感する独特の魅力や地域再生の取り組みが多くの方々の共感を得て、さらに、高松空港の国際化の推進や、日本の豊かな四季を感じられる春・夏・秋の3会期の開催を進めたことも相俟って、世界の注目を集めるものとなりました。世界中から人々が集い、そこに暮らす人々との新たな出会いが生まれ、それが地域の元気につながり、移住者の増加や男木島の学校の再開、インフラ整備の維持・強化、「SETOUCHI」のブランド化など、芸術祭の取り組みが少しずつ社会的変化を生んできたことは喜ばしいことです。

今回の瀬戸内国際芸術祭2022について、夏会期の閉幕までを振り返ってみると、瀬戸内国際芸術祭実行委員会総会で開催が正式決定され準備が本格化した2020年4月の段階から、すでに新型コロナウイルス感染症が大きな問題となっており、島民の皆様の声もうかがいながら、福武総合プロデューサーや北川総合ディレクターとも相談を重ねて対策に取り組んだことが、まず思い出されます。

当初、私としては、瀬戸内国際芸術祭は、会場が屋外中心であり、比較的、感染症には強いイベントではないかと考えていました。しかし、2021年12月に、先行事例として、千葉県市原市で開催されていた「房総里山芸術祭 いちはらアート×ミックス2020＋」の感染対策を視察したところ、あくまで、医療体制が比較的充実した都市近郊の陸地での取り組みであり、会場の多くが医療体制の脆弱な離島である瀬戸内国際芸術祭では、よりいっそうの対策が求められるということを感じました。

そうした経験も踏まえ、瀬戸内国際芸術祭2022に向けては、感染症対策の指針を独自に策定し、マスクの着用や手洗い・消毒、換気などの基本的な対策に加え、来場者の検温や島での有症状の発生時の対応など、会場の島ごとの状況に応じた対策を行うこととしました。当初は、開催自体を懸念する声もありましたが、指針に沿った適切な対策が講じられたことで、最後まで大きな問題が生じなかったことを嬉しく思っています。

今回、特に印象に残ったこととして、春会期に、寬仁親王妃信子殿下に御視察いただいたことがあげられます。地域の文化芸術や地方の状況等に高い関心をお持ちの信子殿下の瀬戸内国際芸術祭御視察は、2016年と2019年に続いて、3回目となりました。今回は、2日間の日程で、駆け足になりましたが、屋島山上交流拠点施設「やしまーる」や直島の《ヴァレーギャラリー》などを御案内し、改めて芸術祭に対する高い評価をいただきました。瀬戸内国際芸術祭2022が殿下の御視察により、いっそう、意義深いものとなりましたことを、この場をお借りして、お礼申し上げます。

また、今回は、コロナ禍でボランティアサポーターが集まりにくく、大変であったとうかがいました。そうした中、作品の制作や受付に御協力いただいた多くの皆様に感謝申し上げます。夏会期の閉幕日には、「こえび隊」の皆様に、お別れの会として、素晴らしいパフォーマンスを披露していただき、思い出深い1日となりました。

最後になりますが、今後、インバウンドの復活が期待される中で、バリアフリーや脱炭素といった社会的な課題への対応も十分展望していきながら、瀬戸内国際芸術祭が、夢のある国際芸術祭として、また、世界の「瀬戸芸」として益々発展していくことを心より祈念し、お祝いの言葉といたします。

Setouchi Triennale 2022: Reflections

Keizo Hamada
Honorary President, Setouchi Triennale Executive Committee / former Governor of Kagawa Prefecture

I would like to express my sincere congratulations on the successful conclusion of the Setouchi Triennale 2022. The festival welcomed many visitors from within and outside of the prefecture.

I became the governor of Kagawa Prefecture on September 5th, 2010, when the first Setouchi Triennale was being held, and took over the position of Executive Committee president from the previous governor Takeki Manabe. 2022 was the fifth time the Setouchi Triennale was held, and it was also the fifth time I was involved. It happened that on September 4th, 2022, the closing day of the summer session, my term as governor ended, and I handed over the position of president to Toyohito Ikeda.

Amidst drastically changing times, the Setouchi Triennale has, from the very beginning, adopted the slogan of the "Restoration of the Sea". It has a unique appeal – experiencing contemporary art and the beautiful nature, culture, and history of the Setouchi area simultaneously – and works to revitalize the region. This all is clearly speaking to many people. Also, the increase in international flights at Takamatsu Airport, coupled with the festival being held in three sessions (spring, summer, and autumn), allowing visitors to experience Japan's rich seasons, has resulted in the Triennale attracting worldwide attention. As people from around the world have gathered and met people who live in the area, producing local vitality, it is gratifying to see that the efforts of the Triennale have gradually produced social change, such as an increase in the number of new residents, the school reopening on Ogijima, the maintenance and strengthening of infrastructure, and the emergence of Setouchi as an international brand.

Looking back on the Setouchi Triennale 2022 up through the end of the summer session, I recall that COVID-19 infections had already become a major issue in April 2020, when the General Meeting of the Executive Committee officially decided to hold the Triennale and preparations began in earnest, and that we had consulted with the island residents, as well as with General Producer Fukutake and General Director Kitagawa, to adopt anti-infection measures.

Initially, I thought the Setouchi Triennale would be relatively infection-resistant because the venues are mainly outdoors. However, examining the set of infection control measures at the Boso Satoyama Art Festival Ichihara Art x Mix 2020+ held in Ichihara, Chiba, as a precedent, I realized that they were implemented in a mainland area near a city with a relatively well-developed medical system and that more measures would be required at the Triennale, where most venues are on remote islands with weak medical systems.

Drawing from this experience and other information, we formulated our own guidelines for infectious disease countermeasures. In addition to basic measures such as wearing masks, washing and disinfecting hands, and ventilation, we also decided to implement measures appropriate for each venue island, such as temperature checks for visitors and addressing infections that would occur on the islands. Although there were some initial concerns about whether to hold the Triennale, I am pleased that appropriate measures were taken per our guidelines and that no major problems arose.

One of the most memorable events of the spring session was the visit by Her Imperial Highness Princess Tomohito of Mikasa. This was her third visit, following 2016 and 2019. She is very interested in local arts and culture and the situations in areas outside of major urban centers. Although her two-day stay was short, we were able to show her around the *Yashima Mountaintop Park "Yashimâru"* and the *Valley Gallery*. She offered considerable praise of the Triennale. I would like to take this opportunity to thank Her Highness for making the Setouchi Triennale 2022 even more meaningful through her visit.

I also heard that it was difficult to gather volunteer supporters this time due to the pandemic. I would like to express my gratitude to the many people who cooperated in producing artworks and working reception area in. On the closing day of the summer session, the koebi-tai gave a wonderful farewell performance, making it a memorable day.

I am delighted that the Triennale was a success. While addressing social issues such as barrier-free access and decarbonization, I sincerely hope it will continue to grow and develop as a world-class, dream-filled international art festival as inbound tourism returns to normal.

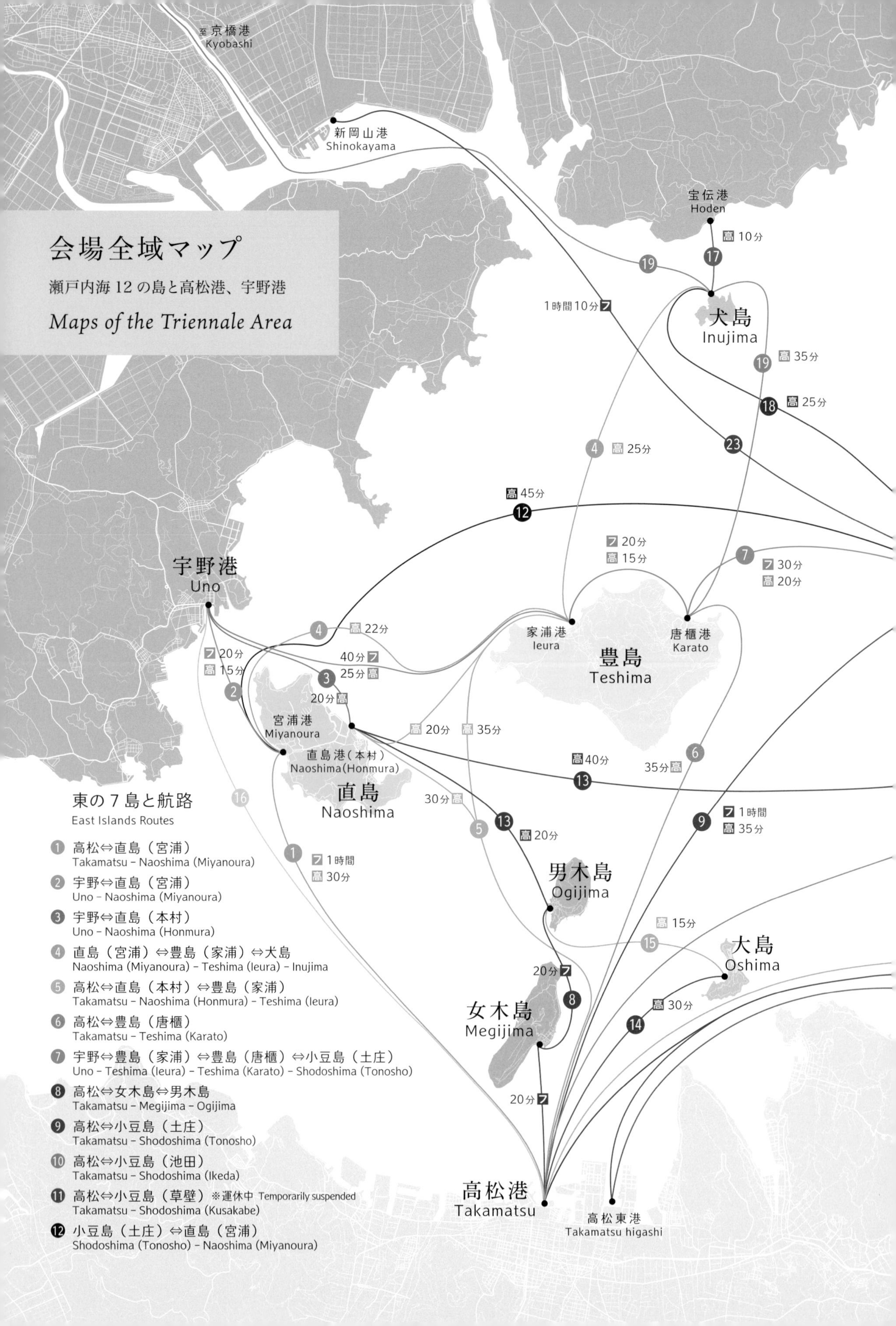

会場全域マップ
瀬戸内海12の島と高松港、宇野港
Maps of the Triennale Area
至 京橋港
Kyobashi
新岡山港
Shinokayama
宝伝港
Hoden
高 10分
1時間10分 フ
犬島
Inujima
高 35分
高 25分
高 25分
高 45分
フ 20分
高 15分
フ 30分
高 20分
宇野港
Uno
高 22分
フ 20分
高 15分
40分 フ
25分 高
20分 高
家浦港
Ieura
唐櫃港
Karato
豊島
Teshima
宮浦港
Miyanoura
高 20分
高 35分
直島港（本村）
Naoshima(Honmura)
高40分
35分 高
直島
Naoshima
30分 高
フ 1時間
高 35分
高 20分
フ 1時間
高 30分
男木島
Ogijima
高 15分
大島
Oshima
20分 フ
高 30分
女木島
Megijima
20分 フ
高松港
Takamatsu
高松東港
Takamatsu higashi
東の7島と航路
East Islands Routes
1 高松⇔直島（宮浦）
Takamatsu – Naoshima (Miyanoura)
2 宇野⇔直島（宮浦）
Uno – Naoshima (Miyanoura)
3 宇野⇔直島（本村）
Uno – Naoshima (Honmura)
4 直島（宮浦）⇔豊島（家浦）⇔犬島
Naoshima (Miyanoura) – Teshima (Ieura) – Inujima
5 高松⇔直島（本村）⇔豊島（家浦）
Takamatsu – Naoshima (Honmura) – Teshima (Ieura)
6 高松⇔豊島（唐櫃）
Takamatsu – Teshima (Karato)
7 宇野⇔豊島（家浦）⇔豊島（唐櫃）⇔小豆島（土庄）
Uno – Teshima (Ieura) – Teshima (Karato) – Shodoshima (Tonosho)
8 高松⇔女木島⇔男木島
Takamatsu – Megijima – Ogijima
9 高松⇔小豆島（土庄）
Takamatsu – Shodoshima (Tonosho)
10 高松⇔小豆島（池田）
Takamatsu – Shodoshima (Ikeda)
11 高松⇔小豆島（草壁）※運休中 Temporarily suspended
Takamatsu – Shodoshima (Kusakabe)
12 小豆島（土庄）⇔直島（宮浦）
Shodoshima (Tonosho) – Naoshima (Miyanoura)

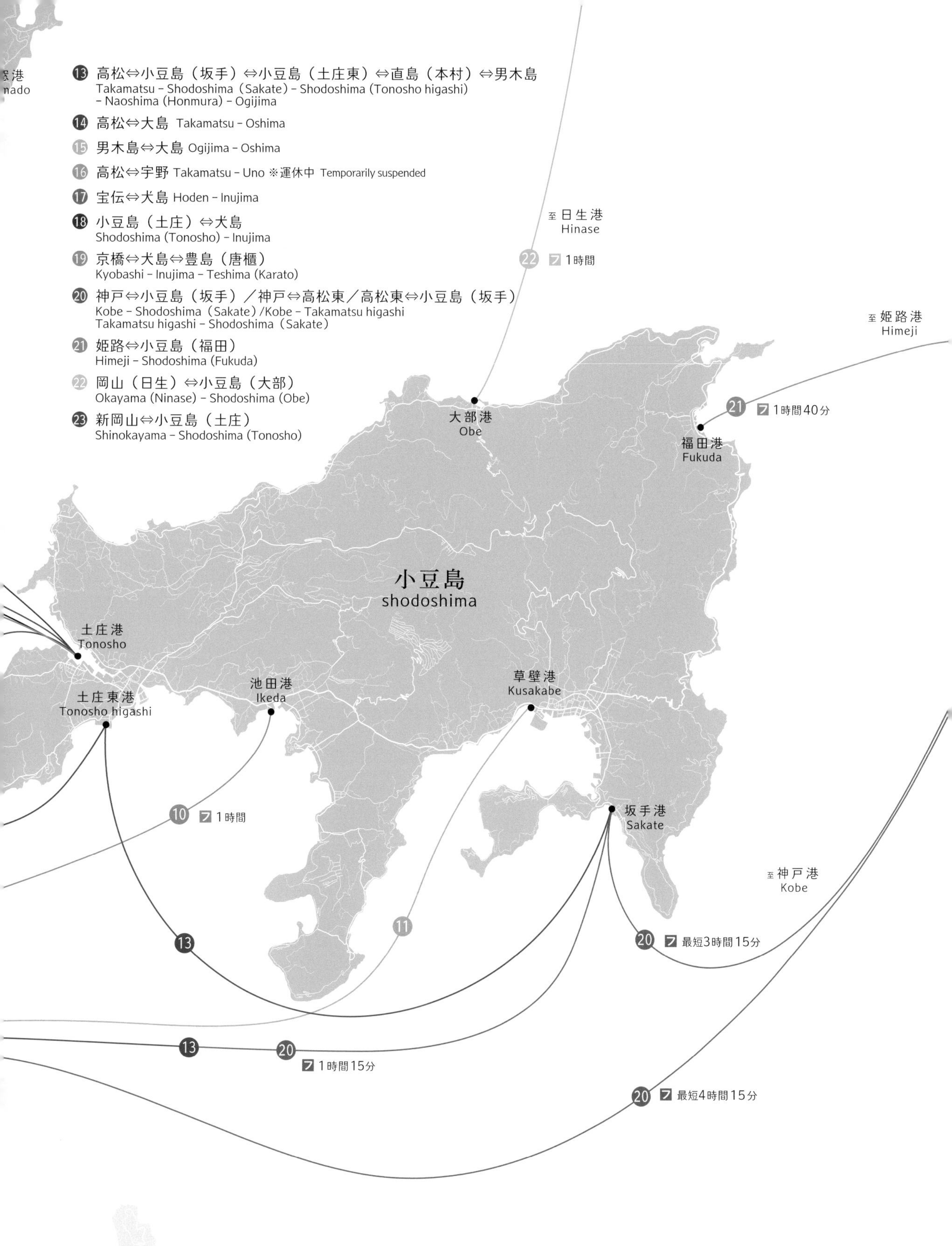

航路は、瀬戸内国際芸術祭 2022 会期中のものです。 フ フェリー 高 高速船
Sea Routes during the Setouchi Triennale 2022 sessions.

西の５島と航路
West Islands Routes

1. 丸亀⇔牛島⇔本島
   Marugame – Ushijima – Honjima
2. 児島観光⇔本島
   Kojima kanko – Honjima
3. 多度津⇔高見島⇔佐柳島（本浦）⇔佐柳島（長崎）
   Tadotsu – Takamijima – Sanagijima (Honura) – Sanagijima (Nagasaki)
4. 須田⇔粟島⇔粟島（上新田）⇔志々島⇔宮の下
   Suda – Awashima – Awashima (Kamishinden) – Shishijima – Miyanoshita
5. 本島⇔高見島⇔粟島
   Honjima – Takamijima – Awashima
6. 観音寺⇔伊吹島
   Kan-onji – Ibukijima

伊吹島
Ibukijima
25分
観音寺港
Kan-onji

航路は、瀬戸内国際芸術祭 2022 会期中のものです。 フ フェリー 高 高速船
Sea Routes during the Setouchi Triennale 2022 sessions.

瀬戸内国際芸術祭の経緯とあゆみ

History of the Setouchi Triennale

2022年、第5回展を迎えた瀬戸内国際芸術祭のこれまでの経緯とあゆみを振り返る

We trace the history of the Setouchi Triennale, and the path it has taken up to the 5th edition in 2022

1985

福武哲彦と三宅親連が出会う 直島

瀬戸内の島に、世界中の子どもたちが集える場を作りたいとの思いを抱いていた福武書店の福武哲彦社長（当時）が、直島の南側一体を教育的な文化エリアとして開発する夢を描いていた三宅親連町長（当時）と出会う。

Tetsuhiko Fukutake, the president and founder of the Fukutake Publishing, met the Mayor Chikatsugu Miyake.

1989

直島国際キャンプ場オープン 直島

1986年に急逝した福武哲彦の遺志を引き継ぎ、福武總一郎（以下、福武）によって子どもたちが瀬戸内の自然を体感できる場所が安藤忠雄監修のもとで整備された。ここから福武と安藤による直島のアートと建築による地域づくりが始まる。

Enacting the vision of Tetsuhiko Fukutake, who suddenly passed away, Soichiro Fukutake opened the Naoshima International Camp Site, which was supervised by Tadao Ando.

1992

ベネッセハウスオープン 直島

Benesse House opened.

1998

本村地区で「角屋」を皮切りに家プロジェクトが始まる 直島

Art House Project opened.

2004

香川県庁若手職員グループ「アートアイランドトリエンナーレ」開催を知事に提言

以前から香川県にはイサム・ノグチや丹下健三など優れたアーティストや建築家の作品が集積しており、その蓄積を生かそうと2003年から「アートツーリズム」を推進する取り組みが始まる。アートによる地域活性化の方策を模索する中、若手職員グループは島々を舞台にした国際美術展の開催を知事に提言した。

A group of young workers at the Kagawa Prefectural Office proposed holding an international art exhibition set on the islands.

地中美術館オープン 直島 Chichu Art Museum opened.

2005

公開シンポジウム「瀬戸内アートネットワークの可能性」開催 高松

（直島福武美術館財団主催、国土交通省四国地方整備局・香川県共催）

The public symposium “The Possibilities of Setouchi Art Network” was conducted.

[SOh]

2006

北川フラム、福武が瀬戸内国際芸術祭を構想

新潟県十日町市・津南町で2000年から始まった「大地の芸術祭　越後妻有アートトリエンナーレ」の第2回展に福武が訪れる。過疎の広大なエリアで展開するアートプロジェクトや、住民やサポーターとの協働に賛同し、第3回展から福武が総合プロデューサーを務めた。2006年秋、総合ディレクターの北川フラム（以下、北川）に、瀬戸内の島々で構想している芸術祭への協力を打診し、瀬戸内国際芸術祭に向けて本格的な動きが始まった。

Soichiro Fukutake asked Fram Kitagawa to collaborate with a planned art festival in the Setouchi Islands.

「直島スタンダード2」が開幕、直島全体を使った展覧会が話題に

"Naoshima Standard 2" started.

2007

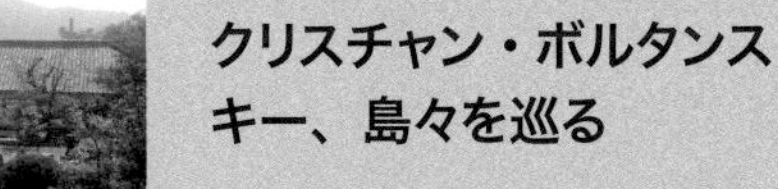

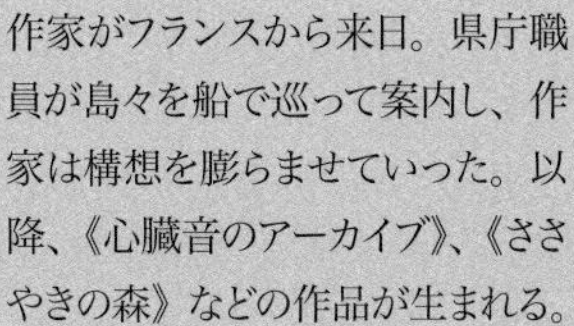

北川、島巡りをはじめる

Kitagawa began examining the islands.

やさしい美術プロジェクト高橋伸行が大島初来島

Artists visited Oshima for the first time.

クリスチャン・ボルタンスキー、島々を巡る

作家がフランスから来日。県庁職員が島々を船で巡って案内し、作家は構想を膨らませていった。以降、《心臓音のアーカイブ》、《ささやきの森》などの作品が生まれる。

Christian Boltanski went around the islands to plan his work.

2008

[DAn]

犬島アートプロジェクト「精錬所※」オープン　犬島

明治時代、銅製錬所ができ一時は人口3,000人にもなった犬島。工場閉鎖後、長い間放置されていた製錬所跡が、アーティスト柳幸典と建築家 三分一博志によって美術館へと生まれ変わった。その後も集落の中でアートや建築を展開する「犬島『家プロジェクト』」や《犬島 くらしの植物園》が続き、作品鑑賞に加え、環境や社会問題を考える場所として多くの人が島を訪れている。

※＝後の犬島精錬所美術館

Inujima Art Project's "Seirensho" (later renamed the Inujima Seirensho Art Museum) opened.

瀬戸内国際芸術祭実行委員会設立

Setouchi Triennale Executive Committee was set up.

2009

初のアーティスト公募ツアーを開催

The first open call for artists took place.

こえび隊が誕生

北川や実行委は、多くの人が主体的に島や芸術祭に関われる仕組みとしてサポーター組織を構想。2009年の夏、県庁職員やサポーター事務局が「大地の芸術祭」のこへび隊に参加し、芸術祭のいろはを学ぶ。秋にこえび隊が発足し、募集が始まった。初回の説明会には約100名が参加。以降、世界中へサポーターネットワークが広がった。

The koebi-tai volunteer group was established.

各島にて住民説明会が始まる

住民を対象に芸術祭の概要やアート作品を紹介する説明会が各島で行われた。それまで観光客があまり訪れなかった一部の島では、芸術祭参加に懐疑的な意見もあったが、県庁職員や北川を中心に熱心な話し合いが行われた。

Orientations explaining the outline of the festival and introducing artwork to local residents were conducted on each island.

瀬戸内国際芸術祭 2010 開催

[ON]

はじめての芸術祭は7月19日に開幕。朝7時、高松港ではこえび隊や県庁職員が集まり朝礼が行われ、エイエイオーの掛け声とともに島に向かった。高松港で開かれた開会式にはアーティストや関係者、さらに近隣の漁船も大漁旗を掲げて駆け付け、青空のもと、賑々しく行われた。開幕当初は戸惑いがちだった島の住民らも、遠方から訪れる来場者に道や島について尋ねられることも多くなり、自主的に案内に立つ人や商品を売る人も現れる。会期半ばには真鍋前知事（当時）から浜田恵造新知事（当時）にバトンが渡された。大岩オスカール作品が火災で焼失し、翌日男木島全島休館という出来事もあった。秋には豊島美術館がオープンし、さらに来場者が増え、90万人を突破。当初予定の3倍以上となった。10月31日、3カ月に渡る芸術祭は閉幕し、一部作品の継続公開が決定した。

本芸術祭は18の国と地域から75組のアーティスト・プロジェクトと16のイベントが参加。会場は直島、豊島、女木島、男木島、小豆島、大島、犬島、高松港。2010年7月19日から計105日間開催した。

Setouchi International Art Festival 2010
The festival featured 75 art projects, and 16 performance events. The participating artists came from 18 countries and regions. The venues were Naoshima, Teshima, Megijima, Ogijima, Shodoshima, Oshima, Inujima, and Takamatsu Port. It was open to the public for 105 days, from July 19th.

2010

島の学校巡回版画展

会場以外の島の子どもたちにも美術の楽しさに触れてほしいと、岩黒島や伊吹島などの学校を訪問して、版画の展示と北川によるレクチャーを行った。

The Island School Print Exhibition Tour for the children of islands that were not part of the festival was held.

アーティストが続々と来島、空き家掃除、作品制作が始まる

住民説明会と並行して、国内外のアーティストたちが来島し、こえび隊と一緒に空き家掃除や作品制作を進めた。全員がはじめての経験であり手探りではあったが、住民の協力もあり、各島で次々に作品が完成していった。

Artists came to the islands one after another. They began cleaning vacant houses and developing their productions with koebi-tai and local residents.

[NM]

李禹煥美術館、豊島美術館がオープン　直島・豊島

The Lee Ufan Museum and Teshima Art Museum opened.

2011

男木島で32年ぶりに結婚式が行われる　男木島

高松市男木交流館のジャウメ・プレンサ《男木島の魂》で、32 年ぶりに結婚式が行われた。新郎新婦が前年の芸術祭で島を訪れたのがきっかけで、当日は島の住民らやこえび隊、北川や大西秀人高松市長も参列し、賑やかな式となった。式のあと新郎新婦は定期船めおんに乗って移動し、女木島で披露宴が開かれた。

A wedding was held in Ogijima for the first time in 32 years, and was celebrated by residents and koebi-tai.

こえび隊による地元の祭りや運動会・文化祭の手伝いが本格的に始まる

芸術祭は地域の理解があってはじめて取り組める活動である。そのためには島をよく知り、丁寧に島に入っていく必要がある。2009 年から少しずつ始まった地域行事への参加が、芸術祭の継続が決まり本格化した。説明会や意見交換会では聞けない住民の声を聞くことができる大切な活動だ。

Koebi-tai started to participate in local festivals, sports days and the cultural festival.

2012

Setouchi Triennale という名称が決まる

The name Setouchi Triennale was decided upon.

[KiT]

瀬戸内海底探査船美術館プロジェクトが粟島で始まる　粟島

初回の芸術祭で将来プロジェクトとして発表した日比野克彦の作品。2011 年のシンポジウム、2012 年の豊島沖調査を経て、2013 年から海洋記念館のある粟島にプロジェクトが引き継がれた。海底の遺物に思いを馳せる《ソコソコ想像所》や海底探査船《一昨日丸》などが登場。2019 年には「種は船プロジェクト」がスタートし、2022 年は「TANeFUNe」が島々を巡った。

Katsuhiko Hibino's *Project for the Museum of Seabed Inquiry Ship in Setouchi* began in Awashima.

島間交流が始まる

かつて漁船などが頻繁に行き交っていた時代は周辺の島との交流や婚姻が盛んだったが、近年は航路がつながっている島のみの交流にとどまっていた。芸術祭を機に舞台となる島同士の交流を促進しようと島間交流が始まる。テレビなどでしか見たことのなかった島へ行き、アート作品の鑑賞や座談会を行った。お互いの地域の課題を共有するなど、住民らにとっても刺激となる取り組みとなった。

Residents of the art festival venues began to visit each other's islands

2013

福武ハウスに参加する7つの地域の団体のキュレーターなどが島々を巡る　小豆島

2009年に閉校になった福田小学校の校舎を利用して「福武ハウス―アジア・アート・プラットフォーム」が構想される。そこをプラットフォームにアジアのさまざまな美術組織がつながり協働しようという動きだ。初の共同展に向けて7つの地域の団体がパートナーとして参加。各団体が選出したキュレーターやアーティストが瀬戸内を訪れた。

Curators and artists from seven regional organizations which took part in Fukutake House went around the islands.

[KiT]

五十嵐靖晃《そらあみ》制作が始まる　与島5島

与島地区5島の住民と作家による、漁網を編む作品づくりがスタートした。瀬戸大橋の架橋によって海のご近所付き合いがなくなってから25年、作品を通して5つの島がつながった。2016年は塩飽諸島の10島で制作、沙弥島・本島で展示し、2019年は14島の約500名が参加した。

The workshops of *Sora-Ami* were held in the Yoshima Goto Area.

2点とも[KiT]

EAT & ART TAROが《島スープ》の試作と島の婦人会メンバーと交流　沙弥島

食とアートを融合させる作家による、島の食にフォーカスを当てた作品。島の特徴を調べ、それぞれ特有のスープを作り提供した。ここから芸術祭の食の可能性が拓かれていく。

Activities by creator of food and art EAT&ART TARO began.

高見島での作品制作が始まる　高見島

京都精華大学有志による「高見島プロジェクト」がスタートした。作家らが家探しや改修を行うなど、会期外も継続的に島に通い、元住民やサポーターらとともに活動した。

The Takamijima Project by a group of artists from Kyoto Seika University began on Takamijima.

瀬戸内国際芸術祭 2013 開催

春・夏・秋に会期を分け、会場は12島へ広がった。小豆島は島全体に作品を展開し、高松港では「高松港・アート工房―ベンガル島―」や「丹下健三生誕100周年プロジェクト」が行われるなど、前回展より規模も内容も充実した開催となった。沙弥島は春、伊吹島は夏、本島・高見島・粟島は秋に開幕。「現代源平屋島合戦絵巻」は歴史的ランドスケープを活かした市民参加型イベントで、パフォーミング・アーツの新たな方向性を打ち出した。女木島の「世界の子ども創作劇プロジェクト『海へのお話～トーベ・ヤンソンに捧ぐ～』」は、大島子どもサマーキャンプのキックオフとして位置づけられ、「瀬戸内国際芸術祭＋三越伊勢丹コラボエキシビジョン」など企業との協働も前進した。

[KiT]

本芸術祭は26の国と地域から200組のアーティスト・プロジェクトと40のイベントが参加。会場は直島、豊島、女木島、男木島、小豆島、大島、犬島、沙弥島、本島、高見島、粟島、伊吹島、高松港、宇野港。2013年3月20日から春・夏・秋の3会期、計108日間開催した。

Setouchi Triennale 2013
The festival featured 200 art projects, and 40 performance events. The participating artists came from 26 countries and regions. The venues were Naoshima, Teshima, Megijima, Ogijima, Shodoshima, Oshima, Inujima, Shamijima, Honjima, Takamijima, Awashima, Ibukijima, Takamatsu Port and Uno Port. It was open to the public for a total of 108 days from March 20th, split between spring, summer, and autumn sessions.

2014

男木小・中学校が3年ぶりに再開　男木島

2011年3月に中学生3名が卒業し、惜しまれつつ休校となった男木小・中学校。その校舎は、2013年の芸術祭で昭和40年会によってユニークで活気のあるアートな学校に生まれ変わった。このときの体験がきっかけとなり数組の家族が島に移住。多くの協力者の署名活動もあり、2014年4月に小・中学校が再開した。全国的にも珍しい事例で、多くのメディアに取り上げられた。

Ogi Elementary and Junior High School reopened three years after closure, thanks to immigration of families.

「島のお誕生会」が始まる　豊島

2010年に唐櫃岡集落にできたアート作品《島キッチン》は、豊島の食の豊かさを伝えるレストランとして人気を博した。継続営業が決まり、より地域に開かれた場所になるべく「島のお誕生会」が始まる。毎月開催される催しでは、島に住む赤ちゃん連れの親子や100歳のおばあちゃん、海外からの来場者も一緒にお祝いをしている。三味線演奏や島の子どもたちのダンスなど老若男女に喜んでもらえる出し物が人気で、毎月の開催前には島の全戸に手書きの新聞を配布、島キッチンを飛び出して、各集落で開催する出張お誕生会も開催している。地域に根付く芸術祭の代表的な取り組み。

The monthly event *Island Birthday Party* began at Shima Kitchen on Teshima.

四国新聞に「こえび新聞号外 瀬戸内海2025年新聞」が掲載

新聞の見開き全面に、12年後の瀬戸内の島々の様子を発表。芸術祭の取り組みが各島の将来にどうつながるかをイラストで描いた。

“Koebi-Shinbun: Seto Islands Sea 2025 Newspaper” was featured in the *Shikoku Shinbun*.

大島の在り方を考える会

ハンセン病療養所のある大島は、芸術祭構想の段階から福武や北川が参加を強く希望した島である。入所者の希望に伴走した丁寧な交流が2007年から続き、島の歴史や入所者の記憶を伝えるアート作品の展示や、こえび隊によるガイド、来島者と入所者をつなぐ《カフェ・シヨル》の運営などを行っている。大島を訪れた来場者の中には大島で起こったことをはじめて知る人も多かった。第1回展で4,800人が大島を訪れ、会期外もこえび隊らの活動が継続。これらを受け、第2回展の開催時、高松市によって「大島の在り方を考える会」が立ち上がる。2014年には芸術祭の取り組みを盛り込んだ「大島振興方策」が策定され、2015年の離島振興対策実施地域の指定につながっていく。

Through exhibitions and explanations by supporters that conveyed the history of Oshima and the memories of the residents at the Hansen’s disease sanatorium there, many people learned about the island. Based on changes brought about by the art festival, Takamatsu City held “Meeting to Discuss Oshima” with specialists, to discuss the future of Oshima.

2015

「瀬戸内『食』のフラム塾」を開講

食はその土地の特徴や生活をよく表す。しかし、島には飲食店が少なく、瀬戸内らしい食事を楽しめる場がないという反省から、第3回展に向けて講座を開講した。100名以上の参加者が全国から集まり、地域の食の大切さや芸術祭における食の展開を学んだ。成果として9つのプロジェクトが認定され、会期中に島や港で受講生らが食を提供。この塾を起点に「本からうまれる一皿　壺井栄と庚申の夜」や「レストラン イアラ女木島」、野村正人《海のテラス》や指輪ホテル「讃岐の晩餐会」など食の展開が一気に拡がった。2017年、"食文化"を明記した文化芸術基本法が成立する。

Seminars to educate about the significance of local food and the development of cuisine at the art festival were held.

直島ホール オープン

Naoshima Hall opened.

[SOg]

[SM]

「大島子どもサマーキャンプ」が始まる　大島

大島がこれからも子どもたちが集う場所になってほしいという入所者の希望から始まった、大島の将来展望へつながる大切な取り組み。小学生～中学生ら約30名が参加し、自然の豊かさに触れ、アート作品を通して大島の歴史やハンセン病を学ぶ2泊3日の夏休みの合宿が始まった。以降、毎年開催され、2021年のコロナ禍はオンラインで入所者と交流した。

Residential educational programs for children, in which they learned about the history of Oshima and Hansen's disease through art, began.

瀬戸内放送局「大島アワー」が始まる　大島

入所者向けのラジオ番組「大島アワー」の放送が大島青松園内で始まった。

Oshima Hour, a radio program for the residents of Oshima Seishoen, was introduced.

2016

[JN]

男木島図書館 オープン

Ogijima Library opened.

《ISLAND THEATRE MEGI「女木島名画座」》の準備が進む　女木島

高松市出身、ニューヨーク在住の依田洋一朗が、2階建ての倉庫を改装し、映画館を作った。年3回行われる「女木島名画座上映会」は人気ツアーになり、その後「島の中の小さなお店プロジェクト」や「女木島名店街」に発展し、多様な商店が増えている。

ISLAND Theatre MEGI was completed. Later developed into *Megijima Meitengai Mall* and the number of stores increased.

江戸一番隊（切腹ピストルズ）の四国八十八カ所巡りが始まる

芸術祭で人気のパフォーミング・アーツが、香川県を飛び出して四国遍路にでかけた。各札所では演奏を奉納。乱れ打ちだが、なるべく歩き遍路を心がけ、トレードマークの藁草履はいつもボロボロに。まだ結願していない。

Edo-Ichiban-tai (Seppuku Pistols) started with a pilgrimage to 88 sacred sites.

2017

うららの台所のお母さんたちによる調理実習が始まる　伊吹島

平均年齢 75 歳のお母さんたちによるお弁当づくりが 2016 年からスタートし、以降毎年、郷土料理の掘り起こしや試作を繰り返している。船の上で食べていた「ふき大根」など、お母さんたちの記憶を辿って、漁とともに暮らしてきた伊吹らしい料理を提供し、人気となっている。

Cooking projects by the women of Ibukijima began. A typical fishing island dish was created and became a popular bento box.

14年ぶりに島で赤ちゃんが誕生　男木島

男木小・中学校の再開を皮切りに、国内外からの移住者がのべ 80 名近くあり、中でも家族の転入が多く、新しい住人たちの子どもが次々に誕生している。島のおばあちゃんたちはまるで自分の孫のように世話を焼き、放課後の港は走り回る子どもたちの声が響いている。この年、40 年ぶりに島に住む住民同士が結婚、花嫁行列が復活した。

A baby was born on Ogijima for the first time in 14 years. Also, a couple living on the island got married for the first time in 40 years.

瀬戸内国際芸術祭 2016 開催

[SM]

食、地元文化、アジアとのつながりに重点をおいて展開。初の開催となった「瀬戸内アジアフォーラム 2016」ではアジア圏 10 カ所の国と地域からアートによる地域づくりに取り組む 26 団体が集い、現代美術や地域発の芸術祭がもつ意味が議論された。伊吹島や本島では島とアジアの国をつなぐ作家を選定。瀬戸内アジア村「タイファクトリーマーケット」「Asia Performing Arts Market in Setouchi2016」は、アジア 12 の国と地域からパフォーマーを招聘し合同公演や島でのワークショップを行った。香川県盆栽生産振興協議会や讃岐獅子舞保存会の参加は、改めて地元文化の魅力を伝えた。協賛企業との協働では、にっぽん丸「芸術祭鑑賞クルーズ」が運行された。

本芸術祭は 34 の国と地域から 226 組のアーティスト・プロジェクトと 37 のイベントが参加。会場は前回と同じ。2016 年 3 月 20 日から春・夏・秋の 3 会期、計 108 日間開催した。

Setouchi Triennale 2016
This time, emphasis was placed on food, local culture, and a connection with Asia. The festival featured 226 art projects, and 37 performance events. The participating artists came from 34 countries and regions. The venues were unchanged from the previous edition. It was open to the public for a total of 108 days, from March 20th, split between spring, summer, and autumn periods.

2018

「瀬戸内フラム塾『地域型芸術祭のつくられ方』」を開催

継続的な活動や芸術祭の取り組みをさまざまな地域に活かしていくための人材育成プログラムを実施。国内外から 67 名が参加した。

A human resource training program, teaching how to develop a regionally-rooted art festival, was held.

「せとうち島旅ガイド研修」が始まる

第 4 回展に向けて、島をより楽しくスムーズに巡るオフィシャルツアーを企画。それに先駆けて島巡りの水先案内人となるガイド養成講座を開催した。全国通訳案内士など多くの方が受講し、芸術祭の趣旨や島の概要、アート作品について学んだ。日替わりでさまざまな島を巡る 1DAY ツアーは、人気の芸術祭の廻り方になる。

A guide training program for new official tours was launched.

「高校生のための瀬戸内アートサマープログラム」が始まる

香川県教育委員会が主催して、県内の高校生が芸術祭や島巡りを通して地域づくりについて学ぶ夏季講習を実施。さまざまな学校から参加した約 100 名の高校生らは、北川の講演や島の現地実習から、島の魅力や課題を見つけて発表。以降、毎年開催している。

Summer classes for high school students to learn about building local communities through art festivals and to tour around the islands was held.

家プロジェクト「角屋」《Sea of Time '98》タイムセッティング 2018 〜継承〜　直島

家プロジェクト第 1 号となった宮島達男による作品の再セッティング。1998 年、125 個の LED 製デジタルカウンターの「タイムセッティング会」が開かれ、直島の 5 〜 95 歳までの 125 名が参加し、それぞれが"時の速さ"を決めた。20 年たった 2018 年、当時参加した 125 名に声をかけ、故人の場合は血縁者に連絡し、タイムセッティングが行われた。

The Art House Project Kadoya: *Sea of Time '98* was re-set for the first time since its placement 20 years earlier.

[SM]

プロジェクト《瀬戸内「　　　」資料館》が開始　直島

旧パチンコ店の建物を改装した宮浦ギャラリー六区で始まった新たなアートプロジェクト。アーティストの下道基行は直島に移住し、調査・収集・展示を通して島内外の人々が集う場所を創出。これまで「緑川洋一」、「百年観光」、「鍰（からみ）造景」、「中村由信と直島どんぐりクラブ」を取り上げている。

Motoyuki Shitamichi began *Setouchi "　　　" Archive.*

National Geographic Traveller（UK版）の「2019年に注目する旅行先」第1位に「瀬戸内」が選ばれる

“SETOUCHI” の注目度は年々高まり、米国の「Condé Nast Traveler」や「The New York Times」、英国の「The Guardian」など各国で発信された。

Setouchi was featured on “The Cool List 2019” by National Geographic Traveller (UK Edition).

海外で初のこえびミーティングを開催

こえび隊発足から、回を重ねるごとに海外からのサポーターが増加。第4回展ではじめて台湾でこえびミーティングを開催し、約100名が集まった。お寺を借りての「こえび寮」は人気で、国内外からのこえび隊が寝食をともにして交流を深めた。2019年芸術祭では、22の国と地域から参加があった。

The first koebi-tai meeting overseas was held.

2019

[SM]

社会交流会館がグランドオープン 高松と大島間の官有船が一般旅客定期航路化　大島

入所者の強い希望であった社会交流会館が完成。元住居を改装し、ハンセン病の正しい知識や大島の歴史を学べる資料展示や図書館、宿泊施設等が設置され、昭和33年の園の様子を再現した巨大なジオラマもお披露目された。アート作品《カフェ・シヨル》も交流会館内に移転した。また、これまで療養所関係者しか利用できなかった官有船が、観光客など不特定多数の人も乗船できる定期航路になった。芸術祭の開催や社会交流会館完成などで来島者が増えることを入所者の多くが望み、実現した。

Oshima Memorial Museum was opened. Also, the route between Takamatsu and Oshima was registered as a regular ferry line for general passengers, with publicly-owned ships.

不法投棄された産業廃棄物がすべて島から撤去される　豊島

1970年代より都市部から不法に持ち込まれた産業廃棄物を巡る豊島事件。2000年の公害調停を経て、2003年から始まった産廃処理は91万トン余り、撤去に16年を要した。しかし自然を再生するためにはまだ長い年月がかかる。

The illegal industrial waste that had been afflicting Teshima for a long time was removed from the island.

2017年3月28日運搬船「太陽」最終運航の様子
March 28th, 2017 State of the last day of “Taiyo”

宇高航路が休止に、109 年の歴史に幕

1910 年から続いた高松港と宇野港を結ぶ航路は、瀬戸大橋架橋前は本州と四国を結ぶ唯一の鉄道連絡船として活躍していた。1947 年の紫雲丸事故を契機に瀬戸大橋建設の声は高まり、1988 年の橋の完成とともに連絡船は廃止。しかしその後も 30 年間フェリーは行き来し、通学通勤する人もいたが、高速道路の値下げなどの影響もあり、ついに航路は休止となった。

The Uko Line ferry route, connecting the mainland and Shikoku, closed after 109 years of operation.

「ハンセン病元患者家族に対する補償金の支給等に関する法律」が成立

The Law Concerning Payment of Compensation to Families of Former Hansen's Disease Patients took effect.

瀬戸内国際芸術祭 2019 開催

[KK]

[SM]

開幕と同時に始まったゴールデンウィーク 10 連休は、多くの来場者で賑わった。2 回目の開催となった「瀬戸内アジアフォーラム 2019」は 15 カ国 38 団体 60 人が参加、各組織の事例紹介やアジアの芸術文化の進むべき方向性が話し合われた。また新たなジャンルの作品展開もあり、宇川直宏による瀬戸内発ライブストリーミング配信「DOMMUNE SETOUCHI」、参加型演劇の「瀬戸内少女歌劇団　せとうち物語ー粟島編ー」、アジアの書籍関係者が 100 組集う「SETOUCHI ART BOOK FAIR」などは参加者の幅を広げた。「SETOUCHI 企業フォーラム」では 21 社が参加し、企業が持続的な成長と文化活動をいかに戦略的につなげるかについて話し合われた。来場者アンケートでは、来場者の約 23% が海外からで、うち 7 割はアジアから、のべ 7,000 人のこえび隊のうち半数近くが海外からの参加者だった。

本芸術祭は 32 の国と地域から 230 組のアーティスト・プロジェクトと 35 のイベントが参加。会場は前回と同じ。2019 年 4 月 26 日から春・夏・秋の 3 会期、計 107 日間開催した。

Setouchi Triennale 2019
The number of overseas visitors greatly increased. The festival featured 230 art projects, and 35 performance events. The participating artists came from 32 countries and regions. The venues were unchanged from the previous edition. It was open to the public for a total of 107 days, from April 26th, split between spring, summer, and autumn periods.

本島送り太鼓が人気に

[SM]

芸術祭終盤になると、各島で島を出るフェリーのお見送りが白熱していく。子どもたちによる太鼓と笛の演奏と旗振りで盛大な本島のお見送り「送り太鼓」が話題になり、それを目的に来島する人もいた。以降、島の住民によるお見送りは各島に拡がった。

The custom of local residents bidding farewell to visitors leaving the islands became widespread.

2020

塩田千春《遠い記憶》お別れ会　豊島

2010年に甲生地区に完成した《遠い記憶》は、集落の元公民館に木製建具約600枚を組み合わせた集落初のアート作品。住民の思い入れも強く、制作時からさまざまな人が関わった。制作に参加したこえび隊の1人は住民らと交流を続け、この作品で結婚式を挙げたときは、集落総出でお祝いした。しかし建物の老朽化が進み解体が決定。住民やこえび隊によるお別れ会が開催され、10年の日々を振り返った。

Distant Memory by Chiharu Shiota was dismantled, and a farewell party was held by local residents and supporters.

新型コロナウイルスの感染拡大を受け、作品の公開やイベントが中止に

Due to the spread of the Covit pandemic, exhibitions of artwork and events were cancelled.

2022年展に向けて市町行政との勉強会が始まる

作品展開を検討するため、10の市町行政との勉強会をはじめた。自治体それぞれの芸術祭あるいは島や地域の位置づけを再確認し、エリアの特徴を学び直して、展開方針を検討した。小豆島・寒霞渓への作品設置や本島の石をテーマにした作品群、多度津町本通の作品展開など成果が出ている。

Study sessions with related local administrators began with regard to the 2022 edition.

2021

「瀬戸内アジアフォーラム 2021 Artists' Breath Live」

コロナ禍の中、世界中の約100人のアーティストから寄せられたブックレットの公開と、30人のアーティストによるライヴレポートで構成したフォーラムをオンラインで開催した。

"Setouchi Asia Forum 2021: Artists' Breath" Live was broadcast online.

2022

海外アーティストによるリモート制作が進む

入国制限の影響で来日が難しい中、海外アーティストは現地スタッフとオンラインで連絡を取り作品づくりを進めた。ロシアのレオニート・チシコフは旧沙弥小・中学校、与島、鍋島灯台での展開に向けて地域のことを調査し、プランを考えた。エカテリーナ・ムロムツェワもオンラインで男木島の子どもたちとワークショップを行い、ともに作品を制作した。

Remote production was conducted by overseas artists.

パンデミック下での地域型国際芸術祭

A Localized International Art Festival During the Covid-19 Pandemic

日本では2020年1月28日に新型コロナウイルス感染症を指定感染症として定める等の政令が公布され、瀬戸内国際芸術祭2022は感染症のパンデミックとその対策の中で準備が進んだ。海外からの入国制限、政府や自治体の感染症対策など、芸術祭へのさまざまな影響は会期終了まで続いた。

In Japan, Covid-19 was officially recognized as Designated Infectious Disease on January 28th, 2020, and the Setouchi Triennale continued its preparations under the conditions of the ongoing pandemic and measures to prevent further spread. As evidenced by the limited entry to the nation, and the various restrictions introduced by national and local governments, the pandemic affected the art festival in many ways and continued through the end of it.

経緯 *Timeline*

■ 2020年

2月29日 新型コロナウイルス感染拡大を受けて2月29日以降、直島・豊島・大島・犬島の作品公開やイベントが中止となった。その後も、感染状況と国や自治体による県外への移動制限や自粛の呼びかけの影響で、アート作品や施設等の開閉館、イベント実施の変更があった。

3月31日 第26回実行委員会総会（以下、「総会」）で瀬戸内国際芸術祭2022の開催が決定。

7月28日 第27回総会で、会期や会場、重点的な取り組みを定めた取組方針を策定。

■ 2021年

3月30日 第28回総会で、取組方針に新型コロナウイルス感染症対策を加えた。

11月9日 東京で企画発表会を開催した。対外的にはじめて感染症対策の概要を発表、パンデミック下での芸術祭開催に向けて対応方針を説明した。

■ 2022年

3月3日 第8回実行委員会本部会議にて「新型コロナウイルス感染症対策の指針」を策定した。会場の多くが離島であること等を踏まえた、基本的な感染症対策やケース別の対応等を盛り込んだ。

4月14日 瀬戸内国際芸術祭2022が開幕

8月5日 夏会期開幕日の8月5日から8月14日まで感染状況を踏まえ、大島の作品を休館とした

9月29日 感染症対策の指針一部改正(来場記録取得を削除)

11月6日 瀬戸内国際芸術祭2022が閉幕

2020

February 29th: As a result of the spread of Covid, the public exhibitions and events in Naoshima, Teshima, Oshima, and Inujima were cancelled from February 29th onwards. Other effects included the closure of artworks and facilities, and changes to events due to shifting infection rates, restrictions of movement between prefectures, and calls for self-restriction by national and local governments.

March 31st: In the 26th General Meeting of the Executive Committee (hereafter "General Meeting"), it was decided to go ahead with the Setouchi Triennale 2022.

July 28th: An organization policy, framing the festival periods, venues, and core principles, was established in the 27th General Meeting.

2021

March 30th: Efforts to prevent Covid infections were added to the key principles of the festival in the 28th General Meeting.

November 9th: A planning presentation was held in Tokyo. The outline of the infection prevention measures was publicly introduced for the first time, explaining the organization's plans for holding the festival during the pandemic.

2022

March 3rd: In the 8th Executive Committee Cabinet Meeting the "Covid-19 Infection Measure Guidelines" were finalized. Considering the fact that many of the venues are remote islands, basic prevention rules were augmented with manuals detailing responses to different cases.

April 14th: The Setouchi Triennale 2022 opened.

August 5th: Due to infection rates at the time, artworks in Oshima were closed in the summer period between August 5th and 14th.

September 29th: Part of the "Covid-19 Infection Measure Guidelines" was amended. The collection of visitor's information was no longer required.

November 6th: The Setouchi Triennale 2022 ended.

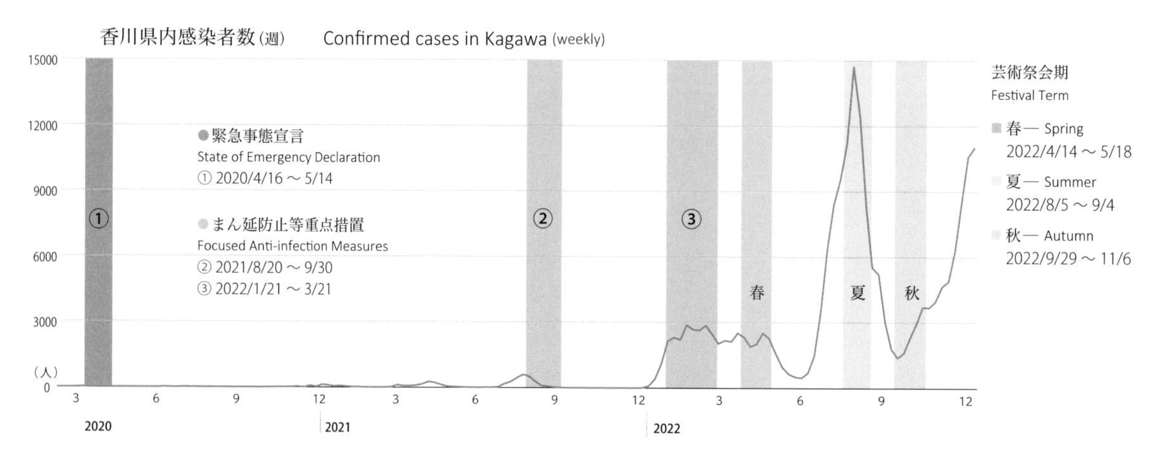

[SM] [SM] [SM]

具体的な影響と対策　*Notable Effects and Counter-Measures*

主な会場である島しょ部は、高齢者が多いこと、医療体制が脆弱であること、船での移動であることなどから、地域から不安の声が寄せられた。

通年開館している直島等の美術館施設は早くから感染症対策を徹底し、状況を考慮しながら運営した。豊島の「島のお誕生会」や各島の作品メンテナンスなども住民や市町と相談しながら実施、大島青松園等との定例会はオンラインで開催するなど、活動を継続し、地域とのつながりをできる限り維持し続けた。

コロナ禍の瀬戸内国際芸術祭第5回展開催に向けては、会期日程の検討や作品鑑賞パスポートの制度設計変更にまで影響が及んだ。各島や集落に対して感染症対策の説明など複数回の意見交換会を行い、独自に「新型コロナウイルス感染症対策の指針」を策定した。準備期間はアーティストらのウイルス検査等のルールを決め、制作現場の感染症対策も工夫した。会期中は、住民や来場者同士が安心して鑑賞できるよう、来場者は港等に設置した検温スポットで体調を確認後、配布したリストバンドを各作品受付で提示し入館した。また来場履歴の取得も行った。有症状者が発生した場合はチャーター船で島外へ搬送する等の対策も整えた。会期中の有症状者発生は1件のみで、クラスターは発生しなかった。

入国制限で海外アーティストの来日や訪日時期などの判断が難しく、作家選考にも影響があった。しかし、アーティストはリモートアクセス等によるリサーチや、地域住民とのワークショップをオンラインで実施するなど、新たな作品制作の方法を模索した。これまで多くの参加があった海外在住のサポーターは今回ほとんど来日できず、サポーター全体の参加人数が減少した。一方で県職員や企業・団体ボランティアの参加の増加があった。

地域の人々とのワークショップやパフォーミング・アーツ、対面型の食のプロジェクト、サポーター同士の交流など人と人がつながる活動が積極的に実施できなかった。状況が異なった島や地域で開催する広域芸術祭の危機管理における有事対応の難しさが課題として残った。

Before the festival, concerns were raised by local residents related to the risks associated with an aging population, weak medical infrastructure, and boats being a major means of transport.

The art facilities in Naoshima and other areas, which are open throughout the year, committed to enforcing strict measures to prevent infection from early in the process, closely examining the situation in order to remain open. Teshima's Island Birthday Party and maintenance of artworks on the islands were conducted in consultation with local residents and administrations, and regular meetings with Oshima Seishoen were held online. All efforts were made to conserve the connections of continuous projects and the local areas as much as possible.

The influence of the pandemic was present throughout the 5th edition, from planning the periods to changing the visitor's passport scheme. Multiple discussion sessions and orientations were held in the islands and villages, outlining prevention measures and developing the unique "Covid-19 Infection Measure Guidelines". During preparation, participating artists were required to take infection tests, and to follow prevention regulations at the production sites. During the festival periods, visitors confirmed their health status at temperature-checking points at each port, and received wristbands enabling them to enter the facilities. The traveling history of visitors was also traced. A chartered boat was in operation, prepared to move anyone displaying symptoms. During the festival period there was just one symptomatic case, and no clusters.

Due to the restrictions on entry to Japan, the ability for international artists to visit the sites and the timing for them to do so was challenging, which affected the selection of participants. However, the artists involved explored new modes of production adapted to the situation, such as research through remote access and online workshops with local residents. Overseas supporters, who had been active in previous editions, could not take part this time, which decreased the total number of supporters. On the other hand, prefectural administration workers and corporate volunteers increased in number.

Activities aimed at connecting people, including workshops with local residents, the performing arts, in-person food projects, and communication between supporters, could not be actively pursued. The difficulty of managing the risks of emergency situations in a festival over such a wide area, involving islands and areas with unique circumstances, remains issue that needs to be carefully examined.

地域と芸術祭の課題、その可能性

北川フラム
瀬戸内国際芸術祭総合ディレクター

第5回の瀬戸内国際芸術祭が2022年11月6日に終了し、その記録集を制作している今、何よりも大事故がなくパンデミック下の芸術祭が終了し、2025年の第6回展に繋げられたこと、2020年1月のコロナ発生以来、日本と各地で検討していた展覧会、公演を含む越後妻有 大地の芸術祭、奥能登国際芸術祭、北アルプス国際芸術祭、いちはらアート×ミックスらのバトンを繋げられたことが嬉しい。

2020年から第5回の芸術祭に向けて動き出しましたが島の意見は厳しいものがありました。更に全入場者の行動履歴をとるという課題も出てきて、集団発生を防ぐための可能な限りの対策を考えました。海外からの来客がないとの予想のなかで、予算的にもコロナ対策の計上を含めて厳しいものがありました。作品制作費は20%減、サポーターも県を超えての移動が抑制されていました。そんな中でも今回は187組のアーティスト（うち海外53組）、新作（展示替えを含む）85件が実施されたことはよかったと思います。結果的には前回までの計り方で来場者723,316人、サポーター参加者5,417人（約4割減）であり、企業協賛も262社・3億2600万円となりました。そんな中でもアーティスト・サポーターは頑張りました。制作を期日中に仕上げた他、エカテリーナ・ムロムツェワの《学校の先生》などでは制作中も、女木島名店街や男木島の《漆の家》などでは作品展示期間中も、盛んにワークショップが行われていたのです。

第4回展の開始時点で、2019年に世界の行くべき場所としてナショナル・ジオグラフィックが瀬戸芸をやっている瀬戸内海を世界1位、ニューヨーク・タイムズが世界7位にあげていたように、日本の地域型芸術祭は世界的に注目されていましたが、2020年にいったんストップになりました。しかし国内では経産省が地方創生として芸術文化による展開の準備に入ったほか、2017年の文化芸術基本法の改正（地域型芸術祭と日本の食文化を重視する）以来の底流があり、文化と観光は国家的なプロジェクトになりつつありました。勿論、個々の文化活動へのサポート、文化イベントへの支援は薄く、文化的インフラは国としてはお粗末ながら、この40年以来衰退し続ける国の産業展開力、教育力のなかで、この列島の固有の魅力と観光こそが起動力だという考えは当然のことだったわけで、突然の休止符が3年間うたれたとはいえ、2023年度からは25年度に向かって多くの人が瀬戸内に関心をもち、来られることは期待できそうです。500年前からの地理上の発見以来の植民地主義が今なお世界地図をつくり、科学技術が人間の均質化、記号化に向かっている今こそ、人間個々の生理の多様性に根ざしている美術の役割を果たしたいと思うのです。

さて第5回展の概括です。

瀬戸芸の場所は12の島と2つの港のある市町です。来場者の増加と島民の数を考えると本土にも作品が必要になります。今回は高松市の屋島と四国村、玉野市の築港商店街を意識するほか、丸亀、多度津、観音寺での展開をはかりました。坂出では沙弥島だけではなく、今までも神戸芸術工科大学が瀬居島で活動を続けてくれているほか、今回は与島や鍋島の灯台、高松からの海岸線が美しい王越にも展開したし、小豆島の福田から寒霞渓までのルートが韓国のイ・スーキュン［李秀京］、山頂の青木野枝の作品によって魅力的になり、拠点からのつながりが延伸しています。

高松ではホテルが増えましたが、宇野でも新しいホテルが2つ出来、それらが町のプロジェクトと連携してくれたことは嬉しいことでした。玉野市の気運が高まっています。

公募は継続していますが、特にパフォーマンス系は人気があります。海外作品は2020年から検討をしていて、可能な範囲で多くの（特になじみのない地域からの）作家は意識しています。コロナ下での困難はありましたが、それなりに展開できました。内容については観客の反応をみたいと思います。課題としては、良品が残る仕組みをつくることと、作品の継続上、メンテナンス費の恒常的な用意がだんだん必要になっています。

今回の海外からのアーティストは次の通りです。ヘザー・B・スワン＋ノンダ・カサリディス、ニコラ・ダロ、大岩オスカール＋坂 茂、ワン・テユ［王德瑜］、エカテリーナ・ムロムツェワ、ソピアップ・ピッチ、スタシス・エイドリゲヴィチウス、ワン・ウェンチー［王文志］、チャールズ・ウォーゼン、フリオ・ゴヤ、シャン・ヤン［向阳］、イ・スーキュン［李秀京］、レオニート・チシコフ、アリン・ルンジャーン、DDMY STUDIO、ケンデル・ギール、ネオン・ダンス、マッシモ・バルトリー

Challenges for Regions and Art Festivals, and Possibilities

Fram Kitagawa

General Director, Setouchi Triennale

The fifth edition of the Setouchi Triennale drew to a close on November 6th 2022, and in the process of creating this archive book, I reflected how glad I was that it concluded without major incidents of any kind and is continuing towards the sixth edition in 2025. I am happy that the baton has passed from festivals like the Echigo-Tsumari Art Triennale, the Oku-Noto Triennale, the Northern Arts Festival, and Ichihara Art x Mix, which included various exhibitions and performances that had been considered since the outbreak of Covid-19 in January 2020.

We began working on preparations for the fifth edition in 2020, but the concerns of the islanders were strong. Additionally, we were required to face the issue of creating records of each guest as part of our stringent measures to prevent clusters. What is more, the anticipated lack of overseas guests resulted in a limited budget, which also had to cover the cost of pandemic prevention measures. The work production budget for this edition was down by 20%, and supporters were under regulations that discouraged movement across prefectural borders. Despite these circumstances, we were still able to work with 187 artists, including 53 from overseas, and introduce 85 new works (including changes of exhibits). The number of visitors, counted conventionally, was 723,316, and there were 5,417 supporters (a reduction of about 40%). Corporate support, from 262 organizations, totaled 326 million yen.

The artists and supporters worked with great dedication in these trying conditions. They not only completed their work on time, but also held many active workshops. For instance, during the production of Ekaterina Muromtseva's *The School Teachers*, in Megijima Meitengai, and during the exhibition of *Maison de Urushi* in Ogijima.

At the opening of the fourth edition, Setouchi was listed at No.1 on *National Geographic*'s "The Cool List 2019" (19 destinations set to hit the headlines in 2019), and No.7 on the *New York Times*' "52 Places to Go in 2019", indicating that this localized art festival in Japan had attracted global attention. But this was halted in 2020. However, on a domestic scale the Ministry of Economy, Trade and Industry began preparing for the development of art and culture as a mode of regional revitalization, and the amendment of the "Basic Act for the Promotion of Culture and the Arts" which recognized the significance of local art festivals and Japanese food culture, underlined the positioning of culture and tourism as a national project.

Of course, the support provided for individual cultural activities and events is not comprehensive, so cultural infrastructure remains under the expectations of the national administration. Yet in the context of a four-decade decline in national industrial development and educational level in the nation, the powerful attraction of the charms unique to each island of Japan with sightseeing as a driving force is undeniable. Even though this was brought to a sudden halt for three years, we are confident many people will be interested in Setouchi and will visit between 2023 and 2025. The colonialism sparked by the discovery of new lands, which began 500 years ago, still defines the world map today, and scientific technology leads towards human homogenization and iconization. We would like to play a role with art that is rooted in the diversity of humanity's individual ways of being.

So how can one summarize the fifth edition?

The location of the Triennale is 12 islands and 2 port cities. Considering the increasing number of visitors and island residents, the festival required some development on the mainland. For this edition, we had Yashima and Shikokumura in Takamatsu, and Chikko shopping street in Tamano in mind, and also pursued development in places like Marugame, Tadotsu, and Kan-onji as well. This year, Kobe Design University, which has been developing art activities in Semijima (part of the city of Sakaide), relocated from Shamijima as their center of activity. Yoshima, Nabeshima Lighthouse, and Ougoshi, with its beautiful coastline that can be viewed from Takamatsu, were also incorporated into the areas of development. What is more, the route between Fukuda and Kankakei in Shodoshima was brightened by the work of Yeesookyung and Noe Aoki. These developments stretched out from the central hubs.

Takamatsu is seeing the opening of several hotels, and there are also two new ones in Uno. I am delighted to see this occurring in areas that cooperated with projects, and I can see the spirits of the towns growing. We have continued open calls for artwork, and the field of performing arts has been very popular. Since 2020, work from overseas has been in consideration, with the aim of featuring as many artists as possible, particularly those from regions we are not familiar with. Despite the difficulties posed by Covid-19, I believe the level of development was strong. For their quality, I defer to the reactions of the audiences. Looking to the future, I am intrigued by schemes to enable great works to remain, and the implementation of a maintenance fee to be used towards continuous installation.

The artists from overseas who participated in this edition are as follows: Heather B. Swann + Nonda Katsalidis, Nicolas Darrot, Oscar Oiwa + Shigeru Ban, Wang Te-yu, Ekaterina Muromtseva, Sopheap Pich, Stasys Eidrigevičius, Wang Wen Chih, Charles Worthen, Julio Goya, Xiang Yang, Yeesoookyung, Leonid Tishkov, Arin Rungjang, DDMY STUDIO, Kendell Geers, Neon Dance, Massimo Bartolini, Adel Abdessemed, Aleksandra Kovaleva & Kei

ニ、アデル・アブデスメッド、アレクサンドラ・コヴァレヴァ＆佐藤敬／ KASA、ゲゲルボヨ、マナル・アルドワイヤン、Asaki Oda、ムニール・ファトゥミ、アイシャ・エルクメン。

また、ここで特筆すべきは小豆島の福武ハウスの活動です。2013 年から始まった 7 の国と地域のアートセンター（組織）の参加による着実な討議と展開は、今回ハウスの近くの 5 つの家屋を使った展示として結晶しました。それぞれがカンボジアのクヴァイ・サムナン、台湾のサマー・ファン＆ツァイ・ジアイン、インドネシアのアナン・サプトト、香港のフィオナ・ウォン・ライ・チンと香港アートセンターチーム、タイのコラクリット・アルナーノンチャイ＆アレックス・グヴォジックによるものですが、福田という地域に焦点をあてたものではないにしろ、それぞれの出身地をベースとしたサイトスペシフィックなものであり、日本や瀬戸内との関係を意識したものもあり、観客の興味を魅（ひ）いたと思います。このような関わり、活動がふえてくるのはよいと思います。日本を含めた北東アジアと、特に瀬戸内で意識している東南アジアのアーティストによる作品の質の向上と交流は、今なお続く植民地主義的な経済動向のなかで、ささやかでも希望のありかを示してくれるように思います。陸地面積世界 62 位でありながら、海岸線世界 6 位の日本列島は古来、海による恩恵を享けており、とりわけ瀬戸内海は、その列島のコブクロのように、豊かで穏やかな、多くの海外からの文物の交易場所でした。その意味でも南条嘉毅、長谷川仁、玉野の食プロジェクトが塩・塩田をテーマにしており、他には台風で損壊し撤去せざるを得なかったアイシャ・エルクメンの四国地図の作品、マナル・アルドワイヤンの中東と瀬戸内海の海・女性漁労者をテーマとした作品など、海と海の繋がりを意識した作品が多かったのも嬉しい。

女木島の商店街については前回の 2019 年に寿荘での店舗からスタートして、今回は集落内で展開しました。寿荘は 8 作家、集落内は 5 作家です。このほかにはもともとレアンドロ・エルリッヒの作品や、依田洋一朗の《女木島名画座》などがありました。実際にこの 3 年間でも女木島には 5 店のカフェやゲストハウス等が進出し、以前に比べて元気になってきたし、その他宿泊施設などの話も聞くようになりました。島の人たちとご相談して長期的な展望をつくっていきたいと思っています。

男木島は島の出身者の家族が 2014 年に帰島して以来私設図書館を作るなど、さまざまな活動が生まれています。現在新居住者は 26 家族 51 人（うち島で生まれた子どもは 5 人）になっていて、もともといろいろな考えを持つ居住者と新住民を含めた試行が行われていると聞いています。

これらの他に玉野市では蓄電池会社の工場設置を機に街づくりをはじめる計画が生まれ、三豊市では世界の海洋環境について調査しているフランスの NPO 団体が、2019 年より日本でワークショップや作品展示を行う拠点を粟島に置いています。

観光の島・小豆島では 2010 年以来 3,000 人以上の移住があり、瀬戸芸とからんで通年で積極的な動きが始まっています。第 5 回展で言えば寒霞渓山頂にも展開したし、広島市立大学のプロジェクトも活発です。今後は町の政策とのすりあわせが必要になるでしょう。

瀬戸芸は国内を代表する地域創生の起爆になる芸術祭であるとともに、観光立国日本の新しい可能性を拓くものとして期待を集めています。国際的にもサイトスペシフィックな美術の成立は、地理上の発見以来の国際的経済連合体主導の国際政治の枠組と地球規模の自然崩壊が続くなかで、空気・水・土・森林といった人類共通の基盤がますます大切になっています。20 世紀の都市景観をかたちづくった、鉄筋にガラスのカーテンウォールからなる共通の風景は、住居、オフィス、ホテル、レストランへ簡単に転用でき、効率のよい居住・都市空間となり、さらにそれらは均等・民主主義・土地の力を捨象した普遍として、空間だけでなく世界を覆う今日のもっとも強力で支配的な思想となりました。これが高い白い壁という美術館・ギャラリーの実験室的空間に使われて、オークション・アートフェアに至る、もっとも効率のよい金融商品となる仕組のベースとなってしまっていますが、瀬戸内の島々で展開されている作品はそのような現代社会のなかでのもうひとつの可能性を示しています。それが最初に述べたように外国からの評価を呼びはじめているし、国を超えた多くのファンを獲得してきたのだと思います。

Sato / KASA, Gegerboyo, Manal AlDowayan, Asaki Oda, Mounir Fatmi, and Ayşe Erkmen.

Worthy of a special mention here are the activities of Fukutake House in Shodoshima. The consistent discussion and development by an art center featuring 7 different countries and regions, which began in 2013, has crystalized as an exhibition in five houses near Fukutake House. These are by Khvay Samnang (Cambodia), Summer Huang & JiaYin Tsai, (Taiwan), Anang Saptoto (Indonesia), Fiona Wong Lai Ching and the HKAC team (Hong Kong) and Korakrit Arunanondchai & Alex Gvojic (Thailand). These are not necessarily works that put a spotlight on the area of Fukuda, but rather site-specific works based on the artists' places of birth, and some of them are highly conscious of their relationships with Setouchi and Japan – all attracting the interest of the audience.

I believe that it is good to have relationships and activities like this. The improvement in quality of work by artists from south-east Asia, and their communication with north-east Asian countries including Japan, is a trend that the Setouchi Triennale is paying attention to. It is showing a hint of where hope might lie in the ongoing colonialist economic movement. Geographically, Japan is 62nd in the world in terms of land area, yet has the 6th longest coastlines, and it has long received the blessings of the ocean. Setouchi in particular was like the womb of the Japanese islands – rich in resources, calm, and a place of trade for many foreign items. For that reason, I am pleased that many works are concerned with the connections between oceans, such as those of Yoshitaka Nanjo, Jin Hasegawa, and the Food Project in Tamano, which has dealt with the themes of salt and salt farms, as well as the piece featuring a map of Shikoku by Ayse Erkmen, which unfortunately had to be removed due to damage from a typhoon, and the work of Manal AlDowayan, which expressed the themes of the seas of the middle east and the Seto Inland Sea, and female fishers.

The shopping street in Megijima grew from only having shops at Kotobukiso in the previous edition in 2019 to having eight artists in Kotobukiso and five more in the village itself. The island also featured work by Leandro Erlich and *Island Theatre Megi* by Yoichiro Yoda. Over the past three years, five cafés and guest houses have opened in Megijima, and I have also heard of plans for new accommodation there: this is a sign of the island becoming more active. We would like to support long-term development in collaboration with the island residents.

Many new activities have been seen in Ogijima, including a new private library, since families originally from the island began returning in 2014. New residents now number 51 people from 26 families, including 5 children who were born on the island, and I have come across new projects undertaken by residents with diverse ideas, as well as the new residents themselves. In addition to this, Tamano has seen a new plan to develop the community, based around the opportunities created by an accumulator factory, and Awashima, which belongs to Mitoyo City, has become a base for a French NPO that investigates the global marine environment for their workshops and art exhibitions.

Shodoshima, an island of tourism, has seen more than 3,000 people settle since 2010, demonstrating the consistent activity prompted in relation to the Triennale. For the fifth edition, some work was developed at the peak of Kankakei, while a project by Hiroshima City University has been ongoing. In the future, further cooperation with local policy will be necessary.

The Setouchi Triennale is an art festival that triggers local revitalization that is an emblem for the nation, and it bears the expectation of being a pioneer for Japan as a country sustaining itself by tourism. Internationally, for site-specific art, elements such as air, water, earth, and forests, which are universal foundations for mankind, are critical in an ongoing global political framework engendered by the international economic paradigm that arose from geographical discovery and environmental destruction. The common view of the curtain walls of reinforced steel and glass that defined the urban landscape of the 20th century was easily transmuted into housing, offices, hotels, and restaurants that offered efficient domestic and urban spaces, and in their abstraction of homogenization, democracy, and power of land, they became the dominant philosophy in the world today, not just in terms of space. It is used in the experimental space of museums and galleries with high white walls, and extends to auctions and art fairs, a philosophy that generates the most efficient financial product. This festival shows another possibility in such a society. As I touched upon at the beginning, it has begun to garner attention from foreign countries, and I believe it has earned a following beyond the nation.

凡例　Explanatory Notes

- 本書の内容は 2023 年 2 月 28 日現在の情報をもとに制作した。
- 作品解説は主に編集部で作成した。
- 各章の扉に記載したデータは、令和 2 年度国勢調査などを参照した。
- 文中において、諸氏の敬称は省略した。

- This book is based on the information available as of February 28th, 2023.
- The descriptions of the artworks were mainly written by editorial staff.
- The data on the areas on the front pages of each chapter is based on Reference Data of the National Population Census 2020, etc.
- Honorifics are omitted in the text.

①施設名　Facility Name
- 施設名がない場合は非表示
- Omitted if there is no facility name

②作家名　Name of the Artist

③作品名　Title of the Artworks

④作品番号　Number of the Artwork
- 14の会場を示すアルファベット2文字と数字の組み合わせによる。Eはイベント、Tは広域に展開する作品、末尾にBがつくものはベネッセアートサイト直島が所蔵・所有するもの。
- A combination of two letters and a number represents one of the 14 venues. E is an event, T is a work in a broad area, and items ending in B are owned by Benesse Art Site Naoshima.

⑤サイト名　Site of the Artwork

⑥施設名（英）Facility Name in English

⑦作家名（英）Name of the Artist in English

⑧国籍／居住地　Nationality / Residential Area
- ユニットの場合は、それぞれの出身地／居住地の間を「,」で区切って示した。
- Nationality / Residential Area for units, the respective nationalities or residential areas are separated by (,).

⑨作品名（英）Title of the Artworks in English

⑩サイト名（英）Site of the Artwork in English

⑪制作年　Production Year

制作後に新規展開があった場合はその年を並記した。

⑫作品説明　Introduction of the Artwork

①…豊島美術館
②…内藤礼［アート］
西沢立衛［建築］
③…母型
④…te13B｜唐櫃岡…⑤

Teshima Art Museum…⑥
Art: Rei Naito｜Japan…⑦
Architecture: Ryue Nishizawa｜Japan…⑧
Matrix…⑨
Karato-oka…⑩
2010…⑪

⑫…瀬戸内海を望む小高い丘の中腹に立地し、周囲には棚田が広がり、自然と建築、アートが融和した美しい環境を作り出している。中では一日を通して「泉」が誕生する作品《母型》が展開される。天井からは光や風、鳥の声が注ぎ、時間の流れや季節の移り変わりとともに無限の表情を伝える。

⑬…Teshima Art Museum, the collaborative creation of artist Rei Naito and architect Ryue Nishizawa, lies partway up a hill overlooking the Seto Inland Sea and is bordered by terraced rice fields, resulting in a beautiful fusion of nature, art and architecture. Inside, new "springs" are constantly born from the work *Matrix*. Light, wind, and the voices of birds enter from above, conjuring an infinite array of impressions with the passage of seasons and the flow of time.

⑭…所蔵・運営＝公益財団法人 福武財団
Collection & Management: Fukutake Foundation

⑬作品説明（英）Introduction of the Artwork in English

⑭クレジット Credit Title
- 設計／ディレクションや主催、構成メンバー等／特別協力／所蔵・運営／協賛・助成の順に記載した。
- 「所蔵」＝作品の所蔵者、施設の所有者。瀬戸内国際芸術祭実行委員会が所蔵・所有するものについては記載を省略した。
- 「運営」＝恒常開館している施設や商品販売・サービス提供をともなう施設の運営者。瀬戸内国際芸術祭実行委員会が運営するものについては記載を省略した。
- 「助成」「協賛」＝2022年度に受けたものを記載した。
- Listed in order are Architecture, Design / Organization, Direction, etc. / Cooperation / Collection, Management / Sponsor, Funding.
- "Collection" denotes the owner of the work or facility. Omitted for items owned by the Setouchi Triennale Executive Committee.
- "Management" denotes the operator of a permanent facility or a facility that sells products and provides services. Omitted for events run by the Setouchi Triennale Executive Committee.
- "Funding" and "Sponsor" list those received in 2022.

写真　Photograph

- 撮影者は同じ頁内に右記の略称で示し、その他コピーライト・提供元等は同じ頁内に記載した。
- 作家、芸術祭事務局などの撮影による場合は、記載を省略した。
- Photographers are credited on the page of the image, with the following abbreviations. Copyright holders and suppliers are also indicated on the same page.
- All photographs without credit, found mainly in the introductions of artworks, are by the artist, secretariat of the executive committee, or editorial staff.

Photo Credit:
表紙　Front Cover: Yoshihiko Ueda
見開き　Facing Pages: Kimito Takahashi...p.2, Hideaki Hamada...p.4, 40, Shintaro Miyawaki...p.32, 38, 70, 88, 102, 134, 156, 166, 194, 264
Osamu Nakamura...p.58, Makoto Tanaka...p.146

Daici Ano [DAn], Daisuke Aochi [DAo], Yoshihiro Asada [YA], Mitsumasa Fujitsuka [MF], Jin Fukuda [JF], Hideaki Hamada [HHa], Naoya Hatakeyama [NH], Hiroyuki Hirai [HHi], Takashi Homma [TH], Yasushi Ichikawa [YIc], Yoshikazu Inoue [YIn], Mitsushige Kida [MK], Keizo Kioku [KK], Takumi Kondo [TK], Yasuhide Kuge [YK], Tomoko Makiura [TM], TAKASHI SAWARAME [TSa], Yoshiro Masuda [YM], Shintaro Miyawaki [SM], Noboru Morikawa [NM], Masatomo Moriyama [MM], Satoshi Nagare [SN], Osamu Nakamura [ON], Junko Nukaga [JN], Shigeo Ogawa [SOg], Seiichi Ohsawa [SOh], KEI OKANO [KO], Hidehiko Omata [HO], Shinkenchiku-Sha [Shinkenchiku-Sha], Koichi Shiraishi [KSh], Tang Shiyao [TSh], Sung Lung-Chuan [SL], Ken'ichi Suzuki [KSu], TADA(YUKAI) [TADA], Akira Takahashi [AT], Kimito Takahashi [KiT], Kai Takizawa [KaiT], Katsumasa Tanaka [KatT], Takahiro Tsushima [TT], Yoshihiko Ueda [YU], Norihiro Ueno [NU], Osamu Watanabe [OW], Tadasu Yamamoto [TY], Kaori Yamane [KY]

直島

Naoshima

「南瓜」草間彌生 2022年 ©YAYOI KUSAMA [TY]

直島　*Naoshima*

27の島々からなる直島諸島は、古くから漁業、海運業、製塩業などが盛んで、多くの人やモノが行き交う海上交通の要衝だった。「保元物語」では、平安時代の保元の乱で破れた崇徳上皇が讃岐に流される際、直島に立ち寄ったと記され、島には上皇ゆかりとされる地名が多く残っている。戦国時代には豊臣秀吉に仕えた高原次利が直島城を築き、江戸時代に幕府領であったため歌舞伎や人形浄瑠璃などの公演が許された。淡路島から伝わった浄瑠璃は「直島女文楽」として現在も続いている。

1910年代に島の北側に製錬所ができ企業城下町として発展、1980年代には島の南側で文化的な観光開発がはじまり、1989年「直島国際キャンプ場」が完成した。以降、現代アートと建築による地域づくりは町や住民とともに活動を展開していく。質の高いアート作品や建築が集積する人口約3,000人の“アートの島”は、世界中から多くの人々が訪れる。

The 27 islands that make up Naoshima have enjoyed prosperity through the fishing, sea transportation, and salt producing industries, and played an important role as a center for ocean traffic, where many people met and goods were exchanged. In *Hogen Monogatari* (“The Tale of the Hogen Rebellion”, which took place in 1156), the retired Emperor Sutoku is said to have stopped off at Naoshima on his way into exile in Sanuki (modern-day Kagawa), and there are many places that have names with imperial roots. In the Sengoku era (the Age of Civil Wars), Takahara Tsugutoshi, who served Toyotomi Hideyoshi, built Naoshima Castle, which was granted permission to host performances of *kabuki* and *ningyo-joururi* (Japanese puppet theater) due to its location on government land. *Joururi*, which was brought from Awajishima, continues to this day as *Naoshima Onna Bunraku*.

In the 1910s, a smelting factory was built in the north of the island, which helped it to become an industrial area. In the 1980s, the south of the island began to pursue cultural tourism, and the Naoshima International Camp opened in 1989. Since then, community-building through contemporary art and architecture has developed alongside the towns and their residents. This “art island”, with a population of 3,000, has collected wonderful art and architectural work, attracting many visitors from across the globe.

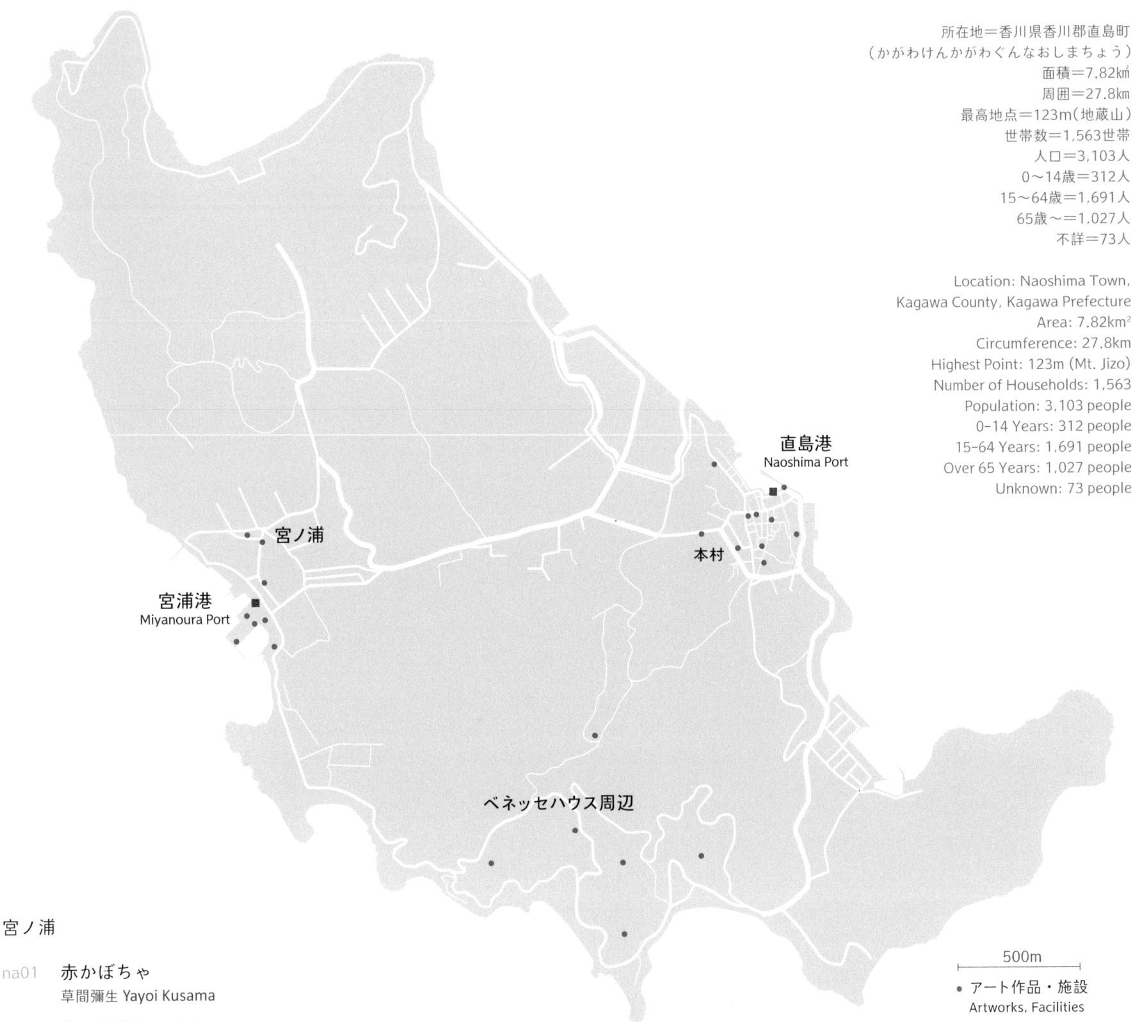

宮ノ浦

na01 赤かぼちゃ
草間彌生 Yayoi Kusama

na02 海の駅「なおしま」
妹島和世＋西沢立衛／SANAA［建築］
Architecture: Kazuyo Sejima + Ryue Nishizawa / SANAA

na03 BUNRAKU PUPPET
ジョゼ・デ・ギマランイス José de Guimarães

na04 直島パヴィリオン
藤本壮介 Sou Fujimoto

na05B 直島銭湯「I ♥ 湯」
大竹伸朗 Shinro Ohtake

na06B 宮浦ギャラリー六区
瀬戸内「　　　」資料館
下道基行 Motoyuki Shitamichi

na23B The Naoshima Plan「住」
三分一博志 Hiroshi Sambuichi

E01 直島女文楽
Naoshima Onna Bunraku

E02 直島建築ツアー
Naoshima Architecture Tour

E03 近代化の歴史にふれる
—直島・犬島の鍰煉瓦を訪ねて—
Naoshima and Inujima Karami Tour
—Exploring Modern History—

E04 杉本雅楽 直島御神楽
Sugimoto Gagaku—Naoshima Mikagura

本村

na07B The Naoshima Plan「水」
三分一博志 Hiroshi Sambuichi

na08 直島ホール
三分一博志 Hiroshi Sambuichi

na09 直島港ターミナル
妹島和世＋西沢立衛／SANAA［建築］
Architecture: Kazuyo Sejima + Ryue Nishizawa / SANAA

na10B ANDO MUSEUM
安藤忠雄 Tadao Ando

na11B 角屋
宮島達男 Tatsuo Miyajima

na12B 護王神社
杉本博司 Hiroshi Sugimoto

na13B 南寺
ジェームズ・タレル James Turrell

na14B 碁会所
須田悦弘 Yoshihiro Suda

na15B 石橋
千住博 Hiroshi Senju

na16B はいしゃ
大竹伸朗 Shinro Ohtake

na17B きんざ
内藤礼 Rei Naito

ベネッセハウス周辺

na19B ベネッセハウス ミュージアム
安藤忠雄［建築］Architecture: Tadao Ando

na24B 杉本博司ギャラリー 時の回廊
杉本博司［アート］Art: Hiroshi Sugimoto

na20B 李禹煥美術館
李禹煥［アート］ 安藤忠雄［建築］
Art: Lee Ufan, Architecture: Tadao Ando

na25B ヴァレーギャラリー
草間彌生、小沢剛［アート］ 安藤忠雄［建築］
Art: Yayoi Kusama, Tsuyoshi Ozawa
Architecture: Tadao Ando

na21B 地中美術館
安藤忠雄［建築］ Architecture: Tadao Ando

na22 桜の迷宮
安藤忠雄 Tadao Ando

[MM]

ヴァレーギャラリー

草間彌生、小沢剛[アート]
安藤忠雄[建築]

ナルシスの庭／スラグブッダ88ー豊島の産業廃棄物処理後のスラグで作られた88体の仏

na25B | ベネッセハウス周辺

Valley Gallery
Art: Yayoi Kusama | Japan
Art: Tsuyoshi Ozawa | Japan
Architecture: Tadao Ando | Japan
Narcissus Garden (1966/2022) / *Slag Buddha 88—Eighty-eight Buddha Statues Created Using Slag from Industrial Waste at Teshima* (2006/2022)
Benesse House Area
2022

[MM]

祠をイメージした小さな建物と周囲の屋外エリアで構成されるギャラリー。谷間に沿うように立つギャラリー内は、二重の壁による内省的な空間でありつつも半屋外に開かれ、外の光や風を感じ取ることができる。建物内と屋外の池では草間彌生の《ナルシスの庭》が展開され、2006年より池の横に恒久展示されている小沢剛の《スラグブッダ88 ー豊島の産業廃棄物処理後のスラグで作られた88体の仏》も一部改変されて公開された。

Valley Gallery is composed of a small building resembling a shrine and the surrounding outdoor area. Built along the valley, which is considered a boundary or sanctuary, the double-walled interior space is introspective, it is semi-open to the outdoors, allowing visitors to directly feel the movement of natural energy, such as light and wind. Yayoi Kusama's *Narcissus Garden* was installed inside the building and in the outdoor pond, and Tsuyoshi Ozawa's *Slag Buddha 88 – 88 Buddhas Made from Slag from Teshima's Industrial Waste Disposal*, which has been on permanent display next to the pond since 2006, was partially modified and exhibited.

設計＝安藤忠雄 | アート・ディレクション＝三木あき子
所蔵＝株式会社ベネッセホールディングス
運営＝株式会社ベネッセホールディングス、株式会社直島文化村

Architecture: Tadao Ando | Art direction: Akiko Miki
Collection: Benesse Holdings Inc.
Management: Benesse Holdings Inc., Naoshima Cultural Village Co., Ltd.

上 [TY]、下 [YA]

ANDO MUSEUM

安藤忠雄

na10B | 本村

ANDO MUSEUM
Tadao Ando | Japan
Honmura
2013

本村地区に残る築約100年の木造民家の中に新しい命を吹き込んだ空間。直島における安藤の活動を伝える資料も展示している。過去と現在、木とコンクリート、光と闇といった対立する要素が重なり合い、安藤建築のエッセンスが凝縮されている。

A space that breathes new life into a 100-year-old traditional wooden house in the Honmura area. It exhibits documents detailing Ando's work in Naoshima. Here, contrasting elements of past and present, wood and concrete, light and shadow overlap in a space which condenses the essence of Tadao Ando's architecture.

設計＝安藤忠雄
所蔵・運営＝公益財団法人 福武財団
Architecture: Tadao Ando
Collection & Management: Fukutake Foundation

上Hiroshi Sugimoto, Glass Tea House "Mondrian", 2014 ©Sugimoto Studio　下 [MM]

杉本博司ギャラリー 時の回廊

杉本博司［アート］

na24B | ベネッセハウス パーク

Art: Hiroshi Sugimoto | Japan / USA
Hiroshi Sugimoto Gallery: Time Corridors
Benesse House Park
2022

作家の創作活動のひとつの原点である直島と、作家の究極の作品とも言われる小田原の《江之浦測候所》とをつなげる形で構想され、代表作品を継続的かつ本格的に鑑賞できる展示施設となった。「時の回廊」は、建築空間や自然環境を回遊し体感することを促す安藤建築の特徴や、作家がこれまで追求し続けてきた時間に対する問いを反映している。鑑賞者は自然の変化や壮大な時間の流れを体感しながら、歴史や生きることについて思索を巡らせる。

Hiroshi Sugimoto Gallery was conceived to connect Naoshima and Enoura, which can be said to be the starting point of Sugimoto's creative activities, as Sugimoto's longtime efforts in Naoshima led to the creation of his ultimate work as an artist: *Enoura Observatory* in Odawara. *Time Corridors* reflect the characteristics of Ando's architecture, which encourages visitors to walk around the architectural space in its natural environment, and Sugimoto's continuous pursuit of solving the question of time.

設計＝新素材研究所（改修）
所蔵・運営＝株式会社ベネッセホールディングス、株式会社直島文化村
Renovation design: New Material Research Laboratory
Collection & Management: Benesse Holdings Inc., Naoshima Cultural Village Co., Ltd.

[TY]

ベネッセハウス ミュージアム

na19B | ベネッセハウス周辺

Benesse House Museum
1992

ベネッセハウスは「自然・建築・アートの共生」をコンセプトに、美術館とホテルが一体となった施設としてオープンした。「ミュージアム」を含む全ての建築が安藤忠雄の設計によるもので、経年とともに環境に溶け込むように構成されている。ミュージアムでは多様な形態の収蔵作品に加え、アーティストたちが自ら場所を選んで制作したサイトスペシフィック・ワークが館内だけでなく屋外まで点在している。

設計＝安藤忠雄
所蔵・運営＝株式会社ベネッセホールディングス、株式会社直島文化村

Benesse House opened as an integrated museum and hotel facility based on the concept of the "coexistence of nature, art and architecture". All of the facilities including Benesse House Museum were designed by Tadao Ando, and they blend into their surroundings as they age. In addition to the museum's diverse collection of artworks, site-specific works are scattered not only inside the museum but also outdoors.

Architecture: Tadao Ando
Collection & Management: Benesse Holdings Inc., Naoshima Cultural Village Co., Ltd.

[MF]

地中美術館

na21B | ベネッセハウス周辺

Chichu Art Museum
Benesse House Area
2004

クロード・モネ、ウォルター・デ・マリア、ジェームズ・タレルの作品を恒久設置する美術館。建物の大半は地下に埋設されているが、館内には自然光が差し込み、空間の表情が時間や季節によって刻々と変化する。

Chichu Art Museum permanently exhibits works by Claude Monet, Walter De Maria, and James Turrell. The vast majority of the building is embedded under the ground, but it is reached by natural light, giving the impression of a space shifting constantly depending on the hour and the season.

設計＝安藤忠雄
所蔵・運営＝公益財団法人 福武財団
Architecture: Tadao Ando
Collection & Management: Fukutake Foundation

安藤忠雄
桜の迷宮
na22 | 広木池

Tadao Ando | Japan
The Labyrinth of Cherry Blossom
Hirogi Pond
2015

[YIc]

直島ダム公園の敷地に約130本のオオシマザクラの苗木が格子状に植えられ、遊歩道が整備された。以前からあるソメイヨシノとともに花を咲かせる。

Approximately 130 Oshima cherry trees have been planted in a lattice pattern on the grounds of Naoshima Dam Park, and a walkway has been paved. The Oshima cherry trees flower along with the long-present Somei Yoshino cherry blossoms.

所蔵＝直島町
Collection: Naoshima Town

[TY]

[TY]

李禹煥美術館
李禹煥[アート]
安藤忠雄[建築]
na20B | ベネッセハウス周辺

Lee Ufan Museum
Art: Lee Ufan | Korea / Japan
Architecture: Tadao Ando | Japan
Benesse House Area
2010

李禹煥の作品が屋内外に展示される個人美術館。1970年代から今日までの作品群が、周囲のなだらかな地形や安藤忠雄の設計による建物と呼応しながら静謐な空間を作り出している。

A private museum featuring the work of Lee Ufan both inside and outside. Many of his works from the 1970s to today create a tranquil space while responding to the gradual slopes surrounding them and the museum building by Tadao Ando.

設計＝安藤忠雄 | 所蔵・運営＝公益財団法人 福武財団
Architecture: Tadao Ando | Collection & Management: Fukutake Foundation

上 [SOg] 下 [Shinkenchiku-Sha]

三分一博志

Hiroshi Sambuichi | Japan

The Naoshima Plann「住」

na23B | 宮ノ浦

The Naoshima Plan "JU"
Miyanoura
2022

直島の個々の建築や街区を通して、島全体の風・水・太陽などの「動く素材」を浮き上がらせ、その価値を再認識する試みである「The Naoshima Plan」。本建築はその一環としての島に移住する人たちが住まう長屋の計画である。建設中の建築を春・秋ごとの進行状況で公開。伝統工法「貫工法」の応用により、耐震性・耐久性と「動く素材」の享受を両立した建築を通して、「地球に知的に『住』まう」とは何かを問いかけた。

The Naoshima Plan attempts to focus on "moving material" such as wind, water, and the sun across the whole island, and reevaluate their importance. As a part of it, this building is designed as collective housing for people migrating to the island. The site was open to the public in spring and autumn, during the building process. The artist uses the penetration method – a traditional approach to building that ensures earthquake resistance and durability and the enjoyment of "moving material" – in his architecture, questioning what it is to "live on the earth intellectually".

The Naoshima Plan「水」

na07B | 本村

The Naoshima Plan "The Water"
Honmura
2019

直島では、多くの古屋敷が流れてくる風を受け渡す南北の続き間を持ち、地下には井戸から井戸へと共有される伏流水がある。作家は風や水、太陽を「動く素材」と呼び、建築の重要な素材と考えている。ここでは旧家の続き間を活かし、水盤を設置することで、来訪者が「動く素材」を肌で感じられる空間を作り出した。

Many old houses in Naoshima have a serial room lying in a north–south arrangement, allowing the wind to blow directly through them, and wells to access the groundwater arteries that flow beneath them. The artist terms the wind, water, and sun as "moving materials", and considers them to be significant materials in architecture. In this site, by placing a water-dish in the serial room of an old house, he created a space where visitors can physically experience this "moving material".

設計＝三分一博志 | 所蔵・運営＝公益財団法人 福武財団
Architecture: Hiroshi Sambuichi | Collection & Management: Fukutake Foundation

[SOg]

直島ホール

三分一博志［建築］

na08 | 本村

Naoshima Hall
Architecture: Hiroshi Sambuichi | Japan
Honmura
2015

ホール・集会所・庭園からなる施設。大屋根は直島に多く見られる「入母屋」という伝統的な形状で、本村の風向に即した風穴と内部の空気循環によってエアコンのないホールを実現するなど、島の自然環境を活かしている。直島女文楽をはじめとした文化活動や、地域の活動拠点として多目的に活用されている。

Naoshima Hall is a facility that features a meeting space and garden along with its main hall. The large roof is in the traditional form of *iri-omoya* (hip-and-gable roof), often seen in Naoshima. The artist utilizes the natural environment of the island, as seen by the implementation of louvers positioned with the wind direction and internal ventilation in the hall dispensing with the need for air conditioning. The facility serves as a center for cultural activities, such as the island's famous Naoshima Onna-Bunraku (all-female Japanese puppet theater troupe) and as a multi-purpose base for other local activities.

設計＝三分一博志
所蔵＝直島町
Architecture: Hiroshi Sambuichi
Collection: Naoshima Town

Event Data

4月18日（月）、24日（日）、5月16日（月）、10月3日（月）、19日（水）、24日（月）9:45～ | 旅行企画実施＝株式会社直島文化村 | 料金＝3,000円 | 参加者数＝48人

April 18th (Mon), 24th (Sun), May 16th (Mon), October 3rd (Mon), 19th (Wed), 24th (Mon); 9:45– | Tour Operation: Naoshima Cultural Village Co., Ltd. | Admission: 3,000 yen | Attendance: 48 people

直島建築ツアー

E02 | 宮ノ浦、本村

Naoshima Architecture Tour
Miyanoura / Honmura
2022

直島では美術施設を中心としたアート活動が活発になる以前から、ユニークな造形の公共建築がつくられてきた。1970年より直島小学校をはじめ体育館や武道館、直島町役場などを石井和紘が設計、近年では三分一博志の設計した直島ホールが日本建築学会賞などを受賞している。直島建築ツアーでは、普段は見学できない直島の公共施設を案内付きで見学するとともに、これらの建築がつくられてきた島の歴史にも触れた。

In Naoshima, even before it became known for art-related activities and the facilities that they center around, uniquely designed public buildings had been constructed. Since 1970, buildings like the Naoshima Elementary School, Gymnastics Hall, Martial Arts Hall and Naoshima Town Office were designed by Kazuhiro Ishii. Recently, Hiroshi Sambuichi's Naoshima Hall won the AIJ Prize (Architectural Institute of Japan). *The Naoshima Architecture Tour* move around, viewing public buildings in Naoshima – many of which are usually closed to the public – with a guide, and provides lectures on the history of the island and how it led to this architecture.

特別協力＝直島町 | Cooperation: Naoshima Town

Travel & Tourism
Recording & Creating
NAOSHIMA STANDARD
香川県
NAO SHIMA
おラボ
窯工研

2点とも [TY

[TY]

宮浦ギャラリー六区

下道基行

瀬戸内「　　　　」資料館

na06B | 宮ノ浦

Miyanoura Gallery 6
Motoyuki Shitamichi | Japan
Setouchi "　　　　" Archive
Miyanoura
2019–, 2022

アーティスト・下道基行による《瀬戸内「　　　　」資料館》は2019年9月から現在まで継続的に展開しているプロジェクトである。直島を中心とする瀬戸内海地域の景観・風土・民俗・歴史などについて調べ、展示・発表するプロジェクトで、住民や専門家とも協働する。このプロジェクトは、かつて島民の娯楽の場であった「パチンコ999（スリーナイン）」を改装した宮浦ギャラリー六区を舞台にしている。2022年はギャラリーに隣接する旧焼き肉屋を改修した空間「へんこつ」も公開を開始した。今回の瀬戸内国際芸術祭では春会期と秋会期に2つの展示を行った。

春会期：瀬戸内「鍰造景」資料館

銅の製錬が盛んに行われていた直島に関係の深い鍰（からみ：鉱石を溶融して金属を製錬するときに分離されたもの）に焦点を当て、鍰が島の景観や人々の暮らしにどのように関わったかを紹介した。

秋会期：瀬戸内「中村由信と直島どんぐりクラブ」資料館

直島出身の写真家・中村由信（なかむらよしのぶ・1925〜1990）と、中村が友人たちと結成した写真団体「直島どんぐりクラブ」に着目し、彼らの撮影した写真や資料を通して1950〜60年代の直島の人々の営みや瀬戸内の風景が紹介された。

設計＝［宮浦ギャラリー六区］西沢大良、［へんこつ］能作文徳
キュレトリアル・アドバイス＝三木あき子
印刷物デザイン＝SO（橋詰宗）
所蔵・運営＝公益財団法人 福武財団

Setouchi "　　　　" Archive, by Motoyuki Shitamichi, is ongoing project started in 2019 to present. It is a research project that examines the landscapes, culture, customs, and history of the Setouchi area – with Naoshima at its center – and exhibits its results. It is also a collaboration with local residents and specialists in various fields. The project is based in the Miyanoura Gallery 6, a refurbishment of Pachinko 999, a former pachinko parlor, which was once a popular amusement location for the islanders. In 2022, "Henkotsu" a refurbished space in the former *yakiniku* grill restaurant next to the gallery was also opened. In this edition of the Setouchi Triennale, different exhibits were presented in spring and autumn.

Spring: Setouchi "Slagscape" Archive

Focusing on slag – the waste substance produced in the process of melting ore to smelt metal – which has a historical association with Naoshima, a former center for copper refinement, this project introduced the ways in which slag impacted the view of the island and the lives of people there.

Autumn: Setouchi "Yoshinobu Nakamura and Naoshima Donguri Club" Archive

Concentrating on the photographer Yoshinobu Nakamura (1925–1990) and the photography group that he and his friends formed, named "Naoshima Donguri Club", this archive presented images of the daily lives of the people of Naoshima and views of Setouchi in the 1950s–60s.

Architecture: [Miyanoura Gallery 6] Taira Nishizawa, [Henkotsu] Fuminori Nousaku
Curatorial advice: Akiko Miki
Printing design: SO (So Hashizume)
Collection & Management: Fukutake Foundation

近代化の歴史にふれる —直島・犬島の鍰（からみ）煉瓦を訪ねて—

Naoshima and Inujima *Karami* Tour —Exploring Modern History—

E03 | 直島、犬島　Naoshima / Inujima

直島で鍰の煉瓦や瓦が残されている場所を訪ね、犬島の製錬所跡地（犬島精錬所美術館）を見学。日本の近代化の背景を体感した。

Visitors encountered locations where slag bricks and tiles remain in Naoshima, and went to the ruins of a former copper refinery in Inujima (Inujima Seirensho Art Museum) to experience the background of Japanese modernization.

Event Data

4月16日（土）、5月11日（水）10:00〜 | 旅行企画実施＝株式会社直島文化村
料金＝12,000円、15歳以下10,000円 | 参加者数＝3人

April 16th (Sat), May 11th (Wed); 10:00 | Tour Operation: Naoshima Cultural Village Co., Ltd. | Admission: 12,000 yen, Children (under age 15): 10,000 yen | Attendance: 3 people

[OW]

大竹伸朗
直島銭湯「I♥湯」
na05B | 宮ノ浦

Shinro Ohtake | Japan
Naoshima Bath "I ♥ 湯" (I Love YU)
Miyanoura
2009

実際に入浴できる美術施設。直島島民の活力源として、また国内外から訪れる来場者と島民との交流の場として作られたこの銭湯は、外観・内装はじめ、浴槽、風呂絵、モザイク画、トイレの陶器に至るまで大竹伸朗の世界が反映されている。

An art installation that doubles as a public bath. "I ♥ 湯" was created to provide both a place for Naoshima residents to rejuvenate and as a venue for exchanges between Japanese and international visitors and locals to take place. The exterior and fittings of the bathhouse, from the bath itself to the pictures decorating the walls, the mosaics, and even the toilet fittings, all reflect the universe of the artist.

所蔵＝公益財団法人 福武財団 | 運営＝NPO 法人直島町観光協会
Collection: Fukutake Foundation | Management: Town-Naoshima Tourism Association

草間彌生
赤かぼちゃ
na01 | 宮浦港緑地

Yayoi Kusama | Japan
Red Pumpkin
Miyanoura Port Square
2006

宮浦港で人々を出迎える大きな南瓜の作品。作家は「太陽の『赤い光』を宇宙の果てまで探してきて、それは直島の海の中で赤カボチャに変身してしまった」と語っている。

This is the first thing you see when the ferry enters Naoshima's Miyanoura Port. According to the artist, a red sunbeam searched the outer reaches of the universe only to metamorphose into a red pumpkin in the sea off Naoshima.

所蔵＝直島町
Collection: Naoshima Town

©YAYOI KUSAMA [DAo]

海の駅「なおしま」
妹島和世＋西沢立衛／SANAA［建築］

na02 | 宮浦港

Marine Station “Naoshima”
Architecture: Kazuyo Sejima + Ryue Nishizawa / SANAA | Japan
Miyanoura Port
2006

広くて薄い鉄板屋根を細いポールが支える軽やかな平屋建ては、開放感のあるデザイン。観光案内所やカフェ、特産品販売店などの施設で構成される。

A light structure with a huge flat steel-sheet roof supported by thin columns, the terminal is designed to feel open. Inside, it houses a tourism information office, café, and gift shop.

所蔵＝直島町
Collection: Naoshima Town

[JF]

藤本壮介
直島パヴィリオン

na04 | 宮浦港

Sou Fujimoto | Japan
Naoshima Pavilion
Miyanoura Port
2015

27の島からなる直島町の「28番目の島」がコンセプト。三角形のステンレスメッシュ約250枚を組み合わせてできた形は「浮島現象」に着想を得ている。

The concept is a 28th island of Naoshima, which actually consists of 27 islands. The shape, created by the combination of 250 triangle pieces of stainless mesh, is inspired by the phenomenon of mirages appearing on the ocean surface.

所蔵＝直島町
Collection: Naoshima Town

[YIc]

ジョゼ・デ・ギマランイス
BUNRAKU PUPPET

na03 | 宮浦港

José de Guimarães | Portugal
BUNRAKU PUPPET
Miyanoura Port
2006

伝統的な「直島女文楽」の人形の動きや着物の裾さばきに着想を得た立体作品。昼間は青い原色が鮮やかに映え、夜はカラフルにライトアップされる。

A three-dimensional work inspired by the movements of traditional Naoshima Onna-Bunraku puppet theater dolls and their flowing *kimono*. During the day, the primary blue color is striking, while at night it is colorfully illuminated.

所蔵＝直島町
Collection: Naoshima Town

[DAo]

直島港ターミナル
妹島和世＋西沢立衛／SANAA［建築］

na09 | 直島港

Naoshima Port Terminal
Architecture: Kazuyo Sejima + Ryue Nishizawa / SANAA | Japan
Naoshima Port
2017

宮浦港の水平に広がる海の駅「なおしま」と対をなす立体的な建物。直径4mのFRP球13個を積み上げた高さ約8 mの建物内には、半透明の球を通して外の光が明るく入り込む。

This building is designed to emphasize the vertical in contrast to the striking horizontal lines of Marine Station “Naoshima”, an island landmark, and the two seem like opposite halves of a pair. The building is 8 meters high and comprised of thirteen 4 meter-diameter translucent fiberglass spheres, through which light filters brightly.

設計＝妹島和世＋西沢立衛／SANAA | 所蔵＝直島町
Architecture: Kazuyo Sejima + Ryue Nishizawa / SANAA | Collection: Naoshima Town

家プロジェクト | *Art House Project*

所蔵・運営＝株式会社ベネッセホールディングス、株式会社直島文化村
Collection & Management: Benesse Holdings, Inc., Naoshima Cultural Village Co., Ltd.

本村地区における、1998 年の「角屋」には始まったプロジェクト。古い家屋などを改修・改築し、空間そのものを作品化する。現在 7 軒が公開されている。

The *Art House Project* is an art project underway in Honmura district, in which old houses were modified and restored to recreate their spaces as artworks, began with Kadoya (1998). A total of seven houses are currently exhibited.

[NU]

[KSu]

角屋

宮島達男

Sea of Time '98
Naoshima's Counter Window
Changing Landscape

na11B | 本村

Kadoya
Tatsuo Miyajima | Japan
Sea of Time '98 / Naoshima's Counter Window / Changing Landscape
Honmura
1998, 1999, 2018

築約 200 年の家屋を改修。直島町の人々が《Sea of Time '98》の制作に参加するなど、現代アートが地域に介在する契機になった作品。

A renovated house built approximately 200 years ago. Residents of Naoshima participated in the creation of *Sea of Time '98*, a work that became an opportunity for contemporary art to intersect with the community.

設計＝山本忠司（修復監修）
Restoration supervision: Tadashi Yamamoto

2 点とも [OW]

碁会所

須田悦弘

碁会所

na14B | 本村

Gokaisho
Yoshihiro Suda | Japan
Gokaisho
Honmura
2006

日本画家・速水御舟《名樹散椿》に着想を得た作品。庭と屋内には、本物の竹や椿と、それらを精巧に木彫で作った作品とが同時に存在している。

The work is inspired by the masterpiece *Meiju Chiritsubaki* by the Japanese painter Gyoshu Hayami. In the garden and indoors, real bamboo and camellias coexist with elaborate wood carvings of them.

設計＝須田悦弘、秋元雄史（空間デザイン）、本多忠勝（修復監修）
Spatial design: Yoshihiro Suda, Yuji Akimoto, Restoration supervision: Tadakatsu Honda

©Hiroshi Sugimoto

護王神社

杉本博司

Appropriate Proportion

na12B | 本村

Go'o Shrine
Hiroshi Sugimoto | Japan / USA
Appropriate Proportion
Honmura
2002

江戸時代から続く護王神社の改築に合わせて設計。伊勢神宮など初期の神社建築の様式を引用しつつも、作家の美意識が活かされた空間となっている。

The project began with the renovation of the Go'o Shrine which dates from the Edo period. The main and front structures are based on the architectural style of early shrines (such as the Ise Shrine) while reflecting the artist's own aesthetic sensibilities.

設計＝杉本博司 | 特別協力＝木村優・設楽敏生／アートステーション（設計）
Architecture: Hiroshi Sugimoto | Design cooperation: Masaru Kimura and Toshio Shitara / Art Station

[KSu]

はいしゃ

大竹伸朗

舌上夢／ボッコン覗

na16B | 本村

Haisha
Shinro Ohtake | Japan
Dreaming Tongue/BOKKON-NOZOKI
Honmura
2006

歯医者兼住居だった建物を作品化。タイトルの「舌上夢」は何かを口にしたときの味覚・嗅覚からたどる夢の記憶のプロセスを表す。

Haisha, meaning "dentist", was once the home and office of a dentist, and the entire building was converted into a work of art. The title of the work, *Dreaming Tongue*, represents the process of holding something in one's mouth and recalling a dream by retracing the taste and scent.

設計＝秋元雄史、本多忠勝（修復監修） |
Restoration supervision: Yuji Akimoto, Tadakatsu Honda

[KSu]

南寺

ジェームズ・タレル

バックサイド・オブ・ザ・ムーン

na13B | 本村

Minamidera
James Turrell | USA
Backside of the Moon
Honmura
1999

黒々とした焼板で覆われた木造建築の中には真っ暗な闇が広がり、かつてここに実在した寺が人びとの精神的な拠り所であったという記憶をとどめている。

The wooden architecture, covered with pitch-black burnt cedar planks that hold a deep darkness, preserving the memory that the temple on this site once functioned as a spiritual center for the people.

設計＝安藤忠雄 | Architecture: Tadao Ando

[KSu]

[OW]

石橋
千住博
ザ・フォールズ／空の庭

na15B｜本村

Ishibashi
Hiroshi Senju | Japan
The Falls / The Garden of Kū
Honmura
2006, 2009

明治に製塩業で栄えた石橋家の家屋で展開。作家は瀬戸内の風景や歴史に向き合いながら、5年の歳月をかけて「場の持つ記憶」を空間ごと作品化した。

The project is housed in the building of the Ishibashi family, who were prosperous in the salt industry during the Meiji period. The artist spent five years studying the landscape and history of the Seto Inland Sea, expressing "the memory of the place" in his work.

設計＝千住博、福武總一郎（空間デザイン）、秋元雄史、本多忠勝（修復監修）
Spatial design: Hiroshi Senju, Soichiro Fukutake,
Restoration Supervision: Yuji Akimoto, Tadakatsu Honda

[NH]

きんざ
内藤礼
このことを

na17B｜本村

Kinza
Rei Naito | Japan
Being Given
Honmura
2001

伝統的な技術を使いながら、小さな家屋の全体を作品化した。足元から射す光によって、多様な素材で微細に構成された空間が浮かび上がる。

A small house has been transformed into artwork based on traditional techniques. The space lit up by the light from the floor reveals delicately composed space made with various materials.

設計＝木村優・永田直／アートステーション（実施設計）
Detailed design: Masaru Kimura and Sunao Nagata / Art Station

---

杉本雅楽 直島御神楽

E04｜本村・護王神社

Sugimoto Gagaku—Naoshima Mikagura
Go'o Shrine, Honmura

老朽化した社殿を、家プロジェクトの一環として杉本博司が全面改修を行い、2002年に公開した護王神社。2022年に遷座20周年を迎えたことを祝い「杉本雅楽 直島御神楽」を上演した。

As part of the *Art House Project*, Hiroshi Sugimoto completely refurbished the aging building of Go'o Shrine, and it was opened to the public in 2002. For its 20th anniversary in 2022, the event *Sugimoto Gagaku – Naoshima Mikagura* was held.

主催＝護王神社20周年記念奉賛事業実行委員会
Organization: Executive Committee for the 20th Anniversary of Go'o Shrine Dedication Project

Event Data 10月9日（日）14:00～、16:30～
October 9th (Sun); 14:00– , 16:30–

直島女文楽

麗春の舞

E01 | 本村・直島ホール

Naoshima Onna Bunraku | Japan
Dance of Beautiful Spring
Naoshima Hall, Honmura
2022

江戸時代、天領だった直島は古くから芸能が盛んに行われていた。「直島女文楽」はその代表的なもので、今のように人形の使い手が女性だけになったのは昭和23年から。一度は下火になりかけていた文楽を女性3人の手により再興した。昭和30年に県無形文化財となり、現在も県無形民俗文化財として受け継がれている。今回は「壺坂観音霊験記〜山の段〜」と「伽羅先代萩 政岡」を上演。ゲストの津軽三味線小山流三代目・小山豊が演奏した。

During the Edo period (1603–1868), the performing arts flourished on Naoshima, a territory belonging to the emperor. One example is *Naoshima Onna Bunraku*, an all-female puppet theater, although the troupe only became all-female in 1948. The traditional art, which had almost died out by that time, was revived by three women. In 1955, it was designated a prefectural intangible asset and continues to be passed down as an intangible folk-cultural asset. This time, performances were held of *The Miracle at Tsubosaka Kannon Temple: The Mountain* and *Meiboku Sendaihagi: Nursing Mother Masaoka* (The Disputed Succession of the Date Family), accompanied by a guest appearance by Yutaka Oyama, the third head of the Oyama school of *tsugaru-jamisen* (three-stringed Japanese banjo of Aomori).

Event Data

4月23日（土）14:30〜 | 出演＝直島女文楽、小山豊
料金＝一般1,500円、小中高生800円、ほか | 来場者数＝159人

April 23rd (Sat); 14:30– | Cast: Naoshima Onna Bunraku, Yutaka Oyama | Admission: General 1,500 yen, Children (ages 6–18) 800 yen, etc. | Attendance: 159 people

3点とも [SM]

豊島

Teshima

豊島　*Teshima*

東備讃瀬戸の中央に位置する島。海がまだ淡水だった9,000年前の貝塚があり、縄文時代から人が住んでいたことがわかっている。漁業や海運業をはじめ、近年まで豊島石の採掘加工や酪農も盛んだった。現在はノリ養殖などの漁業、イチゴ、オリーブなどの栽培をしている。

標高340 mの檀山にはスダジイの原生林が茂り、山全体が水を湛え島のあちこちから水が湧き出る。この水を活用し緩斜面を棚田に変えて古くから稲作が行われた。最盛期は島外へ米を出荷していたが、1960年代から過疎高齢化に伴う担い手不足で、125haあった棚田の約80%が荒廃してしまう。1970年代以降、都市部から産業廃棄物が運び込まれ日本最大の不法投棄事件が起こる。環境汚染、健康被害、風評被害に苦しみ、住民運動や産廃処理に費やした年月は50年近くにも及ぶ。

2007年、棚田のある唐櫃岡に美術館建設計画が持ち上がり、荒廃した棚田の再生がはじまった。豊島美術館が完成した2010年以降、徐々に島のイメージは“豊かな自然とアートの島”へ変化し、観光客や移住者が増えている。

Located in the central area of East-Bisan Seto, between Okayama and Kagawa. A shell mound from about 9000 years ago, when the sea was still a body of fresh water, shows that Teshima has been inhabited since the Jomon period (14000–1000BC). Until recently, mining and processing of Teshima rock and milk farming were active industries, alongside fishing and ocean transport. Today, its major businesses are seaweed farming, fishing, and strawberry and olive farming.

The 340-meter Mt. Danyama is forested with primeval *Itaji chinkapin*, and the island has many natural springs, as the whole mountain is rich with water. Rice farming in terraced paddy fields dug into the gentle slopes has been conducted with this water since a long time ago. At its peak, rice was exported from the island, but since the 1960s the aging and decreasing population has limited the number of workers, and 80% of the 125 hectares of terraced fields have been abandoned. Additionally, from the 1970s, industrial waste from cities was disposed of on the island in the largest illegal waste dumping in Japanese history. Suffering from environmental pollution, associated health issues, and rumors, it took the island more than 50 years of public activity and waste disposal to recover.

In 2007, a plan to establish an art museum in Karato-oka, which formerly had terraced paddies, and to regenerate the ruined fields began. After 2010, when the Teshima Art Museum was completed, the image of the island gradually began to shift, becoming “a place of rich nature and art”, and seeing an increase in tourists and new settlers.

所在地＝香川県小豆郡土庄町
（かがわけんしょうずぐんとのしょうちょう）
面積＝14.5㎢
周囲＝18㎞
最高地点＝340m（檀山）
世帯数＝410世帯
人口＝768人
0〜14歳＝47人
15〜64歳＝334人
65歳〜＝387人

Location: Tonosho Town, Shozu County, Kagawa Prefecture
Area: 14.5km^2
Circumference: 18km
Highest Point: 340m (Mt. Danyama)
Number of Households: 410
Population: 768 people
0–14 Years: 47 people
15–64 Years: 334 people
Over 65 Years: 387 people

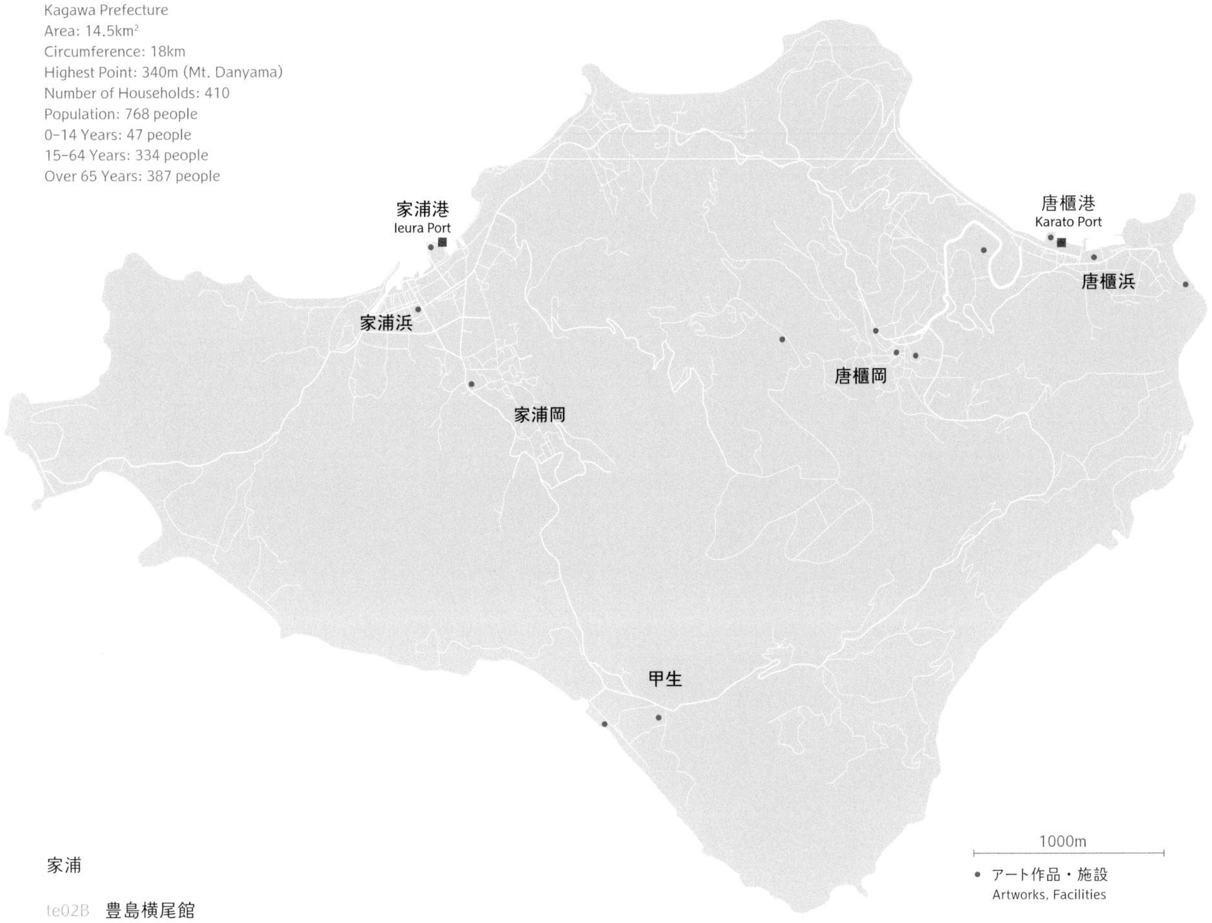

家浦港
Ieura Port
家浦浜
家浦岡
唐櫃港
Karato Port
唐櫃浜
唐櫃岡
甲生

1000m
• アート作品・施設
Artworks, Facilities

家浦

te02B 豊島横尾館
横尾忠則［コンセプト・アート］ 永山祐子［建築］
Concept, Art: Tadanori Yokoo, Architecture: Yuko Nagayama

te03B 針工場
大竹伸朗 Shinro Ohtake

唐櫃岡

te08 空の粒子／唐櫃
青木野枝 Noe Aoki

te09 あなたの最初の色（私の頭の中の解〈ソリューション〉一私の胃の中の溶液〈ソリューション〉）
ピピロッティ・リスト Pipilotti Rist

te10 島キッチン
安部良［建築］ Architecture: Ryo Abe

te12B ささやきの森
クリスチャン・ボルタンスキー Christian Boltanski

te13B 豊島美術館《母型》
内藤礼［アート］ 西沢立衛［建築］
Art: Rei Naito, Architecture: Ryue Nishizawa

te18B 西本喜美子写真展〜ひとりじゃなかよ〜
西本喜美子 Kimiko Nishimoto

唐櫃浜

te14 勝者はいない一マルチ・バスケットボール
イオベット＆ポンズ Llobet & Pons

te15B 心臓音のアーカイブ
クリスチャン・ボルタンスキー Christian Boltanski

甲生

te19 海を夢見る人々の場所
ヘザー・B・スワン+ノンダ・カサリディス
Heather B. Swann + Nonda Katsalidis

te20 かげたちのみる夢（Remains of Shadowings）
冨安由真 Yuma Tomiyasu

E06 島のお誕生会
Island Birthday Party

3点とも [KK]

冨安由真

かげたちのみる夢
(Remains of Shadowings)

te20 | 甲生

Yuma Tomiyasu | Japan
Remains of Shadowings
Kou
2022

築100年余りの古民家を舞台にしたインスタレーション作品。小泉八雲の小説『影 (Shadowings)』の一編「和解」に着想を得た作家は、家にあるものの配置を詳細に決定し、それらを描いた絵画を部屋、廊下など12の空間に1点ずつ潜ませた。家の中を通り抜けた最後の部屋には12のモニターが並び、密かに設置されたカメラを通して、各部屋に置かれた絵画の様子が映されている。鑑賞者はもの・絵画・映像によって、この家に虚実が混じった何層もの時空が存在したことを知る。

A work set in a 100-year old house. Inspired by the short story "The Reconciliation" from the novel *Shadowings* by Yakumo Koizumi, the artist planned the placement of items in the interior of the house in detail, and hid a painting of those items in each room and corridor: 12 different spaces and 12 pieces in total. 12 monitors are placed in the final room visitors enter, showing each piece in its space. Visitors realize that there are multiple layers of time and space, with reality and falsity, through items, paintings, and video images.

ヘザー・B・スワン+ノンダ・カサリディス
海を夢見る人々の場所
te19 | 甲生

Heather B. Swann + Nonda Katsalidis | Australia
Place for Sea Dreamers
Kou
2022

男木島をのぞむ甲生集落の海岸に作られた、長さ約 6m にわたる鉄製のベンチ。有機的な形は漁網や流木、動物や船などさまざまなモチーフから着想され、アーティストのスワンと建築家のカサリディスとのコラボレーションによって実現した。人々が腰掛けて海と向き合いながら、その向こうにある景色や自分たちのいる世界について想像をめぐらせる場所となる。

This 6-meter-long steel bench, a collaboration between sculptor Swann and architect Katsalidis, stands on the Kou beach overlooking Ogijima island. The work's organic form was inspired by animals and driftwood, fishing nets and vessels, and it was conceived as a place where people can sit, face the sea, and contemplate the world in which they live, and the worlds beyond.

助成=オーストラリア大使館
Funding: Australian Embassy Tokyo

2点とも [KK]

クリスチャン・ボルタンスキー

ささやきの森

te12B | 唐櫃岡・檀山

Christian Boltanski | France

La forêt des murmures

Karato-oka, Danyama

2016

コーディネーション＝白羽明美
所蔵・運営＝公益財団法人 福武財団

Art coordination: Akemi Shiraha
Collection & Management: Fukutake Foundation

森の中で無数の風鈴が音を奏でるインスタレーション。風鈴の短冊には誰かの大切な人の名前が記され、個人の記憶や魂の神秘性が音とともに感じられる。

An installation in which the sound of many wind chimes proliferates through the forest. Strips attached to each chime hold the name of a person who is important to someone, conveying the memories of individuals and the mysteriousness of the soul through sound.

[YIc]

2点とも [YK]

クリスチャン・ボルタンスキー
心臓音のアーカイブ

te15B | 唐櫃浜

Christian Boltanski | France
Les Archives du Cœur
Karato-hama
2010

美しい浜に建つ、世界中の人々の心臓音を収集する小さな美術館。心臓音に合わせて電球が明滅する「ハートルーム」、希望者の心臓音を採録する「レコーディングルーム」、世界中から集められた心臓音を検索し聴くことができる「リスニングルーム」で構成される。訪れた人々は人間の個々の固有性と、記憶のもろさ、はかなさを体感する。

A small museum standing on a beautiful shore, collecting the sounds of the hearts of people from all over the world. It consists of "Heart Room", where light bulbs flash with the sound of heartbeats, "Recording Room", where visitors can have the sound of their heart recorded, and "Listening Room", where they can search and listen to the sounds of hearts collected from across the world. Visitors experience human individuality, and the faintness and impermanence of memory.

所蔵・運営＝公益財団法人 福武財団
Collection & Management: Fukutake Foundation

豊島美術館

内藤礼[アート]
西沢立衛[建築]
母型
te13B | 唐櫃岡

Teshima Art Museum
Art: Rei Naito | Japan
Architecture: Ryue Nishizawa | Japan
Matrix
Karato-oka
2010

瀬戸内海を望む小高い丘の中腹に立地し、周囲には棚田が広がり、自然と建築、アートが融和した美しい環境を作り出している。館内では1日を通して「泉」が誕生する作品《母型》が展開される。天井からは光や風、鳥の声が注ぎ、時間の流れや季節の移り変わりとともに無限の表情を伝える。

Teshima Art Museum, the collaborative creation of artist Rei Naito and architect Ryue Nishizawa, lies partway up a hill overlooking the Seto Inland Sea and is bordered by terraced rice fields, resulting in a beautiful fusion of nature, art and architecture. Inside, new "springs" are constantly born from the work *Matrix*. Light, wind, and the voices of birds enter from above, conjuring an infinite array of impressions with the passage of seasons and the flow of time.

所蔵・運営＝公益財団法人 福武財団
Collection & Management: Fukutake Foundation

2点とも [NM]

[SM]

大竹伸朗
針工場
te03B | 家浦岡

Shinro Ohtake | Japan
Needle factory
Ieura-oka
2016

メリヤス針の製造工場跡に、宇和島の造船所に残されていた漁船用の木型が持ち込まれることで、異質なものが出会い新たな磁場を産み出している。

A former manufacturing facility for latch needles, this location, which features a fishing boat that remained in the shipbuilding yard in Uwajima, gains a magnetism through encounters with alien items.

設計＝津田朋延、奥野雄（改修）
所蔵・運営＝公益財団法人 福武財団
Renovation design: Tomonobu Tsuda, Yu Okuno
Collection & Management: Fukutake Foundation

[TY]

豊島横尾館
横尾忠則[コンセプト・アート]
永山祐子[建築]
te02B | 家浦浜

Teshima Yokoo House
Concept, Art:
Tadanori Yokoo | Japan
Architecture:
Yuko Nagayama | Japan
Ieura-hama
2013

古民家を改修した美術館。「母屋」「倉」「納屋」で構成される屋内に平面作品11点を、石庭と池、円筒状の塔にそれぞれインスタレーションを展開。作家が長きに渡り主題としてきた「生と死」のテーマに深く迫る場所となっている。

A museum set in a refurbished old house. The interior, that consists of the "main house", "warehouse", and "outhouse", is host to 11 pieces of two-dimensional work, as well as installation work – a stone garden, a pond, and a cylindrical tower. It is a place to delve deeply into "life and death", a theme that the artist has long dealt with.

設計＝永山祐子
所蔵・運営＝公益財団法人 福武財団
Architecture: Yuko Nagayama
Collection & Management: Fukutake Foundation

イオベット&ポンズ
勝者はいない
―マルチ・バスケットボール
te14 | 唐櫃浜

Llobet & Pons | Spain
No one wins – Multibasket
Karato-hama
2013

島の人や来場者たちがバスケットボールを楽しめる作品。リングがたくさんあるボードで、思い思いのルールで楽しめる。

This artwork creates a place where local residents and visitors can enjoy basketball. Unlike the regular game, there are multiple hoops. Players must use their imagination and make up their own rules.

[ON]

島キッチン

安部良[建築]

te10 | 唐櫃岡

Shima Kitchen
Architecture: Ryo Abe | Japan
Karato-oka
2010

大きな屋根が全体を包む開放的なレストラン。地元の食材を使った食事を提供するほか、「島のお誕生会」をはじめ地域のプラットフォームとして定着している。

A restaurant under a large roof that extends over the whole building, creating a sense of openness. It not only serves meals using local ingredients, but is also a well-established center in the local area, hosting events such as *Island Birthday Party*.

設計＝東京藝術大学美術学部建築科金田研究室（構造）
特別協力＝株式会社丸ノ内ホテル | 運営＝NPO 法人瀬戸内こえびネットワーク

Structural design: Professor Kanada's lab at Department of Architecture of Tokyo University of the Arts | Cooperation: Marunouchi Hotel Co., Ltd. | Management: Setouchi Koebi Network

島のお誕生会

E06 | 唐櫃岡・島キッチン

Island Birthday Party
Shima Kitchen, Karato-oka
2022

毎月開催している「島のお誕生会」。2014 年から続き、毎回さまざまな楽しいゲストを迎えて、延べ約 400 名以上をお祝いしてきた。豊島に住んでいる方や島を訪れた方が、一緒にお誕生月を迎えた方々をお祝いする。日頃なかなか外出する機会のないおじいちゃんやおばあちゃん、豊島に住む子どもたち、国内外からの来島者、この日のために駆けつけたボランティアサポーターこえび隊など、いろいろな人が自由に参加できる会。

Island Birthday Party, held once a month on the island, has been continuing since 2014, with various fun guests each time, and it has celebrated more than 400 birthdays. The people of Teshima and visitors wish happy birthday to everyone born in that month. Elderly people who do not have many opportunities for a day out, children from the island, visitors from Japan and overseas, koebi-tai volunteers – all kinds of people can freely come and enjoy themselves.

Event Data

4/17（日）「春うらら～テラスに人形劇がやってくる！」ゲスト＝人形歌劇団パペレッタ（田所俊一）
5/8（日）「カチ♪カチ♪キャッチ！けん玉で遊ぼう！」ゲスト＝青木勇
6/12（日）「身体も心もスッキリ！癒しのヨガ体験♪」ゲスト＝長屋諒子
7/10（日）「ワクワク！楽しい！すご技大道芸がやってくる！」ゲスト＝ホワイトアスパラガス
8/7（日）「豊島ブギウギ♪夏の昭和歌謡ショー」ゲスト＝虎姫一座
9/11（日）「ポンポ～ン♪華麗なジャグリングショー！」ゲスト＝とっしゃん
10/10（月祝）「聞いてうっとり、食べて美味しい！？ちくわ笛がやってくる！」ゲスト＝住宅正人
11/3（木）「秋風と優しいウクレレのコンサート♪」ゲスト＝高嶋秀明
各日 14：00 ～ | 参加者数＝ 272 人

April 17th (Sun): One Fine Day – Puppet Theater Comes to the Terrace Guest: Puppet Opera Company Pupperetta (Shunichi Tadokoro) | May 8th (Sun): Kachi Kachi Catch! Let's Play Kendama Guest: Yu Aoki | June 12th (Sun): Refresh Body and Mind! Healing Yoga Experience Guest: Ryoko Nagaya | July 10th (Sun): Exciting! Fun! Amazing Street Performer Skills Guest: White Asparagus | August 7th (Sun): Teshima Boogie-Woogie – Summer Pop Songs from Showa Guest: Tora-Hime Ichiza | September 11th (Sun): Pom-pon! Astonishing Juggling Show! Guest: Tosshan | October 10th (Mon): Sounds Great, Tastes Nice?! Fish Stick Whistle Guest: Masato Sumitaku | November 3rd (Thu): Autumn Breeze and Gentle Ukulele Concert Guest: Hideaki Takashima | Each day starts 14:00– | Attendance: 272 people

西本喜美子

西本喜美子写真展　〜ひとりじゃなかよ〜

te18B | 唐櫃岡

Kimiko Nishimoto | Japan
Kimiko Nishimoto Photo Exhibition
Karato-oka
2022

70 代に入ってから友人の勧めで写真をはじめ、90 歳を超えた今もなお仲間を増やしながら、カメラのレンズ越しに新しいチャレンジを続ける作家。唐櫃岡で実際に使われていた民家にて、作家著書『ひとりじゃなかよ』の言葉を交えながら写真を展示し、人生を楽しむその姿から豊かに生きる術を垣間見ることができる空間をつくり出した。

The artist began photography in her 70s at the recommendation of a friend, and today, at over 90, she continues to explore through her lens, broadening her circle of friends. In a venue in Karato-oka that was formerly a house, Nishimoto exhibited work with excerpts from her book *Hitori Ja Nakayo* (You Are Not Alone), creating a space in which visitors can see the philosophy of a fulfilled life through images created in her enjoyment of living.

[ON]

青木野枝

空の粒子／唐櫃

te08 | 唐櫃岡・清水霊泉

Noe Aoki | Japan
Particles in the Air / Karato
Shimizureisen, Karato-oka
2010, 2013

空に粒子が舞うかのように円形の鉄の彫刻をつなぎ合わせ、貯水タンクを囲んで設置された作品。2013 年には水源の鉄扉やベンチが追加された。

Overlapping steel hoops hover like particles dancing in the air above a water tank. The iron grating and a bench were added in 2013.

[ON]

ピピロッティ・リスト

あなたの最初の色(私の頭の中の解〈ソリューション〉―私の胃の中の溶液〈ソリューション〉)

te09 | 唐櫃岡

Pipilotti Rist | Switzerland
Your First Color (Solution In My Head — Solution In My Stomach)
Karato-oka
2011

島キッチン敷地内にある蔵の 2 階部分に円形の映像が浮かんでいる。チューリップやイギリスの道などカラフルな映像が投影され、鑑賞者を幸福感で包む。

This visual work was projected on to a round screen installed on the second floor space of a warehouse in the yard of Shima Kitchen. The work features images such as tulips and British streetscapes. with the aim of enveloping the viewer in a feeling of happiness.

女木島

Megijima

[SM]

女木島　*Megijima*

南北に細長い形の島。2つの山頂から東西に海まで斜面が続いている。高松港からフェリーで20分の場所に位置し、東側にやや広い平地があり港や民家が集まる。西側にも十数軒の家が建つ。冬は「オトシ」と呼ばれる海水を巻き上げた強風が集落に吹きつけるため、島の東海岸は「オオテ」と呼ばれる巨大な防風防潮用の石垣がずらりと並んでいる。

平地には畑が点在するが、人口が多かった昭和初期頃は、山頂近くまで段々畑であった。現在もニンニクやトウモロコシ、ミカンの栽培が盛んで、半農半漁で暮らしてきた島である。江戸時代は直島・男木島とともに幕府領に、明治期には男木島と雌雄島村となり、昭和期に高松市に編入された。北側の標高186mの鷲ヶ峰では1930年代に穴丁場跡の洞窟が発見され、観光資源として桃太郎伝説とつなげて島は「鬼ヶ島」と呼ばれるようになる。夏は海水浴で多くの人で賑わい、8月には太鼓台を担いで海に入る勇壮な祭りがある。

An island thinly stretched between north and south, with long slopes extending to the sea in the east and west from the peaks of two mountains. It is located 20 minutes from Takamatsu port by ferry, and its port and local houses are positioned on a relatively large flat plain on the east side. On the west side there are few more than ten houses. In winter the island experiences such strong winds, called "*otoshi*", that the seawater is blown upwards and into the village. As a result, the east shore features a huge stone wall called "*oote*", set up as a wind breaker and tidal embankment.

Flat land with vegetable fields is scattered here and there these days, but in the Showa era, when the population was larger, terraced fields reached almost to the top of the mountains. Today, garlic, corn, and tangerines continue to be grown, supporting the island's farming and fishing life. In the Edo era, Megijima became government territory along with Naoshima and Ogijima, in the Meiji era it became Shiyujima village paired with Ogijima, and in the Showa era it became part of Takamatsu city. In the 186-meter Washigamine, in the north of the island, there is a cave where traces of stone mining were discovered in the 1930s. The island became known as Onigashima, tied to the legend of Momotaro, which boosted tourism. In summer, many people come to enjoy swimming at the beach, and August sees a festival where brave people enter the sea carrying *Taiko-dai* on their shoulders.

女木島中心部

mg01 カモメの駐車場
木村崇人 Takahito Kimura

mg02 20世紀の回想
禿鷹墳上 Hagetaka Funjo

mg05 Café de la Plage／カフェ・ドゥ・ラ・プラージュ
ヴェロニク・ジュマール Véronique Joumard

mg06 ヘアサロン壽
宮永愛子 Aiko Miyanaga

mg08 ピンポン・シー
原倫太郎＋原游 Rintaro Hara + Yu Hara

mg09 ランドリー
レアンドロ・エルリッヒ Leandro Erlich

mg11 ティンカー・ベルズ　ファクトリー
中里繪魯洲 Eros Nakazato

mg13B 女根／めこん
大竹伸朗 Shinro Ohtake

mg14 ISLAND THEATRE MEGI「女木島名画座」
依田洋一朗 Yoichiro Yoda

mg15B 不在の存在
レアンドロ・エルリッヒ Leandro Erlich

mg17 段々の風
杉浦康益 Yasuyuki Sugiura

E07 女木島名画座上映会
Screening of Megijima

500m

• アート作品・施設
Artworks, Facilities

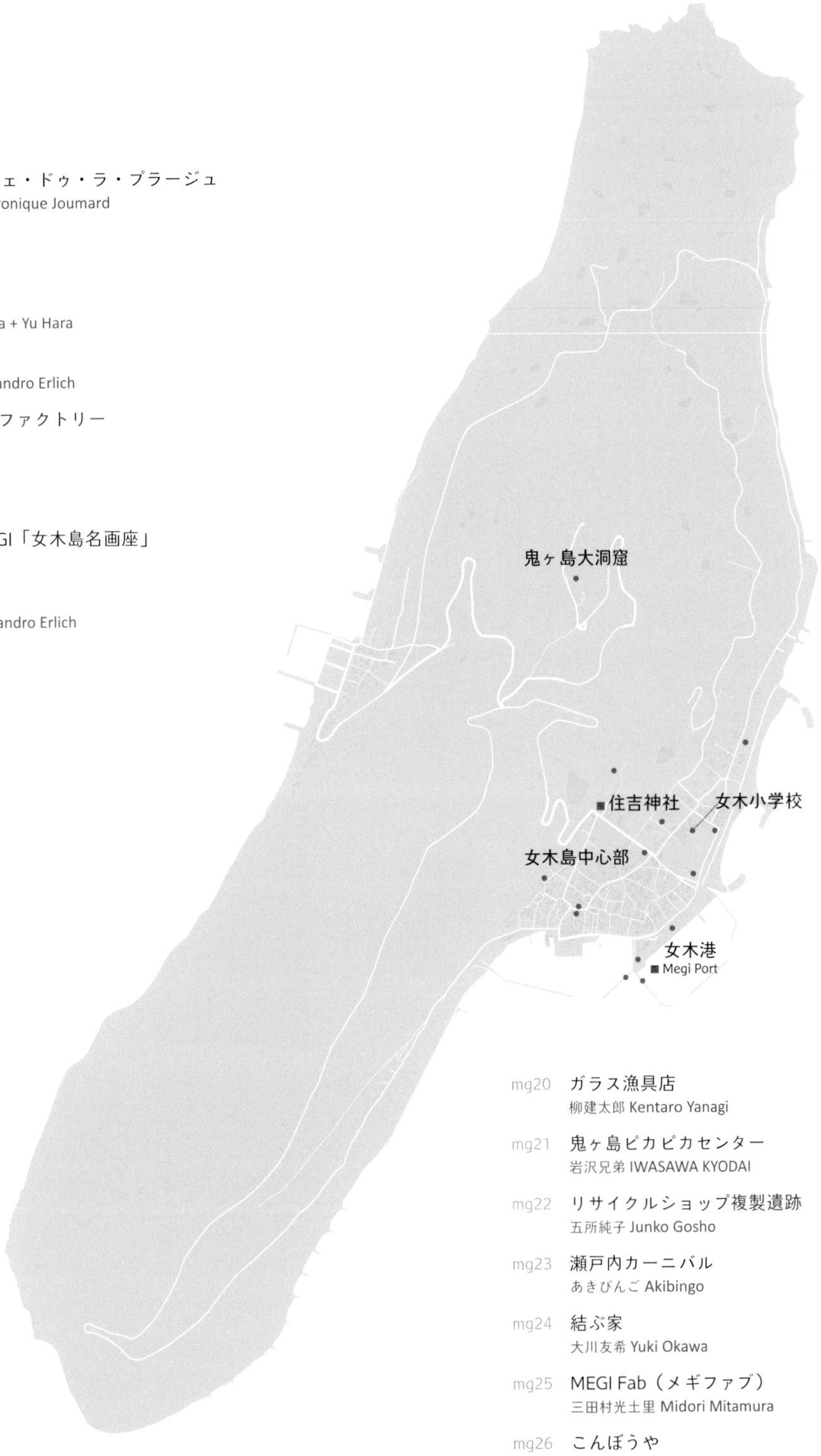

所在地＝香川県高松市
（かがわけんたかまつし）
面積＝2.62㎢
周囲＝7.9㎞
最高地点＝216m
世帯数＝81世帯
人口＝125人
0～14歳＝4人
15～64歳＝30人
65歳～＝88人
不詳＝3人

Location: Takamatsu City, Kagawa Prefecture
Area: 2.62km²
Circumference: 7.9km
Highest Point: 216m
Number of Households: 81
Population: 125 people
0-14 Years: 4 people
15-64 Years: 30 people
Over 65 Years: 88 people
Unknown: 3 people

mg20 ガラス漁具店
柳建太郎 Kentaro Yanagi

mg21 鬼ヶ島ピカピカセンター
岩沢兄弟 IWASAWA KYODAI

mg22 リサイクルショップ複製遺跡
五所純子 Junko Gosho

mg23 瀬戸内カーニバル
あきびんご Akibingo

mg24 結ぶ家
大川友希 Yuki Okawa

mg25 MEGI Fab（メギファブ）
三田村光土里 Midori Mitamura

mg26 こんぼうや
小谷元彦 Motohiko Odani

mg27 ナビゲーションルーム
ニコラ・ダロ Nicolas Darrot

鬼ヶ島大洞窟

mg19 オニノコ瓦プロジェクト2
オニノコプロダクション Oninoko Production

女木島名店街　*Megijima Meitengai Mall*

2019年にささやかにはじまった「島の中の小さなお店プロジェクト」が前身となり、2022年に本格始動した「女木島名店街」。アーティストが感じた新鮮な土地の固有性をグッズやサービスとして購入できる、新たな価値観を持ったさまざまな名店で島が活気づくことを目指し、地域の人が利用できて来島者が楽しめる場所を創出してきた。かつての民宿「寿荘」を中心に島内の空き家を活かして、ヘアサロン、金物加工店、卓球場、カフェ、コインランドリーが開店し、今回新たに釣具店、本屋、こんぼう屋、手芸店、リサイクルショップ、照明器具の店が加わった。寿荘にはコンシェルジュ機能を持つ総合レジ受付のほか、島の新鮮な野菜や惣菜、瀬戸内の特産品やスイーツを扱うフードマーケットが開いた。アートの非日常と島の日常が交差した、新たな島の風景が生まれつつある。

Following on from the small-scale 2019 project *Little Shops on the Island*, the Megijima Meitengai Mall opened in 2022, aiming to bring visitors closer to the life of the island. It works through a system in which the things that artists find attractive from the island can be purchased as goods and services. Using empty houses with the former bed and breakfast Kotobukiso at the center, there is a hair salon, a metalwork shop, a table tennis space, a café, and a laundry shop that were operating before, along with newly opened shops for fishing goods, sticks, hand-made crafts, recycling, and lighting equipment. The hub, the general information center in Kotobukiso, has a concierge service, and visitors can enjoy workshops held in each of the shops. It created a new landscape on the island where the extraordinary in art and the ordinary in life intersect with one another.

寿荘営業時間＝9:20〜16:30
名店街運営管理＝NPO法人 瀬戸内こえびネットワーク
Opening hours : 9:20–16:30
Management: Setouchi Koebi Network

[SM]

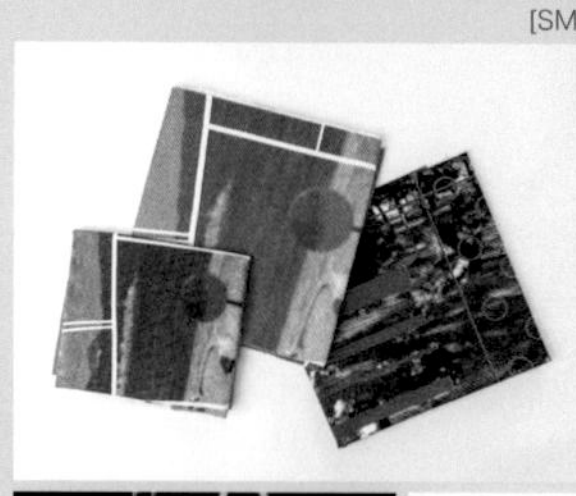

[SM]

[HO]

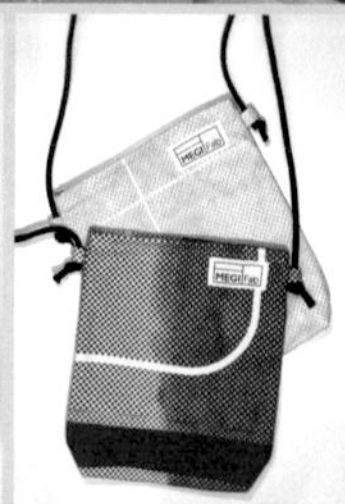

5点とも [SM]

GOODS & SERVICE

カフェメニュー＝ドーナツ、メロンクリームソーダ、チョココーヒーフロート、ほか
Café Menu: Donuts, Melon soda, Chocolate coffee float, etc.

ヴェロニク・ジュマール

Café de la Plage／
カフェ・ドゥ・ラ・プラージュ
mg05 | 寿荘

Véronique Joumard | France
Café de la Plage
Kotobukiso
2019

海を臨む浜辺のカフェ。コーヒーカップの熱や太陽の光でテーブルや壁の色が変わる空間で、時間を気にせず過ごせるよう、秒針だけの時計を設置している。来訪者は作品巡りの合間に一息つき、ドリンクや手作りドーナツを味わった。

A café overlooking the sea. The warmth of the coffee cups and the sunlight change the colors of the tables and walls in the space. In order for visitors to enjoy a moment without minding time, the clock only has a second hand. Visitors took the opportunity to rest here while they went around viewing the art, enjoying drinks and hand-made donuts.

2点とも [SM]

原倫太郎＋原游

ピンポン・シー

mg08 | 寿荘

Rintaro Hara + Yu Hara | Japan
Ping-Pong Sea
Kotobukiso
2019, 2022

かつて民宿だった建物のピロティにある、誰でも自由に遊べる卓球テーマパーク。複数人でプレイできる巨大卓球台や、球が跳ねる場所で音が変わる卓球台に加え、今回はボルダリングのホールドがついた新たな卓球台が現れた。

A table tennis space open to all is set in the courtyard of a former bed and breakfast. In addition to an existing giant table for multiple players appeared a new one that emits various tones when the ball bounces, and one that features rock-climbing holds.

GOODS & SERVICE
料金＝ラケット貸出 1 人 100 円
販売商品＝絵本「逃亡者おむすびころりん」
Fee: Rental Racket 100 yen / person
Products: Picture book *The Runaway Riceball*

宮永愛子

ヘアサロン壽

mg06 | 寿荘

Aiko Miyanaga | Japan
Hair Salon Kotobuki
Kotobukiso
2019

海辺のヘアサロン。ナフタリンや塩を用いた刻々と変化する作品が置かれた空間で、光や風を受け表情を変える海を眺めながら散髪した自分もまた少しだけ変化する。作家が島巡りのなかで出会った美容師と協力して実現した。

A hair salon on the beach. Within the space of an artwork that utilizes naphthalene and salt so that it changes by the minute, you can look out on the sea, also fluctuating with light and wind: having your hair cut here, you realize that you have changed a little. The project was realized in collaboration with a hair stylist that the artist met while moving around the island.

特別協力＝玉木ひろ子（ヘアカット等）
Cooperation: Hiroko Tamaki

[KK]

GOODS & SERVICE
ヘアサロンメニュー＝カット 3,500 円、ブロー 1,500 円、シャンプー 1,000 円
Hair Salon Menu: Cut 3,500 yen, blow dry 1,500 yen, shampoo 1,000 yen

[KK]

レアンドロ・エルリッヒ

ランドリー

mg09 | 寿荘

Leandro Erlich | Argentina
Laundry
Kotobukiso
2019

現実と仮想が交差するコインランドリー。本物の洗濯機と乾燥機の対面に洗濯物が回転する映像が流れ、鑑賞者を惑わせる。実際に利用することも可能。

A laundromat where fantasy and reality combine. A video installation of washers with rotating laundry covers one wall, opposite real coin-operated washers and driers, playing with the minds of the viewers. The real washing machines are available for use.

所蔵＝公益財団法人 福武財団
Collection: Fukutake Foundation

GOODS & SERVICE
料金＝洗濯 1 回 300 円、乾燥 10 分 100 円
Fee: Washer 300 yen, Dryer 100 yen / 10 min

[KK]

[KK]

[TADA]

[TADA]

岩沢兄弟
鬼ヶ島ピカピカセンター
mg21 | 寿荘

IWASAWA KYODAI | Japan
Onigashima pika-pika Centre
Kotobukiso
2022

GOODS & SERVICE

販売商品＝鬼をモチーフにした「紙袋吊り下げ鑑賞キット」、バッジ、ほか
Products: "Paper Bag Hanging Observation Kit" with a motif of an *oni*, badge, etc.

特別協力＝株式会社 Office Toyofuku（制作ディレクション）
Production direction: Office Toyofuku Co., Ltd

「島でみつけたものをピカピカにしていく」をコンセプトに、扇風機や採集コンテナ、ソフトクリーム看板など本来の目的を終えたものたちを照明器具に生まれ変わらせた。鬼の洞窟をイメージした奥のほの暗い空間では、島の住民から集めた紙袋がユーモラスに光る。自分で紙袋のランプシェードを制作できる「おにのかみぶくろ」キットなども販売され、あったかもしれない鬼と人との関係性を想像させる空間になった。

With the concept of "illuminating what is found on the island", IWASAWA KYODAI repurposed an electric fan, a harvesting box, and ice cream signage – all of which having finished their initial roles – into lighting equipment. In the dim space at the back, evoking the cave of an *oni* (Japanese Ogre), paper bags collected from the islanders are illuminated humorously. "Oni Paper Bag" sets of DIY lampshade making kits are sold as well. The work became a space to imagine the relationships between *oni* and humans that may have once been.

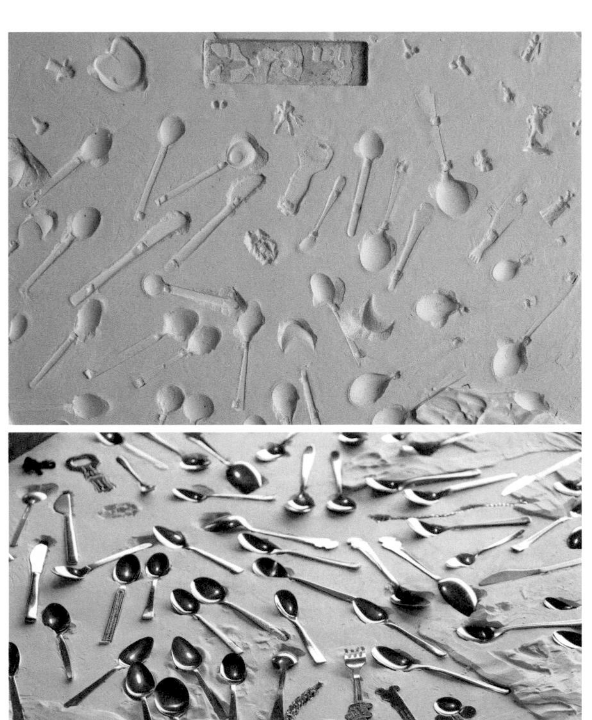

3点とも [KK]

五所純子

リサイクルショップ複製遺跡

mg22 | 寿荘

Junko Gosho | Japan
thrift shop duplication remains
Kotobukiso
2022

物語が交差するリサイクルショップ。島の内外から集まったさまざまな物品を石膏の壁に埋め込み、展示販売した。購入された物品は石膏から「発掘」され、ある物品は「島の道具」から「記念品」となり、「ストーリー」が次の所有者に受け継がれもする。物と人が交易し、交配した痕跡が「遺跡」のように残る石膏は、壁として会期中も増えていった。また文筆家でもある作家が行った古い物品にまつわる聞き書きを、海岸を見渡す窓辺の席で読むことができた。

A space where people interact through objects and the stories within them. The artist gathers items from places on and off the island and presses them into a plaster wall. Objects sold are removed from the panels, shifting from "a tool of the island" to "a souvenir", with stories handed down to a new owner. Things and people interact in trades at the plaster wall, and exchanges remain on it like a historical record. The number of panels increased during the festival period. The artist, also being a writer, conducted interviews about the old items, and they could be read at the seats by the window overlooking the sea.

特別協力＝株式会社 Office Toyofuku（制作ディレクション）、松本弦人
Production direction: Office Toyofuku Co., Ltd., Cooperation: Gento Matsumoto

GOODS & SERVICE

販売商品＝作家セレクト雑貨（リサイクル品）、書籍『薬を食う女たち』
Products: Recycled product selected by Artist,
Junko Gosho's book, *kusuri wo kuu onna tachi*

[KK]

[SM]

中里繪魯洲

ティンカー・ベルズ ファクトリー

mg11 | 寿荘

Eros Nakazato | Japan
Tinker Bell's Factory
Kotobukiso
2022

妖精ティンカーベルの金物加工店。2019年に制作された「こころのマッサージチェア」に座ってハンドルを回すと、不思議を信じる心が成長する。今回はチェアに加え、アップサイクルの作品群の展示とファクトリーが登場した。「ティンカー」には、巡回する金物修理屋、鋳掛屋、いじくり回して壊してしまう、放浪者などの意味がある。会期ごとに作品が増え、ファクトリーでは鉄玉を叩く体験などのワークショップを開催。島の人々が鍋釜の修理を頼める工房になった。

The metalwork shop of the fairy Tinker Bell. Sit on the "mind massage chair" created in 2019 and pull the handle, and your mind to believe in the mysterious will grow. This year, in addition to the chair, an exhibition of up-cycled work and a factory appeared. The word "tinker" can refer to a traveling metal repair worker, a pot or pan fixer, a wanderer, or a naughty child who breaks things. With each festival period, the number of works increases, including a workshop in the factory to hammer iron balls. It has developed into an atelier for local residents to come to repair their cookware.

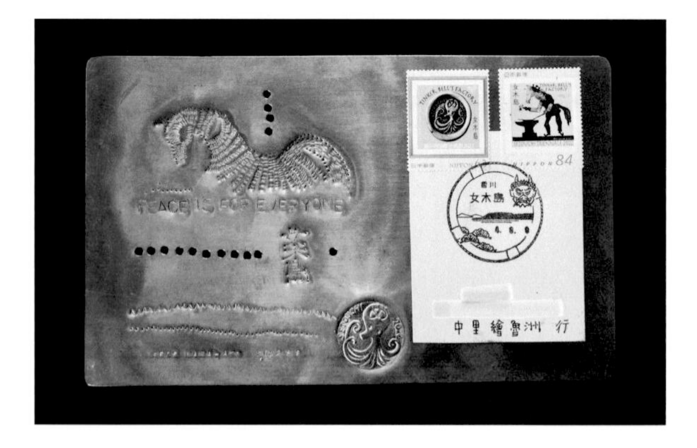

GOODS & SERVICE

販売商品＝鉄メダル、鉄のペーパーウェイト、女木島ペーパーウェイト、真鍮製の葉書「女木島からの便り」、ほか
Products: Iron medal, Iron paperweight, Megijima paperweight, Brass postcard "A Letter from Megijima", etc.

[KK]

[SM]

[SM]

[KK]

柳建太郎
ガラス漁具店
mg20 | 寿荘

Kentaro Yanagi | Japan
Glass fisherman
Kotobukiso
2022

ガラスの釣り針でできたハートのシャンデリアが、光を反射させて暗い室内に浮かびあがった。漁師でもある作家の「大気で空想を釣りあげる」をコンセプトにした釣具屋。漁具をモチーフにしたガラスのルアーやアクセサリーを展示販売した。会期中は作家が工房に滞在し、美しい色彩のガラス棒をバーナーであぶったオリジナルマドラーづくりのワークショップを連日開催した。

A heart-shaped chandelier made from glass fishhooks floats in a dark room, reflecting the light. The artist and fisherman created a shop with the concept of "fishing your imagination with the air". Glass lures and accessories with fishing tool motifs were exhibited and sold. During the festival period, the artist stayed in the atelier to conduct workshops, teaching how to make muddlers by hand by heating a beautiful glass stick with a burner.

特別協力=株式会社 Office Toyofuku（制作ディレクション）
Production direction: Office Toyofuku Co., Ltd.

[SM]

GOODS & SERVICE

販売商品=釣り針のペンダント、ガラスのルアー、ハートと釣り針のガラスのピアス／イヤリング、天使のショットガンシェル、ほか
Products: Fishhook pendant, Glass lure, Glass fishhook heart earrings, Angel's shotgun shell, etc.

3点とも [KK]

あきびんご

瀬戸内カーニバル

mg23 | 女木島中心部

Akibingo | Japan
Setouchi Carnival
Megi Community Area
2022

栗林公園から移設されたと伝わる松林横の古民家で、屏風型の大型絵本を展開。芸術祭の会場の島々や広島県の尾道、岡山県の倉敷などを舞台に、たくさんの生き物たちが瀬戸内地域を巡る物語を描いた。別の部屋では世界各地に伝わる鬼やなまはげを描いたドローイング174点を展示したほか、古本屋「なタ書」監修の本棚では瀬戸内に関する書籍を展示販売し、また作家の絵本も販売した。子どもから大人まで本と物語の楽しさを味わえる場所となった。

In an old house said to have been relocated from Ritsurin Garden, large folding screens of picture books were exhibited. Centering on the islands that are part of the art festival, along with Onomichi in Hiroshima and Kurashiki in Okayama, various creatures travel around the Setouchi area in the story. In another room, 174 drawings of *oni* and *namahage* from all over the world are displayed. On a bookshelf curated by the second-hand bookshop Natasyo, books about Setouchi were on sale, along with books by the artist himself. It was a place for both children and adults to enjoy books and stories.

特別協力＝なタ書（古書販売）
Cooperation: Natasyo

GOODS & SERVICE

販売商品＝作家の絵本、瀬戸内に関する書籍
Products: Artist's Picture Books, Books about Setouchi

[KK]

上 [KK] 下 [SM]

大川友希
結ぶ家

mg24 | 女木島中心部

Yuki Okawa | Japan
House of Knots
Megi Community Area
2022

私たちの一番近くで一緒に記憶を体験している衣服を素材に、5,000本を超える「記憶の紐」で、民家の内外を覆いつくしたインスタレーション作品。作家と島民、訪れた人々の作業を通して、服に宿る記憶が編み上げられたほか、ゲスト講師を招いて服飾にまつわるワークショップも行われた。この土地を守りつづける人々の記憶と時間の断片を集めて結び合わせ、地元の人々や鑑賞者をつなぎたいという作家の想いがこめられている。

Using clothes, which experience memory akin to our own, as materials, an installation piece made with over 5,000 "threads of memory" was produced, covering the interior and exterior of a house. Through the process of creation, which involved the artist, residents of the island, and visitors, the memories residing in clothes were interwoven. Workshops about clothing were also held, with guest lecturers. This work is filled by the artist's hope of developing a connection between the local residents and visitors by collecting and knotting together fragments of memory and time of the people who have always protected the island.

特別協力＝株式会社 Office Toyofuku（制作ディレクション）、高橋彩水／L'ANIT、橋村春樹／KERFMANN（ワークショップ）
Production direction: Office Toyofuku Co., Ltd., Workshop cooperation: Ayami Takahashi / L'ANIT, Haruki Hashimura / KERFMANN

GOODS & SERVICE

販売商品＝刺繍Tシャツ、ワッペン、ステッカー
Products: Embroidered T-shirts, Emblem, Sticker

[KK]

2点とも [SM]

三田村光土里

MEGI Fab（メギファブ）

mg25 | 女木島中心部

Midori Mitamura | Japan

MEGI Fab

Megi Community Area

2022

改装途中のままだった古い長屋の大きな窓や縁側の開放的な空間を活かした布地・手芸店。会期中、鑑賞者が「女木島の風景」を持ち帰ることができるよう、島で撮影した景色の断片でデザインしたオリジナルプリントを販売した。作家のアトリエも兼ねており、会期ごとに新作を作って展示販売。また手芸店としての可能性を広げるべく、高松のボタンのアカネヤが特別出店した。

A handcraft shop in an old tenement house that was abandoned halfway through renovation, utilizing its big windows and the open space of its veranda. During the festival, an original print textile composed with fragments of landscapes shot on the island allowed visitors to take a "Megijima view" home with them. The shop also functioned as an atelier for artists, so new work was produced and exhibited for sale in each period. In order to widen the potential of the handicraft shop, Akaneya, a button shop in Takamatsu, was also a special participant.

特別協力＝株式会社 Office Toyofuku（制作ディレクション）、
ボタンのアカネヤ（アンティーク雑貨等の販売）

Production direction: Office Toyofuku Co., Ltd., Cooperation: Akaneya

GOODS & SERVICE

販売商品＝オリジナルプリント布地とそれを使った雑貨（サコッシュ、エプロン、ほか）、
手芸雑貨（ボタン、ブローチ、ほか）

Products: Original print fabric and goods using it (sacoche, apron, etc.), handicraft goods (buttons, brooches, etc.)

3点とも [HO]

小谷元彦

こんぼうや

mg26 | 女木島中心部

Motohiko Odani | Japan
KONBO-YA
Megi Community Area
2022

鬼ヶ島とも呼ばれる女木島に現れた「こんぼうや」。荒れ果てた状態の空家を訪れた作家は、立派な梁や全体の雰囲気を気に入りこの場所を選んだ。善悪の二項対立を無効化し、超越する正体不明の鬼という存在を再解釈する作品。地獄絵などで鬼がもつ棍棒に着目。敵や闇を追い払う道具であり、人類最初の木彫だったとも考えられる棍棒を公開制作した。古からの日本人の潜在意識を顕在化させ、記憶の集合体を現実に還元する試みである。

KONBO-YA appeared in Megijima, also known as "*Onigashima*", as though from the legend of *Momotaro*. The artist visited an abandoned house that had been left to ruin and, liking the strong beams and atmosphere, decided to place the work there. The concept is the reinterpretation of *oni*, an unidentifiable presence that dismantles the dualism of good and evil and transcends it. In public displays, he created wooden sculptures referencing the clubs that *oni* hold in pictures of hell. The first wooden sculptures created by mankind are thought to have been clubs used to drive off enemies and dark forces. The work is an attempt to visualize the subconscious of Japanese people from ages past, and to restore the aggregate of memory into reality.

特別協力＝株式会社 Office Toyofuku（制作ディレクション）
Production direction: Office Toyofuku Co., Ltd.

GOODS & SERVICE

販売商品＝こんぼう、御朱印
Products: *Konbo* (Club), *Goshuin* (Red Ink Stamp Card)

依田洋一朗

ISLAND THEATRE MEGI「女木島名画座」

mg14 | 女木小学校周辺

Yoichiro Yoda | Japan
ISLAND THEATRE MEGI
Around Megi Elementary School
2016

[Ylc]

古い倉庫を活用し、ニューヨーク42番街シアターの記憶を凝縮したインスタレーション作品。館内には名作映画から描かれた絵画を多数展示し、スクリーンでは作家が撮影したドキュメンタリーや古い短編映画を上映した。

This installation, utilizing an old warehouse, has the essence of a movie theater on 42nd Street in New York. In the theater, many paintings taken from old masterpieces of cinema were exhibited, and old short films were screened.

設計＝林幸稔／林幸稔建築設計事務所（実施設計）、梅岡恒治（空間デザイン）
Detailed design: Yukinori Hayashi / Yukinori Hayashi Architect & Associates, Spatial design: Koji Umeoka

女木島名画座上映会

E07 | 女木島

Screening of Megijima
Megijima
2022

3点とも [SM]

総合ディレクターの北川フラムが案内人となってツアー形式で開催する「女木島名画座上映会」。春は俳優 樹木希林の遺作にして世界デビュー作となった『命みじかし、恋せよ乙女』、夏は松居大悟監督を迎えての『アイスと雨音』、秋は山岡信貴監督を迎えて案内人も出演した『アートなんかいらない！（特別編集版）』を上映した。定期船最終便後の女木島を巡るナイトプログラムや食事も楽しめる特別なツアーとなった。

Screening of Megijima was held in a tour format with general director Fram Kitagawa as a guide. In spring, *Cherry Blossoms and Demons* – the first overseas work of the late Kirin Kiki, which was released posthumously – was shown; in summer *Ice Cream and the Sound of Raindrops* was presented with director Daigo Matsui as a guest; and in autumn a film featuring the guide himself, *Art Nanka Iranai (I Don't Need Art): Special Edited Version*, was screened with Nobutaka Yamaoka, the director. It was a special tour combined with a night program on Megijima held after the last ferry, with a meal included.

Event Data

5月7日（土）『命みじかし、恋せよ乙女』（2019年／ドイツ／117分）| 8月27日（土）『アイスと雨音』（2017年／日本／74分）ゲスト＝松居大悟 | 10月22日（土）『アートなんかいらない！』（特別編集版）ゲスト＝山岡信貴 | 料金＝12,000円 | 参加者数＝67人

May 7th (Sat); *Cherry Blossoms and Demons*, 2019, Germany, 117 min. | August 27th (Sat); *Ice Cream and the Sound of Raindrops*, 2017, Japan, 74 min., Guest: Daigo Matsui | October 22nd (Sat); *Art Nanka Iranai (I Don't Need Art): Special Edited Version*, Guest: Nobutaka Yamaoka | Admission: 12,000 yen | Attendance: 67 people

[OW]

大竹伸朗
女根／めこん

mg13B | 女木小学校

Shinro Ohtake | Japan
MECON
Megi Elementary School
2013, 2016

巨大なブイと島で育った大きな椰子の周りに、タイルのモザイクやワニのオブジェ、船材などを配置。休校中の小学校と植物、作品が響き合う。

A collage of diverse elements, including tile mosaics, boat parts, and an alligator, surround a large palm that once grows the island. The work resonates with the unused school building and vegetation.

設計＝建田朋延、奥野雄（建設・美術制作サポート）、西畠清順／そら植物園（植物監修・植栽サポート）
所蔵＝公益財団法人 福武財団

Design & art production support: Tomonobu Tsuda, Yuu Okuno, Botanical design: Seijun Nishihata / SORA BOTANICAL GARDEN Project Inc.
Collection: Fukutake Foundation

[OW]

レアンドロ・エルリッヒ
不在の存在

mg15B | 女木小学校周辺

Leandro Erlich | Argentina
The Presence of Absence
Around Megi Elementary School
2010

空家の中庭に見えない誰かの足跡が現れる《Invisible（見えないもの）》と、鏡の世界と現実が混在する茶室《Double Tea（二重の茶室）》の2作品を展開。併設する図書室では自由に本を閲覧できる。

In the courtyard of an empty house two works appear: *Invisible*, showing the footsteps of someone unseen, and *Double Tea*, a tea room where the world of mirrors and reality mix. Visitors are invited to freely read at the library on the site.

設計＝後藤哲夫／VAKA（実施設計）
所蔵＝公益財団法人 福武財団

Detailed design: Tetsuo Goto / VAKA
Collection: Fukutake Foundation

[KK]

ニコラ・ダロ

ナビゲーションルーム

mg27 | 女木島海水浴場周辺

Nicolas Darrot | France
Navigation Room
Around Megijima Beach
2022

女木島東海岸の元海の家に現れた、架空の海を航行するためのナビゲーションシステム。銀河を模した長さ12mの紙をオルゴールが読み込み、12カ月に対応するオリジナル曲を奏でる。六分儀やスティックチャート（貝殻や枝で作成された海図）を組み合わせた中央の装置は、音楽と連動して天体の動きや太陽光の減衰を表すプラネタリウムとなる。ホメロスの叙事詩オデュッセイアからインスパイアされた一つ目の灯台とおしゃべりな口が、想像力の航路を照らした。

Appearing in a former beach house on the east shore of Megijima is a navigation system to sail on an imaginary sea. A 12-meter paper resembling a galaxy was read by a music box, playing original tunes corresponding to the different months of the year. The central device with a sextant and stick chart (a sea map made with shells and twigs) combined to become a planetarium, displaying the movement of the planets and the attenuation of the sunlight together with the music. Inspired by Homer's epic *The Odyssey*, the lighthouse with one eye and a verbose mouth shone on the sailing route of the imagination.

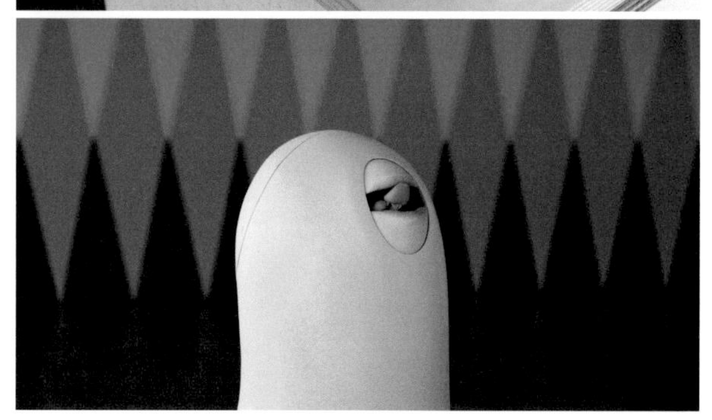

設計＝長尾勝彦＋デザインオフィス（内装）
特別協力＝エティエンヌ・シャリー（音楽）、アンスティチュ・フランセ日本
Interior design: Katsuhiko Nagao + Design Office
Music: Etienne Charry, Cooperation: Institut français du Japon

[ON]

木村崇人
カモメの駐車場
mg01 | 女木港周辺

Takahito Kimura | Japan
Sea Gulls Parking Lot
Around Megi Port
2010, 2013

女木港に入ると、約300羽のカモメの風見鳥が迎えてくれる。風の向きが変わるとカモメもいっせいに方向を変える。風の流れを可視化した作品。

Visitors to Megi Port are greeted by nearly 300 seagull weathercocks. The seagulls create a perfectly straight line that changes direction in unison whenever the wind blows.

禿鷹墳上
20世紀の回想
mg02 | 女木港周辺

Hagetaka Funjo | China / Japan
20th Century Recall
Around Megi Port
2010

海岸沿いに設置された、青銅製のグランドピアノと4本の帆からなるサウンド・インスタレーション。ピアノから流れる音楽が海の波の音と呼応する。

A sound installation comprised of a bronze grand piano and four sail masts. The piano plays a melody in response to the sound of waves lapping against the nearby shore.

[KiT]

杉浦康益
段々の風
mg17 | 住吉神社周辺

Yasuyuki Sugiura | Japan
Terrace Winds
Around Sumiyoshi Shrine
2013

かつて段々畑だった場所に約400個の陶のブロックを設置。作品と女木島の町並みと海を見渡す光景が一体化し、瀬戸内海の大パノラマを見せる。

In a place that used to be terraced fields, about 400 ceramic blocks were positioned. The work merged with the townscape of Megijima in a huge panoramic view of the Seto Inland Sea.

オニノコプロダクション
オニノコ瓦プロジェクト2
mg19 | 鬼ヶ島大洞窟

Oninoko Production | Japan
Oninoko Tile Project 2
Onigashima Ogre's Cave
2013, 2019

鬼の洞窟で、膨大な鬼瓦を見せるプロジェクト。香川県の中学生約3,000人が参加し、伝統工芸士の指導のもと、それぞれの鬼瓦を制作した。

At the cave of the *oni*, numerous *oni-gawara* tiles (Japanese gargoyle rooftiles) were shown. About 3,000 junior high school students from Kagawa Prefecture participated by making their own tiles under the instruction of traditional craftsmen.

企画＝香川県立ミュージアム
特別協力＝神内俊二（伝統工芸士）

Planning: The Kagawa Museum
Cooperation: Shunji Jinnai (Traditional Craftsman)

男木島
Ogijima

[SM]

男木島　*Ogijima*

女木島と豊島の間に位置する島。女木島からフェリーでさらに20分、岬を回ると急斜面に張り付くように並ぶ家々の風景が眼前に広がる。細い急な坂道は集落の中を縫うように走り、中腹の豊玉姫神社に通じる。ほとんどの家の窓から瀬戸内海を望むことができ、西向きの集落からは瀬戸大橋越しに沈む夕陽が見られる。島の北にある灯台は総御影石造りで、映画「喜びも悲しみも幾歳月」の舞台となった。周辺は水仙の群生が広がり2月頃に白い花が咲く。農業と漁業で暮らしを支え、昭和初期までは牛を飼い四国本土に農耕用に貸し出しをした「借耕牛」という習慣があった。

1950年代には1,000人近くいたがその後は過疎化が進み、2010年の芸術祭開始時は180人まで落ち込んだ。2011年3月に中学生3名が卒業して男木小・中学校が休校となったが、芸術祭をきっかけに移住者が増え、2014年に小中学校が再開、保育所の再開も続いた。その後も国内外からのべ80人が島に移住し、飲食店や私立図書館ができ、新たに5名の子どもが島で生まれている。

Located between Megijima and Teshima. It is a 20-minute ferry ride away from Megijima, and as the boat goes around the cape, houses come into view as though they are gripping on to the severe mountainside. A narrow and steep slope runs through the village, on to Toyotama-hime Shrine in the hills. Most houses have views of the Seto Inland Sea, and those that are west-facing can enjoy sunset over the Seto Ohashi Bridge. The lighthouse in the north of the island is carved out of granite rock, and is famous as the set of the film *Times of Joy and Sorrow*. Colonies of narcissus spread around it, blooming with white flowers in February. Farming and fishing have sustained the lives of the islanders, and until the early Showa era there was a custom of “lending farming cows”, in which they bred cows and then lent them to farms on the Shikoku mainland.

In the 1950s the island had a population of about 1,000, but it has decreased since then, and when the first art festival was held in 2010 there were only 180 residents. In March 2011, three junior-high students graduated, resulting in the closure of Ogi Elementary School and Junior High School. However, the festival triggered an increase in movement to the island, and the schools and nursery reopened again in 2014. Since then, about 80 people have settled in Ogijima, restaurants and a private library have opened, and 5 children have been born on the island.

男木集落

og01 男木島の魂
ジャウメ・プレンサ Jaume Plensa

og02 タコツボル
TEAM 男気 TEAM OGI

og03 生成するドローイング—日本家屋のために2.0
村山悟郎 Goro Murayama

og05 男木島 路地壁画プロジェクト wallalley
眞壁陸二 Rikuji Makabe

og07 瀬戸で舞う
川島猛とドリームフレンズ Takeshi Kawashima + Dream Friends

og08 アキノリウム
松本秋則 Akinori Matsumoto

og14 漆の家
漆の家プロジェクト "Maison de Urushi" Project

og15 部屋の中の部屋
大岩オスカール Oscar Oiwa

og18 男木島パビリオン
大岩オスカール＋坂 茂 Oscar Oiwa + Shigeru Ban

og19 No. 105
ワン・テユ ［王徳瑜］ Wang Te-yu

og20 学校の先生
エカテリーナ・ムロムツェワ Ekaterina Muromtseva

E08 Come and Go／MAMMOTH
ひびのこづえ Kodue Hibino

男木漁港

og05 漣の家
眞壁陸二 Rikuji Makabe

og16 歩く方舟
山口啓介 Keisuke Yamaguchi

og17 青空を夢見て
レジーナ・シルベイラ Regina Silveira

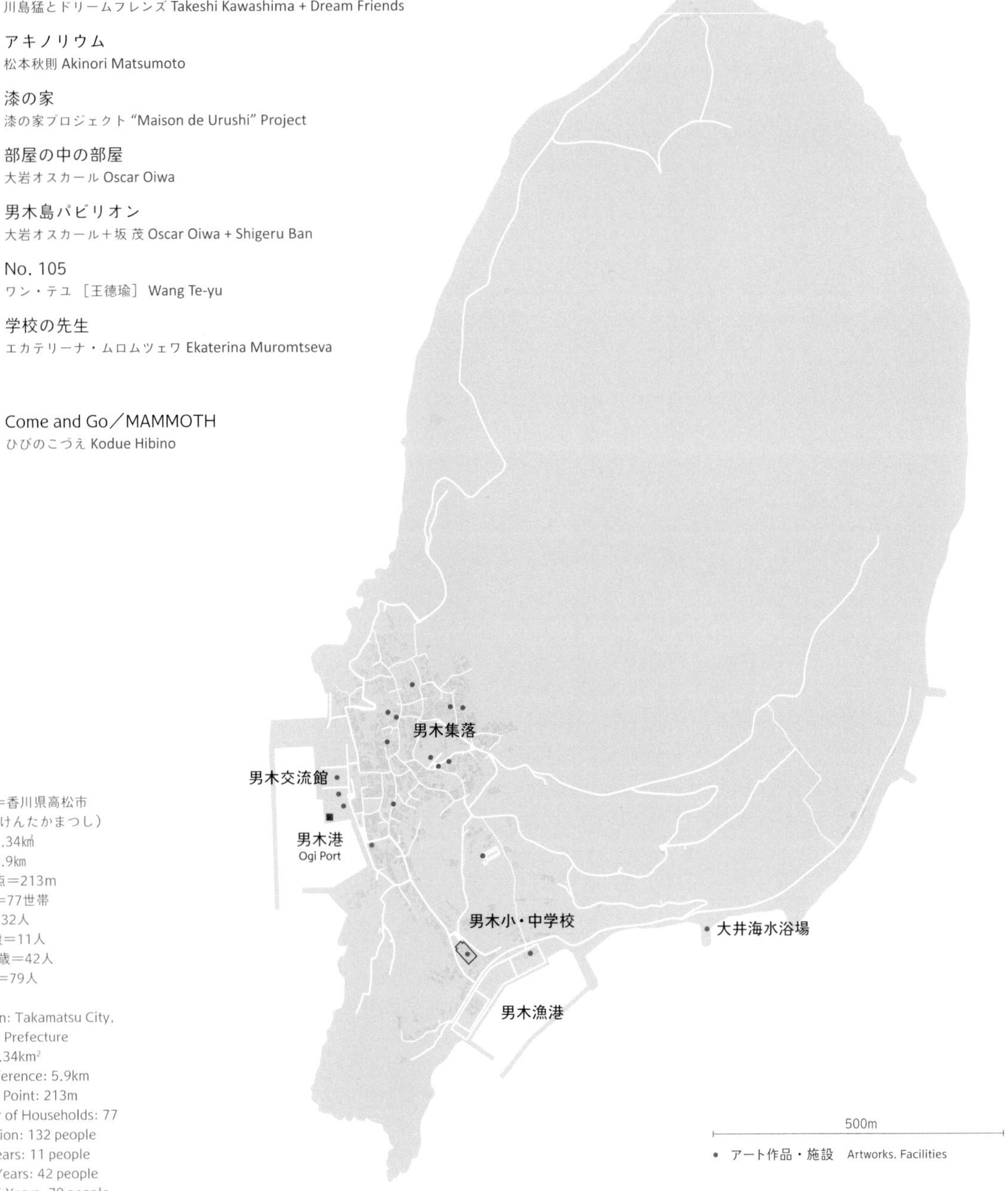

所在地＝香川県高松市
（かがわけんたかまつし）
面積＝1.34㎢
周囲＝5.9km
最高地点＝213m
世帯数＝77世帯
人口＝132人
0〜14歳＝11人
15〜64歳＝42人
65歳〜＝79人

Location: Takamatsu City, Kagawa Prefecture
Area: 1.34km²
Circumference: 5.9km
Highest Point: 213m
Number of Households: 77
Population: 132 people
0-14 Years: 11 people
15-64 Years: 42 people
Over 65 Years: 79 people

大岩オスカール+坂 茂

男木島パビリオン

og18 | 男木集落

Oscar Oiwa + Shigeru Ban | Brazil / USA, Japan
Ogijima Pavilion
Ogi Village
2022

神社参道の急な階段脇に建つ作品は、建築家とアーティストのコラボレーションによって実現した。坂の代表的な建築資材である紙管を使用した建物で、大きなガラス窓越しに家々の黒い瓦が広がり、その先には港や海、遠くには瀬戸大橋が見える。大岩はこの実際の風景と想像の世界を1つにしたいと考え、窓から見える風景をキャンバスに、ユーモラスな空想の世界を描いた。3枚のガラス窓を重ねると新たな絵が出現する。

This work, standing on the steep stairs of a road leading to a shrine, was realized through collaboration between artist Oscar Oiwa and architect Shigeru Ban, using cardboard tubes – a familiar architectural material for Ban. Through the large glass windows, the black roof tiles of many houses can be seen, and beyond them the port, the sea, and even the Seto Ohashi Bridge are visible in the distance. With the aim of merging the real landscape and the world of imagination, Oiwa painted a humorous imaginary world. When the three glass windows are layered, a new painting appears.

設計=坂茂建築設計 | 助成=駐日ブラジル大使館
Architecture: Shigeru Ban Architects | Funding: Embaixada do Brasil em Tóquio

[HHi]

[HHi]

[KK]

[Ylc]

大岩オスカール

部屋の中の部屋

og15 | 男木集落

Oscar Oiwa | Brazil / USA
The room inside of the room
Ogi Village
2016

床の間のある6畳の和室が90度回転した、だまし絵のようなインスタレーション作品。襖絵には巨大なタコや海を渡るフェリー「めおん」などが描かれている。

An installation like an optical illusion, depicting a Japanese room with six *tatami* mats and a *tokono-ma* shelving rotated 90 degrees. On the *fusuma* sliding doors, a gigantic octopus and the ferry "Meon" cross the sea.

設計＝林幸稔／VAKA（実施設計）
Detailed design: Yukinori Hayashi / VAKA

村山悟郎

生成するドローイング
―日本家屋のために2.0

og03 | 男木集落

Goro Murayama | Japan
Generative Drawing for Japanese Paper House 2.0
Ogi Village
2019, 2022

生命理論や科学哲学をテーマとする作家が、かつて商店だった築 90 年の家の室内に、数学などの研究で利用される「セルオートマトン」の法則に基づいたパターンを利用して描いた ウォールドローイング。1階は島の植物をモチーフに、2階は有機的な図柄を持つ貝殻をモチーフに展開。今回は 19 年の作品をアップデートし、家が持つ「時」、植物や貝殻の持つ「時」、そして作家や観客が持つ「時」がゆるやかに連動した展示空間になった。

The artist, who investigates the themes of organismal theory and the philosophy of science, created wall drawings in the interior of a 90-year-old house that used to be a store, using biological patterns generated by the special rules of "cellular automata", which are investigated in mathematical research. The first floor uses the motif of island plants, while the second uses that of seashells with organic patterns. This time, the 2019 work has been updated, creating an exhibition space in the house in which the "time" of the house, the "time" of the plants and shells, and the "time" of the artist and audience are loosely linked.

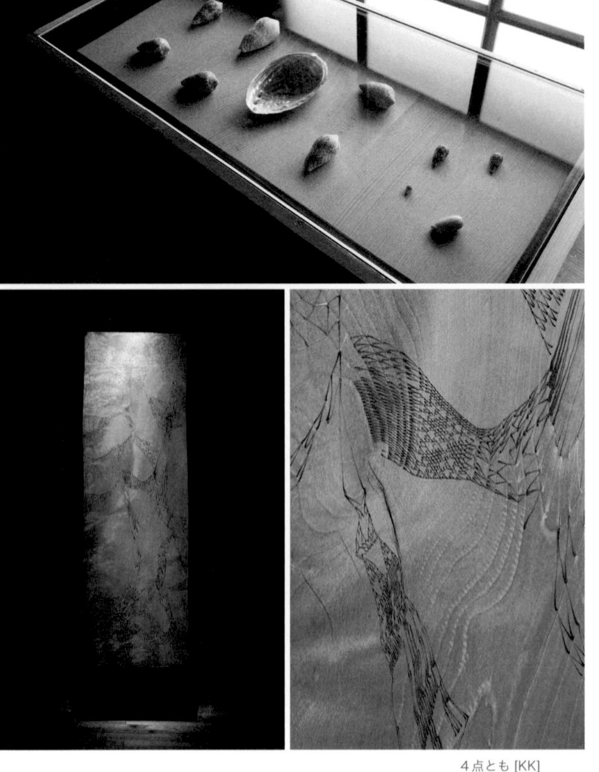

4点とも [KK]

エカテリーナ・ムロムツェワ
学校の先生
og20 | 男木集落

Ekaterina Muromtseva | Russia / USA
The School Teachers
Ogi Village
2022

朝顔の咲く民家に現れた、３つの水彩のインスタレーション作品。記憶に残る先生を古代の仮面のように描いた作品《学校の先生》は、先生という存在を哲学的なアプローチで解体する作家のレクチャーとともに展示した。リモートワークショップも開催し、島の子どもたちの絵も加わった。限られたルールでプレイヤーの創造性を問うゲーム型作品《手をあげよう》や、年齢や性別に関係なく、互いに学び合えることを批評的に描いた《授業の歴史》も展開した。

Three watercolor installation pieces appeared in a house with morning glory blooming. Depicting teachers the artist recalls, *The School Teachers* is like ancient face masks, and was exhibited along with a lecture by the artist herself, analyzing the presence of teachers from the perspective of philosophy. A remote workshop was also held, where the children of the island added their own paintings. Additionally, *Raise Hands*, a game-based piece, challenged the creativity of a player within its pre-set rules, and *History Lessons*, which critically examined what it is to learn from others unbound by age and gender, were also exhibited.

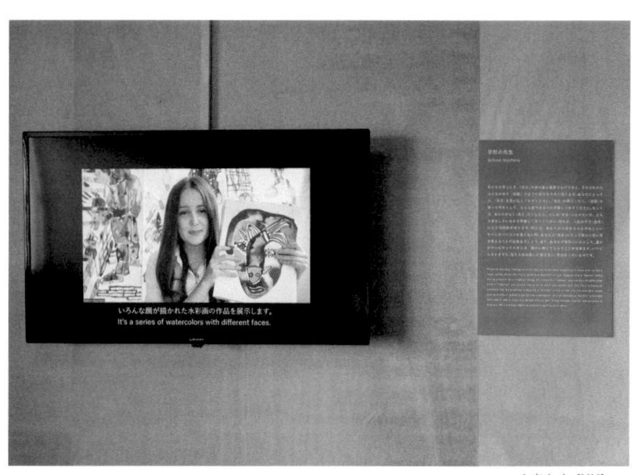

4点とも [KK]

《漣の家》

眞壁陸二

男木島 路地壁画プロジェクト wallalley

漣（さざなみ）の家

og05 | 男木集落／男木漁港周辺

Rikuji Makabe | Japan

Project for Wall Painting in Lane, Ogijima Wallalley

SAZANAMI HOUSE

Ogi Village / Around Ogi Fishing Port

2010, 2022

2010年より《男木島 路地壁画プロジェクト wallalley》を展開している作家の新作。コロナ対策で人を隔てるアクリル板を素材に制作。会期中にワークショップを開催し、島民など55名の参加者がそれぞれの海のイメージを描いた。ひとつひとつ異なる大きさと色彩の250枚のピースを、海岸沿いに佇む倉庫の壁一面にコラージュした。十人十色の個性によって形成する多様性のある社会を表現している。

A new work which utilizes the acrylic partitions that have isolated people during the coronavirus pandemic as a material, by an artist who has been developing *Project for Wall Painting in Lane, Ogijima Wallalley* since 2010. During the festival periods, workshops were held, with 55 participants – including islanders – who painted their own images of the sea. The 250 pieces, all of different sizes and colors, were displayed in collage on the wall of a warehouse on the shore. It expresses diversity in society formed by the individuality of each person.

特別協力＝三嶋公宏、大久保剛、ともひろかなこ
Cooperation: Kimihiro Mishima, Takeshi Okubo, Kanako Tomohiro

《男木島 路地壁画プロジェクト wallalley》[ON]

[KiT]

山口啓介

歩く方舟

og16 | 大井海水浴場周辺

Keisuke Yamaguchi | Japan

Walking Ark

Around Oi Beach

2013

旧約聖書のノアの方舟に着想を得た立体作品を、海に突きでた堤防に展示。白と青の4つの山をもった方舟から脚がのび、海に向かって歩き出す。

A three-dimensional piece inspired by Noah's Ark from the Old Testament was exhibited at the pier, which extends out into the sea. From the ark featuring four mountains of blue and white, legs stretch out as though it is poised to walk into the water.

設計＝林幸稔／VAKA（実施設計）
Detailed design: Yukinori Hayashi / VAKA

[KK]

ワン・テユ［王德瑜］

No. 105

og19 | 男木集落

Wang Te-yu | Taiwan

No. 105

Ogi Village

2022

鉄線加工の工場廃墟に現れた、触覚を刺激するサイトスペシフィックな作品。訪れた人々は建築現場で使用される足場で上下の展示空間を回遊できる。大きなバルーンのスリットから内部に入りこむことで、海に飛びこむ瞬間のような環境が変容する感覚を味わえる。大きなバルーン内部の小さなバルーンは、瀬戸内の海と山を表現しており、作品を外部と内部から鑑賞することで、新しい視点で空間と形態を感じることができる。

Placed in the ruin of a steel wire factory is a site-specific piece that stimulates the sense of touch. Visitors can move between the higher and lower sections of the exhibition space using scaffolding, often seen at construction sites. Entering through a slit in a big balloon, they experience an instantaneous change, like the moment of diving into the ocean. Smaller balloons inside represent the mountains and sea of Setouchi. By observing the piece from both outside and inside, visitors gain a new perspective of its space and form.

助成＝台湾文化部
助成協力＝台北駐日経済文化代表処台湾文化センター
Funding: Ministry of Culture, Taiwan | Funding Cooperation: Taiwan Culture Center, Taipei Economic and Cultural Representative Office in Japan

上［KK］下［SM］

ジャウメ・プレンサ
男木島の魂
og01 | 男木交流館

Jaume Plensa | Spain
Ogijima's Soul
Ogi Exchange Center
2010

[ON]

島を訪れた人を迎え入れる交流館。屋根にはさまざまな文化圏の文字が組み合わされ、日中はその影が建物の内と外の地面に映し出される。白い屋根は水面に映り、近海で採れる二枚貝のよう。

Ogi Exchange Center welcomes visitors as they arrive. The roof is a combination of letters representing the various cultural regions, which cast shadows on the ground inside and outside of the building. The white roof is reflected in the water surface, giving the appearance of a bivalve shell in the surrounding ocean.

所蔵＝高松市
Collection: Takamatsu City

TEAM 男気
タコツボル
og02 | 男木港周辺

TEAM OGI | Japan
Takotsuboru
Around Ogi Port
2019

[KK]

島の伝統であるタコ漁に使うタコ壺をモチーフとした遊具。男木港近くの空地に子どもたちの遊び場を作った。会期中は作家による見送り旗作りやタコツボペイント等のワークショップを開催。

A playground facility with the motif of *tako-tsubo* (an octopus trap) that is used in the traditional octopus fishing of the island. This playground for kids was placed in a vacant space near Ogi Port, and during the festival period workshops were held by the artists, such as flag-making and painting *tako-tsubo*.

松本秋則
アキノリウム
og08 | 男木集落

Akinori Matsumoto | Japan
Akinorium
Ogi Village
2016

[Ylc]

古民家を舞台にした、からくり仕掛けのサウンドオブジェ作品。1階では影絵が映し出され、2階では天井裏や床に仕掛けられたいくつもの竹などでできたオブジェが動きながら、変化する光と影の中で軽やかな音を奏でる。

Mechanical sound objects using an old Japanese house as a stage. Shadows are projected on the first floor, and upstairs objects created from bamboo and other materials placed in the attic and on the floor play light tunes in the transitions of brightness and shadow.

所蔵＝男木地区コミュニティ協議会
Collection: Ogi Community Council

レジーナ・シルベイラ
青空を夢見て
og17 | 男木小・中学校

Regina Silveira | Brazil
Dreaming of Blue
Ogi Elementary and Junior High School
2016

学校の体育館の壁一面に、刺繍のように見える雲と空が出現。瀬戸内独特の青い空と光、その光が波に反射して輝く景色に感銘を受けた作家が、刺繍のようなタッチで表現した。

Clouds and blue sky seem to be embroidered across the entire wall of a school gym. The blue sky and light of Setouchi, and the shining view of that light reflecting on the waves deeply affected the artist, and she presented it in a style that resembles cross-stitch.

設計＝林幸稔／林幸稔建築設計事務所（実施設計監修）
Detailed design supervision: Yukinori Hayashi / Yukinori Hayashi Architect & Associates

[KK]

川島猛とドリームフレンズ
瀬戸で舞う
og07 | 男木集落

Takeshi Kawashima + Dream Friends | Japan
Dancing in the Seto
Ogi Village
2010–2022

超高層ビルが林立するマンハッタンの空と雲の下の人間ドラマ・人間賛歌から生まれた《Blue and white》シリーズ、その中の一つ《Dance 1983》。50 年以上の月日を経て故郷の瀬戸内海へ帰ってきた作家が、コロナ禍による閉塞感の中、瀬戸内の海や島々で大空に向かって大きく深呼吸し、そこで感じる音からダンスをテーマに再制作した。リニューアルした作品群の中、無音の展示室に訪れた少女が躍りはじめたという。

Dance 1983 comes from the series *Blue and White*, born out of the sky of Manhattan above the skyscrapers, and celebrating the human drama below the clouds. After more than 50 years away, the artist returned to his homeland of Setouchi. Feeling trapped by Covid-19, he took deep breaths of ocean and island air, looking up at the expanse of the sky, and re-made the work using the resonance he felt there, with a theme of dance. Visiting the soundless exhibition room, a girl began to dance amongst the series of works being renewed.

漆の家プロジェクト
漆の家
og14 | 男木集落

"Maison de Urushi" Project | Japan
Maison de Urushi
Ogi Village
2010, 2013

讃岐の漆芸家が集まり、木造家屋を伝統的な漆芸技法でリノベーションした。明るく華やかな色彩が特徴の讃岐漆に伝わる五技法を鑑賞しながら「漆のある暮らし」を考えることができる。

The *urushi* (lacquer-ware) artists of Sanuki were gathered to renovate this wooden house with traditional *urushi* painting. Viewers can see the Five Methods of Painting, with their rich, bright colors, characteristic of Sanuki *urushi*, and imagine a life with lacquer-ware.

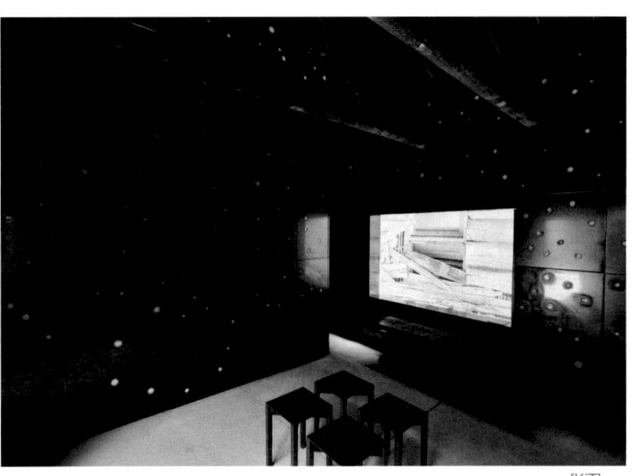

[KiT]

ひびのこづえ

Come and Go
MAMMOTH

E08 | 男木小・中学校グラウンド、高松港

Kodue Hibino | Japan
Come and Go
MAMMOTH
Ogi Elementary and Junior High School's Ground / Takamatsu Port
2022

夕暮れの高松港にマンモスが現れた夏会期の「MAMMOTH」では、藤村港平のダンスパフォーマンスがひびのの衣装に息を吹き込み、島帰りの来場者を釘付けにした。秋会期の「Come and Go」は全国からオーディションで選ばれた19名のダンサーによる全7公演で、男木小・中学校の運動場を舞台に、ダンサーたちは海の生き物の衣装をまとい、寄せては返す海のイメージから宇宙へと広がるダンスパフォーマンスを上演した。

MAMMOTH saw the creature of the title appearing at Takamatsu Port at dusk in the summer period. Kohei Fujimura's dance performance brought life to the costume by Kozue Hibino, commanding the eyes of the audience returning from the islands. *Come and Go*, held in the autumn period, consisted of seven shows by 19 dancers chosen through national auditions. They put on the costumes of sea creatures for their performances, which began with the image of ocean waves coming in, and built to the concept of the universe. The performances were staged in the schoolyard of Ogi Elementary and Junior High School.

「Come and Go」

「MAMMOTH」[SM]

Event Data

MAMMOTH　ひびのこづえ × 藤村港平 × 川瀬浩介

8 月 11 日（木祝）18:00 ～、12 日（金）18:00 ～｜会場＝高松港｜ダンス＝藤村港平｜音楽＝川瀬浩介｜衣装＝ひびのこづえ｜来場者数＝ 380 人

August 11th (Thu); 18:00–, 12th (Fri); 18:00– | Place: Takamatsu Port | Dance: Kohei Fujimura | Music: Kosuke Kawase | Costume: Kodue Hibino | Attendance: 380 people

Come and Go　ひびのこづえ × 島地保武 × 小野龍一 ×OGIJIMA

10月8日（土）15:00～、9日（日）11:30～、15:00～、10日（月祝）11:30～、15日（土）11:30～、15:00～、16日（日）11:30～｜会場＝男木小・中学校グラウンド｜演出・振付＝島地保武｜音楽＝小野龍一｜衣装＝ひびのこづえ｜出演＝生部喜子、岩下愛、上田彩夏、岡田祐介、木村美咲、小林繭子、芝野明日香、資延宏紀、鈴木ミキ、須田珠恵、関口晴、田部井千晶、チャン・クワン・シャン、寺尾茉理加、豊田ちほ、ながやこうた、西村愛香、廣瀬桜子、ふじいみき｜料金＝一般1,000円、小中高生500円、ほか｜来場者数＝645人

October 8th (Sat); 15:00–, 9th (Sun); 11:30–, 15:00–, 10th (Mon); 11:30–, 15th (Sat); 11:30–, 15:30–, 16th (Sun); 11:30– | Place: Ogi Elementary and Junior High School's Ground | Direction/Choreography: Yasutake Shimaji | Music: Ryuichi Ono | Costume: Kodue Hibino | Admission: General 1,000 yen, (ages 6–18) 500 yen, etc. | Attendance: 645 people

小豆島

Shodoshima

所在地＝香川県小豆郡土庄町／小豆島町
（かがわけんしょうずぐん
とのしょうちょう／しょうどしまちょう）
面積＝153.25㎢
周囲＝145.2㎞
最高地点＝816m（星ヶ城山）
世帯数＝11,500世帯
人口＝25,948人
0〜14歳＝2,413人
15〜64歳＝12,256人
65歳〜＝11,264人
不詳＝15人

Location: Tonosho Town / Shodoshima Town,
Shozu County, Kagawa Prefecture
Area: 153.25km^2
Circumference: 145.2km
Highest Point: 816m (Mt. Hoshigajo)
Number of Households: 11,500
Population: 25,948 people
0-14 Years: 2,413 people
15-64 Years: 12,256 people
Over 65 Years: 11,264 people
Unknown: 15 people

[HHa]

小豆島　*Shodoshima*

瀬戸内海で２番目に大きな島。8000 ～ 9000 万年前の花崗岩類の上に 1300 ～ 1500 万年前の瀬戸内火山岩類があり、またサヌキトイドと呼ばれる安山岩が分布するなど異なる地質で成り立っている。花崗岩は採石され大坂城の石垣として搬出されるなど島の産業を支え、多くの採石丁場が今に伝わっている。火山岩類は 1300 万年にわたり侵食され寒霞渓などの景勝地を生んだ。この寒霞渓や対岸の屋島を発端に、瀬戸内海は 1934 年、日本初の国立公園に指定される。中山の千枚田や断崖にある島八十八ヶ所霊場など、起伏に富んだ地形は島特有の景観や文化を育んできた。

海上運送が便利な立地を活かし、そうめんや醤油などの加工産業が盛んで、この 100 年はオリーブの栽培が有名に。映画のロケ地として「八日目の蝉」、島出身の壺井栄原作の「二十四の瞳」などが知られる。秋は島の各地で太鼓台を担ぐ盛大な祭りが行われる。５つの港から本州と四国に航路がつながり交通の便が良く、年間 100 万人が訪れる人気の観光地であり、近年は年間 100 世帯以上が移住している。

The second largest island in the Setouchi area. On 80–90 million-year-old granite lies Setouchi volcanic rock from 13–15 million years ago, along with andesite called *sanukaito*, demonstrating the island's varied geological composition. Granite was mined here and exported for the stone walls of Osaka Castle, supporting the industry of the island, and even today many stonecutting sites remain. Volcanic rock built up by long-term eruptions over a period of 13 million years created well known viewpoints such as Kankakei. These sites, also including Yashima, led to the whole Seto Inland Sea area becoming the first designated national park in Japan. The varied geological features of the island, such as the terraced rice fields of Nakayama, and the Eighty-eight *Reijo* ("sacred places") have nurtured and informed cultures that are unique to Shodoshima.

Utilizing its advantageous position for ocean transport, food processing – including *somen* noodle and soy sauce manufacture – is widespread, and over the last 100 years it has become famous for olive planting. Shodoshima is also known as a film location site, as it was used for *The Eighth Day* and for *Twenty-Four Eyes*, which was written by Tsuboi Sakae, who is from the island. In autumn, there are many large festivals held in different spots on the island, with people carrying huge drum floats. From its five ports, there are routes connecting the mainland and Shikoku island, a feature which makes Shodoshima an important travel destination, seeing 1 million tourists a year. Recently, more than 100 families have moved to the island each year.

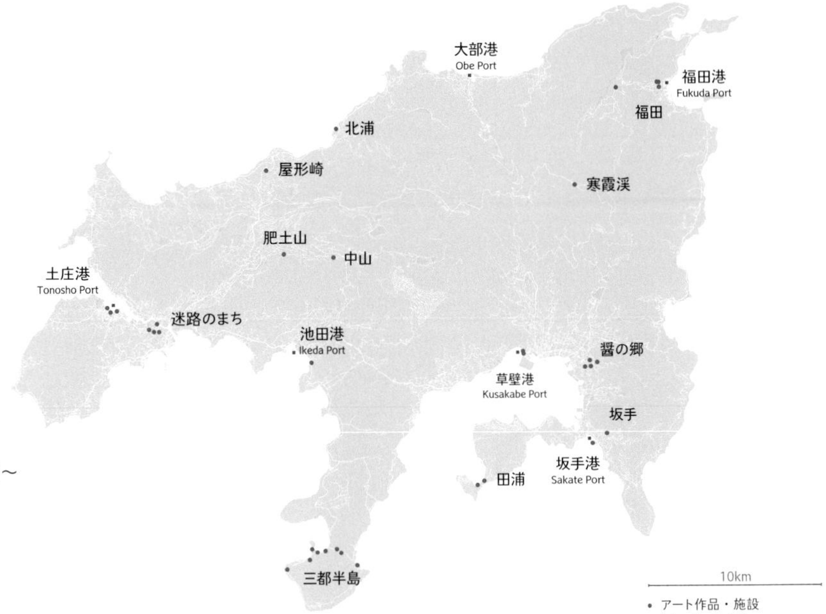

大部港
Obe Port
福田港
Fukuda Port
福田
北浦
屋形崎
寒霞渓
肥土山
中山
土庄港
Tonosho Port
迷路のまち
池田港
Ikeda Port
醤の郷
草壁港
Kusakabe Port
坂手
坂手港
Sakate Port
田浦
三都半島
10km
• アート作品・施設
Artworks, Facilities

土庄港

sd01 太陽の贈り物
チェ・ジョンファ［崔正化］
Choi Jeong Hwa

sd02 対極の美ー無限に続く円ー
コシノジュンコ Junko Koshino

sd03 再び…
キム・キョンミン［金景瞖］
Kim Kyoung Min

迷路のまち周辺

sd04 迷路のまち～変幻自在の路地空間～
目［mé］

sd40 La Danse
ソピアップ・ピッチ Sopheap Pich

sd41 いっしょに／ともだち
スタシス・エイドリゲヴィチウス
Stasys Eidrigevičius

sd42 立入禁止
土井健史 Takefumi Doi

三都半島

sd10 境界線の庭
土井満治 Mitsuharu Doi

sd11 自然の目「大地から」
フリオ・ゴヤ Julio Goya

sd16 潮耳荘
伊東敏光＋康夏奈＋広島市立大学芸術学部有志
Toshimitsu Ito + Kana Kou +
Faculty of Arts, Hiroshima City University

sd19 山声洞
伊東敏光＋広島市立大学芸術学部有志
Toshimitsu Ito +
Faculty of Arts, Hiroshima City University

sd45 ヒトクサヤドカリ
尾身大輔 Daisuke Omi

sd46 ダイダラウルトラボウ
伊東敏光＋広島市立大学芸術学部有志
Toshimitsu Ito +
Faculty of Arts, Hiroshima City University

sd47 ポップストップ
チャールズ・ウォーゼン Charles Worthen

sd48 舟物語
フリオ・ゴヤ Julio Goya

sd49 Utopia dungeon
～ Command from Utopia ～
田中圭介 Keisuke Tanaka

肥土山／中山

sd06 猪鹿垣の島
齋藤正人 Masato Saito

sd44 ゼロ
ワン・ウェンチー［王文志］
Wang Wen Chih

寒霞渓

sd54 空の玉 / 寒霞渓
青木野枝 Noe Aoki

醤の郷周辺／草壁港

sd21 石の島の石
中山英之建築設計事務所
Hideyuki Nakayama Architecture

sd24 おおきな曲面のある小屋
島田陽 Yo Shimada

sd25 オリーブのリーゼント
清水久和 Hisakazu Shimizu

sd26 Umaki camp
ドットアーキテクツ dot architects

sd27 ジョルジュ・ギャラリー／
醤の郷現代美術館
ジョルジュ・ルース Georges Rousse

sd50 辿り着く向こう岸
シャン・ヤン［向阳］Xiang Yang

坂手港／田浦半島

sd30 スター・アンガー
ヤノベケンジ Kenji Yanobe

sd31 アンガー・フロム・ザ・ボトム
美井戸神社
ビートたけし×ヤノベケンジ
Beat Takeshi × Kenji Yanobe

sd32 漁師の夢
入江早耶 Saya Irie

sd33 愛のボラード
清水久和 Hisakazu Shimizu

sd51 小豆島ハウスプロジェクト
新建築社＋SUNAKI
Shinkenchiku-Sha+SUNAKI

北浦／屋形崎

sd38 ダイナマイト・トラヴァース
変奏曲
秩父前衛派 Chichibu Avant-Garde

sd43 はじまりの刻
三宅之功 Shiko Miyake

福田

sd34B アジア・ギャラリー「時代の風景・時代の肖像＋＋＋」
Asia Gallery “The Sceneries and Portraits of the Eras+++”

sd34B 葺田の森テラス
FUKITA NO MORI TERRACE

sd35 葺田パヴィリオン
西沢立衛 Ryue Nishizawa

sd52B 地域紹介展示「福田からのお手紙」
Regional Introduction “Letter from Fukuda”

sd53B アジアアートプラットフォーム2022
協同展「共に在る力」
Asia Art Platform 2022《Communal Spirits》

Songs for living, 2021
コラクリット・アルナーノンチャイ＆アレックス・グヴォジック
Korakrit Arunanondchai & Alex Gvojic

Preah Kunhong (The Way of Spirit), 2016-2017
クヴァイ・サムナン Khvay Samnang

Blessings from Sunshine, 2022
サマー・ファン＆ツァイ・ジアイン Summer Huang & Tsai, JiaYin

EXPLORING FARMER GROUPS JOGJA X FUKUDA, 2022
アナン・サプトト Anang Saptoto

Hong Kong Colours in Shodoshima:
A Ceramics Showcase, 2021～present
香港アートスクールの講師と卒業生
キュレーター：フィオナ・ウォン・ライ・チンと香港アートセンターチーム
Fiona Wong Lai Ching and HKAC team

sd55 そこにいた
イ・スーキュン［李秀京］ Yeesookyung

E09 『竜宮鱗屑譚（せとうちうろくずものがたり）～GYOTS～』
木ノ下歌舞伎 Kinoshita Kabuki

E10 葺田夜祭
川村亘平斎、石田多朗 Koheysai Kawamura, Taro Ishida

E11 ①『あゆみ（短編）』②『反復かつ連続』
ままごと mamagoto

青木野枝

空の玉 / 寒霞渓

sd54 | 寒霞渓

Noe Aoki | Japan
Soranotama / Kankakei
Kankakei
2022

奇岩の渓谷美として知られ、日本書紀にも記述がある寒霞渓に高さ4mの鉄の球体が現れた。細い山道を登ったり降りたりして、鬱蒼とした木の合間を歩いて行くと、ふわっと空へ浮かび上がるように島と海の景色を一望できる展望台が来訪者を迎える。「すごく目立つのではなく、あの場所にそっとある作品をつくりたい」と語った作家が、鋼表面に保護性錆を形成して錆を止める耐性鋼を素材に、時とともに自然に溶け込んでいく作品を制作した。

A 4-meter iron sphere appeared at Kankakei, which is known for the beauty of its unusual rock forms, as mentioned in the *Nihon Shoki* ("Chronicles of Japan", dated at around AD740). After going up and down narrow mountain paths in the deep forests, visitors are welcomed by an observatory to look out on the islands and sea – like a platform floating off into the sky. Rather than obviously standing out, the artist aimed to create a work that quietly sits in place. Aoki produced the piece using weathering steel, which forms a stable rust-like appearance on the surface as a protective layer that prevents rust penetration, and the piece blends deeper into nature as time passes.

設計＝大石雅之建築設計事務所
所蔵＝小豆島町
Architecture: Oishi Masayuki and Associates
Collection: Shodoshima Town

2点とも©Noe Aoki Courtesy of ANOMALY [TY]

イ・スーキュン［李秀京］

そこにいた

sd55 | 福田

Yeesookyung | Korea

You Were There

Fukuda

2022

古来から神聖なものとして象徴されてきた大きな石を起点に、作家が世界各地で発表してきたプロジェクトを、今回は小豆島の福田から寒霞渓へ続く道で展開した。島内で採取した石を、韓国の仏像技術を用いて金箔で覆い、瀬戸内海を臨む２つの地点に配置。時間の蓄積が生んだ神秘的な素材である石の魅力を浮かび上がらせようと試みた。周囲に溶け込みつつも存在感を放つ作品が、山道を通り抜ける人々の目にふと現れる。

With a large rock, a symbol of sacred things from the past, as an originating point, Yeesookyung has exhibited projects all over the world, and she developed one on the route between Fukuda in Shodoshima and Kankakei. Rocks collected on the island were covered with gold foil, using techniques for making statues of Buddha in Korea, and she placed them in two points that overlook the Seto Inland Sea. It is an attempt to convey the charm of stones, a mystical material born out of the accumulation of time. The work blends in with the surroundings, yet gives a sense of its presence as it appears before the eyes of travelers on the mountain road.

2点とも [KK]

福武ハウス　*Fukutake House*

小豆島の東端に位置し、山と海に囲まれた人口 800 名ほどの福田地区から、アジア諸地域をつなぐプロジェクトが、2013 年から旧福田小学校を舞台にはじまった。ローカルとグローバルに同時に焦点をあてる「アジア・ギャラリー」や食プロジェクト、そしてアジアのパートナーが美術を通してお互いの理解を深める「アジア・アート・プラットフォーム」を展開している。

The Fukuda area, located at the eastern tip of Shodoshima, has a population of 800 and is surrounded by mountains and sea. A project to connect regions of East Asia began here in 2013, based in the former Fukuda Elementary School. It has seen the development of *Asia Gallery*, which focuses on global and local food projects, and *Asia Art Platform*, which aims to deepen mutual understanding through art.

運営＝公益財団法人 福武財団
Management: Fukutake Foundation

[Yln]

アジア・ギャラリー「時代の風景・時代の肖像＋＋＋」

sd34B | 福田・福武ハウス

Asia Gallery "The Sceneries and Portraits of the Eras+++"
Fukutake House, Fukuda
2022

ベネッセ賞やアジア各地の調査などで集められたアジア現代美術作品と、空間に合わせて制作された新たな作品を展示。第 12 回ベネッセ賞を受賞したアマンダ・ヘンの写真作品や、日産アートアワード 2020 グランプリを受賞した潘逸舟の新作に加え、これまであまり展示されることのなかった主要な所蔵作品を公開した。

Asia Gallery exhibits contemporary Asian art collected through the Benesse Prize and research conducted in various locations across Asia. In addition to photographic work by Amanda Heng, winner of the 12th Benesse Prize, and work by Ishu Han, who received the Nissan Art Award 2020 Grand Prix, some of the rarely exhibited major pieces of the collection were shown to the public.

アーティスト＝アマンダ・ヘン、Chim↑Pom from Smappa!Group、潘逸舟、ヒルミー・P・スパドモ、インディゲリラ、カンチャナ・グプタ、近藤亜樹、森万里子、森村泰昌、パナパン・ヨドマニー、ズルキフリ・マハムード

Artists: Amanda Heng, Chim↑Pom from Smappa!Group, Ishu Han, Hilmy P. Soepadmo, indieguerillas, Kanchana Gupta, Aki Kondo, Mariko Mori, Yasumasa Morimura, Pannaphan Yodmanee, Zulkifle Mahmod

キュレーション＝三木あき子
特別協力＝株式会社ベネッセホールディングス
所蔵・運営＝公益財団法人 福武財団
Curation: Akiko Miki
Cooperation: Benesse Holdings, Inc.
Collection & Management: Fukutake Foundation

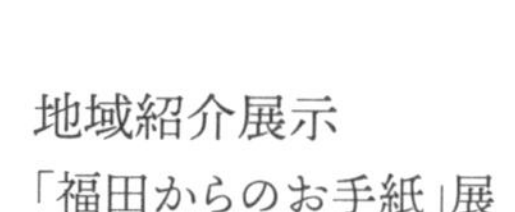

地域紹介展示「福田からのお手紙」展

sd52B | 福田・福武ハウス

Regional Introduction "Letter from Fukuda"
Fukutake House, Fukuda
2022

小豆島の東に位置し海と山に囲まれた福田地区。播磨灘に開いた港を持ち、昔から漁や石材の積み出し港として様々な人が行き交い生活してきた。社叢林を背にした神社や高台から海を望むお寺、秋祭りの太鼓台、獅子舞などの文化資源は今なお豊かに残る。地域の人々から集めた古い写真を通して、今に続く往時の姿を鑑賞者に届けた。

The Fukuda area, surrounded by trees and mountains, is located on the east side of Shodoshima. It has a port opening onto the Harimanada portion of the sea, where many people and goods have entered and left, loading materials for the fishing and stone industries. The area is rich with cultural heritage that still remains, including a shrine with a sacred forest behind it, a temple with a wonderful ocean view from its elevated platform, drum floats in the autumn festival, and a *shishimai* lion dance. Through old photographs collected from the local community, scenes from the past were transmitted to the viewers of today.

主催＝公益財団法人 福武財団、福田地区自治連合会、小豆島町
運営＝公益財団法人 福武財団
Organization: Fukutake Foundation, Fukuda Residents' Association, Shodoshima Town
Management: Fukutake Foundation

[YIn]

葺田の森テラス

sd34B | 福田・福武ハウス

FUKITA NO MORI TERRACE
Fukutake House, Fukuda
2022

ゲストと地域の人々が集い、交流するカフェとして新設。テラスの名前は福田の古い地名「葺田（ふきた）」による。隣接する神社の社叢に大きく開いた半屋外のテラスで、木陰に吹く風を感じながらくつろぐことができる。ウッドデッキは島の間伐材である檜を使用して住民とともに制作された。地域資源を活かすとともに、キッズスペースを設けるなど地元の人々にも親しみを持って利用してもらえる場所を目指した。

設計＝佐々木恵

FUKITA NO MORI TERRACE is a newly opened café for local people and visitors to come together and share their time. The name comes from the old name of today's Fukuda: "*Fukita*". The semi-outdoor terrace opens widely on the sacred forest of a neighboring shrine, and guests can relax in the breeze amongst the trees. The wooden deck was produced with the cooperation of local residents, using lumber from tree thinning on the island. This was not only a way to utilize local resources, but aimed to make the space feel familiar to local people, also seen in the creation of a space for children.

Architecture: Megumi Sasaki

[KiT]

西沢立衛

葺田パヴィリオン

sd35 | 福田・福武ハウス

Ryue Nishizawa | Japan
Fukita Pavilion
Fukutake House, Fukuda
2013

カーブした２枚の鋼板によって生まれた空間が葺田八幡神社とゆるやかに接続し、参拝者が座って休める場所や、子どもの遊び場として利用されている。

Constructed of two curved sheets of steel, the inner space serves as an extension of the shrine grounds, offering visitors a place to sit and rest and children a place to play.

所蔵＝小豆島町
Collection: Shodoshima Town

アジア・アート・プラットフォーム2022協同展「共に在る力」
Asia Art Platform 2022《Communal Spirits》

2013年より継続し、アジアの諸地域と美術を通してつながるプロジェクト。今回は香港、インドネシア、台湾、カンボジア、タイの5つのパートナー団体と連携し、福田集落内の空家に5組のアーティストが作品を展示した。アジア文化の根底に潜在するさまざまな事象をテーマに、かつての先祖が重んじてきたものや生き方を見直し、同時にそれぞれの地域が現在直面している諸問題について焦点を当てる展示となった。

This project, which has been ongoing since 2013, aims to connect East Asian regions through art. This time, through five partner organizations in Hong Kong, Indonesia, Taiwan, Cambodia, and Thailand, five artist units exhibited their work in a vacant house in Fukuda village. With the theme of the various phenomena at the root of East Asian culture, the exhibition reexamined what ancestors regarded as important, and the way they lived, while focusing on the various issues that each region is facing today.

パートナー団体（地域）＝ササ・アート・プロジェクト（カンボジア）、台湾歴史資源経理学会（台湾）、チェメティーインスティチュート・フォー・アート＆ソサイエティ（インドネシア）、香港アートセンター（香港）、ジム・トンプソン・アートセンター（タイ）
アート・ディレクション＝北川フラム
キュレーション＝リノ・ヴス（ササ・アート・プロジェクトアーティスティック・ディレクター）
主催＝公益財団法人 福武財団
特別協力＝福田地区自治連合会、小豆島町

Asia Art Platform Partner (Region): Sa Sa Art Projects (Cambodia), Historical Resource Management Institute (Taiwan), Cemeti- Institute for Art and Society (Indonesia), Hong Kong Arts Centre (Hong Kong), Jim Thompson Art Center (Thailand)
Art direction: Fram Kitagawa
Curation: Lyno Vuth (Sa Sa Art Projects artistic director)
Organization: Fukutake Foundation
Cooperation: Fukuda Residents' Association, Shodoshima town

[YIn]

コラクリット・アルナーノンチャイ＆アレックス・グヴォジック
Songs for living, 2021
sd53B | 福田

Korakrit Arunanondchai & Alex Gvojic | Thailand
Songs for living, 2021
Fukuda
2022

祖父を亡くした後、悲しみ、変化、そして精神的な力を伝える物語を展開するコラクリット・アルナーノンチャイと、撮影監督のアレックス・グヴォジックによる共同作品。生と死を媒介するメタファーとしてウミガメや幽霊・シャーマンなどの神話的なシンボルを映像作品に取り入れた。タイの社会的・政治的現実を示唆すると同時に、人生の出来事に直面しつつ前進しようとする私たちの感覚を映し出した。

This work is a collaboration between Korakrit Arunanondchai, who weaves stories that convey grief, transformation, and spiritual power and cinematographer Alex Gvojic. Mythical symbols like sea turtles, ghosts, and shamans were incorporated into the film as metaphors that mediate life and death. While it suggests social and political reality in Thailand, it also projects the sensation of facing various occurrences in life and continuing to move forward.

2点とも [YIn]

クヴァイ・サムナン

Preah Kunhong (The Way of Spirit), 2016–2017

sd53B | 福田

Khvay Samnang | Cambodia
Preah Kunhong (The Way of Spirit), 2016–2017
Fukuda
2022

東南アジアにおける最後の大森林であるアレン渓谷と、そこに暮らす先住民族チョン族にまつわるパフォーマンス・映像作品。アレン渓谷は近年ダム開発による環境破壊が進み、チョン族は生活の変化を迫られている。1年間チョン族と関係を築きリサーチを行った作家は、振付家・ダンサーのNget Radyとともに、チョン族とその土地とのつながりや、彼らの抵抗の姿を作品に表した。

This is a performance and film work about Areng Valley, the last remaining great forest in southeast Asia, and the indigenous Chong people who live there. Areng Valley has been under the threat of environmental devastation due to the development of a large hydroelectric dam, and the resulting transformation of the indigenous way of life. Khvay built a lasting relationship with the Chong people in their communities for one year to conduct research, and together with choreographer and dancer Nget Rady, expressed the inherent connection of the Chong people with their land, as well as their most powerful form of resistance.

2点とも [YIn]

サマー・ファン&ツァイ・ジアイン

Blessings from Sunshine, 2022

sd53B | 福田

Summer Huang & Tsai, JiaYin | Taiwan
Blessings from Sunshine, 2022
Fukuda
2022

「太陽が地球上の全てを祝福する」というコンセプトの作品。台湾の植物や自然環境から着想した有機的な形を布に描き、台湾の人々による手書きの言葉やドローイングを、日光で青く印画されるサイアノタイプの技法を使って転写した。文字やイメージは太陽光を浴びることで徐々に写し出され、台湾から日本へのメッセージとして、一針、一縫い、一念、一筆を捧げて祝福の気持ちを伝える作品になった。

The work of Summer Huang and JiaYin Tsai is based on the concept that "the sun blesses everything on the earth". Images of the plants of Taiwan and organic shapes inspired by the natural environment are drawn on a cloth, onto which hand-written phrases and drawings by Taiwanese people are printed with a cyanotype method, so that after sunlight exposure the image will appear onto the fabric. Every stich, every sew, every thought, and every stroke is a dedication and blessing from Taiwan to Japan.

2点とも [YIn]

アナン・サプトト
EXPLORING FARMER GROUPS JOGJA X FUKUDA, 2022

sd53B | 福田

Anang Saptoto | Indonesia
EXPLORING FARMER GROUPS JOGJA X FUKUDA, 2022
Fukuda
2022

パンデミック時代の食糧の流れを理解するために、作家が2020年から取り組んできた芸術と農業をつなぐイニシアチブ「Panen Apa Hari Ini (PARI)」による展示。今回はインドネシアのジョグジャカルタと小豆島・福田における食料の供給源や農業の実践について、農家や漁師、子どもたちと調査やワークショップを行い、それらの記録をジョグジャカルタと福田の２拠点で発表した。

In order to understand the distribution of produce in the time of the pandemic, the artist has been working on an initiative connecting art and agriculture called *Panen Apa Hari Ini* since 2020, and this exhibition is a part of it. In this project the artist conducted research and workshops about food sources and agricultural practices of the cities of Yogyakarta, Indonesia, and Fukuda in Kagawa. The results were shown to public in Yogyakarta and Fukuda.

2点とも [YIn]

香港アートスクールの講師と卒業生 キュレーター：フィオナ・ウォン・ライ・チンと香港アートセンターチーム
Hong Kong Colours in Shodoshima: A Ceramics Showcase, 2021〜present

sd53B | 福田

Teachers and alumni of Hong Kong Art School
Curator: Fiona Wong Lai Ching and HKAC team | Hong Kong
Hong Kong Colours in Shodoshima: A Ceramics Showcase, 2021〜present
Fukuda
2022

《香港カラーズ》は自分たちの土地について再発見することを目的に、継続的に実施されるプロジェクト。土の採集から制作に至るまで、人がその場所をどのように発見し、理解し、共に生きているかを重要な要素として取り上げ、その過程から土地の記憶、コミュニティ、地域の文化の関係を見直す。今回は小豆島でこのプロセスを実践し、香港の土地の色に並んで《小豆島カラーズ》を展示した。

Hong Kong Colours is an ongoing project that aims to rediscover the land we live in. Following the process from collecting local clay to its production, the project deals with the process of how a person discovers and understands a place, and lives together with it. By doing so, it seeks to revisit the relationships between memory, community, and culture of a locality. This time, the project took place in Shodoshima, and alongside the colors of Hong Kong clay, *Shodoshima Colours* were also displayed.

[Yln]

川村亘平斎、石田多朗

葺田夜祭

E10 | 福田・福武ハウス

Koheysai Kawamura | Japan
Taro Ishida | Japan
FUKITAYOMATSURI
Fukutake House, Fukuda
2022

Event Data

9月4日（日）屋台出店 16:00～、舞台公演 18:00～20:00
「福田うみやまこばなし 2022―かぼそ雑記」出演＝川村亘平斎、トンチ、カメイナホコ、福田影絵団 | 「ドンス」出演＝石田多朗、小野雄大、小林武文、高岡大祐 | 屋台出店＝Kaina、はるや、TrackTruck×ata rangi、炭火焼き鳥ヒラク、福田自治連合会、葺田の森テラスほか | 料金＝一般 2,500円、15歳以下無料、ほか

September 4th (Sun); Steet Stands 16:00–, Live Performance 18:00–20:00 | Theater performance: Shadow Picture: Short Stories of Fukuda Seas and Mountains 2022 – Kaboso Journal, Cast: Koheisai Kawamura, Tonchi, Nahoko Kamei, Fukuda Kagee-dan | Music Performance: Donsu, Cast: Taro Ishida, Yudai Ono, Takefumi Kobayashi, Daisuke Takaoka | Street Stands: Kaina (baked sweets, drinks, and others), Haruya (pizza), TrackTruck×ata rangi (fish and chips), Charcoal-grilled Yakitori Hiraku (grilled chicken), Fukuda Union of Residents' Association (shooting game, yo-yo catching), FUKITA NO MORI TERRACE (food and drink), etc. | Attendance: General 2,500 yen, Ages 15 and under free, etc.

アーティストと住民が、島の1年の「実り」を演目や屋台として持ち寄る「葺田夜祭」を開催。影絵師の川村は、2020年から福武ハウスの取り組みに関わり、地域住民と交流を重ねてきた。公演では公募で集まった出演者たちと福田に滞在し、「妖怪かぼそ」を軸に小豆島にまつわる物語を影絵として上演。作曲家の石田は、住民の記憶に残る地域の風景や暮らしをテーマに作曲、音楽プロジェクト「ドンス」として、演奏者らとチンドン演奏や音楽ライブを行った。

Artists and residents of the island hold a festival called *Fukita Yomatsuri*, to which they bring the island's "harvest of the year" in the form of performing arts and street stands. Shadow picture artist Koheysai Kawamura has been sharing communication with the residents of the area since he began working on *Fukutake House* in 2022. At the festival, a cast gathered through an open call stayed in Fukuda with the artist and performed a shadow picture work about Shodoshima, with the story of *Ghost Kaboso* at its center. Composer Taro Ishida produced a musical piece with the theme of the landscape and life of the area remaining in the memories of the islanders, which was performed live with a group of musicians as the project *Donsu* .

[Ylc]

島田陽

おおきな曲面のある小屋

sd24 | 馬木・醤の郷

Yo Shimada | Japan
Hut with the Arc Wall
Hishionosato, Umaki
2013

醤油蔵が立ち並ぶ醤の郷に公共トイレを設置。周囲の町並みに溶け込むよう、屋根には瓦を採用。柔らかな曲線を描いて穏やかな空間をつくり出す。

The artist constructed a public restroom in Hishionosato, home to a number of soy sauce breweries. The roof tiles blend in with the traditional houses nearby and the gentle curves evoke a sense of tranquility.

所蔵＝小豆島町
Collection: Shodoshima Town

©Georges Rousse

ジョルジュ・ギャラリー 醤の郷現代美術館

sd27 | 馬木・醤の郷

GEORGES Gallery / MOCA HISHIO
Hishionosato, Umaki
2019, 2022

かつて醤油製造業で栄えた醤の郷で長期的に展開する「小豆島アートプロジェクト」の一環として、アート・文化施設を展開。
ジョルジュ・ギャラリーは、醤の郷の古民家を、フランスの写真家・ジョルジュ・ルースとボランティア約50名の創作活動によって、3つの写真作品と制作の過程を展示する恒久施設として再生。農機具小屋を活かした「コヒラカフェ」を併設する。
醤の郷現代美術館は、90年以上前に建てられた島で最初の鉄筋コンクリート建築である旧醤油会館を、現代美術館・文化施設として再生し2022年4月にオープン。植松奎二、渡辺信子、中川佳宣らが新たに制作した作品のほか、約130点のコレクションを展示する。近接するMOCA HISHIO ANNEXは、かつての工場跡のレンガ倉庫を再生したギャラリー施設で、今回は「ズガコーサク＋クリエイト展」「滑川みざ展」を開催した。

所蔵・運営＝小豆島アートプロジェクト

GEORGES Gallery operates as an art and culture facility as part of the *Shodoshima Art Project* that has been conducted for a long time at Hishionosato, which once enjoyed prosperity through the production of soy sauce.

Through the creative work of photographer Georges Rousse and almost 50 volunteers, an old house in Hishionosato was regenerated as a permanent facility for the exhibition of three of his photographic works and a documentary film about the production process. It also features KOHIRA café, located in a former farm machinery shed.

The former soy sauce memorial hall, built more than 90 years ago, was the first reinforced-concrete building on the island. It was renovated as contemporary art gallery and cultural facility MOCA HISHIO in April 2022.

It exhibits around 130 pieces from its collection, along with new work by Keiji Uematsu, Nobuko Watanabe, and Nakagawa Yoshinobu. MOCA HISHIO ANNEX, built nearby, is a gallery space in a brick warehouse that used to be a factory. It held the exhibitions *ZUGAKOUSAKU & KURIEITO* and *Misa Namekawa*.

Collection & Management: Shodoshima Art Project

ドットアーキテクツ Umaki camp

sd26 | 馬木・醤の郷

dot architects | Japan
Umaki camp
Hishionosato, Umaki
2013

セルフビルドによって作られ、誰でも自由に使えるキッチンやスタジオを備えた木造平屋の施設。今回は夏会期中に「馬木ローカルミーティング」を開催し、地域の人々と馬木に関わってきた建築家たちが集い、これからの島についてをテーマにトークを行った。

A self-built, one-story wooden building with a kitchen and studio open for anyone to use. During the summer session, an “Umaki Local Meeting” was held there, where local people and architects who have been involved in Umaki gathered to talk about the future of the island.

所蔵＝小豆島町
Collection: Shodoshima Town

©SUNAKI Inc. [KY]

新建築社＋SUNAKI
小豆島ハウスプロジェクト

sd51 | 坂手

Shinkenchiku-Sha+SUNAKI | Japan
Shodoshima House Project
Sakate
2022

古民家と比べ「いまいち古くない」昭和期の建物を改修し、新しい価値や活用方法を探求するプロジェクト。母屋はレジデンス機能を備えたワーケーション施設に、離れはギャラリー空間に、蔵は資材倉庫として再生した。会期中は離れでの企画展示や、「都市と移動に関するリサーチ」としてフードトラックでの食事提供、建築ミーティングなど、複数のプログラムを展開した。今後も新建築社の拠点として継続的な活用を予定している。

This project converted buildings from the Showa period, which are "not quite old" in comparison with traditional Japanese houses, in order to seek new values and uses in them. Through the regeneration plan, the main house was transformed into a "workation" facility with residential features, the annex into a gallery, and the warehouse into storage for material. During the festival, it developed various programs including exhibitions in the annex gallery, serving meals from a food truck with the theme of "researching cities and transport", and architectural meetings. It is planned to be used going forward as the base of an architectural firm.

URL ＝ https://www.shodoshimahouse.com/

SUNAKI ＝砂山太一、木内俊克
所蔵・運営＝新建築社
SUNAKI: Taichi Sunayama, Toshikatsu Kiuchi
Collection & Management: Shinkenchiku-Sha Co., Ltd.

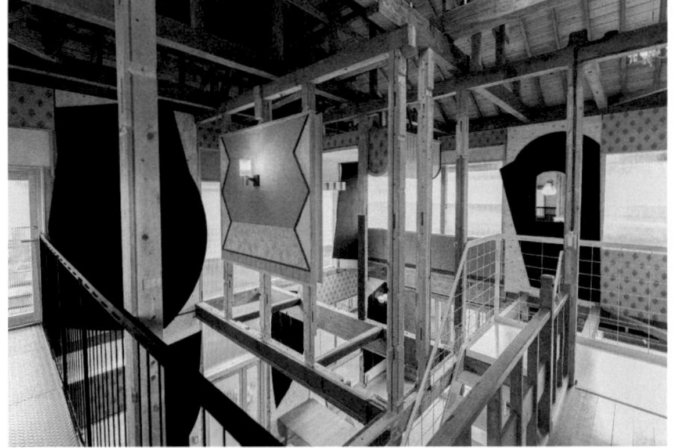

上 © SUNAKI Inc. [KY] 下 [KK]

[Ylc]

ビートたけし×ヤノベケンジ

アンガー・フロム・ザ・ボトム 美井戸神社

sd31 | 坂手

Beat Takeshi × Kenji Yanobe | Japan
Beat Shrine / ANGER from the Bottom
Sakate
2013

自然を破壊する人間に対し、古井戸の底に潜む巨大な化け物が怒りを露わにする様子を表した作品。約8mもの巨大なオブジェが実際の古井戸に出現した。

This work presents the figure of a giant monster hidden at the bottom of an old well, showing anger against humans who destroy nature. The huge, 8-meter tall object was placed inside a real well.

設計＝ドットアーキテクツ（祠）
所蔵＝小豆島町
Design: dot architects
Collection: Shodoshima Town

ヤノベケンジ

スター・アンガー

sd30 | 坂手

Kenji Yanobe | Japan
THE STAR ANGER
Sakate
2013

坂手港の灯台跡地に立つ作品。太陽の形の球体に水の神である龍が鎮座してミラーボールのように回転し、文明によって破壊される地球の「怒り」を表す。

This work was constructed on the former site of the Sakate Port lighthouse. A dragon, the deity of water, sits neatly atop a brilliantly shining orb in the shape of the sun, and the entire installation rotates like a disco ball. The yelling dragon is used to symbolize anger at the earth being destroyed by civilization.

所蔵＝小豆島町
Collection: Shodoshima Town

[KiT]

[KK]

入江早耶

漁師の夢

sd32 | 田浦・二十四の瞳映画村

Saya Irie | Japan
Fisherman's Dream
Twenty Four Eyes Movie Studio, Tanoura
2019

「漁師は魚の絵のコレクターだった」というコンセプトから、世界中の魚の絵や魚拓を展示。それらの一部の絵を消した消しゴム屑から、弁財天や人魚をモチーフにした女神を造形した。

With the concept that "fishermen were collectors of fish paintings", the artist exhibited paintings and fish prints. She molded figures of goddesses from eraser flakes generated by erasing parts of these paintings, with motifs of *Benzaiten* (a Japanese Buddhist goddess) and mermaids.

所蔵＝二十四の瞳映画村
Collection: Twenty Four Eyes Movie Studio

中山英之建築設計事務所

石の島の石

sd21 | 草壁港

Hideyuki Nakayama Architecture | Japan
Stone Island's Stone
Kusakabe Port
2016

小豆島の花崗岩を主材料とするコンクリートで公共トイレを施工。屋内は天井から光が差して明るく、夜は室内照明が街灯の役割も兼ねる。

The work is a public washroom made with concrete containing crushed Shodoshima granite. Sunlight shining through the roof illuminating the interior, while at night the interior lights also serve as street lights.

設計＝満田衛資構造計画研究所（構造）、環境エンジニアリング（設備）、岡安泉照明設計事務所（照明）| 所蔵＝小豆島町
Structural design: Mitsuda Structural Consultants | Equipment design: Kankyo Engineering Co., Ltd., | Lighting design: Izumi Okayasu Lighting Design | | Collection: Shodoshima Town

[Ylc]

[SM]

上 [KK]

シャン・ヤン［向阳］

辿り着く向こう岸

sd50 | 草壁港

Xiang Yang | China
The Shore Where We Can Reach
Kusakabe Port
2022

人々を希望と安寧の待つ「向こう岸」へ導く巨大な船をイメージし、実際の船のように海に面した場所に作られた作品。中国で廃棄された家具や建具を修復し組み合わせ、大小の部屋が並ぶ巨大な構造体が完成した。鑑賞者は実際に中に入り、山水画の輪郭が立体的に浮かび上がる刺繍作品や、美しい装飾を細部まで鑑賞できる。コロナ禍で夏会期からの公開となったが、公開初日には地元の人々による太鼓のパフォーマンスで盛り上がった。

In the image of a huge ship ready to take people “to the other side of the water”, where hope and peace wait, the artwork was placed facing the ocean like a real boat. After repairing furniture and construction parts that were discarded in China, the artist combined them into a huge structure with rooms of different sizes. The viewer can enter to see stitched pieces with the outlines of *shan shui* (Chinese-style landscape painting) raised from the base, along with other decorations. Due to the pandemic, it opened in the summer, and on the opening day local people performed with Japanese drums to celebrate.

特別協力＝タチバナ工業株式会社
Cooperation: Tachibana Industry Co., Ltd.

三都半島アートプロジェクト *Mito Peninsula Art Project*

三方を海に囲まれた三都半島では、集落ごとに固有の文化が形成されてきた。2009年からアーティストインレジデンスやワークショップなどの、地域住民とアーティストの協力・共働によるさまざまな取り組みを展開。2014年からは、広島市立大学芸術学部彫刻専攻が中心となりアートプロジェクトを展開している。2022年は新たに5作品が追加された。

所蔵＝小豆島町

Surrounded by sea on its three sides, Mito Peninsula has developed its own distinct culture. Since 2009, it has undertaken a variety of initiatives involving collaboration between local residents and artists, including an artist-in-residence program and workshops. Since 2014, students majoring in sculpture in the Faculty of Arts at Hiroshima City University have been a driving force in this movement, developing art projects. In 2022, 5 new pieces were added.

Collection: Shodoshima Town

2点とも [Ylc]

伊東敏光＋康夏奈＋広島市立大学芸術学部有志
潮耳荘
sd16 | 神浦

Toshimitsu Ito + Kana Kou + Faculty of Arts, Hiroshima City University | Japan
Shiomimi-so
Song of the Tides Inn
Konoura
2016

海と人間の関係を再認識させる野外彫刻作品。古い木材を重ねた高さ10mほどの小山から海に向かってホルン型集音器が設置され、内部空間全体に波の音を届ける。

An exterior sculpture that reaffirms the audience's awareness of the relationship between humans and the sea. From a 10-meter high mound with layers of old wood off-cuts, a horn-shaped object extends towards the sea, filling the space inside with the sound of the waves.

設計＝林幸稔／林幸稔建築設計事務所（監修）
Design supervision: Yukinori Hayashi / Yukinori Hayashi Architect & Associates

2点とも [KK]

伊東敏光＋広島市立大学芸術学部有志
山声洞
sd19 | 神浦

Toshimitsu Ito + Faculty of Arts, Hiroshima City University | Japan
Yamagoe-do
Mountain Voice Cavern
Konoura
2019

採石場跡地に現れた高さ5mの鉄製の彫刻作品。鑑賞者が地下へ降りると、内部の壁に開いたじょうご形の穴が、鳥や風など森が生み出す周囲の音を響かせる。

A 5-meter high iron sculpture was installed in an abandoned quarry site. A funnel-shaped hole in the interior wall captures and echoes the sounds generated by the forest, such as bird calls and the rustling wind.

[KK]

伊東敏光＋広島市立大学芸術学部有志

ダイダラウルトラボウ

sd46 | 神浦

助成＝広島市立大学
Funding: Hiroshima City University

Toshimitsu Ito + Faculty of Arts, Hiroshima City University | Japan
DAIDARAURUTORABOU
Konoura
2022

高台に腰掛け、神浦集落と海を見下ろす巨人の作品。不要になった神浦地区の小径の石垣や、厳島神社への往来で使われていた廃船、瀬戸内海で集められた流木などを組み合わせて作られ、高さは 9m、長さは 17 mにも及ぶ。訪れた人は曲がりくねった山道を抜けた先に現れる巨人と、その目線の向こうに広がる風景をともに眺めた。

Sitting at a great height, a giant looks down on Konoura Village and the sea. It is made of a mixture of materials, such as unused stone from the alleyways of Komoura, abandoned boats that used to travel to Itsukushima Shrine, and driftwood collected from the Seto Inland Sea. The giant is 9 meters tall, and 17 meters long. Visitors see the giant appear at the end of a winding mountain path, and the view that spreads out before its gaze.

[KK]

尾身大輔

ヒトクサヤドカリ

sd45 | 神浦

助成＝広島市立大学
Funding: Hiroshima City University

Daisuke Omi | Japan
Human Home Hermit Crab
Konoura
2022

家を貝殻に見立てた巨大なヤドカリの彫刻。高さ約 2m のヤドカリは楠を彫って制作している。「ヒトクサヤドカリ」とは、琉球の創世神話で人間の起源として登場するヤドカリと、草原のように繁茂する人々という意味の言葉「人草」に由来。人間の誕生や繁栄のイメージであるヤドカリが、人のいなくなった空家に住みついた作品。

A sculpture of a hermit crab, with a house as its shell. The 2-meter tall crab is created with sculpted camphor wood. The name *Human Home Hermit Crab* (*Hitokusa Yadokari*) comes from the hermit crab (*yadokari*) that is the origin of humans in the Okinawan myth of genesis, and from people enjoying prosperity – like growing grass fields (*hitokusa*). The hermit crab, which symbolizes human birth and prosperity, has sneaked into a human house.

[KK]

田中圭介

Utopia dungeon

〜 Command from Utopia 〜

sd49 | 神浦

Keisuke Tanaka | Japan
Utopia dungeon
–Command from Utopia–
Konoura
2022

木造民家を架空の彫刻家のアトリエとして再生させた作品。家の柱や梁などから掘り出されるかたちは、瀬戸内の人々や自然、作家自身がモチーフになっている。均質に切り出された製材にはらむ「死」のイメージと、そこから紡がれる自然や人間といった「生」のイメージが、空間に対比を生み出した。

Tanaka has regenerated a wooden house into the atelier of an imaginary sculptor. The shapes carved into the pillars and beams are inspired by the people of Setouchi, nature, and the artist himself. The idea of death is present in the material that is uniformly carved out, while the image of life is woven into the figures of nature and humans in the sculptures, creating contrast in the space.

助成＝広島市立大学
Funding: Hiroshima City University

[KK]

チャールズ・ウォーゼン

ポップストップ

sd47 | 神浦西バス停

Charles Worthen | USA / Japan
Popstop
Konoura-Nishi Bus Stop
2022

三都半島方面の終点のバス停を鮮やかに彩る作品。コの字に広がる神浦西バス停の建物を、マリンブルーを基調に魚の鱗や海の波を想起させるパターンのファブリックで覆い、建物全体を作品にした。バスを待つ来場者に、停留所の先に隠れた美しい海を示唆している。

A work coloring the last bus stop in Mito Peninsula. The U-shaped building of the Konoura-West bus stop was covered in fabric with colors and patterns evoking fish scales and ocean waves on its marine blue base, creating a work that utilizes the whole building. For the visitors waiting for their buses, it suggests the beautiful sea hidden beyond.

助成＝広島市立大学
Funding: Hiroshima City University

[KK]

フリオ・ゴヤ
舟物語
sd48 | 神浦

Julio Goya | Argentina / Japan
Story of a Boat
Konoura
2022

漁業者の高齢化によって使われなくなった舟を作品化。2艘の舟を使い、一つは船の中にベンチやテーブルが据えられ、もう一つははばたく鳥の姿へと生まれ変わった。舟の塗装や装飾には地元の人々も協力し、地域のものを活かしたひと休みできる場所が生まれた。

Julio Goya created artwork with the boats that have stopped being used as fishermen retire with age. He placed a bench and a table in one of the boats and transformed another into flying birds. The production, including painting and decoration, was undertaken with the cooperation of the local community, resulting in a place to take a rest made from local objects.

[KK]

フリオ・ゴヤ
自然の目「大地から」
sd11 | 神浦

Julio Goya | Argentina / Japan
Eyes of nature (from the earth)
Konoura
2019

防風林として機能してきた2本のイブキの木を活かしたツリーハウス。木のフォルムを活かしたバルコニーから、島の悠大な景色を眺望できる。

Two Chinese juniper trees growing on the site as windbreaks were used to make a treehouse. From the balcony that utilizes the form of the tree, visitors can look out on the grand landscape of the island.

[KK]

土井満治
境界線の庭
sd10 | 南蒲野

Mitsuharu Doi | Japan
Garden of the Border
Minami Kamano
2016, 2019

土砂災害で生じた土砂の埋立地に、埋もれた鳥居のような彫刻と、参道を思わせる道を制作。山から里そして海へと移動する土の流れや、自然と世俗の境界を意識させる。

The work resembles the top of a shrine gate, looking like its posts are buried in the soil, and a path leading to a shrine. It draws attention to the movement of the earth from the mountain to the village and on into the sea, and makes viewers aware of borders, such as those between the mystical world of nature and the secular world.

[SL]

[SM]

[SL]

ワン・ウェンチー［王文志］

ゼロ

sd44 | 中山

Wang Wen Chih | Taiwan
Zero
Nakayama
2022

中山地区の千枚田が広がる田園風景の中に立つ、第1回の芸術祭から毎回テーマを変えて作り続けてきた竹の巨大な作品。冬に地域住民と協働で切りだした4,000本の竹を素材に制作した。高さ15mのドームの内部は螺旋状になっており、心身ともに守られ、自然と一体になる「調和の精神空間」を体験できる。世界的なパンデミックに襲われた地球が、破壊される前の原始の状態に戻り、希望に満ちた未来を迎えるようにという作家の願いが込められた。

Wang Wen Chih has produced huge bamboo pieces with different themes at each edition of the festival, standing in the terraced rice fields of the Nakayama area. This time, he used 4,000 pieces of bamboo, cut with the cooperation of the local residents. Inside its 15-meter high dome is a spiral, creating the feeling of a "harmonic spiritual space" where the visitors are physically and spiritually protected and united with nature. It is a work that conveys the artist's wish that the earth, under the threat of the global pandemic, can return to a primitive state before its destruction, and that it will have a future with hope.

協賛＝株式会社レクザム
助成＝台湾文化部
助成協力＝台北駐日経済文化代表処台湾文化センター
Sponsor: Rexxam Co., Ltd. | Funding: Ministry of Culture, Taiwan | Funding Cooperation: Taiwan Culture Center, Taipei Economic and Cultural Representative Office in Japan

[KK]

コシノジュンコ
対極の美—無限に続く円—
sd02 | 土庄港アートノショーターミナル

Junko Koshino | Japan
The Beauty of Contrast – Eternal Roundness –
ART no SHOW TERMINAL, Tonosho Port
2022

所蔵＝土庄町
Collection: Tonosho Town

2016年に土庄港待合所をリニューアルして誕生した「アートノショーターミナル」で、「対極の美」をテーマにした作品を展示。日本の提灯の折る・畳む・重ねる機能から着想して作家がデザインしたドレスをモチーフに、幅・奥行約4.5m、高さ約6mの巨大なオブジェが完成した。四角四面・東西南北・合理性を象徴する四角と、波紋・地球・宇宙を象徴する円を組み合わせ、共存し繁栄する美を表現した。

Koshino exhibited a work with the theme of "the beauty of contrast" at Tonosho ferry terminal, which was renewed as *"ART no SHOW TERMINAL"* in 2016. Inspired by the folding, collapsing, and stacking properties of Japanese paper lanterns, the artist designed a dress, and using that as a motif created a huge object – 4.5 meters in width and depth, and 6 meters in height. Precision, compass points, and rationality are often symbolized by squares, and here, together with a circle representing ripples, the earth, and the universe, she expressed beauty in co-existence and prosperity.

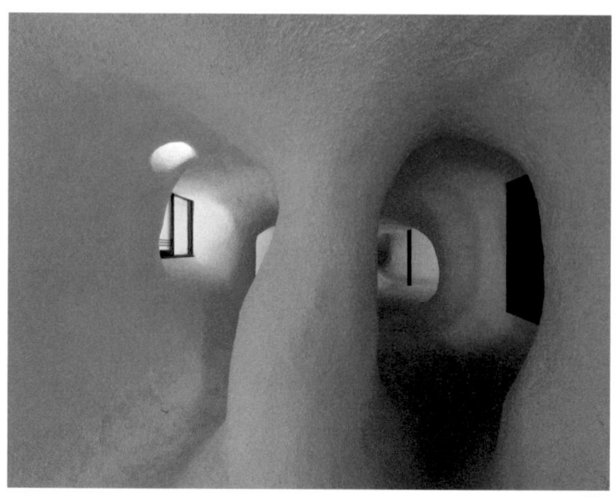

[Ylc]

目 [mé]
迷路のまち
〜変幻自在の路地空間〜
sd04 | 迷路のまち

[mé] | Japan
Maze Town
– Phantasmagoric Alleys –
Maze Town Area
2016

家屋の外壁を室内に延長させ、建物内部に洞窟のように延ばされた路を制作。白い壁のところどころには元々あった家の建具や柱が現れる。

The outside walls were extended within the house to create cave-like paths leading to different spaces. Bits of furniture and parts of the old house emerge from the white walled tunnels.

特別協力＝MeiPAM、柳生忠平
Cooperation: MeiPAM, Chubei Yagyu

左側２点とも [KK]

右側２点とも [KatT]

土井健史

立入禁止

sd42 | 迷路のまち

Takefumi Doi | Japan
KEEP OUT
Maze Town Area
2022

ある場所に「立入禁止」の看板とロープを張ると、その場所は他の部分とは異なり特別な場所となる、と語る作家が、迷路のまちを新しい視点で巡る体験を提案した。作品として街中に設置された 14 カ所の立入禁止は、普段は通り過ぎる風景にフォーカスし、作家の視点とともに、来訪者それぞれの自由な想像と感情をも顕在化させた。会期中には立入禁止を巡るハンドアウトが配布され、来訪者は迷路のまちに迷い込んだ。

The placement of a "*KEEP OUT*" sign and a cordon makes a site different and special, says Takefumi Doi, who invites visitors to experience a tour around the Maze Town Area with a new perspective. 14 "*KEEP OUT*" signs are placed throughout the town as artworks, focusing on landscapes that are usually passed by, and they actualize the free imagination and emotions of each visitor along with the perspective of the artist. During the festival period, handouts locating the signs were distributed, and visitors wandered around the Maze Town Area.

ソピアップ・ピッチ

La Danse

sd40 | 迷路のまち

Sopheap Pich | Cambodia
La Danse
Maze Town Area
2022

カンボジアで身近に使われてきた鍋などのアルミ製品を使って百日紅の木に添わせて型を取り、複数のオブジェを制作。カンボジアの貧しい人々が作家の農地の木を切って盗んだ出来事から、人々の厳しい生活と生育した木の喪失との間で作家が模索しながら構想した。複数の木が円形に林立する様子はアンリ・マティスの絵《La Danse》のような穏やかな一体感がある。江戸時代の陣屋跡地で、かつて存在したものを想い起こさせる作品。

Using aluminum products such as pots and pans that have been used in familiar ways in Cambodia, the artist created multiple objects by molding them to accompany the tropical crepe myrtle trees (*Lagerstroemia*). The artist conceived of this work in response to an incident in which poor people in Cambodia cut down and stole trees from the farmland, as the artist searched for a connection between the people's harsh living conditions and the loss of the trees that had grown there. The circular forest of multiple trees creates a peaceful sense of unity, like Henri Matisse's painting *La Danse*. This work reminds us of what once existed at the former site of an Edo period camp.

2点とも [KK]

スタシス・エイドリゲヴィチウス

いっしょに／ともだち

sd41 | 迷路のまち

Stasys Eidrigevičius | Lithuania / Poland
Together / *FRIENDS*
Maze Town Area
2022

顔をモチーフにしてきた作家が、迷路のまちの離れた空地に設置した2つの彫刻作品。《いっしょに》では2つの顔が組み合わされ、一方が他方にもたれかかる。《ともだち》は小さな部屋のような立体から横顔の形が切り取られ、ドアのように外の世界へと開かれている。その表情の真意や、自分と他者、内と外の世界について想像させる作品。会期後、作品は土庄港近くに移設された。

Stasys Eidrigevičius, who often works with the theme of "faces", placed two pieces of sculptural work in an empty space of the Maze Town Area. In *Together*, two faces are combined, with one seemingly reliant on the other. And in *FRIENDS*, the profile of a face is cut out of a three-dimensional object resembling a small room, opening like a door to the outside world. It is a work that draws the audience into imagining the hidden emotions of facial expressions, the self and others, and internal and external worlds. After the Triennale, the works were relocated near the Tonosho Port.

右中央除く３点とも [KK]

[Ylc]

清水久和
愛のボラード
sd33 | 田浦・二十四の瞳映画村

Hisakazu Shimizu | Japan
Bollard of Love
Twenty Four Eyes Movie Studio, Tanoura
2016

駐車場の一角に設置された巨大なボラード（船を係留するための柱）の作品。周囲の風景を変容させるとともに、海からやってくる「何か」への想像力をかき立て、人々の意識をつなぎとめる。

The work is a huge bollard, or mooring post, placed in the corner of a parking lot. It not only transforms the surrounding landscape, but also stirs the imagination about "something" coming from the sea, anchoring consciousness.

所蔵＝二十四の瞳映画村 | Collection: Twenty Four Eyes Movie Studio

[KiT]

清水久和
オリーブのリーゼント
sd25 | 馬木・醤の郷

Hisakazu Shimizu | Japan
Regent in Olives
Hishionosato, Umaki
2013

オリーブ畑の中に佇む作品。口のようなくぼみには野菜や果物が置かれ、無人販売所にもなっている。地域の人々にも愛され続けている作品。

The work stands in an olive field. In the dimple-like mouth, vegetables and fruits are placed, functioning as an unattended sales point. It is a work that is loved by local residents.

所蔵＝小豆島町 | Collection: Shodoshima Town

[Ylc]

齋藤正人
猪鹿垣の島
sd06 | 肥土山

Masato Saito | Japan
Shishigaki Island
Hitoyama
2013, 2016

約200年前に築かれたとされる猪鹿垣を復興。道祖神や魔除け、陶作品、ピラミッド型の石積みなどを新たに加えつつ、小豆島固有の文化を再現した。

A reconstruction of *shishigaki,* stone walls that are said to have been built about 200 years ago to keep out wild animals. The artist added guardian deities and talismans against the devil, as well as pottery pieces and a pyramid of stones, re-visualizing the unique culture of Shodoshima.

[Ylc]

秩父前衛派
ダイナマイト・トラヴァース変奏曲
sd38 | 北浦・大阪城残石記念公園

Chichibu Avant-Garde | Japan
Dynamite Traverse Variations
Osaka Castle Stone Quarry Memorial Park, Kitaura
2016

小海にある石切り場跡地で、図形のような独自の楽譜を石に刻んだ作品。2016年に移設し、現在は小豆島大坂城残石記念公園に展示している。

In the remains of Koumi stone quarry, original musical scores were carved into stone blocks like graphics. After the 2016 Triennale, the work was moved to Shodoshima Osaka Castle Stone Quarry Memorial Park.

所蔵＝土庄町
Collection: Tonosho Town

[Ylc]

チェ・ジョンファ［崔正化］
太陽の贈り物
sd01 | 土庄港

Choi Jeong Hwa | Korea
Gift of The Sun
Tonosho Port
2013

オリーブの島・小豆島の玄関口である土庄港に設置した、オリーブの王冠の形をした作品。島の小学生約100人が寄せた海へのメッセージが葉に刻まれる。夜はライトアップされ、黄金に輝く。

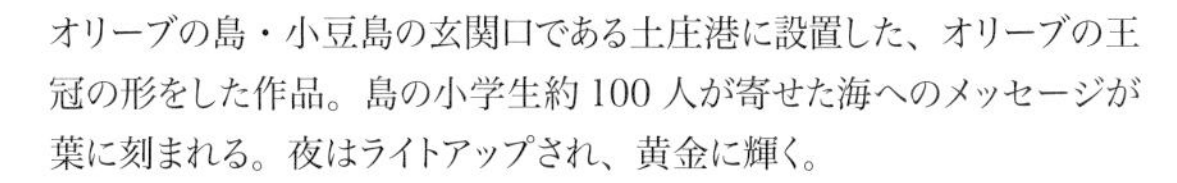

A work in the form of an olive crown located at Tonosho Port, the gateway to Shodoshima, known as the island of olives. Messages written to the sea by around 100 elementary school children from the island are engraved on the leaves. At night, while it is lit up, it shines gold.

所蔵＝土庄町
Collection: Tonosho Town

[KK]

キム・キョンミン［金景暋］
再び…
sd03 | 土庄港

Kim Kyoung Min | Korea
again ...
Tonosho Port
2019

「再びこの島を訪れてもらいたい」という思いが込められた作品。小豆島をかたどった土台と太陽と月をイメージした半円のオブジェが、いつまでも続く自然豊かな小豆島を表した。

The artist imbues her work with the hope that many people come back to visit the island again. The semi-circular object, on a stand in the shape of Shodoshima, evokes the sun and the moon, expressing the eternal existence of Shodoshima, rich in nature.

連携＝UBEビエンナーレ（現代日本彫刻展）| 所蔵＝土庄町
Cooperation: UBE Biennale International Sculpture Competition | Collection: Tonosho Town

三宅之功
はじまりの刻
sd43 | 屋形崎・夕陽の丘

Shiko Miyake | Japan
The Time of the Beginning
Sunset Hill, Yakatazaki
2022

瀬戸内海に沈む夕陽を見おろす丘に、陶でできた高さ約4mの大きな卵が現れた。よく見ると植物が自生していることに気づく。作家は自然と人間の関係性を問いながら「はじまりの刻」を形にした。一期一会の出会いにより受け継がれる命のエピソードは、この地球上に存在するあらゆる生命に共通する普遍的なものである。大きな卵の背に沈む夕陽を見ていると、原始の世界を彷彿とさせ、アートと自然が融合する新しい世界を予感した。

On a hill looking down on where the sun sets on the Seto Inland Sea appeared an egg-shaped sculpture made of ceramic, measuring almost four meters in height. When observed closely, some wild plants can be seen sprouting from earth placed in the cracks in the pottery. The artist questions the relationship between the natural world and the human, while expressing *The Time of the Beginning*. The episodes of life, passed on through once-in-a-lifetime chances are universal, common to every life form existing in on the earth. Looking at the sun setting over the giant egg, the primitive world is evoked; a world in which art and nature emerge.

[KK]

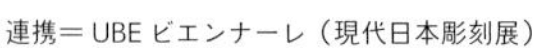

連携＝UBE ビエンナーレ（現代日本彫刻展）
Cooperation: UBE Biennale International Sculpture Competition

上「あゆみ（短編）」[KaiT]
中下３点とも「反復かつ連続」[SM]

ままごと
①『あゆみ（短編）』
②『反復かつ連続』

E11 | 小豆島町池田体育館、豊島・唐櫃公堂

mamagoto | Japan
AYUMI – short version – / Repetitive and Continuous
Shodoshima Ikeda Gym, Shodoshima / Karato Hall, Teshima
2022

2013 年より継続的に小豆島で演劇活動を行ってきた劇団。今回は演劇的な仕掛けに満ちた短編二作品を瀬戸内国際芸術祭バージョンとして再創作した。2008 年初演の「あゆみ（短編）」は、あゆみと未紀、二人の少女が過ごした時間を、複数の俳優が歩きながら紡いでいく作品。本公演では小豆島出身の俳優が出演。「反復かつ連続」は、多重録音を発想の起点として創作され、1人の俳優が演技を重ねることで、ある家族の朝の風景を描き出す。本公演では豊島在住の住民が出演し、新しい家族を演じた。

A theater company who have been conducting performances in Shodoshima since 2013. This time, two early short plays by Yukio Shiba, full of theatrical tricks, were reproduced specially in Setouchi Triennale versions. *Ayumi – short version –*, first performed in 2008, is a piece in which several actors walk to thread the time spent by two girls, Ayumi and Miki. The performance featured actors from Shodoshima. *Repetitive and Continuous* originated with over-dubbing as a starting point. In the play, one actor repeats his actions many times to reveal the morning scene of a family. An actor from Teshima starred in this performance, acting out a new family.

Event Data

「あゆみ（短編）」

11月3日(木祝)13:00～、16:30～ | 会場＝小豆島町池田体育館 | 作・演出＝柴幸男(ままごと) | 出演＝端田新菜、石倉来輝、小山薫子(以上 ままごと)、金田八愛子 | 来場者数＝221人

「反復かつ連続」

11月5日(土)10:45～、15:00～ | 会場＝豊島・唐櫃公堂 | 作・演出＝柴幸男(ままごと) | 出演＝小山薫子(ままごと)、清水里子 | 音響＝COB | 来場者数＝137人

舞台監督＝鐘築隼 | 衣装＝瀧澤日以(PHABLIC×KAZUI) | 宣伝美術＝関田浩平 | 制作＝宮永琢生、加藤仲葉(以上 ままごと) | 協力＝醍醐ビル株式会社、ソシオミュゼ・デザイン株式会社、HUNCH、シバイエンジン | 企画制作＝ままごと[一般社団法人mamagoto] | 料金＝一般1,200円、小中高生500円、ほか

AYUMI – short version –

November 3rd (Thu); 13:00–, 16:30–, | Place: Shodoshima Ikeda Gym, Shodoshima | Direction: Yukio Shiba | Performer: Niina Hashida, Riki Ishikura, Kaoruko Oyama, Yaeko Kaneda | Attendance: 221 people

Repetitive and Continuous

November 5th (Sat); 10:45–, 15:00– | Place: Karato Hall, Teshima | Direction: Yukio Shiba | Performer: Kaoruko Oyama, Satoko Shimizu | Sound: COB | Attendance: 137 people

For both plays; Stage Direction: Hayato Kanetsuki | Costume: Kai Takizawa (PHABLIC×KAZUI) | Publicity Art: Kohei Sekida | Production: Nakaba Kato, Takuo Miyanaga | Cooperation: Daigo Building, SOCIOMUSÉ Design, HUNCH, Shibai-Engine | Planning and Production: General Incorporated Association mamagoto | Admission: General 1,200 yen, Students (ages 6–18) 500 yen, etc.

6点とも [SM]

木ノ下歌舞伎
竜宮鱗屑譚
(せとうちうろくずものがたり)
～GYOTS～

E09 | 肥土山農村歌舞伎小屋

Kinoshita Kabuki | Japan
～GYOTS～ Hidden Stories of the Setouchi Deep Sea World
Hitoyama Rural Kabuki Stage
2022

300年ほど前からはじまったと伝わる肥土山農村歌舞伎の舞台で、木ノ下裕一と白神ももこ（モモンガ・コンプレックス）が制作したオリジナル作品を上演。作家の取材は多岐に及び数多くの素材から、瀬戸内海成立の経緯、民俗学者の宮本常一、ハンセン病と瀬戸内の療養所、源平の屋島の戦いと那須与一、さらには竜宮城伝説も盛り込まれた。浪曲師の玉川奈々福をはじめ、俳優やダンサー、日本舞踊家による異色の共演となった。生演奏とともに海に棲む魚たちが語りだす。

On the stage of Hitoyama Rural Kabuki, with a 300-year history, an original piece by Yuichi Kinoshita and Momoko Shiraga (Momonga Complex) was performed. The research done by the artists showcases a great diversity and range of materials and topics, with the work incorporating the origin of the Setouchi Inland Sea, the folklorist Tsuneichi Miyamoto, Hansen's Disease and the sanatoriums in Setouchi, Nasu-no Yoichi in the Battle of Yashima between the Minamoto and Taira Clans, and even the legend of the underwater palace of the dragon king. It starred an unusual set of performers, such as *rokyoku* (traditional narrative singing) artist Nanafuku Tamagawa, actors and dancers, and a Japanese classical dancer, all in collaboration. Along with the live music, the fish in the sea begin to tell their stories.

Event Data

5月14日(土)、15日(日) 各日17:30～ | 監修・補綴＝木ノ下裕一 | 演出・振付＝白神ももこ(モモンガ・コンプレックス) | 出演＝Aokid、泉秀樹、臼井梨恵、白神ももこ、武谷公雄、玉川奈々福 | 演奏・音楽＝西井夕紀子 | 演奏＝あだち麗三郎 | 美術＝カミイケタクヤ | 照明＝中山奈美 | 音響＝小早川保隆 | 衣装＝大野知英 | 演出助手＝鈴木美波 | 舞台監督＝大鹿展明 | 制作＝本郷麻衣 | 料金＝一般 3,500円、小中高生1,500円、ほか | 来場者数＝459人

May 14th (Sat), 15th (Sun); 17:30– | Supervision/Prosthetics: Yuichi Kinoshita | Direction/Choreography: Momoko Shiraga (Momonga Complex) | Cast: Aokid, Izumi Hideki, Rie Usui, Momoko Shiraga, Kimio Taketani, Nanafuku Tamagawa | Music: Yukiko Nishii | Art: Takuya Kamiike | Lighting: Nami Nakayama | Sound: Yasutaka Kobayakawa | Costume design: Chie Ono | Assistant director: Minami Suzuki | Stage manager: Nobuaki Oshika | Production: Mai Hongo | Admission: General 3,500 yen, Students (ages 6–18) 1,500 yen, etc. | Attendance: 459 people

大島

Oshima

大島　*Oshima*

２つの砂州がつながった島は、古くから人が住み約2000年前の土器が出土している。源平合戦で敗れた平家が落ち延び、今も残る「墓標の松」は800年前に墓に植えられたものと伝えられる。島全体に松が自生し白砂青松の瀬戸内の原風景が残る。春はヤマツツジが咲く。1907年、日本でハンセン病患者を療養所に入所させるための法律ができ、大島には1909年に療養所が開設された。主に中四国からの患者が集められ、1950年代後半には700人が厳しい共同生活を送った。

1996年に「らい予防法」は廃止されたが、ハンセン病に対する社会の差別と偏見は濃く、また高齢化も進んで、故郷に帰れず島で生涯を終えた人も多い。これまで2,000人あまりの方が大島で亡くなっている。2010年から芸術祭がはじまり毎回5,000人ほどが大島を訪れるようになった。

2019年に社会交流会館が完成し、ハンセン病に関する正しい知識を学び、さらに入所者と来島者が交流できる場所が整備される。同年、高松—大島間が一般旅客定期航路化した。

This island with two connected sand bars has been settled by humans for a long time, evidenced by the discovery of clayware from around 2,000 years ago. Following defeat in their battle with the Genji clan, the remains of the Heike clan are believed to have fled here, and the "grave maker pine" is said to have been planted 800 years ago where they lie. Pine trees grow wild across the whole island, showing an unspoiled Setouchi landscape of green pines on white sand. In spring, rhododendrons blossom. In 1907, the national government enacted a law that forced sufferers of Hansen's disease (leprosy) into sanatoriums, and in 1909 a facility opened in Oshima. The majority of patients sent to the island were from Chugoku and Shikoku, and by the late 1950s, about 700 sufferers lived collectively in hardship.

The Leprosy Prevention Law was abolished in 1996, but discrimination and prejudice remained strong in Japanese society, and for that reason, along with advanced age, many patients could not return home and remained on the island. To date, more than 2,000 patients have died on Oshima. Since the establishment of the art festival in 2010, more than 5,000 people have visited the island in every edition.

In 2019, the Oshima Memorial Museum was completed, creating a center for visitors to learn about Hansen's disease, and to communicate with the residents of the sanatorium. In the same year, a route between Takamatsu and Oshima was registered as a regular sea route for general passengers.

大島青松園

os01 青空水族館
田島征三 Seizo Tashima

os02 森の小径
田島征三 Seizo Tashima

os03 「Nさんの人生・大島七十年」－木製便器の部屋－
田島征三 Seizo Tashima

os04 稀有の触手
やさしい美術プロジェクト
Art for the Hospital Project, Yasashii Bijutsu

os05 ｛つながりの家｝GALLERY15「海のこだま」
やさしい美術プロジェクト
Art for the Hospital Project, Yasashii Bijutsu

os06 歩みきたりて
山川冬樹 Fuyuki Yamakawa

os07 海峡の歌／Strait Songs
山川冬樹 Fuyuki Yamakawa

os08 浜辺の歌、月着陸、壁上り
鴻池朋子 Tomoko Konoike

os08 物語るテーブルランナーin大島青松園
鴻池朋子 Tomoko Konoike

os09 ｛つながりの家｝カフェ・シヨル
やさしい美術プロジェクト
Art for the Hospital Project, Yasashii Bijutsu

os11 リングワンデルング
鴻池朋子 Tomoko Konoike

os12 物語る金の豚
鴻池朋子 Tomoko Konoike

os13 声の楔
やさしい美術プロジェクト
Art for the Hospital Project, Yasashii Bijutsu

E12 学ぶ！楽しむ！ オータムスクール
Oshima Autumn School

所在地＝香川県高松市
（かがわけんたかまつし）
面積＝0.62㎢
周囲＝4.2㎞
最高地点＝68m
人口＝53人

Location: Takamatsu City
Kagawa Prefecture
Area: 0.62km²
Circumference: 4.2km
Highest Point: 68m
Population: 53 people

納骨堂
社会交流会館
大島青松園
大島港
Oshima Port

500m

• アート作品・施設
Artworks, Facilities

鴻池朋子
リングワンデルング

os11 | 大島青松園

Tomoko Konoike | Japan
Ringwanderung
National Sanatorium Oshima Seishoen
2019, 2022

作家は大島で《リングワンデルング》《物語る金の豚》《浜辺の歌、月着陸、壁上り》《物語るテーブルランナー in 大島青松園》の 4 つの作品を展開した。

The artist presents four artworks in National Sanatorium Oshima Seishoen: *Ringwanderung, The Golden Pig That Tells a Story, Songs on the Beach, Moon Landing, Climbing the Wall, Storytelling Table Runner.*

昭和 8 年（1933 年）、青松園青年団が島の北の山に切り開いた「相愛の道」という 1.5 km の散策路があった。この道は荒れて閉ざされていたが、2019 年に作品《リングワンデルング》として復活。2022 年の夏、作家は、かつて隔離されていた入所者が、海が凪いだ日は「逃走日和だ」と挨拶していたことを知り、ここからさらに崖下の浜へ降りる《逃走階段》を制作。雑木と落石を利用してつくられた約 30 m の階段を下り波打ち際へと続く階段は、「島」というものが持つ本質的に閉じた地形／場の開口部、またはエスケープルートとなった。

In 1933, a 1.5-kilometer path called "the path of mutual love" was opened by a Seishoen youth group. The path was eventually closed and left to ruin, but it was reopened as *Ringwanderung* in 2019. In the summer of 2022, the artist learned that residents isolated here used to greet each other by saying, "good day for escaping" on days without wind, and she created an *Escape Route* that goes down from the path to the shore at the bottom of the cliff. The stairs that descend about 30 meters, made with tree branches and fallen rocks to reach the sea, became an opening of the geography and site of an island, which is closed in essence: an Escape Route.

[SN]

[KK]

やさしい美術プロジェクト
{つながりの家}カフェ・シヨル
os09 | 大島青松園

Art for the Hospital Project, Yasashii Bijutsu | Japan
{Tsunagari no Ie} Café SHIYORU
National Sanatorium Oshima Seishoen
2010

{つながりの家} カフェ・シヨルは2010年から活動している「大島を味わう」カフェ。現在は社会交流会館で営業している。

運営＝NPO 瀬戸内こえびネットワーク

This café has been active since 2010, with the slogan "Taste Oshima". They currently do business from Oshima Memorial Museum.

Management: Setouchi Koebi Network

鴻池朋子
Tomoko Konoike | Japan

浜辺の歌、月着陸、壁上り
os08 | 大島青松園 カフェ・シヨル

Songs on the Beach, Moon Landing, Climbing the Wall
Café SHIYORU, National Sanatorium Oshima Seishoen
2019, 2022

カフェ・シヨルで上映した3つの映像作品。大島に初上陸したときからの作家の制作の彷徨を、青松園の脇林清さんの写真とともにまとめた《浜辺の歌》《月着陸》のほか、2021年に作家が菊池恵楓園を訪れた日の出来事を収めた《壁上り》と逃走階段の制作過程の映像が新たに加わった。

Three film pieces were screened at café SHIYORU. The wandering production of the artist since she first landed on the island was made into *Songs on the Beach* and *Moon Landing* in combination with photographs by Kiyoshi Wakibayashi of Seishoen. A new film, *Climbing the Wall*, record the day the artist visited Kikuchikeifuen in 2021, and the production of the Escape Route.

特別協力＝長谷川拓郎（映像制作）
Video Production: Takuro Hasegawa

[KK]

[KK]

物語る金の豚
os12 | 大島青松園 カフェ・シヨル

The Golden Pig that Tells a Story
Café SHIYORU, National Sanatorium Oshima Seishoen
2022

熊本県にある国立療養所菊池恵楓園の絵画クラブ「金陽会」の絵、約50点を、カフェ・シヨルに展示。長年、「金陽会」の絵の調査や保存活動を行ってきたキュレーターの藏座江美と作家が出会い、その意欲的な作品の数々に純粋に絵画の可能性を感じ、芸術祭で発表した。タイトルは、金陽会の絵の一つ「奄美の豚」と、それぞれの作品の背後にある「物語」から発想を得た。

About 50 painting works created at the Kinyokai painting club of the Kikuchikeifuen National Sanatorium in Kumamoto were displayed at Café SHIYORU. The artist's encounter with the curator Emi Zoza, who has been working on investigating and preserving the work of Kinyokai, and the highly motivated works themselves, made her see the potential of their paintings as art, and she exhibited them at the festival. The title comes from one of the paintings, *Pig of Amami*, and the stories behind each work.

物語るテーブルランナー in 大島青松園
os08 | 大島青松園 カフェ・シヨル

Storytelling Table Runner in National Sanatorium Oshima Seishoen
Café SHIYORU, National Sanatorium Oshima Seishoen
2019, 2022

作家が人々の語りをもとにさまざまな場所を旅して行ってきたプロジェクト。大島青松園の入所者、看護師、職員らが語った物語を作家が下絵に描き、それを型紙にして手芸でものづくりをする女性たちがランチョンマットを制作。今回、新たにアーティストの弓指寛治が物語の聞き描きに加わり、菊池恵楓園を訪ねた日の旅の出来事や金陽会のエピソードを元に作品を制作した。

This is a project that the artist has conducted in different places she has traveled, based on the words of the people. Stories told by residents, nurses, and workers at Oshima Seishoen were sketched by the artist, and were developed from the pattern paper into a table runner by craftswomen. This time, artist Kanji Yumisashi joined the interviews, creating another work based on their traveling journal detailing the day he visited Kikuchikeifuen, and episodes related to Kinyokai.

やさしい美術プロジェクト

Art for the Hospital Project, Yasashii Bijutsu | Japan

やさしい美術プロジェクトは 2007 年から大島青松園に通い、入所者と交流を深めて記憶、記録を伝える活動に取り組んできた。

Art for the Hospital Project, Yasashii Bijutsu have been frequent visitors of Oshima Seishoen since 2007, deepening their relationship with the residents and working on spreading their memories and records.

2点とも [KK]

声の楔

os13 | 大島青松園

Voice Wedge
National Sanatorium Oshima Seishoen
2022

2007 年から大島に通い続ける作家が、島で触れてきた声を掬い取り、陽のもとに差し出した作品。かつて入所者が植物を育てるのに使っていた温室を再生し、入所者の方々から温室や畑にまつわる歌や句、今伝えたい言葉などを集め、それらを漂流物や石などに書きつけ、インスタレーションとして展開。島で生き抜いてきた入所者の痕跡に触れ、耳をすますと感じる響きがある。温室を介してこの地に響く声の伏流をたずね、深く楔を打ち込む。

This artist group, who have visited regularly since 2007, have collected the voices they encountered on the island and hold them in the light of the sun. They regenerated the greenhouse where residents used to grow plants, while collecting *tanka* and *haiku* poems and words about the greenhouse and fields of the residents. These words were written on driftwood and stones, and exhibited as an installation work. As you touch the traces of people who have survived on the island, and stop to listen, you can feel a sound: an underground flow of voices that echoes through Oshima via the greenhouse, which the artists searched out and opened with a wedge.

{つながりの家} GALLERY15「海のこだま」

os05 | 大島青松園

{Tsunagari no Ie} GALLERY15 "Sea Echo"
National Sanatorium Oshima Seishoen
2013

一般独身寮の 15 寮全室をギャラリーに改装し、寮の床下を掘り、かつて大島で使用された木造舟をまるで浮遊しているかのように展示した。

All of the rooms of "Dormitory 15", a former dormitory for unmarried residents, were renovated to create the gallery. Soil under the floor was dug out to exhibit an old wooden boat from Oshima as though it were floating in the air.

[Ylc]

稀有の触手

os04 | 大島青松園

Rare Feeler
National Sanatorium Oshima Seishoen
2019

大島の歌人、故斎木創の歌「唇や舌は麻痺なく目に代る稀有の触手で探りつつ食う」からタイトルをつけた。大島を撮り続けた入所者、脇林清を撮影した写真群を濃紺の部屋に展示。脇林も所属していた「カメラ倶楽部」の創設者、故鳥栖喬の撮影自助具や部品を設えた一室がある。

"No numbness yet in lips or tongue, rare feelers that serve in place of eyes. Searching, I eat". This poem by the late Oshima-born poet So Saiki inspired the title *Rare Feeler.* A room with deep blue walls displays photographs depicting a resident named Kiyoshi Wakibayashi, who recorded Oshima with his camera. A separate room contained an exhibition of photography by the late Takashi Tosu, who founded the camera club that Wakibayashi belonged to compensate for his disabilities.

[KK]

[KK]

山川冬樹
Fuyuki Yamakawa | Japan

海峡の歌／Strait Songs
os07 | 大島青松園

Strait Songs
National Sanatorium Oshima Seishoen
2019

強制隔離の時代、大島には自由を求めて四国本土の庵治の海岸まで泳いで渡ろうとした人たちがいた。その記憶に呼応するように、作家自らが庵治から大島へ泳いで渡る様子を映像に記録。島に遺る海の短歌を読む庵治の子どもたちの声と重なるインスタレーションを構成した。

In the era of compulsory isolation, some patients tried to swim to the shore of Aji, on the other side of the strait, seeking their freedom. As if responding to their memory, the artist himself swam from Aji to Oshima – a feat captured on film. This was presented with the voices of children from Aji reciting *tanka* poems about the sea that remained on the island, forming an installation work.

2点とも [Ylc]

歩みきたりて
os06 | 大島青松園

Ayumi Kitarite
National Sanatorium Oshima Seishoen
2016

大島に生きた歌人の故政石蒙は、満州へ出征し、終戦後モンゴル抑留中にハンセン病が発覚、二重の隔離の中で短歌を詠みはじめた。作家は政石の足跡を巡って、モンゴル、大島、政石の故郷である愛媛県松野町を旅し、各地で撮影した映像と遺品による作品を展開した。

The poet Masaishi Mo lived in Oshima, and was deployed to the war in Manchuria. During incarceration after the war, he was diagnosed with Hansen's disease, and began writing *tanka* poems in a kind of double-isolation. Yamakawa followed the poet's path to Mongolia, Oshima, and his birthplace of Matsuno town in Ehime, developing work consisting of films shot in those places and Masaishi's possessions.

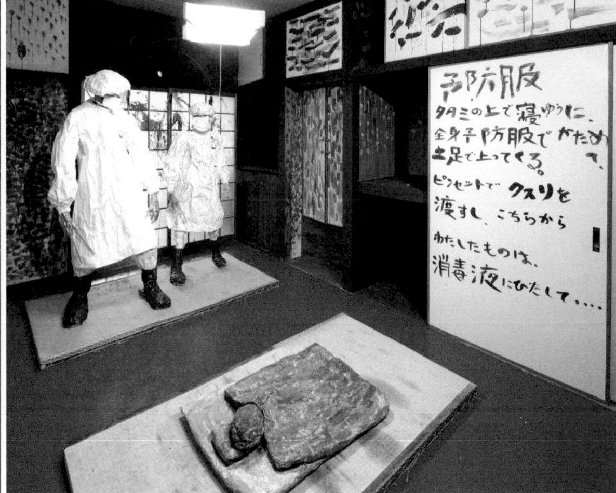

2点とも [KK]

田島征三

Seizo Tashima | Japan

「Nさんの人生・大島七十年」
ー木製便器の部屋ー

os03 | 大島青松園

Life of N: 70 years on Oshima
— A room with a wooden pot —
National Sanatorium
Oshima Seishoen
2019

作家が交流を続けている同郷の入所者の人生を、元独身寮を使い立体絵巻物にした。鑑賞者は５つの部屋を進むと、母親との別れ、島の生活、結婚・中絶、Ｎさんの叫びなど、Ｎ夫妻の人生を辿り知る。寮を出るとＮさんの畑がある。

The life of an island resident originally from the artist's hometown who he has kept in contact with was transformed into a three-dimensional picture scroll using a former accommodation for unmarried residents. The viewer is guided into five rooms, where they trace the path of Mr. and Mrs. N's lives: his separation from his mother, life on the island, marriage, abortion, and his scream. Outside, Mr. N's vegetable fields are visible.

[SM]

森の小径

os02 | 大島青松園

Forest Path
National Sanatorium Oshima Seishoen
2016

かつて独身寮が立っていた場所に作った庭。島に自生するトベラやウバメガシ、山つつじなどを移植。ソテツや入所者が育てる盆栽の松などを合わせた、雑木と雑草による魂の作庭。

A garden created at a site where accommodation for unmarried residents used to be situated. Wild plants from the island, such as mock orange (*pittosporum tobira*), ubame oak, and rhododendron *kaempferi*, were transferred there, alongside *sago cycad* and bonsai pine trees that residents grow. It is a garden with soul, making use of miscellaneous small trees and grasses.

[KiT]

青空水族館

os01 | 大島青松園

Blue Sky Aquarium
National Sanatorium Oshima Seishoen
2013

入所者が暮らしていた長屋に、海底の世界が広がる。大島の歴史から着想を得、漂流物や木の実などを素材に、ビー玉の涙を流し続ける人魚、魚が逃げ出す絵、動く海賊など、部屋ごとに立体絵本が展開する。人形と海賊の話は本にもなった。

In the terraced houses that residents inhabited, a deep sea world spreads. Inspired by the history of Oshima, three-dimensional picture books using driftwood and nuts were set up in different rooms, featuring images such as a mermaid shedding tears of glass beads, fish running away, and moving pirates. The stories of the mermaid and pirates became books as well.

学ぶ！楽しむ！オータムスクール

E12 | 大島青松園

Oshima Autumn School
National Sanatorium Oshima Seishoen
2022

小学１年から中学３年までの子どもたちがハンセン病の歴史を学びながら自然やアートに触れる、２日間のオータムスクールを開催。子どもたちは入所者から話を聞いたり、アート作品の鑑賞を通して大島について学び、また自然を楽しむワークショップに参加した。創作プログラムでは、ミュージシャンの小林武文、武徹太郎を迎えて、一緒に楽器をつくり演奏した。オータムスクールの様子は、毎月園内で放送しているラジオ番組「大島アワー」で発表した。

※夏会期に予定していた「学ぶ！楽しむ！サマースクール」が秋会期に延期して開催した。

An autumn school offering a two-day course to learn the history of Hansen's disease while experiencing nature and art. Children learned about Oshima through the stories of residents in the sanatorium and viewing artwork, and also participated in a workshop to interact with nature. In a creativity program with Takefumi Kobayashi and Tetsutaro Take as guest musicians they created instruments and played them together. The activities of the autumn school were aired in *Oshima Hour*, a monthly radio program broadcast in Seishoen.

*The Oshima Summer School scheduled for the summer period was postponed to the autumn period

Event Data

10月15日(土)～16日(日) | 料金＝7,000円 | 参加者＝8人

October 15th (Sat)–16th (Sun) | Admission: 7,000 yen | Participants: 8 people

主催＝高松市

Organization: Takamatsu City

3点とも [SM]

大島のこれから *Oshima into the Future*

瀬戸内国際芸術祭は、目的と全体的な将来のイメージ、その方法とアートがもつ発見力・媒介力・多様な開口部・協働力をもって、島の住民の願望に沿い、住民の豊かさに少しでも寄与できたら、と進められてきました。大島がアートサイトのひとつとして青松園の入所者に受け入れられたのは2008年。その当時、ハンセン病問題基本法が国会で審議されている中で、各療養所の将来の指針が、全国13カ所のハンセン病療養施設で唯一、この大島青松園は地理的条件から描くことができなかった背景があります。アートによる活動を当時127人おられた入所者の代表である自治会が、将来展望の可能性のひとつとして考えてくれたからです。その出発は2007年の訪問時に目にした、壁に貼られた入所者の3つの願いからはじまっています。

1. 生活の面でも、医療面でも今より悪くならないようでありたい
2. ここで生きざるをえなく、しかし頑張って生きてきたことを知ってもらいたい
3. この白砂青松の美しい島が、子どもたちにとっての素晴らしい場所になってほしい

以来、高橋伸行、田島征三、山川冬樹、鴻池朋子などのアーティストや、こえび隊をはじめとする多くのサポーターが、青松園に関わり、応援してこられた多くの人たちに続いて15年間意識して併走活動をしてきました。それらは次のようなことです。

来島者へのガイド案内／入所者と来島者をつなぐカフェ・シヨルの運営／高松や周辺の島の人と入所者が交流するマルシェや島間交流の実施／子どもたちが大島に親しみハンセン病を学ぶサマーキャンプの開催／大島の様子を伝えるラジオ番組「大島アワー」の園内放送／大島に関わる人をつなげる季刊誌「大島レター」の発行／盆供養や夏祭りなどの大島青松園の行事への参加／陶芸や畑作業、果樹採取やもちつきなどこえび隊と入所者の交流／昭和33年時の園の様子を再現したジオラマ制作／活動を進めるための月1回の自治会・園・市・実行委・こえび隊による定例会の実施

アート作品を制作・展示し、保守するという活動は芸術祭の枠内で行い、子どもキャンプ、ラジオ番組「大島アワー」の放送は高松市の事業として、それ以外の日常の活動ではこえび隊の自主活動として行ってきました。

入所者の生活・医療面は厚生労働省のもとで、さらに高松市や香川県が関わり、社会交流会館のオープンやアートサイトの整備、入所者の記録・記憶を残し発信する作業も端緒につき、大島と高松を結ぶ官有船が一般旅客定期航路化され、そして現在、港が整備されるなど、将来に向けた活動を少しずつはじめる時期にきたように思えます。

それは世界中の子どもが、望むならばこの大島でキャンプをし、この島の記録・記憶を実際に体験し、人類の希望にふれるようにする準備をしていくことだと考えます。

今までも大島サマーキャンプなどでやってきたことを、遊び学び・食べ泊まるという全体性のなかでともに試行していく時期に入ったということです。そのための遊び場の整備などから芸術祭の活動のなかに組み込んでいきたいと考えています。

北川フラム

Setouchi Triennale has progressed with the hope of contributing to the fulfillment of the wishes of people living on the islands and enriching their lives, based upon its clear vision of the future as a whole, through the Triennale itself and art's ability to discover, mediate, and generate diverse viewpoints, and the opportunity for cooperation. It was 2008 when the residents of Oshima Seishoen accepted the inclusion of Oshima as one of the art sites of the Triennale. The Act to Accelerate the Resolution of the Hansen's Disease Problems was under discussion in the Diet at that time, and the futures of the 13 national sanatoriums was being planned - all of them, that is, except Oshima Seishoen, which was unique due to its restrictive geographical situation as a remote island. As a result of this situation, the local council of the island, which represented the 127 residents in the sanatorium at the time, accepted the art activities as one of the potential developments of the island's future. The journey began with three wishes of the residents posted on the wall, seen on our visit to the institution in 2007.

1. In both life and medicine, we want things to be no worse than they are now.
2. We want it to be known that we had no choice but to live here, but that we have been dedicated to our lives here.
3. We want this island with white sand and green pines to be a wonderful place for children.

Since that time, many artists, including Nobuyuki Takahashi, Seizo Tashima, Fuyuki Yamakawa, and Tomoko Konoike, and many volunteer supporters like the koebi-tai have worked side-by-side with Seishoen for 15 years, building on the work of the people who supported the sanatorium before. The following activities have all been conducted.

Guiding visitors around the island / Operating Café SHIYORU to connect residents and visitors / Holding events for residents of the sanatorium and people from other surrounding islands and Takamatsu, including market events and inter-island activities / Holding summer camps to enable children to learn about Oshima and Hansen's disease / Broadcasting the radio program *Oshima Hour* in Seishoen, which communicates reports about the island / Publication of the quarterly journal *Oshima Letter*, aiming to connect people who do work related to Oshima / Participating in events at Oshima Seishoen, such as *bon-kuyo* (a memorial service held for the dead during the Buddhist All Soul's Festival) and summer festivals / Communication between koebi-tai and residents through making pottery, growing vegetables, harvesting fruit, and making *mochi* / Developing a georama re-visualizing how the sanatorium looked in 1958 / Holding monthly meetings with the local council, the sanatorium, the city council, the executive committee and koebi-tai.

The production, exhibition, and preservation of artworks was handled in the framework of the Triennale; the summer camps and radio program *Oshima Hour* were conducted as projects of Takamatsu City; and other daily activities were operated through the voluntary activities of the koebi-tai. Since the involvement of the Triennale, the lives and medical conditions of the residents, which had been managed by the Ministry of Health, Labor and Welfare, have also been supported by Takamatsu City and Kagawa Prefecture, while the Oshima Memorial Museum opened and maintenance of art sites, and the preservation and publication of records and memories of the residents, began. In addition, a route between Takamatsu and Oshima was registered as a regular sea route for general passengers, and gradually the port has begun to be properly maintained. We can see that it is getting close to a time for introducing activities that look out into the future.

These activities include providing the opportunity for children from all over the world to camp in Oshima and experience the records and memories of the island, facilitating an opportunity for them to encounter the hope of mankind.

In summary, what has been achieved through Oshima Summer Camp and other activities belongs to a phase of endeavoring together in comprehensive activities that involve playing, learning, eating and residing. We would like to incorporate them further into projects of the Triennale, starting with the maintenance of the playground.

Fram Kitagawa

犬島
Inujima

犬島　*Inujima*

岡山県岡山市に位置する犬島諸島の本島。「犬島みかげ」と呼ばれる花崗岩の採掘が盛んで、大阪城や江戸城の石垣、鎌倉の鶴岡八幡宮の鳥居などに使われている。現在も島のあちこちに採掘跡の穴や池が見られる。1909 年に銅製錬所が開設され、10 年間稼働し島は一気に発展した。一時は 3,000 人の住民がいたが、銅の価格暴落とともに製錬所は閉鎖され人々は島を離れた。採石の衰退もあり、人口減少に拍車がかかった。

高い煙突が印象的な製錬所の遺構は、2007 年に近代化産業遺産に認定される。さらに 2008 年から「犬島アートプロジェクト」がはじまり、遺構は美術館として再生した。集落内には建築と現代アートによる犬島「家プロジェクト」も展開され、人口 40 人の島には国内外から多くの人が訪れるようになった。

The main island of the Inujima island group, which belongs to Okayama city, Okayama. The island was famous for the mining of granite rock called *Inujima mikage*, which was used in the construction of the stone walls of Osaka and Edo castles, as well as the torii gate of *Tsuruoka Hachimangu Shrine* in Kamakura. Even today, many former mining sites, such as holes and ponds, can be found. In 1909, a copper smelting facility opened, and in the subsequent decade while it operated, the island saw great prosperity. At one point there were 3,000 residents, but the facility closed due to the falling price of copper, and many people left the island. Decreases in mining activity further accelerated the population decline.

The ruins of the copper refinery, with its impressive high chimneys, was registered as a Modern Industrial Heritage in 2007. The *Inujima Art Project* began in 2008, regenerating the ruins as an art museum. The village features house-projects of architecture and contemporary art, making Inujima – with only 40 residents – popular with domestic and international visitors.

所在地＝岡山県岡山市東区
（おかやまけんおかやましひがしく）
面積＝0.54㎢
周囲＝3.6㎞
最高地点＝36m
世帯数＝22世帯
人口＝36人
0〜14歳＝4人
15〜64歳＝13人
65歳〜＝19人

Location: Higashi Ward
Okayama City, Okayama Prefecture
Area: 0.54km²
Circumference: 3.6km
Highest Point: 36m
Number of Households: 22
Population: 36 people
0–14 Years: 4 people
15–64 Years: 13 people
Over 65 Years: 19 people

500m

• アート作品・施設 Artworks, Facilities

大島中心部

in01B F邸／Biota（Fauna / Flora）
名和晃平 Kohei Nawa

in02B S邸／コンタクトレンズ
荒神明香 Haruka Kojin

in03B A邸／Yellow Flower Dream
ベアトリス・ミリャーゼス Beatriz Milhazes

in04B C邸／無題（C邸の花）
半田真規 Masanori Handa

in05B I邸／Self-loop
オラファー・エリアソン Olafur Eliasson

in06B 石職人の家跡／
太古の声を聴くように、昨日の声を聴く
sprouting 01
淺井裕介 Yusuke Asai

in07B 犬島精錬所美術館
柳幸典［アート］ 三分一博志［建築］
Art: Yukinori Yanagi, Architecture: Hiroshi Sambuichi

in08B 中の谷東屋
妹島和世 Kazuyo Sejima

in09B 犬島くらしの植物園
妹島和世+明るい部屋 Kazuyo Sejima + Akaruiheya

in10B フラワーフェアリーダンサーズ
大宮エリー Ellie Omiya

in10B 光と内省のフラワーベンチ
大宮エリー Ellie Omiya

犬島精錬所美術館

柳幸典 [アート]
三分一博志 [建築]
in07B | 犬島

Inujima Seirensho Art Museum
Art: Yukinori Yanagi | Japan
Architecture: Hiroshi Sambuichi | Japan
Inujima
2008

近代化産業遺産である銅製錬所の遺構を再生した美術館。自然エネルギーを活用し、既存の煙突や鍰煉瓦を使って環境に負荷をかけず設計された。内部には、日本の近代化に警鐘を鳴らした三島由紀夫を題材とした作品を展開。現代社会が失ったものを振り返り、未来を考えるきっかけとなる。

The ruins of a copper refinery, a relic of industrial modernization, are reborn as an art museum. The design places minimal load on the natural environment, using renewable energy sources and materials found on the site, including stone and *karami* bricks. The motif of the works within is Yukio Mishima, who warned his country of the dangers of modernization. The museum provides an opportunity to reflect on what contemporary society has lost and to contemplate the future.

所蔵・運営＝公益財団法人 福武財団
Collection & Management: Fukutake Foundation

2点とも [DAn]

犬島「家プロジェクト」
長谷川祐子[アーティスティックディレクション]
妹島和世[建築]

Inujima Art House Project
Artistic Direction: Yuko Hasegawa | Japan
Architecture: Kazuyo Sejima | Japan

2010年に企画展示を目的としたギャラリーを開館。現在、島内に5つのギャラリーと「石職人の家跡」に作品を展開している。集落に点在するギャラリーは、かつて建っていた民家の瓦屋根や古材、透明なアクリル、周囲の風景を映し出すアルミなど多様な素材で作られている。長谷川は、島の風景を見ながら作品を巡る体験を「桃源郷」をテーマにした一連の物語になぞらえている。

This project and galleries have been developed since 2010. Currently, artworks are exhibited at five venues and the former site of a stonecutter's house. The galleries, scattered around the area, are constructed out of a diverse range of materials including roofing tiles and other components of old houses, transparent acrylic glass and aluminum that reflects the landscape. Hasegawa curated for the experience of touring these works through the island's landscape on the theme of the Peach Blossom Spring, a legendary earthly paradise similar to *Shangri-La* or *Arcadia*.

所蔵・運営＝公益財団法人 福武財団

Collection & Management: Fukutake Foundation

[TH]

名和晃平
F邸／
Biota (Fauna / Flora)
in01B | 犬島

Kohei Nawa | Japan
F-Art House /
Biota (Fauna / Flora)
Inujima
2013

動物や植物を想起させるさまざまな形のオブジェや多様な物質の表面からなる彫刻など、複数の作品を建物全体の空間にダイナミックに展示。犬島という場を背景に、新しい生のかたちを表現している。

Using variously shaped small art objects that reminiscent of plants and animals, as well as sculptures made from the surface of diverse materials, Nawa created a dynamic space encompassing countless works as well as the building itself and its courtyards.

[TH]

荒神明香
S邸／コンタクトレンズ
in02B | 犬島

Haruka Kojin | Japan
S-Art House / *contact lens*
Inujima
2013

大きさや焦点が異なる無数の円形レンズを通して周りの景色の形や大きさが歪んで映し出され、見る人に目に見える世界の多様性を促している。

This work distorts the shape and size of the surrounding scenery through the use of numerous lenses of varying sizes and focuses.

[Ylc]

オラファー・エリアソン

I邸／Self-loop

in05B | 犬島

Olafur Eliasson | Denmark
I-Art House / *Self-loop*
Inujima
2015

向かい合う３つの鏡を配置した本作品は、２方向に開かれた窓からの風景を結びつけている。作品中央のある１点において、鑑賞者はタイムトンネルのような無限の空間とつながるスポットにいる自分を見つけ、新しい感覚の旅に誘われる。

This work consists of three mirrors connecting the landscapes seen through the windows on two sides of the house. Standing on one precise position in the work, viewers find themselves in an infinite space, and are invited to a journey with new sensations.

[Yln]

ベアトリス・ミリャーゼス

A邸／Yellow Flower Dream

in03B | 犬島

Beatriz Milhazes | Brazil
A-Art House /
Yellow Flower Dream
Inujima
2018

犬島の自然の中に見られる幾何形体や人々の暮らしの生命感をエネルギーあふれる色を用いて仮想風景として表現。作品はＡ邸の空間にリズムを生み出し、日の光によって多彩な表情を見せながら鑑賞者の想像力を掻き立てる。

This work represents, through the use of colors overflowing with energy, a virtual landscape depicting the vitality of the residents' lives and the geometry seen in Inujima's nature. The work creates a rhythm in the gallery space, and the daylight creates a variety of expressions, stimulating the viewer's imagination.

[YIn]

半田真規

C邸／無題（C邸の花）

in04B | 犬島

Masanori Handa | Japan
C-Art House / *Untitled*
(Flowers at C-Art House)
Inujima
2019

犬島に生きる人々から発せられるエネルギーにインスピレーションを得た作品。C邸にひっそりと置かれた大きな木彫は、まるで神聖な場に奉納された切り花のように静かなエネルギーを内包している。

This work was created by drawing inspiration from the energy of the residents of Inujima. The large wooden sculpture which has been inconspicuously installed in C-Art House contains a quiet energy as if it were a cut flower dedicated to a sacred site.

[TH]

淺井裕介

石職人の家跡／
太古の声を聴くように、昨日の声を聴く
sprouting 01

in06B | 犬島

Yusuke Asai | Japan
Former site of a stonecutter's house /
Listen to the Voices of Yesterday Like the Voices of Ancient Times
sprouting 01
Inujima
2013–2016, 2016

素材や場所そのものに蓄積された記憶に反応するように、描かれた動植物などの生命力あふれるモチーフが犬島の土地に根ざし、さらには敷地を飛び出して集落内の路地にも展開している。

As if responding to the memories accumulated in the materials and place, vibrant motifs of plants and animals arise from the land on Inujima, and extend into the alleys of the village, leaping out from the site.

[TH]

妹島和世

中の谷東屋

in08B | 犬島

Kazuyo Sejima | Japan
Nakanotani Gazebo
Inujima
2010

島を訪れる多くの人に親しまれてきた、アート巡りの休憩所。鏡面仕上げの屋根には空や周囲の風景が映り込み、声や音が空間に美しく反響する。

This is a space for visitors to rest during their exploration of the artworks and the island. The mirrored roof reflects the sky and the surroundings. Visitors can enjoy the echo of their voices and other sounds within the space.

犬島 くらしの植物園

妹島和世+明るい部屋

in09B | 犬島

Inujima Life Garden
Kazuyo Sejima +
Akaruiheya | Japan
2016

長く使われていなかったガラスハウスを中心とした約4,500㎡の土地を、犬島の風土や文化に根ざした植物園として再生。自然のサイクルに身を置き、食べ物からエネルギーに至るまで、自給自足しながら自然とともにくらす歓びを体験できる場づくりをしている。

Roughly 4,500 square meters of land has been used to create a botanical garden reflecting the natural environment and culture of Inujima, with a long-abandoned glass greenhouse as a centerpiece. It is a place where island residents and visitors can enjoy self-reliance in areas from food to energy while experiencing the joy of living within the cycles of nature.

所蔵・運営＝公益財団法人 福武財団
Collection & Management: Fukutake Foundation

2点とも [YIn]

4点とも © ELLIE OFFICE

INUJIMAアートランデブー

大宮エリー

フラワーフェアリーダンサーズ

光と内省のフラワーベンチ

in10B | 犬島

INUJIMA Art Rendezvous

Ellie Omiya | Japan

Flower Fairy Dancers

Self Journey with Flowers and Light

Inujima

2022

人々の交流のきっかけとなるような作品が島内に点在していくプロジェクト。作品を目印にランデブー＝待ち合わせをし、ときに休憩しながら、島を散策できる。子どもからお年寄りまで、さまざまな人がともに時間を享受できる、公園のような環境が広がることをイメージした。
春に公開された《フラワーフェアリーダンサーズ》は、触れることのできる立体作品。島の盆踊りが行われる「ちびっこ広場」に犬島の花が踊る。作品関連イベントとして、初夏には近隣の小・中学生を招いた、作家によるお絵描きワークショップを行った。
秋には《光と内省のフラワーベンチ》が犬島南側の海岸に設置された。自然を眺めながら佇み、考えを巡らせるためのベンチで、光が差し込むと花のシルエットがそっと地面を彩る。

所蔵・運営＝公益財団法人 福武財団

INUJIMA Art Rendezvous is a project involving works of art to encourage people to interact with each other on the island. Both visitors and residents can "rendezvous" (meet up) at these works and take a break from time to time while strolling around the island. They are conceived of a park-like environment, where various people, from children to the elderly, can enjoy their time together.
Flower Fairy Dancers was unveiled in the spring as a work that visitors can physically touch and interact with. The flowers and plants of Inujima transformed into the artwork, where *bon odori* dances, which islanders gather to honor the spirits of their ancestors, are held during the summer. In an event related to the project, elementary and junior high school students from the neighborhood were invited to participate in a drawing workshop facilitated by the artist.
In autumn, a bench entitled *Self Journey with Flowers and Light* was installed on the south shores of Inujima. The bench encourages its occupant to dwell in their thoughts while engrossed in the natural landscapes of the Seto Inland Sea. During the hours when the sun shines through the work, the flower silhouettes overlay the surface, painting the ground with a burst of color.

Collection & Management: Fukutake Foundation

沙弥島
Shamijima

天海地

[SM]

沙弥島　*Shamijima*

備讃瀬戸の海がもっとも狭まる海域に沙弥島・瀬居島・与島・岩黒島・櫃石島がある。周囲の地形を活かし島々を土台にして1988年、世界最長の鉄道道路併用橋、瀬戸大橋が架かった。沙弥島と瀬居島はもともと離島だったが、1960年代後半に番の州臨海工業団地開発のため埋め立てられ陸続きとなった。

沙弥島は旧石器・縄文・弥生時代の古墳や土器の出土があり、万葉の歌人・柿本人麻呂が立ち寄って歌を詠んだことでも有名。現在は東側に隣接して瀬戸大橋記念公園があり、夏は西の浜辺が海水浴客で賑わう。

In the area of the sea where the Bisan-Seto is at its narrowest sit the five islands of Shamijima, Seijima, Yoshima, Iwakurojima, and Hitsuishijima. Making the most of the geological surroundings, the longest road-rail bridge in the world, the Seto Ohashi Bridge, was built with them as a base in 1988. Shamijima and Seijima were originally individual islands, but in the late 1960s, as a result of the development of the Bannosu Coastal Industrial Park, the gap between them was filled and they became connected by land.

Ancient tombs from the Paleolith, Jomon (14000–300 BC), and Yayoi (300 BC–300 AD) eras have been discovered on Shamijima, and it is also known as a place that Kakinomoto no Hitomaro, one of the poets featured in the *Manyoshu* (8th century anthology of Japanese poetry), visited and composed poems about. Today there is the Seto Ohashi Commemorative Park on the east side, and the beaches on the west are popular for swimming.

与島　*Yoshima*

与島は幕末にドイツのシーボルトが立ち寄ったとされ、架橋後は高速道路のパーキングができ、当初は遊覧船が走るなど多くの人で賑わった。与島には歩いて渡れる鍋島があり、国内で7番目に古い石造りの鍋島灯台は国の重要文化財に指定されている。このエリアの島周辺は古くから塩田が広がっていたが、1970年代までに廃止された。採石も盛んで、今もあちこちの島に丁場跡が残る。

Yoshima is an island best known for a visit by Philipp Franz Balthasar von Siebold. When the bridge was constructed, a highway parking area was located on the island, and sightseeing boats ran, making it a popular leisure spot. Another island, Nabeshima, can be visited on foot from Yoshima, and the stone Nabeshima lighthouse – the 7th oldest in the country – is registered as an Important Cultural Property. The area around these islands was surrounded by salt farms for many years, but they had all closed by the 1970s. It was also active in the stone mining business, as can be seen in former sites across the islands.

所在地＝香川県坂出市
（かがわけんさかいでし）
面積＝0.28㎢
周囲＝2km
最高地点＝28m
世帯数＝32世帯
人口＝91人
0〜14歳＝4人
15〜64歳＝52人
65歳〜＝35人

Location: Sakaide City, Kagawa Prefecture
Area: 0.28km²
Circumference: 2km
Highest Point: 28m
Number of Households: 32
Population: 91 people
0-14 Years: 4 people
15-64 Years: 52 people
Over 65 Years: 35 people

瀬戸大橋

瀬戸大橋記念公園
沙弥島
Shamijima
旧沙弥小・中学校
西ノ浜
▼至王越
To Ougoshi

500m
• アート作品・施設
Artworks, Facilities

沙弥島・与島・鍋島

sm12 月への道
レオニート・チシコフ Leonid Tishkov

沙弥島

sm01 階層・地層・層
ターニャ・プレミンガー Tanya Preminger

sm10 八人九脚
藤本修三 Syuzo Fujimoto

sm11 幻海をのぞく
南条嘉毅 Yoshitaka Nanjo

E15 万葉茶会と講演 〜香を楽しむ〜
市民煎茶グループ 曙 Tea Ceremony Group Akebono

王越

E14 オーチャード王越
GREEN SPACE

[KiT]

ターニャ・プレミンガー
階層・地層・層

sm01 | 瀬戸大橋記念公園

Tanya Preminger | the former Soviet Union / Israel
Stratums
Seto Ohashi Commemorative Park
2013

香川県で多く産出される花崗土を盛って作られた、高さ6.5mの小高い丘。丘の起伏を感じながら螺旋状の道を昇っていくと、周囲の光景を一望できる。

A mound, 6.5 meters high, was created by heaping up granite soil often found in Kagawa Prefecture. Visitors can climb the gentle spiral slope to enjoy the views from the lookout.

設計＝林幸稔／VAKA（監修）| Design supervision: Yukinori Hayashi / VAKA

レオニート・チシコフ

月への道

sm12 | 旧沙弥小・中学校
与島・浦城バス停
鍋島灯台

Leonid Tishkov | the former Soviet Union / Russia
The Way to the Moon
Former Shami Elementary and Junior High School / Urajo Bus Stop, Yoshima / Nabeshima Lighthouse
2022

月への憧れを抱いた人類の壮大な物語を、島から島へと渡りながら体験する作品。実在の宇宙飛行士・科学者・詩人にまつわる複数の展示室がかつての学校に現れ、校庭には沙弥島にゆかりある柿本人麻呂の和歌にもちなんだ月のオブジェが佇む。物語は瀬戸大橋の向こうへと続き、与島のバス停には家族や故郷に別れを告げて月へ飛び立とうとする宇宙飛行士の姿があり、物語の終着点である鍋島灯台の中には宇宙の星々が込められた立方体が浮かんだ。

This piece enables viewers to experience the grand story of mankind and its aspirations towards the moon as they travel around the islands. Exhibition rooms related to a real astronaut, a scientist, and a poet appear in a former school, while a moon object stands in the playground, inspired by a *waka* poem by Kakinomoto no Hitomaro, who is related to Shamijima. The story continues beyond the Seto Ohashi Bridge. At the bus stop of Yoshima there is the figure of an astronaut bidding farewell to his family and homeland before blasting off to the moon, and in the Nabeshima Lighthouse — the final stop in the adventure — a cube containing stars in the universe floats.

特別協力＝株式会社 Office Toyofuku（制作）、鴻野わか菜
Production: Office Toyofuku Co., Ltd., Cooperation: Wakana Kono

7点とも [KK]

南条嘉毅

幻海をのぞく

sm11 | 西ノ浜

Yoshitaka Nanjo | Japan
Peering into the Seabed
Nishinohama
2022

3点とも [KK]

島々の歴史と変化をテーマにした作品。一軒家の中に再現された瀬戸内海の地形に水が静かに満ち、海底から採掘された砂が天井から降り注ぐ。周辺の海や自然の映像が投影され、サヌカイトを叩いた音やピアノの音が会場に響く。この家に残された家具や調度品がこれらの演出と交錯し、西側の廊下に置かれた三面鏡を覗くと現在の海岸の風景が見える。鑑賞者は暗い空間で目を凝らし耳を澄ましながら、現在まで続く悠大な瀬戸内海の歴史を体感した。

This work deals with the history and changes of the islands. Water penetrates a geographical representation of the Setouchi area reconstructed in a house, and sand collected from the bottom of the sea falls from the ceiling. Footage of the surrounding sea and nature is projected, and sounds of *sanukite* and piano echo through the space. The furniture remaining in the house intersects with the direction of these pieces, and if you look into the three-sided mirror placed in the west corridor you can see a view of the current shore. Viewers observe items in a dark room and listen carefully to experience the history of the grand Seto Inland Sea that remains to this day.

特別協力＝カミイケタクヤ（制作）、鈴木泰人／ OBI（特殊照明）、阿部海太郎（音楽）、坂出市立大橋記念図書館（資料提供）
Production support: Takuya Kamiike, Special Lighting: Yasuhito Suzuki / OBI, Music: Umitaro Abe, Historical pictures: Sakaide Ohashi Memorial Library

[KiT]

藤本修三

八人九脚

sm10 | 瀬戸大橋記念公園

Syuzo Fujimoto | Japan
Nine Legs of Eight People
Seto Ohashi Commemorative Park
2013

瀬戸大橋記念公園内にある、９本脚８人掛けのカラフルなベンチ。島巡りの合間に腰を下ろし、瀬戸大橋を一望する絶景を楽しめる。

A colorful bench with 9 legs and 8 seats, placed in the Seto Ohashi Commemorative Park. Visitors can take a break in their tour around the island to take in the amazing view of the entire Seto Ohashi Bridge.

[SM]

市民煎茶グループ 曙

万葉茶会と講演 〜香を楽しむ〜

E15 | 坂出市万葉会館

Tea Ceremony Group Akebono | Japan
Appreciating Japanese Incense
Sakaide City Manyo Hall
2022

1987年から毎年「万葉茶会」を開催してきた市民煎茶グループ曙。今回は御家流香道二十三世宗家・三條西堯水を迎え、香についての講演やデモンストレーションを行った。また万葉集で柿本人麻呂が沙弥島に訪れた際に詠んだ「玉藻よし／讃岐の国は／国柄か」にはじまる長歌にちなみ、人麻呂の句を読みながら万葉の風情を味わう茶会を開催した。

The tea ceremony group Akebono has held the ceremony *Manyo-chakai* every year since 1987. This time, they invited Gyousui Sanjonishi, the 23rd head of the Oie school of *kohdo* (traditional incense burning), and held seminars about incense burning, and demonstrations of the practice. With reference to a *choka* (traditional long-form poem) that was read by Kakinomoto no Hitomaro when he visited Shamijima and is in the *Manyoshu* poetry book (beginning *Tamamo yoshi / Sanuki no Kuni wa / Kunigaraka...* "The beautiful green algae of Sanuki Province could never be tired of, perhaps due to the region's nature..."), they held tea ceremonies to enjoy the ancient atmosphere of *Manyo*, accompanied by poems by Hitomaro.

Event Data

4月17日(日) 講演10:00〜11:20、茶会11:30〜16:30 | 会場＝坂出市万葉会館 | 講師＝三條西堯水 | 茶会・お茶＝市民煎茶グループ曙 | 料金＝講演無料、茶会300円 | 来場者数＝講演140人、茶会277人

April 17th (Sun); Talk 10:00–11:00, Tea Ceremony 11:30–16:30 | Place: Sakaide City Manyo Hall | Lecture and Demonstration Speaker: Sanjonishi Gyosui | Tea Ceremony Organizer: Tea Ceremony Group Akebono | Admission: Free Lecture, 300 yen for Tea Ceremony | Attendance: Lecture 140 people, Tea Ceremony 277 people

[SM]

GREEN SPACE

オーチャード王越

E14 | 王越

GREEN SPACE | Japan
Orchard Ougoshi
Ougoshi
2022

現代の「庭」を追究する庭づくり集団が、美しい原風景の色濃く残る王越で、さらなる魅力となるような場所づくりに挑戦するプロジェクト。キックオフとなる今年は敷地の土起こしと土壌改良を行い、イベント前日と当日で３本のオリーブを植樹し、地域の住民や芸術祭で訪れた人々も参加した。今後は敷地全体にオリーブと花を植え、庵治石を使った小道や農小屋とギャラリーを兼ねた建物を造設し、地域の交流のスペースとなることをめざす。

A gardening company who pursue the "garden" in contemporary time worked on a project in Ougoshi, where beautiful, pristine landscapes remain, in order to augment its attraction. Starting this year, they dug up earth in the area and improved the land. They also planted three olive trees on the event day and preceding day, with the participation of local residents and visitors to the art festival. In the next stage, they plan to plant more olive trees and flowers, pave paths with Aji-stone, and build a space that will function as both a farming shed and a gallery, to create an area of exchange for the local community.

Event Data

10月22日(土)10:00〜 | 来場者数＝40人

October 22nd (Sat); 10:00– | Attendance: 40 people

本島

Honjima

本島汽船
瀬戸内国際芸術祭2022
Setouchi Triennale 2022
タサイクル
申込書

[SM]

本島　*Honjima*

大小 28 の島々からなる塩飽諸島の中心の島。塩飽（しわく）は、塩作りにちなむ「藻塩焼く」や激しい潮流を意味する「潮湧く」がいわれとされる。島周辺の早くて複雑な潮流は高い操舵技術を生み出し、水夫たちは塩飽衆や塩飽水軍と呼ばれ古くから活躍した。

豊臣秀吉が船乗りに島の領地を認めたことから人名（にんみょう）という独自の制度がはじまる。大名でも小名でもない塩飽諸島 650 人の船方衆による自治で、政務を取り仕切る 4 名の年寄は名字を名乗り帯刀を許されていた。人名制度は徳川家康にも引き継がれ、江戸時代は幕府の御用船方として活躍、幕末には咸臨丸の乗組員に選ばれ太平洋を横断した。また船乗りたちは船大工でもあり、江戸時代から明治にかけて宮大工などに転業し中・四国の寺社などを手掛け、塩飽大工と呼ばれた。当時の政所は現在「塩飽勤番所跡」として朱印状や史料、海図などを保管・展示している。笠島地区は水軍の根拠地として発展し、現在は国の重要伝統的建造物群保存地区に指定され、当時の景観を保っている。

Located in the center of the Shiwaku Islands, a group of 28 islands of different sizes. "Shiwaku" is thought to have derived from *moshio-yaku* ("making salt"), or from *shio-waku* ("rapid ocean current"). The powerful and complex tidal streams around the islands required excellent boat-handling skills, and the sailors of the region were called the Shiwaku fleet, or Shiwaku navy, in recognition of their ability.

After Toyotomi Hideyoshi granted the sailors governance of the island, a unique organization called *ninmyo* began. It was neither *daimyo* (run by a feudal lord), nor *shomyo* (run by a minor feudal lord): it was self-governed by 650 sailors of the Shiwaku Islands, of whom four senior members were permitted to take surnames and carry swords. The *ninmyo* system continued into the time of General Tokugawa Ieyasu's government in the Edo era, when they were respected as the government's mariners. At the end of the era, they were selected as crewmembers of the ship Kanrinmaru that sailed across the Pacific Ocean. These sailors were also shipwrights, and from the Edo era to the Meiji era they transitioned into carpenters specializing in temple and shrine manufacture, known as Shiwaku carpenters. They worked on temples and shrines in the Chugoku and Shikoku regions. The local government office from that time, now known as the Shiwaku Sentry Office Remains, today preserves and exhibits the old shogunate trade license, historical documents, and sea maps. The Kasashima area saw development as a naval base. It is now designated as a National Important Preservation District of Historical Buildings, and views of the past remain.

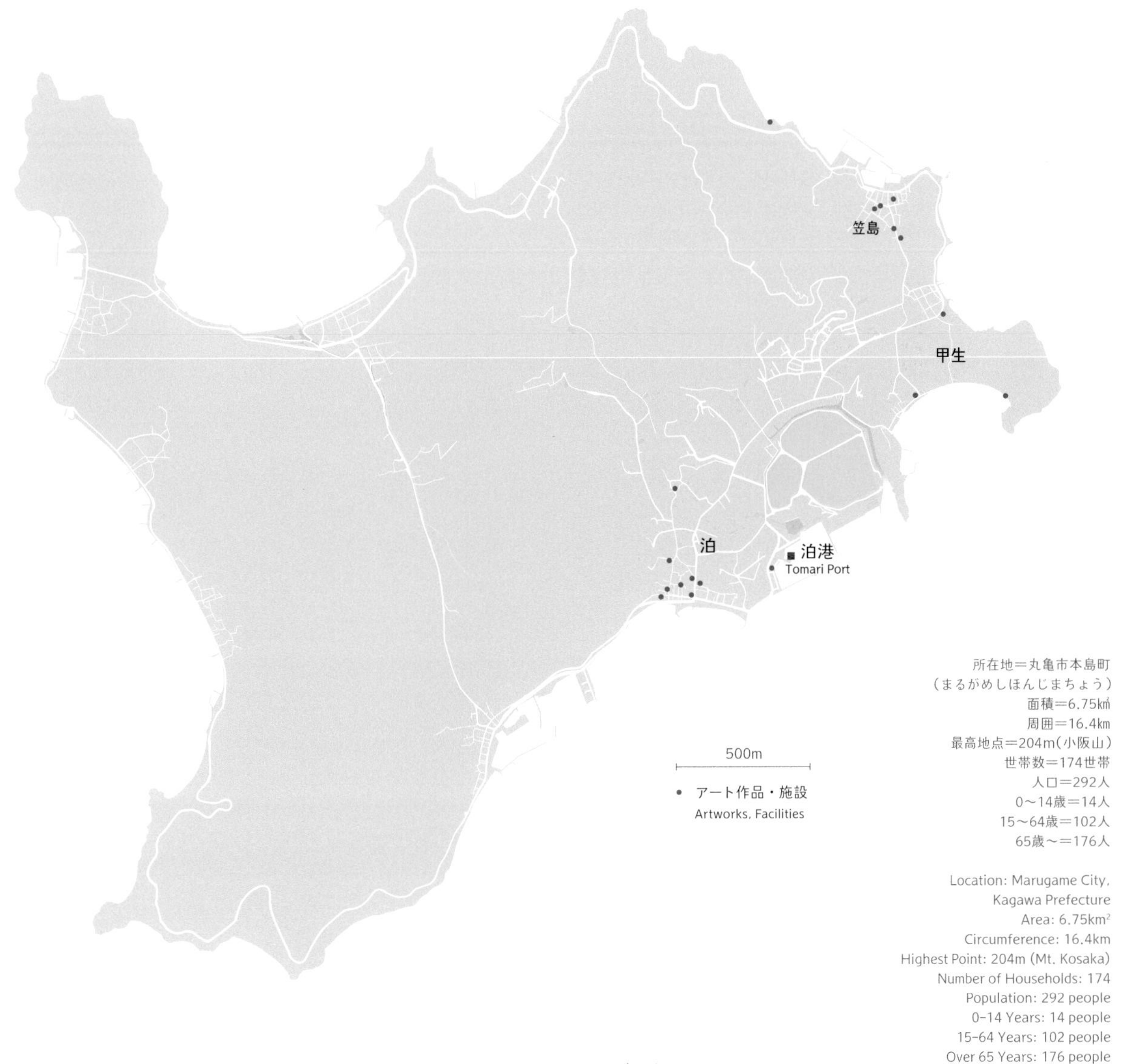

所在地＝丸亀市本島町
（まるがめしほんじまちょう）
面積＝6.75㎢
周囲＝16.4㎞
最高地点＝204m（小阪山）
世帯数＝174世帯
人口＝292人
0〜14歳＝14人
15〜64歳＝102人
65歳〜＝176人

Location: Marugame City,
Kagawa Prefecture
Area: 6.75km^2
Circumference: 16.4km
Highest Point: 204m (Mt. Kosaka)
Number of Households: 174
Population: 292 people
0–14 Years: 14 people
15–64 Years: 102 people
Over 65 Years: 176 people

笠島

ho09　善根湯×版築プロジェクト
齊藤正×続・塩飽大工衆 Tadashi Saito×Shiwaku Carpenters

ho10　Moony Tunes
ツェ・スーメイ Su-Mei Tse

ho12　レボリューション／ワールドラインズ
アリシア・クヴァーデ Alicja Kwade

ho13　水の下の空
アレクサンドル・ポノマリョフ Alexander Ponomarev

ho14　無二の視点から
藤原史江 Fumie Fujiwara

ho15　SETOUCHI STONE LAB
川島大幸 Hiroyuki Kawashima

ho16　石が視力を失っていないように、
盲人も視力を失っていない。
アリン・ルンジャーン Arin Rungjang

泊／甲生

ho01　Vertrek「出航」
石井章 Akira Ishii

ho05　漆喰・鏝絵かんばんプロジェクト
村尾かずこ Kazuko Murao

ho06　咸臨の家
眞壁陸二 Rikuji Makabe

ho08　産屋から、殯屋から
古郡弘 Hiroshi Furugori

ho17　遠くからの音
DDMY STUDIO

E16　せとうち物語一塩飽編一
瀬戸内少女歌劇団 Setouchi Girl's Theater

丸亀港周辺

ho18　丸亀市猪熊弦一郎現代美術館
Marugame Genichiro-Inokuma Museum of Contemporary Art

石の島　*Stone Island*

本島には大坂城築城時に使われた高無坊山（たかんぼうやま）石切丁場の跡があり、「石の島」として日本遺産に登録されている。丁場跡の西側に位置する笠島集落は、戦国期から江戸初期に活躍した塩飽水軍の根拠地として栄えた。重要伝統的建造物群保存地区として美しい町並みを残す集落を舞台に、国内外から5人のアーティストが、異なるアプローチで石に注目した作品を制作。島と丸亀市街地をつなぐ試みとして、丸亀市市民交流活動センター マルタスで川島大幸と藤原史江のサテライト展示も行った。

There is a stone cutting site on Honjima's Mt. Takanbo that was used for the construction of Osaka Castle, which is a designated Japan Heritage called *Ishino-shima* —"the island of stones". The village of Kasashima, to the west of the site, was a prosperous base for the Shiwaku fleet, which was active from the Sengoku into the early Edo era. Within this village, which has retained its beautiful townscape as an Important Preservation District of Historic Buildings, five artists from Japan and abroad created works that take different approaches to dealing with stone. A satellite exhibition of Hiroyuki Kawashima and Fumie Fujiwara was also held in Marutasu (Marugame City Civic Center) with the aim of forging a connection between the island and Marugame city.

ツェ・スーメイ
Moony Tunes
ho10 | 笠島

Su-Mei Tse | Luxembourg / Germany
Moony Tunes
Kasashima
2016

築100年以上の廃屋に現れた、石と月のインスタレーション作品。海や、潮汐を引き起こす月や、宇宙のつながりの中に存在するこの島を、月の痕跡と音を素材に隠喩的に表現した。天井から吊るされた火成岩は、まるで時間の中を漂うかのように、追憶の瞬間を強調している。

Stones and the moon, which creates the ebb and flow of the tides, are expressed in this space, an abandoned house that is more than 100 years old. The installation, with traces and tunes from afar is a metaphorical reflection of the island, positioned between the sea and the great cosmos. Igneous rocks hanging from the ceiling as if floating in time underscore this created moment of reminiscence.

特別協力＝ジャンカルロ・ヴァルカーノ（音楽）、ジャン＝ルウ・マジェリュス
Music: Giancarlo Valcano | Cooperation: Jean-Lou Majerus

川島大幸

SETOUCHI STONE LAB

ho15 | 笠島

Hiroyuki Kawashima | Japan
SETOUCHI STONE LAB
Kasashima
2022

稼働中の採石場で滞在し、採取される原石や埋め立てに用いられる栗石などを素材に作品を制作。石の重さを秤り、ぴったり1kgの石を他の石と差異化して展示することで美術空間における石の価値を再構成した作品《JUST STONES：1,000 kg stone and many other stones》の他、3Dスキャンした採石場の模型に砕石音を組み合わせた作品など、デジタルと伝統２つの技術を用いて、４つの作品を展開した。

Staying in a working quarry, the artist collected raw stones and cobblestones used for landfill and utilized them as material to produce work. In *JUST STONES: 1000 kg stone and many other stones*, he weighed each stone and exhibited those of exactly 1 kg separately from the others, reconstructing the value of a stone in the sphere of art. In addition, he created a piece with 3D-scanned models of the quarry in combination with the sound of rocks being crushed. Altogether, four pieces of art using both digital and traditional approaches were displayed.

3点とも [KK]

[KK]

藤原史江

無二の視点から

ho14 | 笠島

Fumie Fujiwara | Japan
The World from One and Only Perspective
Kasashima
2022

石そのものを画材として絵画を制作する作家は、全ての存在に唯一無二の視点と立場があり、無価値な存在の象徴である『路傍の石』も地球の長い歴史を体現する証人だと語る。サンドペーパーに削られた石粉が付着して絵が生まれるプロセスは、まさに石が身を粉にして自らの見た世界を描くようである。会場には全 25 点の作品が展示され、本島や丸亀城をはじめ瀬戸内のさまざまな場所の石が使われた。

Creating paintings using stone itself as a material, Fujiwara has a unique perspective and position regarding existence as a whole. A stone by the roadside, a symbol of a pointless existence, is also witness to the long history of earth. Her process of creation, attaching stone powder scraped with sandpaper, is like a stone painting the world from its own perspective in a kind of self-sacrifice. 25 works were displayed at the venue, made with stone from various places in the Seto Inland Sea, including Honjima and Marugame Castle.

上 [KK]

4点とも [KK]

アリン・ルンジャーン

石が視力を失っていないように、
盲人も視力を失っていない。

ho16 | 笠島

Arin Rungjang | Thailand
The blindman is not missing sightedness just as the stone is not missing sightedness
Kasashima
2022

人間が規定したものの概念を解体し、詩的に再構成する作品。1階には39個の石が並び、石に敷かれた赤い糸が天井に吊るされた273個の竹製の風鈴と結びついている。土間には連続した抽象的なイメージの3D映像があり、2階では天井から垂れ下がる白い糸が床で人の頭ほどの円を描く。赤と白の糸はサイシンと呼ばれる神聖なもの。この作品は私たちが現実の事象に対し、どうすれば異なった見方ができるかという問題を投げかけた。

A work that dissembles and poetically reconstructs the concept of things as they are defined by people. The first floor is lined with 39 stones, linked by red thread to 273 bamboo wind chimes hanging from the ceiling. Abstract 3D images continuously shift on the earth floor. Upstairs, white threads hanging from the ceiling trace circles on the floor, roughly the size of a human head. The red and white threads are sacred *saishin*. This work questions how we can view phenomena in reality from a different perspective.

上《レボリューション》下《ワールドラインズ》2点とも [KK]

アリシア・クヴァーデ

レボリューション
ワールドラインズ

ho12 | 笠島

Alicja Kwade | Poland / Germany
Revolution / WorldLines
Kasashima
2019

塩飽大工が建てた家の畳や建具の尺貫法の規格を利用し、対にした日用品と鏡によって実像と虚像が混在する《ワールドラインズ》。島の自然石とステンレスのリングを組み合わせ、惑星の軌道をイメージした作品《レボリューション》。作家の空間認識と宇宙観を表した。

WorldLines uses the *shakukan* standard for *tatami* and house fittings for a house built by Shiwaku carpenters, and creates a combination of the real and the virtual through pairs of daily items and mirrors. *Revolution* combines the island's local stones and stainless steel rings to portray the orbits of planets. It speaks of the artist's perception of space and cosmology.

[Ylc]

古郡弘

産屋から、殯屋（もがりや）から

ho08 | 甲生

Hiroshi Furugori | Japan
From Birthing Hut to Mourning Rites
Kosho
2016

島に降り立った時にゆったりと流れる密度の濃い気配を感じた作家は、死者を埋葬する場所と霊をまつる場所を区別する両墓制の習俗に着目。大地から湧き出てくるエネルギーを作品にした。

Landing on the island, the artist felt the sense of a dense, mellow atmosphere, and was fascinated by the *ryobosei* system of double graves, one for the body and the other to enshrine the spirit. He created a work with energy that springs from the earth.

[SM]

アレクサンドル・ポノマリョフ

水の下の空

ho13 | 笠島

Alexander Ponomarev | the former Soviet Union / Russia
Bottom Sky
Kasashima
2016

海辺に現れた和船を思わせる３つの巨大な立体作品。船底の古い網やロープは幻想的な町のようなレリーフになり、船の下の鏡からその町を俯瞰できる。風を受けて揺れる姿が、悠久の時を感じさせる。

設計＝林幸稔／林幸稔建築設計事務所（実施設計） | 特別協力＝鴻野わか菜

Three huge three-dimensional works that resemble Japanese-style ships appeared on the beach. Old nets and ropes placed on the frames of the ships create the image of a fantastical town, which you can see in a mirror below them. As they sway in the wind, you can feel the endlessness of time.

Detailed design: Yukinori Hayashi / Yukinori Hayashi Architect & Associates
Cooperation: Wakana Kono

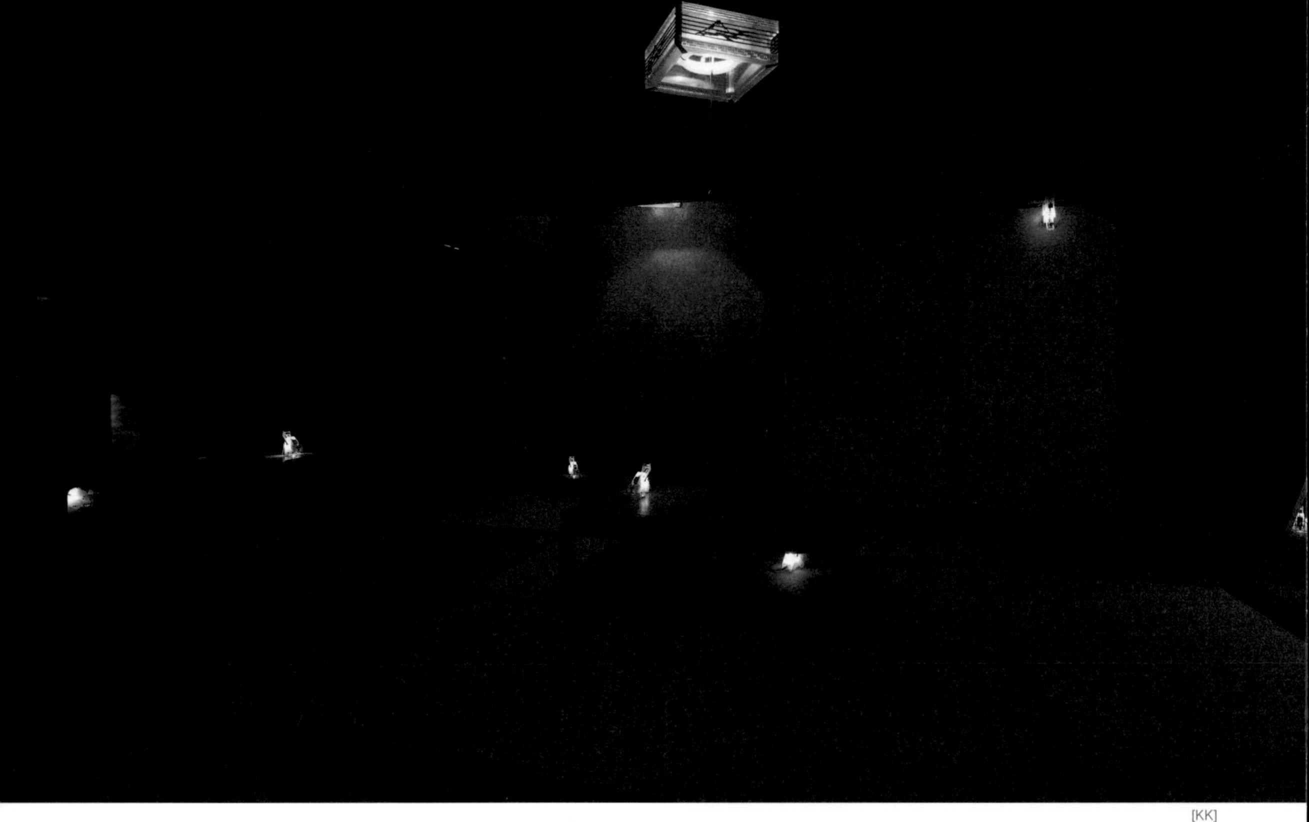

[KK]

DDMY STUDIO
遠くからの音
ho17 | 甲生

DDMY STUDIO | Thailand
The Sound from Distance
Kosho
2022

ロボットを利用した、人と自然のつながりを探求するインタラクティブな作品。タイの田舎町で育った作家は、コオロギの音色や蛍の光を美しく感じた幼少期の記憶と、自然に対して敬意をもった距離が大切という両親の教えを原点に作品を制作。暗い室内の各所で音や光を発する29体の虫型ロボットは、鑑賞者が近づくと音や光を止め、一定の距離で再び動き出す。美しい音や光を維持するために必要な、自然と人間の適切な距離を表現した。

An interactive work that uses robots to examine the connections between humans and nature. The artist, who grew up in a rural town in Thailand, created an installation based on childhood memories of experiencing beauty in the sound of crickets and the light of fireflies, and being taught to keep a respectful distance from nature by his parents. 29 bug-like robots emit sounds and light in different spaces in a dark room. These sounds and lights cease as a viewer approaches, starting again a certain distance away. This installation expresses an appropriate distance between nature and humans, one that is necessary for maintaining the beauty of sound and light.

上 [KK]

[TH]

齊藤正×
続・塩飽大工衆
善根湯×版築プロジェクト

ho09 | 笠島

Tadashi Saito ×
Shiwaku Carpenters | Japan
Zenkonyu x Tamping Earth
Kasashima
2013

版築の技術を用い、高さ８メートルの塔が印象的な構造物を制作。かつて塩飽諸島には優秀な船大工が多くおり、江戸中期以降、宮大工や家大工となった。その復活を願い、続・塩飽大工衆として建設した。

The Shiwaku islands once had many brilliant shipbuilders. In the late 18th century, many became shrine and house carpenters. Aiming to revive their craft, the team built this rammed earth structure with an 8-meter tower using traditional techniques.

特別協力＝株式会社LIXIL、香川トヨペット株式会社、株式会社川上板金工業所、大企建設株式会社
Cooperation: LIXIL Corporation, Kagawa TOYOPET Co., Ltd., Kawakami Bankin Kogosho Co., Ltd., Taiki Kensetsu Co., Ltd.

[KiT]

村尾かずこ
漆喰・鏝絵
かんばんプロジェクト

ho05 | 泊

Kazuko Murao | Japan
A Project of Signboards of Shikkui and Kote-e
Tomari
2013

島民から聞いた言い伝えや、島に活気があふれていた時代のエピソードを調査し、図案化。漆を用いた「鏝絵（こてえ）」と呼ばれるレリーフの絵看板にして、集落の至るところに設置された。

Round painted signboards are installed all around the village. These signboards, known as *kote-e*, are reliefs based on plaster, taking their motifs from folktales told by islanders and episodes from a more vibrant era.

眞壁陸二
咸臨の家

ho06 | 泊

Rikuji Makabe | Japan
Kanrin House
Tomari
2016

咸臨丸の水夫だった横井松太郎氏の生家を舞台に、江戸時代の杉戸絵やモスクのタイル画、教会のモザイク画などを発想の原点として、多様性が混在するカラフルな空間を作りあげた。

In the house where Shotaro Yokoi, a sailor on the Kanrinmaru, was born, Makabe produced a diverse and colorful space, inspired by Edo Period *sugido-e*, mosque murals, and church mosaics.

特別協力＝HIPSQUARE | Cooperation: HIPSQUARE

[KiT]

石井章
Vertrek「出航」

ho01 | 泊

Akira Ishii | Japan
Departure
Tomari
2013

往年の航海を思わせる鋼の彫刻作品。1860年に日本ではじめて太平洋を往復した咸臨丸には、塩飽諸島出身の船員が多く乗船していた。帆を上げ宙に浮く咸臨丸の彫刻が島を訪れる人々を迎える。

A steel sculpture recalling ancient voyages. The Kanrinmaru was the first ship to sail from Japan across the Pacific and back in 1860. Many of its crew members were from the Shiwaku Islands. Working from this fact, Ishii created a sculpture of the Kanrinmaru with hoisted sails, floating in mid-air.

4点とも [SM]

瀬戸内少女歌劇団
せとうち物語 ―塩飽編―
E16 | 本島

Setouchi Girl's Theater | Japan
The Story of Setouchi —Shiwaku ed.—
Honjima
2022

2019年にはじまった、北川フラム総合ディレクター原案の演劇プロジェクト。前回の「せとうち物語 ―粟島編―」に続き、今回は本島に登場し、塩飽諸島のエピソードを演劇化。参加者自身が塩飽石工になったという設定で演劇がはじまり、島内をバスや徒歩で移動しながら、物語を鑑賞した。今回は丸亀市内で演劇ワークショップに参加している小中学生も出演。芸術祭終了後も瀬戸内の物語を演劇化して上演する活動を継続している。

A theater performance project featuring the planning of the festival's general director, Fram Kitagawa, which began in 2019. Continuing from the previous *The Story of Setouchi – Awashima ed. –*, this time Honjima appeared in the dramatized episodes of the Shiwaku Islands. The audience themselves are positioned in the role of Shiwaku stone-makers as the play begins, and they watch while moving around the island on bus or by foot. This time, it featured schoolchildren who had participated in workshops in Marugame city, Kagawa. Even outside of the festival, the project continues, perform the narratives of Setouchi converted to theater.

Event Data

10月22日(土)、23日(日)、29日(土)、30日(日)各日11:30〜、15:00〜(土曜日は15:00〜のみ)|原案=北川フラム|演出=三好真理|演出助手=永井純子|出演=兼久ゆかり、白川夢華、泊愛、中川有紀子、まなべななこ、谷本桂子、平木恭子、オーヤマユイキ、大垣里花、佐藤亜沙美、冨永公未佳、森國真帆、いずみ、えりん、大林充希、河村心平、ゆあん、葛石悠史、葛石日葉里|衣装=山本哲也(POTTO)|宣伝美術=薗田奈緒美、瀬戸内彩|音響=永井雅樹|撮影=鉢峯輝敏|制作=1PO(横山桂子、諸岡君代)|料金=一般2,000円、小中高生800円、ほか|来場者数=223人

October 22nd (Sat), 29th (Sat); 15:00–, 23rd (Sun), 30th (Sun); 11:30–, 15:00– | Planning: Fram Kitagawa | Direction: Mari Miyoshi | Cast: Setouchi Girl's Theater | Production: 1PO (Keiko Yokoyama, Kimiyo Morooka) | Admission: General 2,000 yen, Students (ages 6–18) 800yen, etc. | Attendance: 223 people

[YM]

「今井俊介 スカートと風景」[KO]

丸亀市猪熊弦一郎現代美術館

ho18 | 丸亀市中心市街地

Marugame Genichiro-Inokuma Museum of Contemporary Art
Marugame City Community Area
2022

丸亀市ゆかりの画家・猪熊弦一郎の収蔵作品の展示や現代美術の企画展を開催する美術館。「美術館は心の病院」という猪熊の考え方から、誰もが気軽に立ち寄り、美しい空間で作品を見て心が元気になる場所をめざす。会期中は２期の展覧会を開催。

A museum that holds exhibitions from its collection of work by Genichiro Inokuma, a painter with roots in Marugame, and special exhibitions of contemporary art. It presents work from the concept that "an art museum is a hospital for the mind", aiming to be a place where anyone can freely enter and nurture the wellbeing of their mind by viewing artwork in a beautiful space. During the festival, it held two exhibitions.

企画展「生誕120周年記念 猪熊弦一郎回顧展 美しいとは何か」
常設展「猪熊弦一郎展　○と□」

猪熊弦一郎が約70年にわたり追求してきた「美」の表現に注目し、これまでの作品の数々と、「色」「形」「単純化」「バランス」などのキーワードをはじめとした作家の言葉を展示し、美の探究の軌跡をたどる企画展を開催。常設展では猪熊の1975年以降の作品、中でもこの時期に増えた「○と□」といった2つのものがタイトルに登場する作品を中心に紹介した。

会期　2022年4月2日（土）～7月3日（日）

Special Exhibition *Genichiro Inokuma: Beautiful*
Permanent Collection Exhibition *Genichiro Inokuma: ○ and □*

With a focus on the expression of "Beauty" that Genichiro Inokuma pursued over a period of 70 years, this exhibition was a retrospective that examined the work and periods of the artist with regard to key concepts such as "color", "shape", "simplification", and "balance", tracing the development of his aesthetics. The exhibition from the collection concentrated on the post-1975 work of Inokuma, especially those featuring ○ and □ in the titles, many of which were created around this time.

April 2nd (Sat) – July 3rd (Sun)

企画展「今井俊介　スカートと風景」
常設展「猪熊弦一郎と新収蔵作品による鈴木理策展」

現代の美術作家・今井俊介の美術館における初個展を開催。揺れるスカートの模様や積み重なるファストファッションの色彩などに着想を得た、絵画を中心とする多様な作品群を展示した。常設展では猪熊弦一郎が描いた椅子に座る人の絵画に焦点を当てたほか、2021年度に新収蔵品となった写真家・鈴木理策の「知覚の感光板」シリーズほか7点を公開した。

会期　2022年7月16日（土）～11月6日（日）

Special exhibition *Shunsuke Imai: Skirt and Scene*
Permanent Collection Exhibition
Genichiro Inokuma and Risaku Suzuki

The first solo exhibition in a museum by contemporary artist Shunsuke Imai. Inspired by the patterns on swaying skirts and the layering of colors in fast fashion, Imai's diverse work centered around painting was presented. The exhibition from the collection focuses on paintings of figures on chairs that Genichiro Inokuma worked on, along with the series *La Plaque Sensible* by photographer Risaku Suzuki, which was recently added to the gallery's collection, and seven other works.

July 16th (Sat) – November 6th (Sun)

「今井俊介 スカートと風景」展
助成＝一般財団法人自治総合センター、芸術文化振興基金、
協力＝ホルベイン画材株式会社、HAGIWARA PROJECTS

Shunsuke Imai: Skirt and Scene
Funding: General Incorporated Foundation Jichi Sogo Center, Japan Arts Council
Cooperation: Holbein Art Materials, HAGIWARA PROJECTS

休館日＝毎週月曜 | 企画展観覧料＝一般950円、大学生650円（常設展の料金を含む）
常設展観覧料＝一般300円、大学生200円、高校生以下または18歳未満無料
主催＝丸亀市猪熊弦一郎現代美術館、公益財団法人ミモカ美術振興財団

Closed on Mondays | Special Exhibition Tickets: General 950 yen, University Students 650 yen (including access to the Permanent Collection Exhibition) | Permanent Collection Exhibition Tickets: General 300 yen, University Students 200 yen, Age 18 and under, or high school students free | Organization: Marugame Genichiro-Inokuma Museum of Contemporary Art, The MIMOCA Foundation

高見島
Takamijima

高見島　*Takamijima*

山頂に古い社叢が残る標高約 297 mの龍王山を中心に島全体が緑に覆われ、東側斜面の一部に家々が立ち並ぶ。江戸時代の大火のあと、人名が中心となって石垣を築き計画的に作られた浦地区の集落は、細い路地と階段が交差する独特の風景で、映画のロケ地にもなった。浦・浜地区には埋め墓と参り墓に分けて弔う「両墓制」の墓がある。昭和初期まで殺虫剤の原料に使われた除虫菊の栽培が盛んで、5 月になると島は一面の白い花で覆われた。化学物質が用いられるようになると除虫菊栽培は衰退した。人口は戦後 1,000 名を超えていたが、現在は 20 名前後。

Centered around the 297-meter Mt. Ryuou, topped with an ancient sacred shrine forest, the entire island is covered with green, and houses are gathered on part of the east slope. After a big fire in the Edo era, the *ninmyo* government led people to building stone walls, and the carefully planned villages in the Ura area have a distinctive network of interlocking narrow paths and stairs, as featured in some films. The Ura and Hama areas still retain the culture of having one grave for the body and a separate one for the soul. Until the early Showa era, pyrethrum (insect flower) was grown actively, and the white blossoms covered the island in May. After chemical insect repellant became common, pyrethrum cultivation declined. At the end of World War II, the population of the island was about 1,000, but it has decreased to only around 20 today.

多度津町本通　*Tadotsu Town Hondori*

多度津は、金毘羅参りの玄関口として、また北前船の寄港地として発展した。江戸時代後期から明治時代にかけては廻船業等で財をなした「多度津七福神」と呼ばれる豪商が活躍。鉄道、電力会社、銀行などを設立し、四国の近代化をけん引した。金毘羅街道として栄えた多度津町本通周辺には豪商たちが建てた家や蔵が今も残り、風情のある町並みがみられる。

Tadotsu developed as a gateway for visitors to the Kotohira-gu Shrine (*konpira-mairi*), and also as a port of call for western-route cargo shipping. Between the late Edo to the Meiji era, large-scale businessmen called the "Tadotsu Seven Gods", who made fortunes as shipping agents, were active. They founded a railway, an electric company, and a bank, leading to the modernization of the Shikoku region. Around the Tadotsu Hondori area, popularly known as Konpira Street, many of the houses and warehouses were built by the businessmen, giving it a historical look.

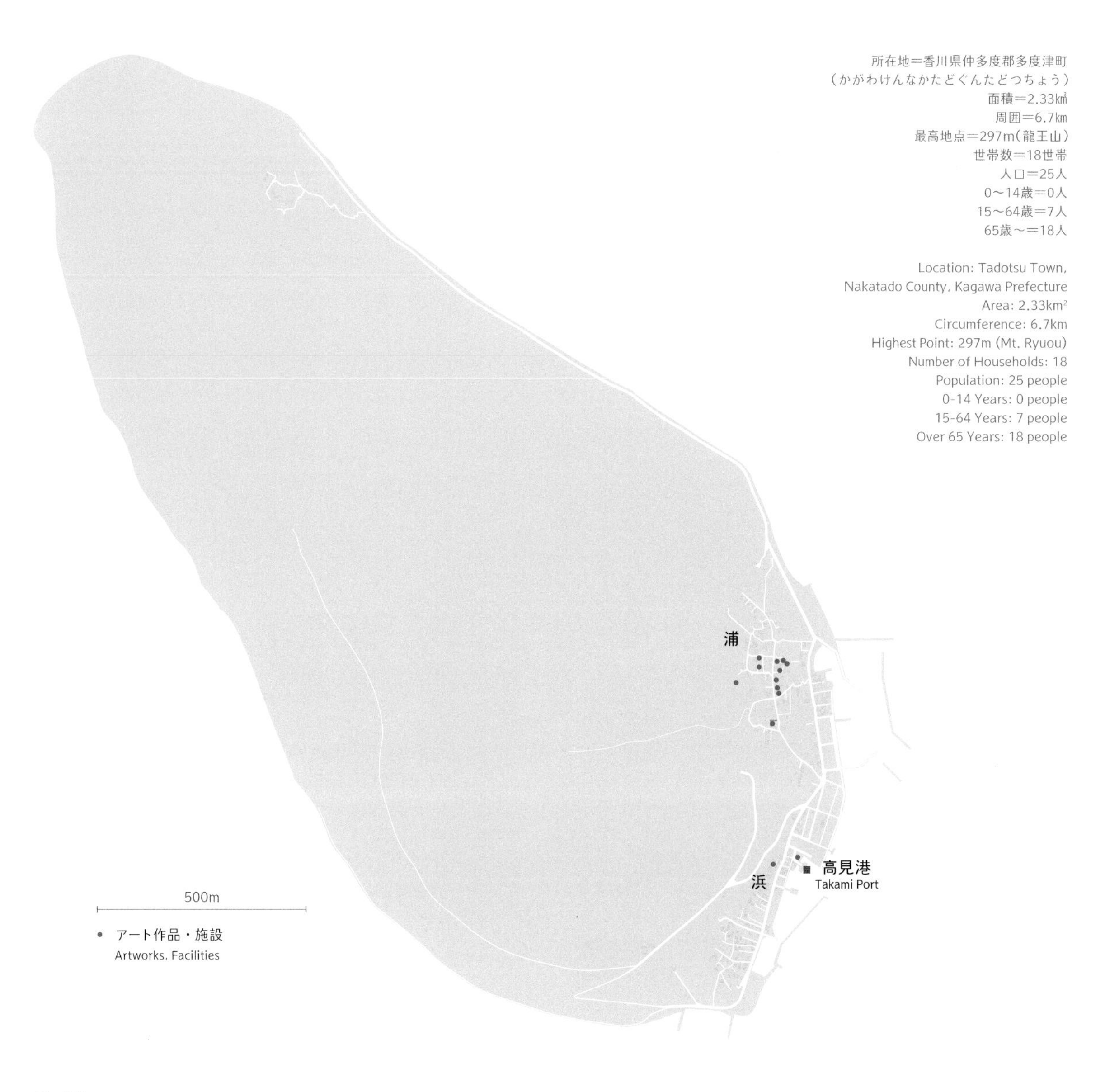

浜／浦

ta02 時のふる家
中島伽耶子 Kayako Nakashima

ta05 まなうらの景色2022
村田のぞみ Nozomi Murata

ta07 過日の同居2022
藤野裕美子 Yumiko Fujino

ta08 うつりかわりの家
中島伽耶子 Kayako Nakashima

ta10 はなのこえ・こころのいろ
小枝繁昭 Shigeaki Koeda

ta11 海のテラス
野村正人 Masahito Nomura

ta13 〜 melting dream 〜 / 高見島パフェ 名もなき女性（ひと）達にささぐ…
西山美なコ Minako Nishiyama

ta14 The Waiting Point
Eri Hayashi

ta15 かたちづくられるもの
鈴木健太郎 Kentaro Suzuki

ta16 高見島の木
竹腰耕平 Kohei Takekoshi

ta17 通りぬけた家
鐵羅佑 Yuu Tetsura

ta18 Merry Gates
内田晴之 Haruyuki Uchida

ta19 Re:mind
山下茜里 Akari Yamashita

ta20 FLOW
ケンデル・ギール Kendell Geers

E17 瀬戸内土のレストラン
bacilli

多度津町本通

ta21 多度津町一海陸交通の発展・近代化を支えた商人たち一

ta21 Nocturne (Tadotsu)
山田悠 Haruka Yamada

ta21 海と路／一太郎やあい
尾花賢一 Kenichi Obana

E18 身体と物体を超えて
ネオン・ダンス Neon Dance

2点とも [KSh]

ケンデル・ギール

FLOW

ta20 | 浦・海のテラス

Kendell Geers | South Africa / Belgium
FLOW
Terrace of Inland Sea, Ura
2022

瀬戸内海と瀬戸大橋を一望する《海のテラス》に現れた彫刻作品。幅6m、高さ3mの焼杉板と鏡、そして窓で構成されている。この作品のタイトルでもあり、壁面の模様の中にも隠されている「FLOW」という単語は、充実感をもって集中している精神状態を表している。窓から望む水平線や鏡に映りこむ島の緑を媒介に、観客の想像力と周囲の自然とが調和し「FLOW」できるような仕掛けを作り出している。

A sculptural piece that appeared at *Terrace of Inland Sea*, overlooking the Seto Inland Sea and the Seto Ohashi Bridge. The piece consists of burned cedar boards, mirrors, and windows, and it stands 6 meters wide and 3 meters high. The word *"flow"* – the title of the work – is hidden in the pattern on the wall, expressing the mental state of being fulfilled and focused. Using the horizon viewed from the windows and the green of the island reflected in the mirrors as the medium, the imagination of the audience and the surrounding nature harmonize to create a path to *"flow"*.

設計＝野村正人建築研究所（実施設計）
Detailed design: M. Nomura Associates

[KK]

野村正人
海のテラス
ta11 | 浦

Masahito Nomura | Japan
Terrace of Inland Sea
Ura
2013

設計＝野村正人、鎌田吉敬／野村正人建築研究所
特別協力＝楠原裕子（華月流生け花）、山田俊彦／パストジータ（料理監修）、野村俊明（料理）、寺井弘征、寺井祐子、渡邉美喜子

Architecture: Masahito Nomura and Yoshinori Kamada / M. Nomura Associates
Cuisine supervision: Toshihiko Yamada / PASTOSITA, Cuisine: Toshiaki Nomura,
Cooperation: Hiroko Kusuhara (Ikebana, Kagetsuryu), Hiromasa Terai, Yuko Terai, Mikiko Watanabe

過疎化した高見島の再興をめざす食プログラムとして2013年から継続しているプロジェクト。雲をイメージしたテントと白い円形テーブルで海とテラスが一体化している。2019年より集落内の見晴らしのよい高台に移設し、瀬戸内海を一望するオープンエアのイタリアンレストランを営業した。

An ongoing project since 2013, this food program aims at the restoration of Takamijima, which is suffering from de-population. A tent reminiscent of a cloud and white tables merge the ocean and the terrace. In 2019, the project moved to a higher site in the same village with a wonderful view, as an open-air Italian restaurant overlooking the Seto Inland Sea.

2点とも [SM]

bacilli
瀬戸内土のレストラン
E17 | 浦・海のテラス

bacilli | Japan
Setouchi Dirt Restaurant
Terrace of Inland Sea, Ura
2022

Event data

10月9日（日）15:00〜、16:00〜 | 各回12名定員 | 料金無料
October 9th (Sun); 15:00– 16:00–

bacilli（バシライ）＝南条嘉毅、ジェームズ・ジャック、吉野祥太郎
bacilli: Yoshitaka Nanjo, James Jack, Shotaro Yoshino

瀬戸内の土を巡る1日限定のレストラン。小豆島、女木島、高松港など各地で採取した土や、その土で育った野菜を使った土のフルコースなどを、島の方のお話とともに提供。「土のレストラン」は、高見島での開催を出発点に、今後、瀬戸内海の島々の土にまつわる話や郷土料理の調査・研究を重ね、瀬戸内海の人々が暮らす風景に出会い、新しいストーリーを紡ぎだしていく試み。参加者は目、耳、舌、そして鼻を使って土を味わった。

Experience fragrances and tastes of stories within Setouchi dirt at this event. Together with residents of Shodoshima, Megijima and Takamijima, memories of the land become the basis for cuisine linked to the unique histories of each island. Through one's ears, eyes, hands, tongues, noses and more, dirt becomes the focus of a three-course meal composed of sky, mountain, and sea. The recipes, research, and encounters born here will continue to sprout in new directions.

高見島プロジェクト　*Takamijima Project*

京都精華大学の有志が中心となり、2013 年から作家が継続的に島と関わり続けているプロジェクト。島に残された時間の痕跡を借景として、集落の空家や荒れ地などを舞台に、旧作を含めて 12 作品が展開。また、これまでの参加作家の作品などを販売するスペースも新設された。

This project has been in progress in Takamijima since 2013, with artists from Kyoto Seika University. Aiming to develop a trace of time in the island as a borrowed landscape, the project has seen 12 pieces of artwork installed, with places such as empty houses and derelict land as their stage. This year, a new space to sell the work of artists who have participated in the project to date was established.

助成＝公益財団法人 福武財団
特別協力＝京都精華大学
Funding: Fukutake Foundation
Cooperation: Kyoto Seika University

左《うつりかわりの家》 右《時のふる家》2 点とも [Ylc]

中島伽耶子

時のふる家
ta02 | 浜
うつりかわりの家
ta08 | 浦

Kayako Nakashima | Japan
Time Falls
Hama
2016
Transition House
Ura
2013

無数の小さな穴に埋め込まれた直径 1 ㎝のアクリル円柱を通じて自然光が室内を柔らかく照らす《うつりかわりの家》。カットしたアクリル板から光が古家の内部に鋭く差しこみ、刻々と変化する光が家を貫通する《時のふる家》。それぞれの光は、変化の象徴として、優しくも暴力的に家という縄張りに介入し、内部を静かに照らしだした。

Transition House is a piece in which light shining through a multitude of small holes softly illuminates the interior of an abandoned house. In *Time Falls*, the artist pierced the walls of acrylic panels, introducing sharp lines of light that slice like arrows through the interior. The light, changing every moment, shines through the house. Each light functions as a symbol of transition, and intervenes with the territory of the house softly yet violently, to illuminate its heart.

2点とも [KK]

藤野裕美子

過日の同居2022

ta07 | 浦

Yumiko Fujino | Japan
Staying in past days 2022
Ura
2022

島の廃村である板持地区への取材を繰り返して制作する作家の継続的な作品。1階では、家財道具と植物が折り重なるように描かれた大きな絵画作品が障子のように空間を隔て、人の生活感が残る家の内部との対比を作り出している。今回は新たに、水平に伸びる梁がある屋根裏の空間を斜めに横断するような大型の絵画作品を展開。板持地区の空き家に残されたオブジェから感じる戦争の気配をコラージュした作品を展示した。

This ongoing work is produced through repeated research about Itamochi area, an abandoned village on the island. On the first floor, paintings of furniture and plants are expressed in folded layers, dividing the space like paper sliding doors, and creating a contrast between the interior of the house and the feeling of human life. This time, the artist presented new large-scale paintings in the attic, seemingly slashing the horizontal beams diagonally. The work developed a college of the sense of war, conveyed through objects left in the abandoned houses of Itamochi area.

2点とも [KK]

鈴木健太郎

かたちづくられるもの

ta15 | 浦

Kentaro Suzuki | Japan
A "figure" formed by the "ground"
Ura
2022

家の多くが廃屋となっている浦地区で、数十年取り残された家を舞台に、人と人とのつながりをテーマにしたインスタレーション作品。かつて住んでいた人の生活の痕跡を、太陽の光で露光するサイアノタイプという技法で収集し、神社仏閣に無数に貼られた千社札のイメージを重ね合わせて制作した。時を超えて対話する1つの形が表現されている。

Suzuki's installation work deals with the theme of connections between people, set in a house that has been abandoned for many decades, in the Ura area where many similarly derelict houses exist. Traces of the lives of the people who used to live there were collected with a method called cyanotype, which functions through exposure to sunlight, and layered with images of countless *senjafuda* (paper slips attached to shrine pillars by pilgrims). The work expresses a form of communication that transcends time.

鐵羅佑

通りぬけた家

ta17 | 浦

Yuu Tetsura | Japan
Blown through
Ura
2022

朽ちていく家に、新しいアプローチで風の通り道をつくった作品。建物の半分が崩れ落ち、壁が抜けて、屋根が下に落ちていた木造の廃屋を改修し、かつてあった家の一部を鉄板で再構築した。強固な外観とは裏腹に、中に入ると構造の軽さ、脆さを象徴する隙間から、外光が有機的に差し込み、時間や家の存在を浮き彫りにしている。人の営みがなくなりつつある島で、家と人の関係を考えさせられる作品。

Blown Through creates a path for the breeze, with a new approach in a house falling into disrepair. Half of the wooden house had collapsed, with no walls remaining and the roof on the ground. The artist reconstructed the building, using iron plates to compliment some parts of the house that had previously existed. In contrast to the sturdy appearance of the exterior, the lightness and frailty of the structure is symbolized in the interior by gaps through which the light enters organically. In an island where the life of people is slowly disappearing, the work forces consideration of the relationship between houses and people.

3点とも [KK]

村田のぞみ

まなうらの景色2022

ta05 | 浦

Nozomi Murata | Japan
Remains in the Mind's Eye 2022
Ura
2022

古民家の中で、痕跡から家の記憶を思い出すように細いステンレス線を無数につなぎ合わせて制作されたインスタレーション作品。まぶたの裏を意味する「まなうら」という言葉には、かつてこの家が見た姿や景色、そして未来について想像するための空間になればという作家の願いが込められている。2019 年作品の再制作となり、今回は島を取り囲む荒々しい海と静寂な海という対照的な存在をテーマにした。

An installation work produced with many thin stainless steel wires linked together in an old house, as though tracing back the memory of the house. By using the title *Manaura,* meaning "the back of the eyelid", the artist conveys her desire for the work to be a space for imagining the landscapes and figures that the house used to see, and its future. This is a re-working of a 2019 piece, and this time the artist deals with the contrary presence of ocean surrounding the island – by turns rough and calm.

2点とも [KK]

2点とも [KK]

西山美なコ

~ melting dream ~ / 高見島パフェ
名もなき女性(ひと)達にささぐ...

ta13 | 浦

Minako Nishiyama | Japan
~ melting dream ~ / TAKAMIJIMA
parfait dedicated to many unknown women...
Ura
2022

特別協力=日新製糖株式会社
Cooperation: Nissin Sugar Co., Ltd.

屋根裏部屋に現れた、時間と共に変容してゆくインスタレーション作品。島の廃屋でみつけたグラスや持ち込んだ家具に、砂糖で制作した350個あまりの薔薇の彫刻がパフェのように盛られ、時間とともに融けて朽ちていく。砂糖の薔薇は甘い夢がとろけるようなイメージと同時に、時が強要する抗い難い現実をも表現している。作家は、この島でかつて生活して男性を支えていたであろう女性の時間にも焦点を当てた。

Appearing in the attic is an installation work that transforms as time passes. More than 350 sculpted roses made of sugar were placed like parfait on objects such as glasses found in an abandoned house on the island and furniture that the artist brought in. Over time the sugar sculptures melt and eventually dissolve. These roses express not only the concept of sweet dreams melting, but also the irresistible reality of time's power. The artist focused on the time of women who used to live on the island in support of the men.

[SM]

2点とも [KK]

竹腰耕平

高見島の木

ta16 | 浦

Kohei Takekoshi | Japan
Takamijima tree
Ura
2022

空き家の庭にある切り株周辺の地面を円柱状に掘り、根を露出させた作品。その根は家の床下まで延びており、家屋の床を剥がして露わになった地面の穴からも見ることができる。上部が切られてしまった木の命を感じさせると同時に、瀬戸内海を一望しながら、自然との在り方を問いかける作品。

Takekoshi dug a cylindrical shape in the earth around a cut tree in the garden of an empty house to expose the roots. The roots extend beneath the floor of the house, and can be seen by visitors, as flooring has been removed to reveal the holes in the ground beneath. The life of a tree with its upper part cut off can still be a presence: the work questions our way of living with nature, at a site overlooking the Seto Inland Sea.

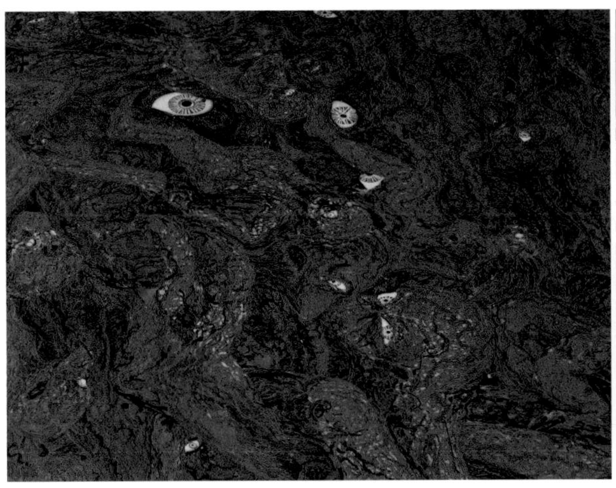

2点とも [KK]

山下茜里
Re:mind

ta19 | 浦

Akari Yamashita | Japan
Re:mind
Ura
2022

古い建物に残された“もの”の「気配」を可視化したインスタレーション作品。かつてそこに暮らしていた人々が消え去ったあと、少しずつ膨らんで充満するモノの気配。作家はその隠れていたモノたちが、何を思うのかに想像を巡らせた。真っ赤な身体と目として象徴的に描かれたその気配は、1階の16畳の畳の下から現れた。急な階段で2階へ登ると、薄暗い部屋の押し入れや箪笥、壁の隙間から溢れるように、鑑賞者を見つめている。

This installation work visualizes the atmosphere of "things" that were left in an old building. After the people who used to live there have disappeared, the atmosphere of things slightly swells to fill the space. The artist explored her imagination of what these things hold in their minds. The atmosphere, personified in the form of red bodies and eyes, appears from underneath the 16 *tatami* on the first floor. Going up the steep stairs to the second floor, they stare at visitors through gaps in the closet, chest, and walls, as though they are about to spill out.

2点とも [KK]

Eri Hayashi
The Waiting Point

ta14 | 浦

Eri Hayashi | Japan
The Waiting Point
Ura
2022

高見島には空海が開基したといわれるお寺がある。空から見た高見島の形が、作者には空海がつけ忘れた「、」に見えたというエピソードからはじまり、連想ゲームのように「弘法も筆の誤り」からドイツ語の諺へと展開していく。ブルーキューブにはささやき声と、島の形を花弁や雲、星や石鹸に見立てたグラフィック作品が配置され、海を望むホワイトキューブでは、詩と本の作品で、取り残された点の物語がさらに詳しく語られた。

On the island of Takamijima there is a temple that is said to have been opened by the monk and calligrapher Kukai. The work is a story, derived from the idea that the island of Takamijima from the sky looks like a Japanese comma "、". The artist posits that this could be a comma that Kukai forgot, building on the saying, "Even Kukai's handwriting has mistakes" in a kind of word association, leading on to a German proverb. In a blue cube are whispers and graphic work that likens the shape of the island to flower petals, a cloud, a star, and soap, while in a white cube stories of abandoned dots are examined in more detail in poems and a book.

２点とも [KK]

小枝繁昭

はなのこえ・こころのいろ

ta10 | 浦

Shigeaki Koeda | Japan
Voice of Flowers･Color of Hearts
Ura
2019

高見島の花たちとの出会いを、写真、襖絵、陶製オブジェの形でカラフルに表現した作品。写真とペインティングを組み合わせた独自の制作手法で「見ること」と「感じること」を行き来して制作する作家が、花を見る瞬間の眼差しについて問いかける。

Koeda has created a space celebrating the joy of discovery and a “comfortable physicality” using photos, partition paintings, and ceramics, all of which were produced in the process of discovering the flowers on Takamijima.

[KK]

[MK]

内田晴之

Merry Gates

ta18 | 浜

Haruyuki Uchida | Japan
Merry Gates
Hama
2022

高見港に設置した、高さ約３m、横幅７mを超える屋外彫刻作品。ステンレススチールを素材に制作し、磁力を内蔵した三角の土台に乗ったパーツは、風とともに上下に揺れて来訪者を迎える。あちらとこちらをつなぐ境界として、「いつもの見慣れた景色から一歩門をくぐれば“違う場所”、幸運な方向に人々が向かうための一歩になるように」という作家の願いがこめられている。

An exterior sculpture measuring around 3 meters in height and 7 meters in width is placed in Takami port. The stainless steel parts swing up and down with the wind on a triangular magnetic base, welcoming visitors. The work presents a border connecting this side with the other, encompassing the artist’s thought that “a step into the gate from the familiar will take you to a different place, and this step is towards somewhere happy”.

多度津街中プロジェクト　*Tadotsu Town Project*

多度津は、古くから金毘羅参詣のため多くの人で賑わい、また北前船の寄港地として讃岐の交易の玄関口であった。明治初期の四国の鉄道発祥の地でもあり、多度津町本通界隈に残る大きな土蔵や町家、近代の豪商として街を支えた多度津七福神の家、合田邸が今も当時の繁栄を思わせる。多度津駅と島への玄関口多度津港との動線にある合田邸や土蔵などに作品を展開した。

The new Tadotsu Town Project began with a focus on the Tadotsu Hondori street, long known as Konpira Street, which many people passed through on their pilgrimage. Tadotsu enjoyed prosperity as a port of call for western-route cargo shipping in the Edo era, and large warehouses and terraced houses still remain today. At the house of the Goda family, formerly of one of the "Tadotsu Seven Gods" who supported the town as large-scale merchant, an exhibition showed the history and changes of the town.

4点とも [KK]

尾花賢一

海と路／一太郎やあい

ta21 | 本通・旧塩田家土蔵（旧石川金物店）

Kenichi Obana | Japan
Sea and Road
Sending off Ichitaro
Former Warehouse of Shiota Family (Ishikawa Hardware Store)
Hondori
2022

旧塩田家土蔵を舞台にした劇画調のインスタレーション作品。戦争中、教科書にも取り上げられた愛国美談「一太郎やあい」の物語を空間に再構築し、海と人が織り成してきた様々な営みを表現した。1階では史実と作家の体験、創作が入り交じる物語を鑑賞者が歩きながら読み進めるドローイングで表現。薄暗い2階は多度津の古い広報物や写真を用いたイメージの海に船の模型が航海しているような作品を展開した。

An installation piece akin to a picture story show was set in a former warehouse of the Shiota family. The story of *Sending off Ichitaro* – a patriotic exploit that even appeared in a war-era textbook – was reconstructed in the space to convey the various exchanges between the sea and the people. On the first floor, the story, with a mixture of history and the artist's experience and creation, was expressed in drawing so the viewers could take in the narrative while walking. In the dim upstairs space was another piece, featuring a model of a ship seeming to sail on a sea of images from old publicity materials and photographs of Tadotsu.

[KK]

山田悠

Nocturne (Tadotsu)

ta21 | 本通・旧吉田酒造場

Haruka Yamada | Japan
Nocturne (Tadotsu)
Former Yoshida Sake Brewery, Hondori
2022

特別協力＝Daisuke Tanabe（サウンド）
Sound: Daisuke Tanabe

旧酒造場を改築した不思議な空間に現れた、月と街が連動する映像作品。作家は1時間に約15度西に動く月に合わせて多度津の街中を歩き、多度津駅近くの線路沿いから多度津港旧外港東防波堤まで、建物や電線といった街の輪郭をなぞるように月を追いかけた。

Opening in a strange location, a renovated former *ake* brewery, this film piece correlates the moon and the town. Yamada walked the streets of Tadotsu in accordance to the moon, which moved about 15 degrees west each hour, from the rail tracks near Tadotsu station to the former east pier of Tadotsu port. The artist followed the moon along the outline of the town, threading buildings and electric wire.

多度津町—海陸交通の発展・近代化を支えた商人たち—

ta21 | 本通・合田邸

Tadotsu Town—Development of Sea-Land Transportation・Merchants who supported modernization—
Goda House, Hondori
2022

多度津港へ流れ込む桜川の河口はかつて川湊として栄え、金毘羅参詣船が多く寄港していた。海運の発達した江戸時代には北前船の寄港地となり、港町多度津はさらに賑わいを増していった。やがて海から陸へと人・物資の流れが大きく変わっていく中でも、鉄道や電力会社の開設などで町の近代化を支えたのは、のちに「多度津七福神」と呼ばれる豪商たちである。本展では、七福神の邸宅では唯一現存する合田邸において、近世から現在に至る多度津の変化について年表や記録映像とともに紹介した。

The estuary of Sakuragawa river, as it flows into Tadotsu Port, once flourished as a river port where the boats of many pilgrims bound for Konpirasan stopped. In the Edo era, when marine transport developed, it became a stopping point for western-route shipping, and the port town Tadotsu became increasingly lively. Eventually, the flow of people and goods shifted from sea to land, but the modernization of the town was supported by the large-scale merchant known as "the Tadotsu Seven Gods", who pioneered the region's railway and electric businesses. In this exhibition at Goda House – the only remaining house of those businessmen today – the transition of the town of Tadotsu from the modern into the contemporary was introduced with chronology and documentary footage.

ネオン・ダンス
身体と物体を超えて
E18 | 本通・旧吉田酒造場

Neon Dance | UK
Beyond Body and Things
Former Yoshida Sake Brewery, Hondori
2022

現代において、なぜ「孤独」の問題がこれほど蔓延しているのかを探求した参加型パフォーマンス。会場には一面に砂が敷かれ「亀」をモチーフにした2体のロボットがいる。1体は、観客がカメラに向かって手を動かすと、それに反応して移動する。もう1体は、会場壁面に投影された、世界のどこかから生中継されたダンサーのパフォーマンスに反応して遠隔で動く。公演後、人間とロボットが呼応した痕跡が砂絵のように現れた。

An interactive performance exploring why loneliness is spreading so widely in the contemporary moment. The floor of the exhibition space is covered with sand, and in it are two turtle-shaped robots. One changes position in response to the hand movements of the audience to a camera; the other moves in response to remote operation by the performance of a dancer broadcast in real time from somewhere in the world. After the performance, the traces of human and robot communication appear on the ground like sand art.

特別協力＝Swindon Dance, University of Bristol, The Place, Wellcome Collection, Bristol Beacon, Dance4, South East Dance, Reversible Destiny Foundation（リバーシブル・デスティニー財団）& 荒川修作＋マドリン・ギンズ東京事務所
協賛＝Arts Council England National Lottery Project Grants, Brigstow Institute, 英国笹川財団 & EPSRC Impact Acceleration Fund.

Cooperation: Swindon Dance, University of Bristol, The Place, Wellcome Collection, Bristol Beacon, Dance4, South East Dance, Reversible Destiny Foundation & Arakawa + Gins Tokyo.
Sponsor: Arts Council England National Lottery Project Grants, Brigstow Institute, The Great Britain Sasakawa Foundation & EPSRC Impact Acceleration Fund.

2点とも [SM]

Event Data

11月3日(木祝)、4日(金)、5日(土)17:00〜 | コンセプト・ディレクション＝エイドリアン・ハート | 振付＝エイドリアン・ハート、高瀬譜希子 | ロボットデザイン・コンセプト＝ブリストルロボット工学研究所（ヘマ・フィラモア、アリックス・パートリッジ、カラム・ゲラスピー）| ダンスアーティスト＝高瀬譜希子 | 音楽＝セバスチャン・レイノルズ | 衣裳＝坂部三樹郎（MIKIO SAKABE）| 料金＝一般1,500円、小中高生800円、ほか | 来場者数＝91人

November 3rd (Thu), 4th (Fri), 5th (Sat) 17:00– | Concept / Direction: Adrienne Hart | Choreography: Adrienne Hart, Fukiko Takase | Robot Design & Concept: Bristol Robotics Lab (Hemma Philamore, Alix Partridge & Calum Gillespie) | Dance Artist: Fukiko Takase | Music: Sebastian Reynolds | Costume: Mikio Sakabe | Admission: General 1,500 yen, Student (ages 6–18) 800 yen, etc. | Attendance: 91 people

粟島
Awashima

粟島　*Awashima*

塩飽諸島、最西の島。上から見ると３枚のスクリューのような形の島は、３つの砂州がつながったと言われる。北前船の寄港地として栄え廻船業も盛んだったが、近代化により和船から汽船へと移行していった明治期、操船の国家試験の導入に合わせて、1897年、日本初の国立海員養成学校が設立された。90年にわたり優秀な船員を輩出し、今も多くの元外航船員が島に住む。海を望むライトグリーンの元校舎は現在「粟島海洋記念館」として船舶機器や当時の資料を展示している。

毎年３月の「粟島ももて祭」は袴を着た男性らによる弓射儀礼で、厄払いや大漁・豊作・海上安全などを祈願する。初夏から秋にかけて、夜になると岸壁や砂浜が海ほたるの青い光で幻想的に瞬く。

The island on the western tip of the Shiwaku Islands. From above, the island is shaped like three propeller wings. This is said to have been caused by the connection of three sand bars. The island was known for its shipping agents, and was a busy port of call for western-route cargo shipping. With modernization, Japanese ships progressed to steam power, and in the Meiji era officials introduced a state license for ship handling. This island was the site of the first national mariner training school, established in 1897. For over 90 years it produced excellent mariners, and even today many ex-ship workers live on the island. The light green former school building, overlooking the sea, is preserved today as Awashima Maritime Museum, exhibiting ship equipment and documents from the time.

"Awashima Momote Festival" is held each March, and consists of a *yumiire* ("shooting") ceremony conducted by men in *hakama* costumes praying for protection from bad fortune, success in fishing and farming, and safety at sea. Between early summer and autumn, the coastal walls and sand beaches are graced by fantastical flickers of blue light from sea-fireflies.

所在地＝香川県三豊市
（かがわけんみとよし）
面積＝3.67㎢
周囲＝16㎞
最高地点＝222m（城ノ山）
世帯数＝102世帯
人口＝154人
0〜14歳＝0人
15〜64歳＝26人
65歳〜＝127人
不詳＝1人

Location: Mitoyo City, Kagawa Prefecture
Area: 3.67km²
Circumference: 16km
Highest Point: 222m (Mt. Jyono)
Number of Households: 102
Population: 154 people
0-14 Years: 0 people
15-64 Years: 26 people
Over 65 Years: 127 people
Unknown: 1 people

西浜
粟島芸術家村／旧粟島中学校
旧粟島小学校
旧粟島幼稚園
粟島港
Awashima Port

500m
• アート作品・施設
Artworks, Facilities

粟島中心部

aw01 瀬戸内海底探査船美術館プロジェクト 一昨日丸／ソコソコ想像所／Re-ing-A
日比野克彦 Katsuhiko Hibino

aw03 TARA
TARA TARA

aw04 粟島大絵地図（あわしまおおえちず）
佐藤悠 Yu Sato

aw04 いのちの声を聴く
森ナナ Nana Mori

aw06 思考の輪郭
エステル・ストッカー Esther Stocker

aw07 過ぎ去った子供達の歌
ムニール・ファトゥミ Mounir Fatmi

aw11 種は船 TARA JAMBIO アートプロジェクト
日比野克彦 Katsuhiko Hibino

西浜

aw12 スティルライフ
マッシモ・バルトリーニ Massimo Bartolini

aw13 「い・ま・こ・こ」
アデル・アブデスメッド Adel Abdessemed

須田港周辺

aw10 須田港待合所プロジェクト「みなとのロープハウス」
山田紗子 Suzuko Yamada

山田紗子
須田港待合所プロジェクト「みなとのロープハウス」
aw10 | 須田港

Suzuko Yamada | Japan
Suda Port Waiting Space Project “Rope House”
Suda Port
2013, 2022

漁業用のロープが張り巡らされた定期船の待合所。今回はこれまでの白いロープから、赤と青の鮮やかな２色のロープにリニューアルして公開された。

The waiting room for a regular ferry route is surrounded by fishing ropes. This time, the previously used white rope was renewed with vivid red and blue ropes.

所蔵＝三豊市
Collection: Mitoyo City

7点とも [KK]

日比野克彦

種は船 TARA JAMBIO アートプロジェクト

aw11 | 粟島港ほか

Katsuhiko Hibino | Japan
TANeFUNe TARA JAMBIO Art Project
Awashima Port, etc.
2022

作家が2003年から行う「明後日朝顔プロジェクト」での、朝顔の種から着想を得て5,000人以上の協力のもと2010年に完成した「TANeFUNe」。各地で活動を行ってきたTANeFUNeが、今回は海洋環境をテーマに活動する調査船へとアップデートした。2019年から「ソコソコ想像船長小屋」を展開する喜多直人が船長を務め、春は小豆島・池田港、夏は豊島・甲生漁港、秋は粟島港へと周遊して活動。来場者は実際に船に乗って漂流物の収集に参加した。

Inspired by seeds of morning glory (*asagao*), familiar from *the Asatte Asagao Project* that the artist has led since 2003, *TANeFUNe* was completed in 2010, with the support of over 5,000 people. The boat *TANeFUNe* toured many places, and has been redeveloped as an investigative ship with the target of the marine environment. Since 2019, Naoto Kita, who organizes the *Sokosoko Sozo Captain's Cabin* has been the captain of the ship, which conducts investigations around Ikeda Port, Shodoshima in spring, Kou Fishing Port, Teshima in summer, and Awashima Port in autumn. Visitors were welcomed on board, taking part in the collection of driftwood.

特別協力＝Tara Ocēan 財団、喜多直人

Cooperation: The Tara Océan Foundation, Naoto Kita

左《ソコソコ想像所》右《一昨日丸》2点とも [KK]

日比野克彦
瀬戸内海底探査船美術館プロジェクト
一昨日丸／ソコソコ想像所／Re-ing-A

aw01 | 旧粟島中学校ほか

Katsuhiko Hibino | Japan
Project for the Museum of Seabed Inquiry Ship in Setouchi
Ototoimaru / Sokosoko Sozosho / Re-ing-A
Former Awashima Junior High School, etc.
2013, 2016

2010年からはじまった、瀬戸内海周辺の海底遺物を探索し収集・展示するプロジェクト。海の遺物が展示される海上の美術館《一昨日丸》、海底から収集されたものに思いを巡らせる《ソコソコ想像所》、そして《一昨日丸》の活動で発見した粟島沖の海底に沈んだ船から引き揚げたレンガで制作した象の彫刻《Re-ing-A》の3作品を展開。ソコソコ想像所は粟島海洋記念館の改装に伴い、旧粟島中学校に移設された。

This project, which began in 2010, explores remains found at the bottom of the Seto Inland Sea and exhibits what is collected. It includes a museum of the ocean, *Ototoimaru*, where the relics are shown, a place where visitors can imagine what has been collected, *Sokosoko Sozosho*, and an elephant sculpture, *Re-ing-A*, which was created with bricks collected from a ship that sunk in the outside sea of Awashima, and was found in the activities of *Ototoimaru*. *Sokosoko Sozosho* was moved to the former Awashima Junior High School due to the renovation of Awashima Maritime Museum.

特別協力＝板倉辰也（運航）
Cooperation: Tatsuya Itakura

《Re-ing-A》[KK]

[KK]

TARA
TARA

aw03 | 旧粟島中学校

TARA | France
TARA
Former Awashima Junior High School
2019, 2022

世界中の海洋調査を通して、気候変動と環境破壊が海洋にもたらす影響を研究する科学捜査船タラ号の活動紹介展示。タラ号乗船アーティストでもある日比野克彦、大小島真木、ニコラ・フロックの作品も展示された。今回は旧粟島中学校に移設され、活動記録やマイクロプラスチックに関する展示が新たに追加された。

This exhibition introduces the activities of *Tara*, a scientific research vessel, which studies the world's oceans and researches the impacts of climate change and environmental destruction on the seas. The artists on the vessel – Katsuhiko Hibino, Maki Ohkojima, and Nicolas Floc'h – exhibited their artwork as well. This time, the exhibition was moved to the former Awashima Junior High School, with new additions related to the activity log and microplastics.

所蔵＝三豊市
協賛＝agnes b.、Tara Océan 財団
Collection: Mitoyo City
Sponsor: agnes b., The Tara Océan Foundation

粟島芸術家村 *Awashima Artists' Village*

ディレクション＝日比野克彦｜主催＝三豊市
Direction: Katsuhiko Hibino | Organization: Mitoyo City

2010年より旧粟島中学校を拠点に、アーティストインレジデンスプログラムを実施。2014年からディレクターに日比野克彦を迎え「日々の笑学校」として再始動した。今回は佐藤悠と森ナナが4～5カ月間の滞在制作を行い、島の生活や文化、自然環境からアイディアを得て、作品を発表した。

An artist in residence program that has been running since 2010, based in the former Awashima Junior High School. From 2014 onwards, Katsuhiko Hibino has been the director, and it was reimagined as "Hibino Shogakko". This time Yu Sato and Nana Mori stayed for 4 to 5 months to produce and exhibit their works, which were inspired by the life, culture, and natural environment of the island.

2点とも [KK]

森ナナ

いのちの声を聴く

aw04｜粟島芸術家村

Nana Mori | Japan
Listen to the Voice of Life
Awashima Artists' Village
2022

書をベースとする作家が、海を泳いで島に渡るイノシシを駆除する島民の猟に同行した体験から生まれた作品。捕獲したイノシシの皮と骨から膠を抽出し、自生する竹を燃やした煤と合わせて、島の素材で自作の墨を作る。その制作過程を島の住民とともに試行錯誤するプロセスを経て、大きな紙全面に住民の姿を写しとった（＝拓をとった）。作品には、人間と動植物、島民と作家が交流した、いのちの声が記録されている。

The artist, whose work is based in calligraphy, went along with islanders hunting to get rid of wild boar, which swim over the sea to the island. Glue is extracted from the skin and bones of the slain creatures, and by mixing that with the soot of locally grown bamboo she makes an ink that is original to the island. The production process was a series of trial and error in collaboration with the island residents. The work itself, rubbings of the residents on a big piece of paper, expresses the voice of life after exchanges between humans, animals, and plants, and between the islanders and the artist.

2点とも [KK]

佐藤悠

粟島大絵地図（あわしまおおえちず）

aw04｜粟島芸術家村

Yu Sato | Japan
Awashima Grand Picture Map
Awashima Artists' Village
2022

島民の故西山恵司が2008年に作成したパノラマの粟島絵地図から着想を得て、島民や来場者に「あなたの見た粟島を描きませんか？」と声をかけ、それぞれの記憶の印象から、幅10mの《粟島大絵地図》を制作した。また粟島芸術家村がどのように生まれ、変遷していったのかを関係者12名にインタビューした約260頁に及ぶ『粟島芸術家村文庫2022』を発行。芸術家村のこれまでとこれからを考えるための記録となっている。

Inspired by a panoramic picture map of Awashima that was completed in 2008 by the late Keiji Nishiyama, a resident of the island, Sato invited local people and visitors to draw Awashima in their eyes. From their memories and impressions of the island, he created the 10-meter wide *Awashima Grand Picture Map*. He also interviewed 12 people who talked about how Awashima Artists' Village was born and developed, and published the *Awashima Artists' Village Book 2022*, which runs to about 260 pages. It is a document that examines the past and future of the village.

2点とも [Ylc]

ムニール・ファトゥミ
過ぎ去った子供達の歌
aw07 | 旧粟島小学校

Mounir Fatmi | Morocco / France
The song of the children all Gone
Former Awashima Elementary School
2016

廃校になった小学校を舞台にした作品。3人の子どもの銅像が校庭の中心で黒と白のポールに囲まれて佇み、校内では学校に残された備品などを使ったインスタレーションを展開。作家が編集した瀬戸内海の波音や校歌、チャイム音などが、誰もいなくなった校内に響く。

This work is situated in the grounds of a closed school. Bronze statues of three children are positioned in the center of the schoolyard, surrounded by black and white poles, and an installation work using items left behind was developed inside the building. Edited by the artist, the sound of the waves of the Seto Inland Sea, school songs, and chimes echo through the vacant classrooms.

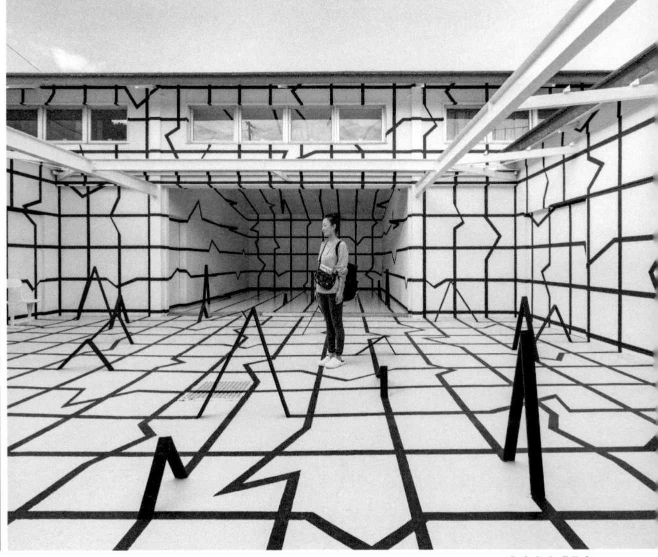

2点とも [Ylc]

エステル・ストッカー
思考の輪郭
aw06 | 旧粟島幼稚園

Esther Stocker | Italy / Austria
Contours of Thinking
Former Awashima Kindergarten
2016

かつての幼稚園の壁や床を白く塗り、うねりのある黒線で空間を構成。黒線は所々立体的に立ち上がり、2次元と3次元のはざまを楽しめる。2つの保育室には白と黒の対照的な空間が広がっている。

The walls and floors of a former kindergarten are painted white, and the space is composed with curved black lines. These lines are raised three-dimensionally at points, allowing viewers to feel a gap between two and three dimensions. In two nursery rooms, contrasting spaces of black and white are developed.

[KK]

マッシモ・バルトリーニ

スティルライフ

aw12 | 西浜

Massimo Bartolini | Italy
Still Life
Nishihama
2022

西洋絵画の代表的な主題である「静物」を再解釈したインスタレーション作品。山なみが見える休耕地に40㎡ほどの人工の池が現れ、その中央にガリレオ・チーニがデザインした花瓶が浮かんでいる。空の花瓶には蓮の花が描かれており、風景―花瓶―水―花という内と外の関係が反転する。周囲に群生するエビスグサという白い花は、制作中に休耕地を耕した際、かつてここで育てられていたハブ茶の種が活性化し育ったもので、一帯が自然発生的に花畑となった。

This installation work reinterpreted a fundamental theme in Western painting: still life. In a fallow field with a view of the mountains, a 40-square-meter artificial pond was created, in the center of which a vase designed by Galileo Andrea Maria Chini was set. Lotus flowers are painted on the empty vase, reversing the roles of inside and outside, as a landscape-vase-water-flower. Groups of white flowers, called Chinese senna, grow in the surrounding land, resulting from habu tea seeds germinating, and the whole area spontaneously became a flowerbed.

[KK]

アデル・アブデスメッド

「い・ま・こ・こ」

aw13 | 西浜

Adel Abdessemed
| Algeria / France
Out, out, brief candle
Nishihama
2022

住む人がいなくなった西浜の集落にある空き家に映しだされた、生と死を示唆する短い映像作品。洞窟に入り込むように薄暗い室内を進むと、ロウソクの火を足で踏み潰す映像がエンドレスで流れている。英題の《Out, out, brief candle》はシェイクスピアの『マクベス』第5幕第5場の有名な一節で、死を覚悟したマクベスが妻が亡くなった知らせを受けて、人生の無意味を語るシーンから引用された。

A short film is projected in a vacant house in the uninhabited village of Nishihama, suggestive of life and death. Moving through the dim room, like going into a cave, the viewer is met by footage of a foot stamping on a candle light is played in a loop. The English title, *Out, out, brief candle* is a famous phrase from Act V Scene V of *Macbeth*, taken from the scene in which Macbeth receives news of his wife's death and speaks of the meaninglessness of life.

3点とも [KK]

伊吹島
Ibukijima

伊吹島　*Ibukijima*

瀬戸内海の真ん中に位置する燧灘（ひうちなだ）は、北は鞆の浦を有する備後灘、西はしまなみ海道の島々が並ぶ。伊吹島は燧灘の東にあり、瀬戸内火山岩類の花崗岩や安山岩からなる台地型の島で、急斜面の崖に囲まれている。海流の流れから島周辺には魚が集まり、古くは鯛しばり網漁、近代からはイリコ漁などが盛ん。朝鮮半島沖など外洋への漁もあった。出産前後の女性たちが共同で暮らした「出部屋」が400年続くなど漁労文化が島に根づいている。

台地の上に集落があり、細い路地が迷路のように走る。海岸沿いはイリコの加工場が並ぶ。現在15軒ある網元の漁船は2つの港に集まり、6月のイリコ漁が解禁になると、島外からの人が増え、漁船のエンジン音が響いて島は活気づく。春は島の北にある波切不動尊周辺の200本の桜が咲く。秋祭りは神輿を乗せた漁船が島を一周し、太鼓台が急坂を登る。島で話される言葉は平安時代のアクセントが残る特殊な方言。

Hiuchinada is a portion of the Seto Inland Sea that lies south of Bingonada (which includes Tomonoura), and east of the Shimanami Kaido path. Ibukijima is in the east of Hiuchinada, and is a flat island consisting of granite, Setouchi volcanic rock, and andesite, edged by steep cliffs. The ocean current encourages fish to gather around the island, so in the past a type of net-fishing was used to catch sea bream. Nowadays, *iriko* (small sardine) is a common catch. Islanders also went out to the open sea to fish, even reaching the waters of the Korean peninsula. The culture of fishing is deeply rooted in the island, as seen by the group house *debeya*, for mothers to live with newborn babies, which lasted for 400 years.

A village is situated on the plateau, with narrow alleyways that run like a maze. Along the eastern shore, *iriko* processing sites can be seen. The ships of the fishermen, of which 15 remain today, are moored at two ports, and once the *iriko* fishing season opens in June, the number of visitors from offshore increases, and the island reverberates with the sound of fishing boat motors. In spring, 200 cherry trees around the Namikiri Fudoson temple blossom. In the autumn festival, a boat carrying a *mikoshi* shrine travels around the island, and *taiko-dai* goes up the steep hills. The island has a unique dialect that retains some features of accents from the Heian era (794–1185).

伊吹島中心部

ib01 トイレの家
石井大五 Daigo Ishii

ib03 イリコ庵
みかんぐみ＋明治大学学生
MIKAN + Students of Meiji University

ib05 伊吹の樹
栗林隆 Takashi Kuribayashi

ib06 パサング
メラ・ヤルスマ+ニンディティヨ・アディプルノモ
Mella Jaarsma + Nindityo Adipurnomo

ib08 ものがみる夢
アレクサンドラ・コヴァレヴァ＆佐藤敬 / KASA
Aleksandra Kovaleva & Kei Sato / KASA

ib09 つながる海
ゲゲルボヨ Gegerboyo

ib10 浜辺の歌
マナル・アルドワイヤン Manal AlDowayan

観音寺市中心市街地

E19 よるしるべ 2022
Yorushirube 2022

所在地＝香川県観音寺市伊吹町
（かがわけんかんおんじしいぶきちょう）
面積＝1.05㎢
周囲＝5.4㎞
最高地点＝121.5m（鉄砲石）
世帯数＝164世帯
人口＝323人
0〜14歳＝18人
15〜64歳＝140人
65歳〜＝165人

Location: Ibuki Town,
Kan-onji City, Kagawa Prefecture
Area: 1.05km²
Circumference: 5.4km
Highest Point: 121.5m (Teppou Stone)
Number of Households: 164
Population: 323 people
0-14 Years: 18 people
15-64 Years: 140 people
Over 65 Years: 165 people

アレクサンドラ・コヴァレヴァ＆佐藤敬／KASA
ものがみる夢
ib08 | 旧伊吹小学校

Aleksandra Kovaleva & Kei Sato / KASA | Russia / Japan
The Dreaming of Things
Former Ibuki Elementary School
2022

伊吹島の暮らしを支えていた民具を収集し、2つの風景《海の庭》と《島の庭》で現した作品。漁が盛んな伊吹の漁網を幾層に重ねて海に見立て、窓の外の瀬戸内海の景色へと続いていく《海の庭》は、網のほつれや縫った跡が、波のように陽を浴びて煌めいた。《島の庭》は、カラフルな金網が草花のように教室に広がり、その上に水に関する道具類が並ぶ。水不足に悩まされ、水を大切にしてきた島の暮らしを示唆した。

This work presents two landscapes, a *Sea Garden* and an *Island Garden*, through the collection of the tools that supported life on Ibukijima. The *Sea Garden* is made with many layers of fishing nets from the island, which is a fishing community, like a sea that extends through the window of the house into the scenery of the Seto Inland Sea. In these nets, frays and traces of maintenance glisten in the sun like waves. In the *Island Garden*, colorful wire netting is spread like flowers in a classroom, and tools with a connection to water are placed on it. It speaks of life on the island, which has been beset by water shortages and places high value on water.

3点とも [KK]

ゲゲルボヨ

つながる海

ib09 | 旧郵便局

Gegerboyo | Indonesia
THROUGH THE SEA
Former Post Office
2022

6人で協力して1つの絵を完成させる作家が、インドネシアの伝統的な素材や技法を用いて滞在制作したインスタレーション作品。インドネシア11代目首相が唱えた、海は島々を隔てるのではなくつないでいるという「ジュアンダ宣言」をコンセプトに、便りを通して人々をつないだ場の記憶を表現した。アジアの中でも自然災害が多く、それゆえ自然を崇拝してきたインドネシアと日本に共通している世界観が、築95年の旧郵便局舎に現れた。

An installation work produced in residence by an artist unit of six, who use traditional Indonesian materials and techniques in their paintings. Based on the Declaration of Djuanda 1957, advocated by the 11th Prime Minister of Indonesia, which states that the sea does not separate islands, but rather links them, the work expresses the memories of a place that connected people through letters. The post office, which is 95 years old, represents a shared world view between Japan and Indonesia, both of which are prone to natural disasters and have therefore worshipped nature.

[TT]

マナル・アルドワイヤン

浜辺の歌

ib10 | 旧造船所

Manal AlDowayan | Saudi Arabia
Songs from the Shore
Former Shipyard
2022

伊吹島の海岸沿いにある旧造船所を舞台に、海との関係性を探求した作品。垂直に重ねた漁網に、サウジアラビアの椰子の葉を素材にした200個の篭を設置。作家はこれらの篭を島の参加者とともに燃やし、その火を海水につけて鎮めるという、アラビア湾岸文化圏で女性たちが船乗りの無事を祈る儀式を行った。儀式の記録は、島の女性が歌う声とアラビア語の真珠漁の歌とがオーバーラップする映像で展示。島の漁師、そして彼らとともにある日本の海への、作家の祈りが込められている。

Located in an old shipyard on the coast of Ibukijima, this work examines relationships with the sea. 200 baskets made from palm leaves from Saudi Arabia were placed on stacked fishing nets. These baskets were set alight and, with the participation of local residents, submerged in seawater to quench the flames in a ritual by which women prayed for the safety of sailors in Arabian culture. A video of the ceremony was exhibited along with the overlapping voices of women singing on the island and Arabic pearl fishing songs. This piece expresses the artist's prayers for the fishermen of the island, and the Japanese sea that is with them.

上 [TT] 下 [TSa]

[TT]

石井大五
トイレの家
ib01 | 旧伊吹小学校

Daigo Ishii | Japan
House of Toilet
Former Ibuki Elementary School
2013

旧伊吹小学校の校庭に、島の四季や時間帯によって異なる表情を見せるトイレを設置。天井や壁のスリットは島から世界6都市への方向を示す。そこから射し込む光は、迷路のような島の路地を連想させる。

A public washroom was installed in the schoolyard of the defunct Ibuki Elementary School, which closed in 2010. The toilet shows different expressions depending on the season and the time of day. Slits in the ceiling and walls indicate the direction of six cities around the world. The light shining through resembles the labyrinthine alleys on the island.

所蔵＝観音寺市
Collection: Kan-onji City

[TT]

みかんぐみ＋明治大学学生
イリコ庵
ib03 | 伊吹八幡神社周辺

MIKAN+Students of Meiji University | Japan, France
Iriko Retreat
Around Ibuki Hachiman Shrine
2016

2013年に《伊吹しまづくりラボ》を手がけたみかんぐみが、2016年に建設した「島の小さな集会所」。建築素材に、イリコの乾燥に使われていたせいろなどを使用している。会期中、お茶会が開かれた。

MIKAN, the team that created *the Island Planning Lab* in 2013, constructed a small gathering place on the island. The building material was basket steamer mesh, used to dry small sardines. During the exhibition it hosted a tea party.

所蔵＝観音寺市
Collection: Kan-onji City

2点とも [SM]

よるしるべ2022
まるみデパート、槙黄州、斉藤幹男
E19 | 観音寺市中心市街地

Yorushirube 2022
Marumi Depart,
Kosyu Maki, Mikio Saito | Japan
Kan-onji City Community Area
2022

Event data

10月28日（金）～30日（日）、11月3日（木祝）～5日（土）18:00～21:00
October 28th (Fri) – 30th (Sun), November 3rd (Thu) – 5th (Sat); 18:00–21:00

企画＝一般社団法人 AIS プランニング | 主催＝よるしるべ実行委員会
助成＝瀬戸内国際芸術祭観音寺市実行委員会
Planning: General Incorporated Association AIS Planning | Organization: Yorushirube Executive Committee | Funding: Setouchi Triennale Kanonji Exhibition Executive Committee

夜の観音寺市街地を巡る「よるしるべ」は、観音寺の街や人々の魅力にスポットを当てながら、光のアートやプロジェクションマッピングを用いて街の日常風景に新たな価値を見いだす実験的なアートイベント。2011年にはじまり10回目となる今年は瀬戸内国際芸術祭の公式イベントとして参加。寺院や路地を舞台に点在する20カ所の作品が道しるべとなり、幻想的な風景が夜の街に現れた。

Yorushirube, an experimental art event which began in 2011, marks its 10th iteration this year. People stroll around the town of Kan-onji at night, and illuminations and projection mapping shine a light on the charm of the town and its people, highlighting a search for new value in the everyday scenes of a town. It was first an official Setouchi Triennale event in 2013. About 20 pieces on the corners of temples, shrines and back streets guide viewers, showing the illusionistic landscape of a town at night.

[KK]

栗林隆
伊吹の樹
ib05 | 旧伊吹産院（出部屋）跡地

Takashi Kuribayashi | Japan / Indonesia
Tree of Ibuki
Former Ibuki Maternity Clinic (*debeya*)
2019

伊吹島にはかつて「出部屋」という出産前後の女性たちが集団生活し、養生する場所があった。命の誕生の場であったその跡地に、作家は生命の樹を制作。子宮に見立てた大樹の中を覗くと、一面の鏡が万華鏡のように島の景色を映し出す。母体からこの世界に生まれたことを暗示させる。

Ibukijima used to have a place called *debeya*, where women went after childbirth to live in groups and care for themselves. The artist created a tree of life on this site where life began. Looking into the large-like tree, a mirror on one side reflects the scenery of the island like a kaleidoscope. The work encapsulates the idea that you entered this world from your mother's body.

２点とも [KK]

メラ・ヤルスマ+ニンディティヨ・アディプルノモ
パサング
ib06 | 伊吹島民俗資料館ほか

Mella Jaarsma + Nindityo Adipurnomo | the Netherlands, Indonesia
Pasang
Ibuki Folklore Museum, etc.
2019,2022

「パサング」とはインドネシア語で潮流、またはペアを意味する。航海の安全を願うお守り「船霊（ふなだま）さん」や、２艘１組で網を引く漁船から着想を得て、2019 年に島民と協働で制作。今回は、一部展示方法を変え、島の４カ所で再公開した。

In Indonesian, the word *pasang* means either "current" or "a pair (of items)". This project was produced in 2019 in collaboration with the islanders, and was inspired by tales of the paired *funadama-san* charms that fishermen placed in their boats to pray for safety at sea, and by pairs of boats pulling nets together. For this edition, the mode of display was slightly different, and it was re-produced in four locations on the island.

高松港

Takamatsu Port

所在地＝香川県高松市
（かがわけんたかまつし）
面積＝375.41㎢
最高地点＝946m（大滝山）
世帯数＝18,7511世帯
人口＝417,496人
0～14歳＝52,018人
15～64歳＝233,651人
65歳～＝115,270人
不詳＝16,557人

Location: Takamatsu City,
Kagawa Prefecture
Area: 375.41km²
Highest Point: 946m (Mt. Otaki)
Number of Households: 187,511
Population: 417,496 people
0-14 Years: 52,018 people
15-64 Years: 233,651 people
Over 65 Years: 115,270 people
Unknown: 16,557 people

高松港　*Takamatsu Port*

安土桃山時代、生駒親正によって築かれた海城は別名「玉藻城」と呼ばれ、明治期には「讃州讃岐は高松さまの城が見えます波の上」と唄われた高松城。その周辺の町は築城とともに発展し、1910年に四国と本州を結ぶ宇高航路が開設されると“四国の玄関口”として栄えた。現在も多くのフェリーや旅客船が出入りし、船舶乗降人員は約270万人で全国4位。船は島に住む人々の大事な“足”であり、また観光客の旅の楽しみとして日々行き交う。

JR・私鉄・バスなどの路線が港周辺に集まり、交通の利便性が良く、高松空港へ40分で移動できる。近年、高松空港とアジアの都市を結ぶ国際線が拡充し、外国人観光客が急増した。芸術祭をきっかけに市内の宿泊施設が増え、インバウンド対応のサービスも充実するなど変化が起きている。

The Sea Castle, Takamatsu Castle, built by Ikoma Chikamasa in the Azuchi-Momoyama era (1558–1600) was also known as “Tamamo Castle”. In the Meiji era it appeared in the song *Sanshu-Sanuki with Takamatsu Castle on the Ocean Wave*. The town around the castle developed as it was built, and saw prosperity as a gateway to Shikoku when a route connecting it with Honshu opened in 1910. Today, many ferries and passenger ships arrive here, and the number of alighting passengers has reached 2.7 million, making it the fourth busiest port in Japan. Boats are essential transport for the people living on the islands, and also for the enjoyment of tourists. They travel to and from every day.

Many other forms of transportation are located near the port, including JR trains, private trains, and buses, making it convenient for travel. Takamatsu airport can be reached in just 40 minutes, and with the recent widening of international flights connecting the airport with Asian cities, there has been a rapid increase in the number of foreign tourists. With the art festival, accommodation options in the city have increased, and different services for incoming visitors have become more common, one of the transformations that has occurred.

高松港

tk01　Liminal Air -core-
大巻伸嗣 Shinji Ohmaki

tk03　「銀行家、看護師、探偵、弁護士」
ジュリアン・オピー Julian Opie

tk04　待つ人／内海さん
本間純 Jun Homma

tk13　香川県立ミュージアム
The Kagawa Museum

tk14　高松市美術館
Takamatsu Art Museum

tk24　プロジェクト「同じ月を見た日」
《ドキュメント―同じ月を見た日》《ここに居ない人の灯り》
渡辺篤（アイムヒア プロジェクト） Watanabe Atsushi (I'm here project)

tk25　PAPER SEA
Asaki Oda

あじ竜王山公園

tk18　Watch Tower
ジョン・クルメリング John Körmeling

高松空港

tk19　ウエルカム／ファニーブルー
ヴェロニク・ジュマール Véronique Joumard

五色台

tk26　瀬戸内海歴史民俗資料館
Seto Inland Sea Folk History Museum

屋島

tk15　Suitcase in a Bottle
ラム・カツィール Ram Katzir

tk20　四国村ミウゼアムエントランス「おやねさん」
川添善行[建築] Architecture: Yoshiyuki Kawazoe

tk21　装う神さま
本山ひろ子 Hiroko Motoyama

tk22　高松市屋島山上交流拠点施設「やしまーる」
周防貴之[建築] Architecture: Takashi Suo

tk23　屋島での夜の夢
保科豊巳 Toyomi Hoshina

tk24　プロジェクト「同じ月を見た日」―《月はまた昇る》
渡辺篤（アイムヒア プロジェクト） Watanabe Atsushi (I'm here project)

E20　瀬戸内仕事歌＆四国民話オペラ「二人奥方」
香川大学×瀬戸内の伝統生活文化・芸術発信プロジェクトチーム
Kagawa University × Setouchi Traditional Life Culture and Art Project

あじ竜王山公園
屋島
高松港
Takamatsu Port
高松駅
ことでん高松築港駅
◀至五色台
To Goshikidai
香川県立ミュージアム
四国村ミウゼアム
高松市美術館
▼至高松空港
To Takamatsu Airport
5000m
• アート作品・施設 Artworks, Facilities

高松市屋島山上交流拠点施設「やしまーる」
周防貴之［建築］

tk22 | 屋島

Yashima Mountaintop Park "Yashimâru"
Architecture : Takashi Suo | Japan
Yashima
2022

©SUO

©SUO

屋島山上に新設された周辺地域の自然、歴史、文化を発信する交流拠点。全長200mにわたるガラス張りの回廊が、起伏のある地形と呼応して、蛇行する川のように一周している。有機的な曲線に沿って展望スペースやホールなどの機能があり、屋根には高松市の特産品である庵治石で制作した瓦が約3万枚使われている。開放的な空間設計が瀬戸内海の美しい展望と周囲の緑を建物内部に取り入れ、自然と建築が一体となって来訪者を迎える。

A newly built community base at the top of Mt. Yashima, which serves as a hub for information about the nature, history, and culture of the surrounding area. The 200-meter corridor, covered in glass that resonates with the uneven terrain, is circular, in the shape of a serpentine river. Along the organic curve are an observatory and a hall, and the building features 30,000 roof tiles produced from Aji stone – a specialty of Takamatsu. The spatial planning creates an open feeling, bringing the beautiful views of Setouchi and the surrounding greenery into the interior and welcoming guests to a blend of nature and architecture.

所蔵・運営＝高松市
Collection & Management: Takamatsu City

[KK]

設計＝西村雄輔、加来悠、田中健吾（構造）| 特別協力＝得重聖治、楊帆、鐘亮、劉泳奇、藩佳辰、唐詩堯、Sheikh Afzal、候候、李漳文（絵画制作）| 所蔵＝高松市
Structural Design: Yusuke Nishimura, Yu Kaku, Kengo Tanaka | Painting production: Seiji Tokushige, Yang Fan, Zhong Liang, Liu Yongqi, Fan Jia Chen, Tang Shiyao, Sheikh Afzal, Hu You, Li Zhangwen | Collection: Takamatsu City

保科豊巳
屋島での夜の夢
tk23 | 高松市屋島山上交流拠点施設「やしまーる」

Toyomi Hoshina | Japan
One Night's Dream in Yashima
Yashima Mountaintop Park "Yashimâru"
2022

平安時代末期の源平合戦における「屋島の戦い」から発想を得て、現代にも通じる人間の戦いと自然の脅威、そして「平家物語」にも描かれているような無常観を表現した「パノラマ館再現プロジェクト」。約5 m × 約40 mの絵画とその前面に広がるジオラマで、自然界や人間界の様々な時空間のドラマを複合的に構成。鑑賞者は日本唯一となるパノラマ館で、朝、昼、夜の1日をドラマチックな物語として体験することができる。

Inspired by "The Battle of Yashima" between the Genji and Heike clans at the end of the Heian Period, Hoshina's *Panorama Hall Reconstruction Project* expressed human conflict, the threat of nature, and the transience of life, which are also themes in the tale of Heike. The work was a 5x40 meter painting, with a georama placed before it, featuring dramatic events from different times in the worlds of nature and mankind presented simultaneously. Viewers in this panorama hall, the only one exiting in Japan today, can experience a day flow from morning to night, and from night to day, as a dramatic story.

[TSh]

渡辺篤(アイムヒア プロジェクト)

プロジェクト「同じ月を見た日」—《月はまた昇る》《ドキュメント—同じ月を見た日》《ここに居ない人の灯り》

tk24 | 屋島・れいがん茶屋 / 高松シンボルタワー

Watanabe Atsushi (I'm Here Project) | Japan

Project "The Day We Saw the Same Moon" / The Moon Will Rise Again, Documentary "The Day We Saw the Same Moon", Lights for People Who are Not Here

Reigan café, Yashima / Takamatsu Symbol Tower

2022

《月はまた昇る》は、ひきこもりの人やコロナ禍の孤独を抱えた人が各自の居場所で撮影した月の写真2500枚以上を集め、満ち欠けする月の映像インスタレーションにした作品。サンポート高松では、孤立を感じる誰かが遠隔操作で光を明滅させている作品《ここに居ない人の灯り》の展示や、《ドキュメント—同じ月を見た日》の上映が行われた。国際芸術祭「あいち2022」出展作品とも連携し、屋島山頂から国内外の人々の思いをつないだ。

The Moon Will Rise Again is a work constructed from more than 2,500 photographs of the moon, by *hikikomori* (people living in social withdrawal) and those in isolation due to the coronavirus pandemic, taken from where they were. These images are transformed into a film installation expressing the tides of the moon. At Sunport Takamatsu, *Lights for People Who Are Not Here*, in which those who feel alone can flash a light by remote operation, was exhibited, along with screenings of the *Documentary "The Day We Saw the Same Moon"*. Working in conjunction with work at another art festival, Aichi Triennale 2022, the emotions of people in and outside of the country were connected from the peak of Mt. Yashima.

特別協力＝《月はまた昇る》らばんか、Ayako、marmotte、たかはしじゅんいち、道後ミカ、増山士郎、蒼晶、渡辺篤／アイムヒア プロジェクト（月の写真）|《ここに居ない人の灯り》アイムヒア プロジェクトメンバー（遠隔ライト操作）|《ドキュメント「同じ月を見た日」》井上桂佑（撮影）、布村善和（構成・編集）

Cooperation: *The Moon Will Rise Again*, Photos of the moon: Rabanka, Ayako, marmotte, Junichi Takahashi, Mika Dogo, Shiro Masuyama, Akira Aoi, Atsushi Watanabe / I'm here project | *Lights for people who are not here*, Remote light operation: I'm here project members | *Documentary "The Day We Saw the Same Moon"*, Filming: Keisuke Inoue, Composition & Editing: Yoshikazu Homura

上《月はまた昇る》 下《ここに居ない人の灯り》2点とも [KK]

高松市美術館

特別展「みる誕生 鴻池朋子展」

tk14 | 高松港周辺

Takamatsu Art Museum

Tomoko Konoike The Birth of Seeing

Takamatsu Port Area

2022

鴻池は生まれたての体で世界と出会う驚きを「みる誕生」と名づけた。観客は眼だけではなく、手で看(み)る、鼻で診(み)る、耳で視(み)る、そして引力や呼吸で観(み)て、眠っていた感覚を目覚めさせたことだろう。エントランスホールには《皮トンビ》が飛翔し、展示室には《どうぶつの糞》などが人間の痕跡である美術館のコレクションとともに展示された。また最後の部屋「インタータイダル・ゾーン(潮間帯)」では、大島でも展示した絵画クラブ「金陽会」の作品や、手芸《物語るテーブルランナー》などが波のように寄せ合っていた。

Konoike termed the encounter of the world by a body just born "the birth of seeing". The audience does not just use vision – they also feel with their hands and sense with their noses and ears, opening an awareness of gravity and breathing that had been dormant. *Leather Kites* flew at the entrance hall and, in the exhibition room, *Animal Dung* and other objects were on display alongside the museum collection, which can be described as "a trace of the human". In the final room, the Intertidal Zone, the handicraft work *The Storytelling Table Runner,* and works produced by the Kinyokai art club, were shown as though waves were coming together.

5点とも [SN]

7月16日(土)~9月4日(日) | 休館=月曜日(7月18日、8月15日は開館)、7月19日(火) | 料金=一般 1,000円、大学生 500円、小中高生無料、ほか | 来場者数=8,090人

関連イベント=鑑賞会「みる誕生会」鴻池朋子、担当学芸員 | クロストーク「絵の波打ち際から」蔵座江美、鴻池朋子 | クロストーク「糞土思想から "みる" 驚き」伊沢正名、鴻池朋子 | 「筆談ダンス Dance in Writing」木下知威、鴻池朋子 | 学芸員とボランティア civi によるトポストーク | 学芸員によるこども鑑賞プログラム | ふらっとアート「ウンチをつくろう!」 | 学校と美術館のためのプログラム | ミニコンサート「動物たちの音楽会 2022」香川大学、青山夕夏

主催=高松市美術館
助成=一般財団法人自治総合センター、公益財団法人朝日新聞文化財団

July 16th (Sat) –September 4th (Sun) | Closed: Mondays (Open on July 18th, August 15th), July 19th (Tue) | Admission: General 1,000 yen, University Students 500 yen, Age 18 and under free, etc. | Attendance: 8,090 people

Related Events: Viewing session: *The Birth of Seeing* by Tomoko Konoike and Museum Curator | Cross Talk Session: *Intertidal Zone*, Emi Zoza and Tomoko Konoike | Cross Talk Session: *Surprises from the Perspective of Excrement Ecology*, Masana Izawa and Tomoko Konoike | *Dance in Writing*, Tomotake Kinoshita and Tomoko Konoike | *Topos Talk*, Museum Curator and volunteer group Civi | *Kids Viewing Program*, Museum Curator | Workshop: *"Let's Make a Poo!"* | School and Museum Program | Mini Concert: *Recital by Animals 2022*, Yuka Aoyama (Supported by Kagawa University)

Organization: Takamatsu Art Museum
Funding: Japan Center for Local Autonomy, The Asahi Shimbun Foundation

「せとうちの大気　美術の視点」[SM]

香川県立ミュージアム

tk13 | 高松港周辺

The Kagawa Museum
Takamatsu Port Area
2022

春「戦後デザイン運動の原点 ―デザインコミッティーの人々とその軌跡」

川崎市岡本太郎美術館と共同企画。戦後デザイン運動の先駆けとなった国際デザインコミッティー（現・日本デザインコミッティー）の創立から1960年代頃までを中心に、創立メンバーらの家具・プロダクトデザイン、建築作品の模型、写真、壁画や絵画作品等を展示。

夏「せとうちの大気　美術の視点」

香川県や瀬戸内に所縁のある美術家や写真家、映像作家、デザイナーなど10名の作家が、様々な視点から瀬戸内の魅力を引き出す作品を展示。音や映像、光など、様々な手法で描き出された情景が鑑賞者の五感を刺激した。

秋「風景が物語る瀬戸内の力ー自然・歴史・人の共鳴ー」

＜ユートピア＞＜自然＞＜生活＞＜名所＞＜近現代そして未来＞の5つのテーマをもとに、厳選された約100点の絵画を展示。各地の瀬戸内海の姿を表した中世から現代までの作品が一堂に会し、歴史、民俗、美術、自然など、これまでにない多面的な視点から瀬戸内海の魅力を紹介した。

春＝4月9日（土）～5月29日（日）| 休館＝毎週月曜日（5月2日は開館）| 料金＝一般1,200円、小中高生無料、ほか | 来場者数＝5,423人 |
関連イベント＝講演会「グラフィックデザインの現在（いま）」色部義昭 | スペシャルトーク・佐藤玲子 | ワークショップ「ピンホールカメラで撮影しよう」| ワークショップ「わたしの好きなデザイン」| ワークショップ「ペーパークラフトでつくる県庁インテリア」| ワークショップ「つくろう！ ミニチュア・坐ることを拒否する椅子」| 学芸講座「社会に開かれたデザインへ ー 香川県庁舎をめぐって」日置瑶子
助成＝一般財団法人地域創造

夏＝8月5日（金）～9月4日（日）| 休館＝毎週月曜日 | 料金＝一般1,200円、小中高生無料 | 来場者数＝2,824人 | アーティスト＝浅見貴子、北村大樹、藏本秀彦、得丸成人、南条嘉毅、水谷一、三村昌道、宮武かおる、宮脇慎太郎、矢野恵利子
関連イベント＝出品作家によるラウンドトーク | 出品作家や担当学芸員によるナイトトーク
助成＝公益財団法人朝日新聞文化財団

秋＝9月23日（金・祝）～11月6日（日）| 休館＝毎週月曜日（10月10日は開館）、10月11日（火）| 料金＝一般1,200円、小中高生無料 | 来場者数＝4,289人 |
関連イベント＝講演会「大地の成り立ちから見た瀬戸内の風景」長谷川修一 | 講演会「くらしが紡ぐ瀬戸内の風景」上杉和央 | 学芸講座「瀬戸内を旅する」川邉優佑 | 学芸講座「画家たちが眺めた瀬戸内海」窪美酉嘉子 | 学芸講座「讃岐十景と讃岐百景」田井静明 | ワークショップ「瀬戸内ロックバランシング」| ワークショップ「屋島は物語る」長谷川修一
助成＝独立行政法人日本芸術文化振興会

主催＝香川県立ミュージアム

Spring : *The Origin of Japanese Design Movement After WWII : The Tracks of Design Committee*

An exhibition held in cooperation with the Taro Okamoto Museum in Kawasaki. Focusing on the period from the foundation of the Design Committee, a pioneer of the post-war design movement, to the 1960s, it exhibited furniture and product design by the founders, including architectural models, photographs, murals, and paintings.

Summer : *Atmosphere Filling SETOUCHI*

10 creators linked to the Kagawa and Setouchi areas, consisting of artists, photographers, filmmakers, and designers, exhibited work that draws out the appeal of Setouchi from various perspectives. These works utilize a range of methods, such as sound, film, and light to express the scenery and stimulate the senses of the viewers.

Autumn : *The Energy of SETOUCHI found in its Scenery —the Symphony of Nature, History and Human—*

100 carefully selected pieces were exhibited, under the five themes of utopia, nature, life, tourist spots, the modern and the contemporary, and the future. Work from the middle ages through to contemporary times that express different views of Setouchi were collected in one place, introducing the attraction of the Seto Inland Sea from the most diverse of perspectives – from history, tradition, art, and nature.

Spring: April 9th (Sat)–May 29th (Sun) | Closed: Mondays | Admission: General 1,200 yen, Age 18 and under free, etc. | Attendance: 5,423 people | Related Events: Lecture *The Current Moment in Graphic Design*, Yoshiaki Irobe | Special Talk by Reiko Sato | Workshop *Shooting with a Pin-hole Camera* | Workshop *My Favorite Design* | Workshop *Prefectural Office Interior in Papercraft* | Workshop *Make a Miniature "Chair Refusing to Seat Anyone"* | Cultural Seminar *Design Open to Society: On Kagawa Prefectural Office*, Yoko Hioki | Funding: Japan Foundation for Regional Art-Activities

Summer: August 5th (Fri)–September 4th (Sun) | Closed; Mondays | Admission: General 1,200 yen, Age 18 and under free | Attendance: 2,824 people | Artists: Takako Azami, Daiki Kitamura, Hidehiko Kuramoto, Naruhito Tokumaru, Yoshitaka Nanjo, Masamichi Mimura, Hajime Mizutani, Kaoru Miyatake, Shintaro Miyawaki, Eriko Yano | Related Events | Round table discussion by participating artists | Night talk by participating artists and curators | Funding: The Asahi Shimbun Foundation

Autumn: September 23th (Fri)–November 6th (Sun) | Closed: Mondays (Open on October 10th), October 11th (Tue) | Admission: General 1,200 yen, Age 18 and under free | Attendance: 4,289 people | Related Events | Lecture: *Views of Setouchi from the Perspective of the Composition of the Land*, Shuichi Hasegawa | Lecture: *The Landscape of Setouchi Woven by Life*, Kazuhiro Uesugi | Cultural Seminar: *Traveling Around Setouchi*, Yusuke Kawabe | Cultural Seminar: *Seto Inland Sea in the Eyes of Painters*, Yukako Kubomi | Cultural Seminar: *"Ten Views of Sanuki" and "A Hundred Views of Sanuki"*, Yoshiaki Tai | Workshop: *Setouchi Rock Balancing* | Workshop: *Yashima Tells its Story*, Shuichi Hasegawa | Foundation: Japan Arts Council

Organization: The Kagawa Museum

[KK]

大巻伸嗣

Liminal Air -core-

tk01 | 高松港

Shinji Ohmaki | Japan
Liminal Air -core-
Takamatsu Port
2010

港にそびえ立つ、高さ８ｍの２本の柱。カラフルな装飾の一部が鏡面になっていて、周囲の情景を映し出す。港の移りゆく景色が作品の様々な表情を作っている。

Two 8-meter high pillars stand at Takamatsu Port. Partly covered with mirrors, the colorful pillars reflect the views of the surrounding port, the sea, and the buildings, altering their appearance depending on where the viewer stands, the time of day, and other circumstances.

[KK]

Asaki Oda

PAPER SEA

tk25 | 高松港旅客ターミナルビル

Asaki Oda | Japan / USA
PAPER SEA
Takamatsu Port Passenger Terminal Building
2022

芸術祭を訪れた人々が集うターミナルビルに、海の世界を想像させるインスタレーション作品が現れた。紙で造形されたウミガメやスナメリなど表情豊かな生き物たちが、目の前の瀬戸内海から飛び出してきたかのように群れをなして空間を泳ぎ回り、島へ行く旅人たちを歓迎した。

An installation piece evoking the world of the sea appeared at the terminal building. Lively creatures like sea turtles and whales made of paper swim together in a pod, as though they are coming out of the Seto Inland Sea before the eyes of the visitors, welcoming them as they travel out to the islands.

本間純

待つ人／内海さん

tk04 | 高松駅南交通広場待合所

Jun Homma | Japan
Waiting for / Mr. Inland Sea
Takamatsu Station South Traffic Square, Waiting Area
2013

[KiT]

高速バス待合所の外壁に隠れている、島の人々の姿を表した彫刻作品《待つ人》。待合所内では映像作品《内海さん》を上映している。バスを待つ時間を豊かにしてくれる作品。

Waiting For, a sculpture portraying the people of the island, hides on the outer wall of the waiting room at the express bus terminal. Inside the waiting room, a film called *Mr. Inland Sea* plays. The time spent waiting for the bus is enriched by these two works.

所蔵＝高松市 | Collection: Takamatsu City

ジュリアン・オピー

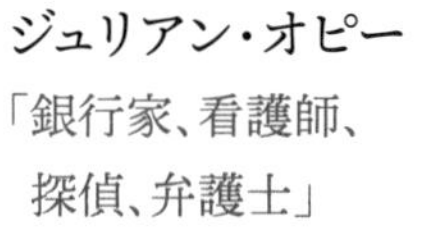

「銀行家、看護師、探偵、弁護士」

tk03 | ことでん高松築港駅付近

Julian Opie | UK
Banker, Nurse, Detective, Lawyer
Around Kotoden Takamatsu-Chikko Station
2015

2点とも [AT]

地元産の石などを用いた４つの彫刻。白大理石の「銀行家」、庵治石の「看護師」、石灰岩の「探偵」、黒御影の「弁護士」が、街を歩く人々に混じって並んでいる。

Four stone sculptures stand, made with local stone. A *Banker* in white marble, *Nurse* in Aji stone, *Detective* in limestone, and *Lawyer* in black granite are lined up among the people walking in street.

所蔵＝高松市 | Collection: Takamatsu City

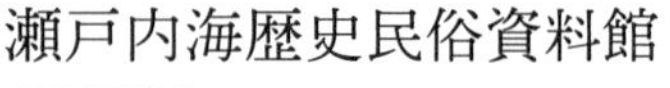

瀬戸内海歴史民俗資料館

tk26 | 五色台

Seto Inland Sea Folk History Museum
Goshikidai

2点とも [KK]

瀬戸内地方の11府県全域を対象とした歴史や民俗に関する資料を収集・研究・展示する広域資料館。山本忠司による建築は1975年に日本建築学会賞（作品賞）を受賞し、香川県を代表する建築物として評価されている。瀬戸内とその周辺地域から収集した木造船や漁撈用具、船大工用具、背負運搬具など国指定重要有形民俗文化財を中心とする民俗資料を常設展示するほか、会期中には「戦後香川の“新たな産業工芸”創出―ジェトロ収集海外優秀商品と古民芸に学ぶ―」などの企画展を開催。長きにわたる瀬戸内の人々の営みを今に伝える。

A large museum that collects and exhibits references related to the history and traditions of all 11 regions of Setouchi. The building by Tadashi Yamamoto won the Prize of AIJ (the Architectural Institute of Japan) in 1975, and is considered a landmark building of Kagawa. The permanent collection includes wooden boats, fishing tools, shipbuilding tools, and implements for carrying things on the back – folk materials, of which many are designated as National Important Tangible Folk Cultural Properties. During the festival periods it held special exhibitions, including *Creation of a New Craft Industry in Post-War Kagawa: Learning from the JETRO Collection of Foreign Products and Traditional Folk Crafts*. The museum tells the long history of life in Setouchi up to the current day.

所蔵＝香川県 | Collection: Kagawa Prefecture

[Ylc]

ジョン・クルメリング

Watch Tower

tk18 | あじ竜王山公園

John Körmeling | the Netherlands
Watch Tower
Aji Ryuozan Park
2016

設計＝野村正人建築研究所 | 特別協力＝Hamer Körmeling（鳥制作）| 所蔵＝高松市
Architecture: M. Nomura Associates | Bird production: Hamer Körmeling | Collection: Takamatsu City

庵治町竜王山の山頂に佇むアーチ状の作品。Watchという単語の2つの意味をもじって、腕時計(watch)の形で「見晴塔」(Watch Tower) を制作した。時計の文字盤部分には日時計の目盛りが刻まれている。

An arch-like watchtower stands at the peak of Aji Ryuozan Park. Playing on the double meaning of the word "watch", it was created in the shape of a wristwatch. A sundial is placed on the face.

左《ウエルカム》右《ファニーブルー》2点とも [KiT]

ヴェロニク・ジュマール

ウエルカム

ファニーブルー

tk19 | 高松空港旅客ターミナルビル国際線ロビー

Véronique Joumard | France
Welcome / Funny Blue
International Flight Lobby, Takamatsu Airport Terminal Building
2013

吹き抜けから下がる金色のシートが風を受けて揺れる《ウエルカム》と、虹色に光るフィルムが外の景色を鮮やかに彩る《ファニーブルー》。高松空港の風景を取り込んで変化する作品。

In the installation *Welcome*, reflective gold sheets hung from the ceiling sway in the wind. *Funny Blue* is a work of rainbow-colored film attached to window glass, coloring the outside view. They take the landscape of Takamatsu Airport and transform it.

四国村ミウゼアム　*Shikokumura Museum*

屋島山麓にある広大な野外博物館。江戸時代から大正時代に建てられた住居や蔵、砂糖づくりの作業小屋など、実際に使われていた民家や建造物が移築復元され、四季折々の豊かな自然を感じながら散策ができる。また安藤忠雄設計の「四国村ギャラリー」や、古民家を移築したうどん店「わら家」もある。

A huge outdoor museum extending at the bottom of Mt. Yashima. Formerly used houses, warehouses, and a sugar-making workshop, all built between the Edo and Taisho eras, were moved and reconstructed, allowing visitors to walk around them, and experience them in the rich nature of each season. The museum also features the Shikokumura Gallery, designed by Tadao Ando, and the udon restaurant Wara-ya, which was developed from a former Japanese house.

[KK]

四国村ミウゼアムエントランス「おやねさん」

川添善行［建築］

tk20 | 四国村ミウゼアム

Shikokumura Museum Entrance “Oyanesan”
Architecture: Yoshiyuki Kawazoe | Japan
Shikokumura Museum
2022

四国村の入口に新設されたエントランス棟。なだらかな曲線を描く特徴的な屋根は、伝統的な切妻屋根形式を現代の技術によってアレンジし建物の機能と調和させたもので、「おやねさん」の愛称の由来でもある。1階にはチケット売り場やミュージアムショップがあり、2階には四国村に関する資料が観覧できる展示スペースも。高松市のシンボルでもある景勝地・屋島の麓の新たなランドマークとなった。

A newly constructed building placed at the entrance of the Shikokumura Museum. The characteristic roof (*yane*) with a gentle curved line is in a traditional Japanese gable roof form, with modern technology enabling it to harmonize with the main building. The nickname *Oyanesan* derives from this roof, too. On the first floor there is a ticket counter and a museum shop, and there is a space on the second floor for viewing documents related to Shikokumura. The museum is a landmark at the bottom of Mt. Yashima, known both for its splendid views and as a symbol of Takamatsu.

所蔵・運営＝公益財団法人 四国民家博物館

Collection & Management: Shikokumura Museum Foundation

[KK]

ラム・カツィール

Suitcase in a Bottle

tk15 | 四国村ミウゼアム

Ram Katzir | Israel / the Netherlands
Suitcase in a Bottle
Shikokumura Museum
2019

古びたスーツケース状のオブジェが入った大きなボトル。移民と絶滅の問題を題材にする作家が、四国村の池に浮かべた。2022年の開催期間には、村内の「砂糖しめ小屋」に展示された。

This installation featured a weathered suitcase set inside an enormous bottle. The artist, who deals with issues of migration and extinction in his work, floated it in the pond at Shikokumura Museum. It was later relocated to a sugar-making workshop, in the village for display.

所蔵・運営＝公益財団法人 四国民家博物館
Collection & Management: Shikokumura Museum Foundation

3点とも [KK]

本山ひろ子

装う神さま

tk21 | 四国村ミウゼアム

Hiroko Motoyama | Japan
Deity in Disguise
Shikokumura Museum
2022

古い集落には路地裏やそこかしこに「なにか」がいる、と語る作家が制作したのは、四国村に居ついた神さまがもののけに姿を換えた化身の彫刻作品。うどん狐、雨降使、なでうさぎ、ご隠居猿、花咲かヒツジさんや人鳥が、四国村の各所に現れ、その場所に居つくことになった理由が「むかしむかしのおはなし」として添えられた。四季折々の自然とともに点在する歴史的な建築物を巡るみちしるべとなり、かつてそこにあった人々の営みを想起させる。

In the back streets and hidden corners of old villages, "something" exists, says the artist, who created sculptural works depicting the gods inhabiting Shikoku Mura village transfiguring into *mononoke* (animal ghosts). An udon-fox, a sea slug, a rabbit for stroking, old monkeys, flower-blooming sheep, and half-human half-bird appear across the village, and the process of each god settling there was explained as a "Tale from Long Ago". These were information points for people walking around the historical architecture which remains in many places, compliments the seasons of nature, and evokes the lives of the people who used to reside there.

所蔵・運営＝公益財団法人 四国民家博物館 | 協賛＝カトーレック株式会社

Collection & Management: Shikokumura Museum Foundation | Sponsor: Katolec Corporation

香川大学×瀬戸内の伝統生活文化・芸術発信プロジェクトチーム
瀬戸内仕事歌&四国民話オペラ「二人奥方」

E20 | 四国村ミウゼアム・小豆島農村歌舞伎舞台

Kagawa University × Setouchi Traditional Life Culture and Art Project | Japan
The Setouchi Work Songs & Shikoku Folktale Opera: "The Two Madams"
Shodoshima Rural Kabuki stage, Shikokumura Museum
2022

2点とも [SM]

瀬戸内地域に暮らす人たちの生活から生まれ、職人・農民・漁師・浜子たちが歌った音楽を、郷土の仕事風景とともに蘇らせた「瀬戸内仕事歌」。香川の芸術、文化界の先人たちによって57年前に生み出され、四国に狐がいない理由を物語る痛快な民話オペラ「二人奥方」。2つの公演は、瀬戸内地域の音楽芸術の魅力発見と発信につながった。

In *The Setouchi Work Songs*, the music born from the lives of people in Setouchi, sung by artisans, farmers, fishermen, and workers in the salt fields, was revitalized through reenactment of labor in the region. *The Two Madams* is a poignant folktale opera created 57 years ago by cultural predecessors, explaining why there are no foxes in Shikoku. These two performances supported the discovery of the musical art of Setouchi and promoted it.

[SM]

Event Data

5月15日(日)15:00〜、18:00〜 | 料金＝一般3,000円、小中高生1,500円、ほか | 来場者数＝411人

第１部　瀬戸内仕事歌

芸術監督・演出＝若井健司 | 映像原画＝古草敦史 | 舞踊振付＝森ゆかり | MC＝中越恵美 | 助演＝香川大学生 | 出演＝石切り唄保存会、讃岐民謡保存会、桑山会宇多津社中、現代舞踊研究会「土曜族」

第２部　民話オペラ「二人奥方」

作曲＝菅野浩和 | 台本＝瀬川拓男 | 芸術監督・演出＝若井健司(香川大学) | 指揮・編曲＝岡田知也(香川大学) | コンサートマスター＝青山夕夏(香川大学) | 音楽アドバイザー＝東浦亜希子(香川大学) | 出演＝國方里佳、佐治名津子、三木伸哉、綾智成、樫村誠、中越恵美 | 合唱＝高松市立屋島中学校合唱部 | 助演(黒子・腰元)＝香川大学生 | アンサンブル＝香川大学生・OB・教員

音響＝津村哲治 | 照明＝西山和宏 | 舞台監督＝田和伸二(タワ・スタッフコラボレーション) | 演出助手＝大平伊織(四国二期会) | 衣装＝原和裁専門学院、ほか | メイク・かつら、ほか＝認定NPO法人農村歌舞伎祇園座保存会、ほか

May 15th (Sun); 15:00–, 18:00– | Admission: General 3,000 yen, Students (ages 6–18) 1,500 yen, etc. | Attendance: 411 people

The First Part: *The Setouchi Work Songs*

Artistic Director: Kenji Wakai | Original picture of video: Atsushi Furukusa | Choreographer: Yukari Mori | Host: Emi Nakagoshi | Supporting performance: Kagawa University Students | Performance: Ishikiri-Uta Preservation Society, Sanuki Folk Song Preservation Society, Souzan-Kai Utazu Group, Study group of modern dance “Doyō-Zoku”

The Second Part: *Shikoku Folktale Opera “The Two Madams”*

Composition: Hirokazu Sugano | Scenario: Takuo Segawa | Artistic director: Kenji Wakai | Conducting and Arrangement: Tomoya Okada | Concertmaster: Yuka Aoyama | Music advisor: Akiko Higashiura | Cast: Rika Kunikata, Natsuko Saji, Shinya Miki, Tomonari Aya, Makoto Kashimura, Emi Nakagoshi | Chorus: Takamatsu City Yashima Junior High School Chorus Club | Supporting performance as *Kuroko* and *Koshimoto*: Kagawa University Students | Ensemble: Kagawa University Students, Graduates, Teachers

Sound: Tetsuji Tsumura | Lighting: Kazuhiro Nishiyama | Stage Manager: Shinji Tawa (TAWA Staff Collaboration) | Assistant director: Iori Ohira (Shikoku Niki-Kai) | Costume: HARA Wasai Professional School, etc. | Make and Wig: Approved Specified Nonprofit Organization Rural Kabuki Gionza Preservation Society and more.

宇野港

Uno Port

所在地＝岡山県玉野市
（おかやまけんたまのし）
面積＝103.58㎢
最高地点＝403.1m（金甲山）
世帯数＝24,090世帯
人口＝56,531人
0〜14歳＝5,608人
15〜64歳＝28,734人
65歳〜＝21,774人
不詳＝415人

Location: Tamano City, Okayama Prefecture
Area: 103.58km²
Highest Point: 403.1m (Mt. Kinkou)
Number of Households: 24,090
Population: 56,531 people
0-14 Years: 5,608 people
15-64 Years: 28,734 people
Over 65 Years: 21,774 people
Unknown: 415 people

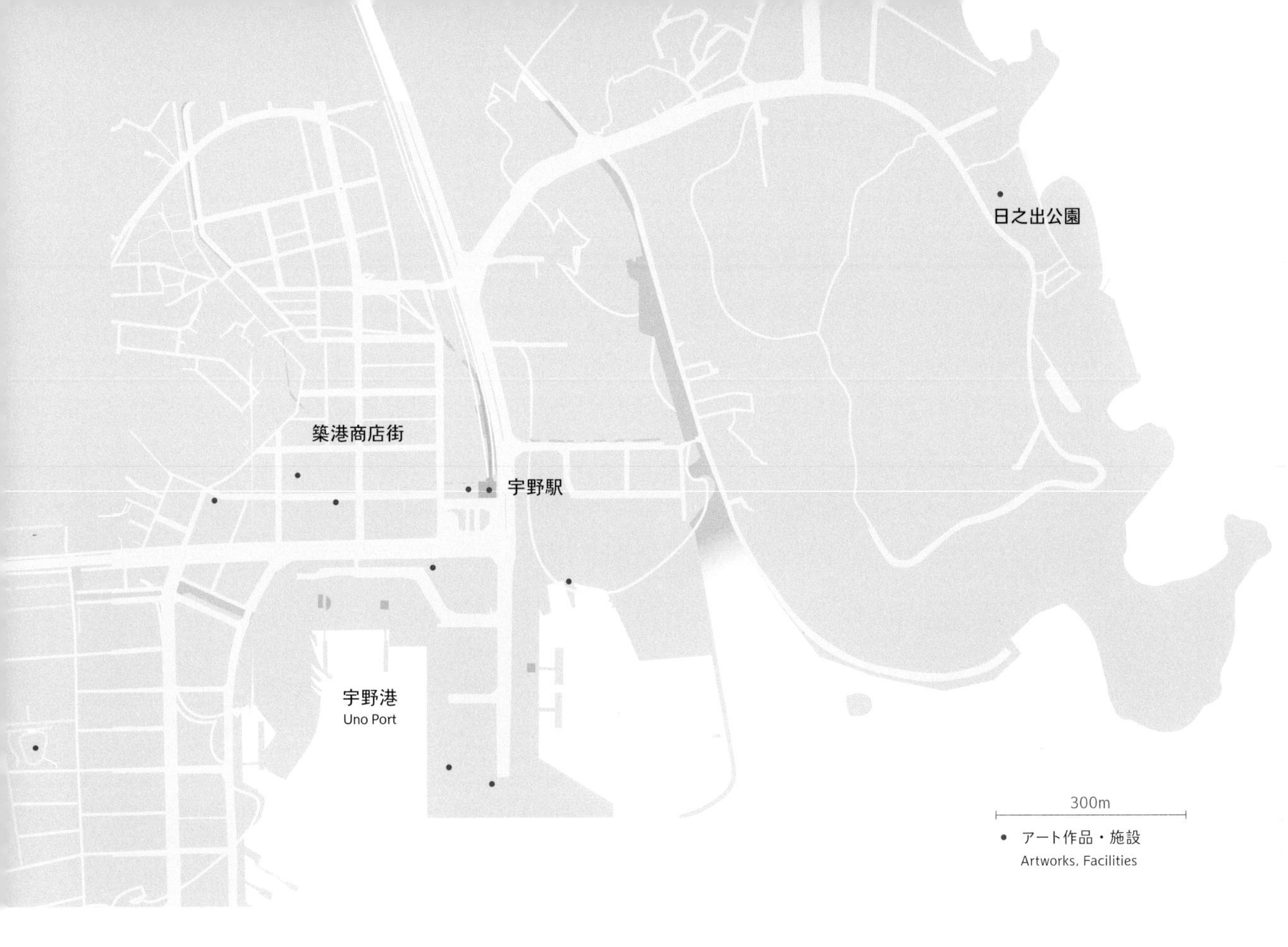

築港商店街

un10 実話に基づく
ムニール・ファトゥミ Mounir Fatmi

un11 時間屋
長谷川仁 Jin Hasegawa

un12 赤い家は通信を求む
片岡純也＋岩竹理恵
Junya Kataoka + Rie Iwatake

宇野港周辺

un02 舟底の記憶
小沢敦志 Atsushi Ozawa

un03 終点の先へ
小沢敦志 Atsushi Ozawa

un04 宇野のチヌ／宇野コチヌ
淀川テクニック Yodogawa Technique

un05 JR宇野みなと線アートプロジェクト
エステル・ストッカー Esther Stocker

un08 海の記憶
内田晴之 Haruyuki Uchida

un13 本州から見た四国
アイシャ・エルクメン Ayşe Erkmen

日之出公園

un14 S.F. (Seaside Friction)
金氏徹平 Teppei Kaneuji

宇野港　*Uno Port*

岡山県の南端に位置する玉野市の港で、児島半島の根元にある天与の良港。1988 年の瀬戸大橋の開通まで約 90 年間活躍した宇高連絡船の本州側の発着地として、多くの人とモノが行き交う重要な物流の拠点だった。今もフェリーなどの定期航路や大型クルーズ船の寄港地として港町の雰囲気が漂う。玉野市沿岸部では古くから土器による製塩が行われ、明治期に塩田が広がっていた。現在、塩田の風景を見ることはできないが、今もなお現役の製塩工場があり、塩づくりを続けている。また、約 1km の白砂青松の海岸線をもち、夏は海水浴で賑わう渋川海岸は、1100 年代に西行法師が訪れたとされ、海辺に暮らす人々の歌を詠んだ。

新幹線が停車する岡山駅から宇野駅まで約 1 時間で移動でき、近年は島への玄関口として国内外の人が行き交う港となった。港近くの築港商店街周辺には宿泊施設や飲食店が増えている。

A port in Tamano, at the southern tip of Okayama, which is naturally blessed with a location at the root of the Kojima Peninsula. Until the opening of the Seto Ohashi Bridge in 1988, Uno was an important hub for people and goods as a terminal on the mainland of the Uko Renrakusen route, which was used for 90 years. It still retains the atmosphere of a port, as a stop for regular ferry routes and huge cruise ships. Salt production using stoneware has been conducted on the coast of Tamano since long ago, and in the Meiji era many salt fields spread out. While it is not possible to see the salt fields anymore, salt production is still ongoing in the salt manufacturing factory. Tamano also has a coastline with green pine trees on white sand, and Shibukawa Beach is popular with visitors in the summer. Saigyo Houshi visited this place in the 1100s, and composed poems about the people who lived by the sea.

It takes an hour to travel to Uno Station from Okayama, where the Shinkansen stops, and it has become a frequently used gateway to the islands, full of people from inside and outside of Japan. The Chikko shopping street near the port has seen a proliferation of accommodation and places for dining.

宇野港街中プロジェクト *Uno Port Town Project*

造船や鉄鋼、製塩などで栄えた街の面影を残す宇野港周辺のエリア。かつての商店や病院、民家を活用した３つの屋内作品と、２つの屋外作品を新たに加え、回遊できるアートの街として新展開した。本州から島々への玄関口として新たな魅力が加わり、瀬戸内からの海風が追い風のようになって地域の賑わいが生まれた。

The area around Uno Port retains the atmosphere of a town flourishing with ship-building, steel-making, and salt farming. Three interior pieces of artwork, utilizing a former shop, hospital, and house, as well as two exterior pieces were newly installed here to develop it as a town of art that people can tour around. A new charm has been added to the port that serves as a gateway from the mainland to the islands, where the sea breeze from the Seto Inland Sea is like a following wind bringing liveliness to the town.

４点とも [KK]

片岡純也＋岩竹理恵

赤い家は通信を求む

un12 | 築港商店街

Junya Kataoka + Rie Iwatake | Japan
The Red House wants communication
Chikko Shopping Street
2022

商店街の片隅に佇む赤い小さな家で展開された作品。地球儀、一輪車、バケツ、電灯などが、回転・遠心力のシンプルな動きにより連動する。家の特徴に合わせ、築港の町や宇野の海で撮影した写真やコラージュ、ドローイングが至るところに展示され、床のタイルのはがれた部分にまでユーモラスな視点が潜んでいる。増改築を繰り返した家が、作家の手により通信装置として再生し、外の世界で起こる様々な事象と家の中が共鳴している。

An artwork developed in a small red house in the corner of a shopping street. Items such as a globe, a unicycle, a bucket, and a light spin in concert, with a simple centrifugal force. To match the characteristics of the house, photographs taken of the town of Chikko and the sea of Uno, along with collages and drawings are displayed throughout the house, even as far as the traces of removed floor tiles, where the artists' humorous point of view is hidden. The house, which has been extended and redeveloped, was regenerated at the hands of the artists as a communication device, with various things happening in the outside world and the interior resonating with one another.

特別協力＝両備グループ、ピープルソフトウェア株式会社
協賛＝一般社団法人 玉野青年会議所

Cooperation: Ryobi Group, People Software Corporation
Sponsor: Junior Chamber International Tamano

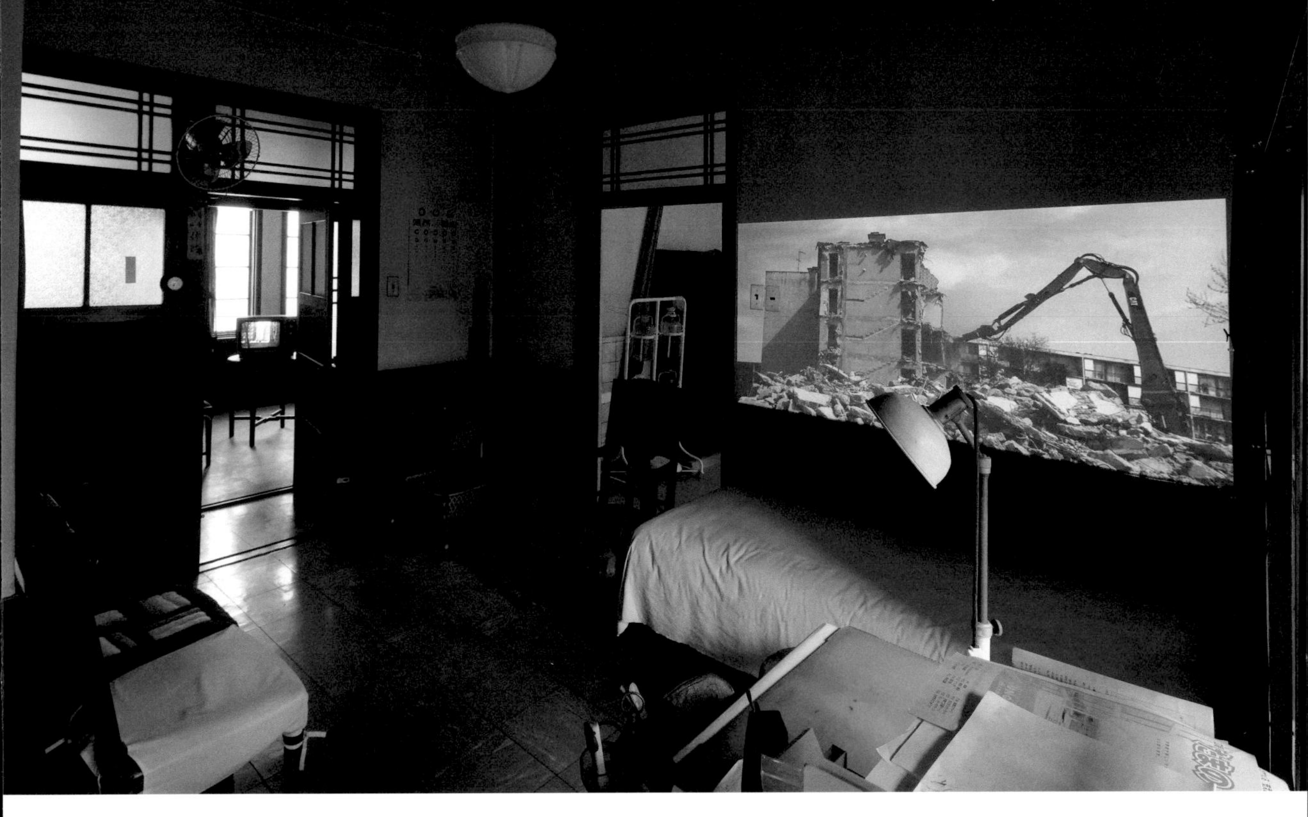

ムニール・ファトゥミ
実話に基づく
un10 | 築港商店街・旧三宅医院

Mounir Fatmi | Morocco / France
Based on True Story
Former Miyake Clinic,
Chikko Shopping Street
2022

建築も人間と同様に「病い」にかかると語る作家が、約40年空家となっていた病院で展開した映像インスタレーション。各部屋に展示したのは、かつて96の国と地域からの移民が暮らしていたパリ郊外の建築物が解体される様子の記録である。これらは2000年から2005年に撮影された15本の映像と16点の写真で構成されており、破壊される様子を遺構となった病院に展開することで、建築物に宿る個々の記憶や感情を現在に伝えた。

For Mounir Fatmi, who developed a film installation in a hospital that has been empty for 40 years, architecture also "gets sick", just like humans. Exhibited in each room is a record of a building demolished in a Parisian suburb, where immigrants from 96 different countries and regions had been living. The work consists of 15 films and 16 photographs shot between 2000 and 2005. By displaying the way it was dismantled in the relic of a hospital, the work communicates the individuality of memory and emotion residing in architecture to the present day.

特別協力＝両備グループ、ピープルソフトウェア株式会社
協賛＝一般社団法人 玉野青年会議所
Cooperation: Ryobi Group, People Software Corporation
Sponsor: Junior Chamber International Tamano

3点とも [KK]

長谷川仁

時間屋

un11 | 築港商店街・旧中山靴店

Jin Hasegawa | Japan
Time Shop
Former Nakayama Shoe Shop,
Chikkou Shopping Street
2022

塩を素材に、はるか昔から続く時間の流れを表現した作品。砂時計の中に入ったような空間に、天井から一筋の塩が流れ落ち続ける。壁には塩の結晶で数字が描かれ、10秒でひと回りする流木の時計があり、止まることのない時間を意識させる。鑑賞者は流れ落ちてくる塩をコップで10秒間受け止めて、今この時間を体験する。コップに入った塩は「46億年分の10秒」として購入できる。併設する展示室では玉野の製塩の歴史について資料展示を行った。

Using salt as a material, this work expresses the flow of time and its continuation from the ancient past. In a space resembling the inside of an hourglass, a stream of salt falls. On the wall, numbers are written in salt crystals, and the hands of a clock constructed of driftwood rotates once every ten seconds, all of which serve to remind the viewer that time never ceases. Each viewer can fill a cup with the falling salt for 10 seconds, experiencing this instant. That salt can be purchased as "10 seconds of 4.6 billion years". In the adjacent exhibition room, documents detailing the history of Tamano's salt-refining were on display.

特別協力＝両備グループ、ピープルソフトウェア株式会社
協賛＝一般社団法人 玉野青年会議所
Cooperation: Ryobi Group, People Software Corporation
Sponsor: Junior Chamber International Tamano

金氏徹平

S.F. (Seaside Friction)

un14 | 日之出公園

Teppei Kaneuji | Japan
S.F. (Seaside Friction)
Hinode Park
2022

玉野競輪場の改修に伴い、不要になった椅子やサイン、元選手の肖像、また新潟・越後妻有の雪景色の写真を使って、カラフルな彫刻作品に再構成した。作品名のSeaside Frictionは「海辺の摩擦」という意味で、元の文脈から切り離されたオブジェは、時間や場所、現実と非現実を複雑に交錯させ、異質であるにもかかわらず、周辺の穏やかな風景とともに不思議な一体感を作りだしている。

Alongside the renovation of the Tamano Keirin Velodrome, the artist recomposed discarded chairs, signboards, old portraits of cyclists, and photographs of snow in Echigo-Tsumari in Niigata to create a colorful sculptural piece. *Seaside Friction* is detached from its initial context, and the work creates complex transpositions of time and place, reality and unreality. While it is not ordinary, it retains a strange sense of unity with the gentle surrounding landscape.

設計＝平野地域計画（実施設計）、有馬建築設計事務所（構造）
特別協力＝株式会社チャリ・ロト

Detailed design: HIRANO Architectural Design Office, Structural design: ARIMA Architectural Design Office | Cooperation: Chariloto Co., Ltd.

3点とも [KK]

[KK]

アイシャ・エルクメン
本州から見た四国
un13 | 宇野港周辺

Ayşe Erkmen | Turkey / Germany
Honshu sees Shikoku
Around Uno Port
2022

かつて本州と四国をつないだ宇高連絡船の宇野港の岸壁遺構の地に立つ作品。一本の線で描かれた四国の輪郭が空に浮かんで溶け込む様子を、鏡面のステンレスパイプを用いた高さ8m・幅5mのオブジェで表し、本州と四国、瀬戸内海の島々で人々が往来し交流してきたことを象徴している。地面にはこの地域の鍰煉瓦が敷き詰められた。9月の台風での損傷により残念ながら撤去となったが、現在もその跡地からは瀬戸内の島々とその向こうの四国の山並みが見える。

The work was situated on the site of the former quay wall at Uno Port, a place where the Uko Ferry connects the mainland and Shikoku. The outline of Shikoku is depicted in a single line by this 8-meter high and 5-meter wide object, made with mirror-finished stainless steel. It symbolizes the movement of people in and out of the mainland, Shikoku, and Setouchi, and their exchanges. The surrounding ground was paved with *karami* (slag) bricks. Unfortunately, due to damage caused by a typhoon in September, the work had to be removed. However, even now, you can view the islands of Setouchi and the mountains of Shikoku from the site.

設計＝平野地域計画（実施設計）、有馬建築設計事務所（構造）
Detailed design: HIRANO Architectural Design Office | Structural design: ARIMA Architectural Design Office

[Ylc]

エステル・ストッカー
JR宇野みなと線
アートプロジェクト
un05 | 宇野駅、備前田井駅、八浜駅、常山駅

Esther Stocker | Italy / Austria
JR Uno Port Line Art Project
Uno Station, Bizentai Station, Hachihama Station, Tsuneyama Station
2016

島々の玄関口である宇野港への移動時間を楽しんでもらうためのプロジェクト。ありふれた景色を、白と黒の3次元的に働きかける構成によって変容させた。

This is a project aimed at entertaining visitors during their journey to Uno Port, which is a gateway to the islands. The usual scenery is transformed by the three-dimensional impact of the black and white structure.

所蔵＝玉野市
Collection: Tamano City

[KK]

小沢敦志
終点の先へ
un03 | 宇野港周辺

Atsushi Ozawa | Japan
Beyond the Last Stop
Around Uno Port
2016

放置自転車に玉野市内で収集した鉄くずを溶接し、アートな自転車へと再生させた作品。レンタルした作品に乗って宇野港を散策することもできる。

Iron scraps collected in the town of Tamano are bonded onto abandoned bicycles to regenerate then as artistic pieces. The art bikes can be rented to cycle around Uno Port.

設計＝林幸稔／林幸稔建築設計事務所（実施設計）| 所蔵＝玉野市
Detailed design: Yukinori Hayashi / Yukinori Hayashi Architect & Associates | Collection: Tamano City

[KK]

小沢敦志
舟底の記憶
un02 | 宇野港周辺

Atsushi Ozawa | Japan
Memory of Ship's Hull
Around Uno Port
2013

旧大日本帝国海軍の船で使われた錨とノルウェーの船のスクリューをベースにした巨大な立体作品。市民が持ち寄った鉄の廃材を海中の付着物のように溶接し、2020 年の高校生向けワークショップでさらに追加された。

These huge three-dimensional works are developed from the anchor of a ship of the former Imperial Japanese Navy and a screw propellor from a Norwegian ship. Just a like accretion at the bottom of the sea or the accumulation of human memory over time, the work multiplies through workshops to this day.

特別協力＝株式会社三井E&S | 所蔵＝玉野市
Cooperation: MITSUI E&S Co., Ltd. | Collection: Tamano City

淀川テクニック
宇野のチヌ
宇野コチヌ
un04 | 宇野港周辺

Yodogawa Technique | Japan
Uno Chinu - the Black Seabream of Uno
Uno Kochinu - the Black Seabream of Uno
Around Uno Port
2010, 2016

「チヌ（クロダイ）」をモチーフに、周辺の島々で採取したゴミや漂流物を使って制作した作品。2010 年にチヌ、2016 年にコチヌが制作され、宇野港のランドマークとなっている。

Using *chinu* (Japanese black seabream) as a motif, this work was created with trash and driftwood collected from the neighboring islands. *Chinu*, created in 2010, and *Kochinu*, in 2016, are landmarks of Uno Port.

設計＝林幸稔／林幸稔建築設計事務所（実施設計）| 所蔵＝玉野市
Detailed design: Yukinori Hayashi / Yukinori Hayashi Architect & Associates | Collection: Tamano City

[Ylc]

内田晴之
海の記憶
un08 | 宇野港周辺

Haruyuki Uchida | Japan
The Sea's Memory
Around Uno Port
2016

御影石の上に据えられた金属の彫刻が、光を受けて海の水面のゆらめきのような表情を見せる。海水を封じ込めた船が空へ漕ぎ出そうとする様子、あるいは生命を運ぶ種子や広大な海のひとしずくを連想させる。

A metal sculpture on a granite base creates the impression of the rippling sea surface reflecting light. It evokes the figure of a boat containing seawater about to sail into the sky, a seed that carries life, or a drop in the vast ocean.

所蔵＝玉野市
Collection: Tamano City

広域・回遊

Island Hopping

山川冬樹＋村山悟郎

大島_男木島 Inter-Island Timescapes

NoNumber | 大島、男木島

Fuyuki Yamakawa + Goro Murayama | Japan
Oshima_Ogijima Inter-Island Timescapes
Oshima / Ogijima
2022

大島、男木島で作品を発表してきた２人の作家による、海を越え交信しながらコラボレーションした映像作品。大島と男木島はそれぞれ異なる時間、文化、歴史と記憶、そして未来を持っている。作家は、大島と男木島で固有に生成される多元的な時間を、自身の身体を媒介しながら結び合せ、アンサンブルを奏でるようにパフォーマンスやドローイングを重ねていくことで、島と島の間に生起するTimescapes＝時間の風景を描き出した。

A film work that is born out the collaboration and communication between two artists who exhibited their work on Oshima and Ogijima that transcends the ocean. The two islands have different frames of time, culture, history, memory and – of course – future. The artists intertwine multi-dimensional time, individually formed on each island, using their physicality as a medium. Through repetition of performance and drawing, as if they are playing in an ensemble, they reveal timescapes, or landscapes in the realm of time, occurring between the two locations.

特別協力＝稲田禎洋（撮影・編集）、渡邉元（撮影）、大橋真日菜、張子宣（撮影助手）

Filming: Yoshihiro Inada | Editing: Yoshihiro Inada, Hajime Watanabe | Filming assistant: Mahina Ohashi, Tzuyi Chang

２点とも [ON]

ジョゼ・デ・ギマランイス

T01 フラワー
T02 ハッピースネーク
高松港ほか各島の港

José de Guimarães | Portugal
Flower
Happy Snake
Takamatsu Port / Islands Port
2010

各地に点在するカラフルな案内看板。地図を載せたサインボード《フラワー》と、花束と幸福の蛇のダブルイメージで「歓迎」を表すポール《ハッピースネーク》は全部で12基あり、その土地固有の歴史や文化をモチーフにした鮮やかな色彩の絵画が描かれている。

Colorful signboards are placed in different locations. The 12 information boards include *Flower*, a signboard with a map, and *Happy Snake*, a welcome pole shaped in the double-image of a bouquet and a snake of happiness. Each sign portrays the history and culture of the location in which they are placed.

切腹ピストルズ

せっぷくぴすとるず瀬戸内神出鬼没

E21 | 沙弥島、高松港、女木島、男木島

Seppuku Pistols | Japan

Seppuku Pistols Setouchi Tours

Shamijima / Takamatsu Port / Megijima / Ogijima

2022

鉦や太鼓を打ち鳴らしながら練り歩く切腹ピストルズが瀬戸内の各所に現れた。１日目は沙弥島の開会式や浜辺に現れたかと思うと、夕方には高松港で島帰りの来場者を出迎えた。２日目は「神出鬼没船」を走らせ海上でパフォーマンスを行い、来場者は太鼓の音に誘われて岸壁から楽しんだ。午後には女木島に上陸し、海水浴場でパフォーマンスを行った。

Seppuku Pistols, parading with the beating of gongs and drums, appeared in various places in Setouchi. On the first day, they showed up at the opening ceremony in Shamijima and on the beach, and in the evening they greeted guests returning from other islands at Takamatsu port. On the second day, they performed at sea on a ship, and guests enjoyed their performance from the wharf, lured by the sound of drums. In the afternoon, they landed on Megijima and performed at the bathing beach.

Event Data

4月16日(土) | マリンドーム〜沙弥島 開会式〜沙弥島 西ノ浜〜高松港 | 4月17日(日) | 女木港付近 海上〜男木港付近 海上〜女木島海水浴場 | 料金=無料 | 来場者数=510人（無料屋外イベントのため、人数は目算）

April 16th (Sat) Marine Dome – Opening ceremony in Shamijima – Nishinohama in Shamijima – Takamatsu port | April 17th (Sun) The sea near Megi port – The sea near Ogi port – Megijima bathing beach | Admission: free | Attendance: 510 (based on an estimate due to it being a free outdoor event)

3点とも [SM]

逃走する芸術船、地球号─コロナの時代に

椹木野衣　［美術評論家］

「瀬戸内国際芸術祭 2022」（以下「瀬戸芸 22」）は、世界が新型コロナウイルス感染症のパンデミックに包まれてから最初の開催となった。観光と文化・芸術の融合をめざしてきたいわゆる芸術祭モデルにとって最大の試練となったのは言うまでもない。感染拡大を防ぐため、国境はおろか都道府県の境を超えるにも留保がつく事態である。まして瀬戸芸は内海に散らばる離島群が主舞台であり、それらの島はいずれも高齢化が進み、人口も限られ、医療体制も十分とはいえない。そのような場で、島を訪れる人と島に住む人たちが国内外の各地からやってくるアーティストを媒介にどのように「触れ合え」ばよいというのか。そうした機会が協働作業や食を媒介とするとなればなおさらだ。ひとつまちがえれば、せっかくの芸術祭がウイルスの感染拡大にとって格好の機会となりかねない。

結論から言えば、「瀬戸芸 22」は無事会期をまっとうし、それでいまわたしもこの文を書いている。国外からの来場者がほぼ壊滅であったことから、総入場者数こそ減ったけれども、感染症対策の徹底や島に住む方々たちの協力、スタッフの尽力はもちろん、リモート技術の駆使や、なにより会期が春・夏・秋とコロナの「波」に柔軟に対応できる設定となっていたこともあり、当初予想された苦戦にもかかわらず、一定以上の成功を収めたと言うことができるのではないか。もっとも、コロナ・パンデミックが収束したわけではいまだない。今後も未知のウイルスによる地球規模の感染症拡大は十分に考えられる。今回のパンデミックでは、中国での地域的感染拡大から驚くほど短期間で地球の隅々にまでウイルスが伝えられた。その背景には、90 年代から爆発的に拡大したグローバリズムの進展と、その後ろ盾となったヒト、モノの迅速な移動や伝達が大量、かつ短期間に集中したことにある。感染拡大抑止のために人が動けなくなれば、おのずと芸術祭へのエネルギーの提供も途切れることにならざるをえない。結果としてこれまでの芸術祭のモデルが、グローバル化時代のメガ観光やインバウンドに大きく依存していたことが明らかになったのは事実だろう。仮に新型コロナ感染症が収束をしたとしても、同じモデルに立ち戻ればそれでよいというわけにはもういくまい。

もっとも、瀬戸芸の運営モデルが観光を主力としていたとしても、その理念が観光そのものに論拠を置いているわけではない。観光による人々の動員はあくまで瀬戸芸の理念を多くの人に知ってもらうためのきっかけであって、感染症によって来場者が減ったからといって、理念そのものを根本から組み立て直すには及ばない。だからこそ今回はこれまでにも増していっそう、当初の理念、すなわち「海の復権」へと立ち帰り、その意義を再確認するためには絶好の機会であったと言えるだろう。

海─それは人類のふるさとそのものだ。あらゆる生命は原点まで遡れば海に由来する。それにしても海とはいったいどのような場所だろう。海という果てしない存在に人類がはじめて出会ったとき、はたしてどんな思いに駆られただろう。その失われた貴重な瞬間はもう二度と戻ってこない。わたしたちは海にあまりにも慣れっこになってしまっているからだ。けれども、幸運なことに（?）わたしはその瞬間についてかすかな覚えがある。わたしは山育ちなので、物ごころがつくまで海というものを実際に見たことがなかった。海はおろか、周囲は四方が山陵の曲線だらけで、地平線さえ知らなかった。映画やテレビで海が出てこないことはなかったけれども、しょせんイメージはイメージにすぎない。そんなわたしがはじめて海を目の当たりにしたのが、小学 5 年生のときに皆で行った千葉の海（岩井海岸）だった。たいへんな衝撃だった。海はあまりにも大きく、水平線は定規で線を引いたように真っ直ぐで、およそ現実のものとは思えなかった。幼いころわたしの遊び場となったのは森や林だったが、そこはありとあらゆる生命の気配に満ちており、まるで万華鏡のような世界だった。ところが海にはまったく生命の気配がなかった。にもかかわらずひとたび水面下を覗き込めば、そこはありとあらゆる形態の生命の坩堝であった。生まれ育った山とのあ

The Fleeing Artship, Earth – in the Covid-19 Era

Noi Sawaragi [Art Critic]

Setouchi Triennale 2022 was the first edition to take place after the Covid-19 pandemic spread around the world. It is needless to say that this was the largest obstacle for the standard model of art festivals, which have pursued a merging of sightseeing, culture, and art. Trying to prevent the spread of the pandemic did not allow for the easy movement between regions, let alone nations. In addition to that, the Setouchi Triennale has developed with the inland sea islands as its main stage, and these islands have not escaped the impacts of an aging society, limited population, and stretched medical system. In such a place, in what way could residents of the islands and visitors "come into contact with one another" with art as a medium? And what about the mediums of workshops and food culture, which are even more problematic? One mistake in the operation could expose the entire art festival to the virus.

To start at the end, the Triennale concluded successfully, and that is why I am in the position to write this. Although the number of visitors from outside the country was almost zero, leading to an overall decrease in attendance, with thorough anti-infection policies, cooperation from the local people, the hard work of the staff, utilization of remote technology, and most importantly the staggering of the festival over three periods – spring, summer, and autumn – in order to remain flexible to pandemic "waves", the festival seems to have been more successful than was initially expected.

However, it is not safe to say that the Covid-19 pandemic has come to an end. And it is equally true that infection by another unknown virus could yet spread across the world again. The pandemic that we experienced expanded from a regional infection in China to every corner of the world in an incredibly short period of time. The background to this phenomenon is the progression of globalism, which has accelerated at an exponential rate since the 90s. The fact that rapid transportation and delivery of goods and people, which facilitated this growth, happened in massive quantities over a short time frame drove the spread of the virus. If movement of people is restricted due to preventative measures, the supply of energy to art festivals would naturally cease. As a result, the reliance of the existing model of art festivals on large-scale sightseeing and inbound visitors became apparent. Even if Covid-19 were completely over, a return to the same model would not guarantee the same kind of success any longer.

That being said, even if the Setouchi Triennale had tourism as a central drive, that does not mean that it was based on tourism alone. Drawing people in by tourism was a trigger for spreading the policy of the festival to many people, so the decrease in visitors precipitated by the infection does not require a rebuild of the festival's fundamental philosophy. That is why it can be seen as an opportunity to refocus on the initial policy and reconfirm its meaning: "the restoration of the sea".

The sea – the very source of humanity. Traced back to the beginning, all life originated in the ocean. What kind of place is the sea? When humans encountered the sea, the eternal presence, for the first time, what kinds of emotions were they driven by? That lost, precious moment will never come back. Nowadays, we are too familiar with the sea. Nevertheless, I have a recollection, far in the distance, of that moment. I grew up in a mountainous area, and never saw the ocean in person until I got slightly older. Surrounded by mountain peaks, I did not know the horizon, let alone the sea. Of course, I knew about it from movies and TV programs, but an image is nothing more than an image. I encountered the sea for the first time in 5th grade, when I went to Iwai beach in Chiba with other people. The impact was tremendous. The sea was too vast and the horizon – like a line drawn with a ruler – too straight, to be anything resembling reality. My playgrounds as a child were the woods and forests, a world filled with signs of life like a

まりの違いにわたしはしばしたじろぎ、言葉を失った。

瀬戸芸とは、そんな海が舞台の芸術祭なのだ。なかなかに大胆なことをしでかすではないか。日本人のやることは細部がていねいでもスケール感に乏しいということがよくいわれるが、どうして、こんな国際現代芸術祭は世界のどこを見ても見つからない。世界でもっとも古い来歴を持つ国際現代美術展にイタリアのヴェネツィアで開かれるビエンナーレ展があり、水都の名にふさわしく街中には運河が縦横に張り巡らされ、ヒトやモノの移動は舟で行われる。実際、会場にもはじめて乗るバポレット（水上バス）で向かった。それにも驚きはしたが、瀬戸芸はなにせスケールが桁違いである。その海を「復権」するのが瀬戸芸の思惑なのだ。まずはそのことをもう一度思い起こす必要がある。

幸いなことに、わたしは2010年に開かれた瀬戸芸の第1回から芸術祭を訪ねることができた。その後も途切れなく毎回足を運ぶことができているから、展示のすべてを見ているとはいえないけれども（それにしても、そのためにはいったいどれくらいの時間が必要なのだろう）、瀬戸芸についてはずっと継続的に見続けている。そのわたしにしても、今回ほど海を舞台に開かれる芸術祭ということの意味について考えさせられたことはない。というのも、海は人と人とを分断すると同時に繋げる意味を併せ持つからだ。陸路を閉ざすには物理的に壁などで封鎖してしまえばよい。ところが海はどこまでも流動的で、安定した地盤などないから、封鎖するのはたいへん難しい。一時期、シリアから大量の難民がギリシャをめざして地中海をゴムボートに乗ってやってきた映像が報道で届けられたが、海は陸と陸とのあいだを隔てて歩いて渡ることこそできないけれども、物理的に封鎖できないぶん、どこまでも開かれている、とも言える。歩いて渡ることができないぶん、権力や監視が行き届かず、逃げ延びるためのあらゆる隙間が存在する―それが海だ。

こういうことをいまここで書いているのは、今回の「瀬戸芸22」でもっとも印象に残った展示のひとつに、大島会場での鴻池朋子による《リングワンデルング》に付け加えられた新たなルート「逃走階段（エスケープルート）」があったからだ。

そもそもわたしと大島との出会いは瀬戸芸の初回に遡る。会期中に瀬戸内に滞在していたわたしたちに対し、ディレクターの北川フラムから、どうしても大島会場を見てほしい、とリクエストが入ったのだ。それに応えることで、わたしははじめて大島が長くハンセン病患者／回復者たちが国の政策でこの小さな島に隔離され、閉じ込められてきた歴史に触れることができた。と同時に、北川が瀬戸芸を推進する原点にこの大島と（お隣の豊島）に残された「負の遺産」を「開く」という思いがあったことを知ったのだった。

大島との交流はその後も続き、「瀬戸芸16」と「瀬戸芸19」の2回は香川県からの委嘱によりアーティストの推薦に関わった。その際、大島会場のためにわたしが強く推したアーティストが山川冬樹と先の鴻池朋子のふたりだった。《リングワンデルング》は、そのふたりのうちのひとり、鴻池が、かつて島から離れることのできない入園者たちがひとときの憩いを求めて歩くための小高い森の一角に張り巡らされた散策路を復活させたものだ。

「瀬戸芸22」の夏、鴻池はこの散策路にかつてなかったルートを切り開いた。およそ道が通じているとは思えない断崖のような斜面を降りる道を新たに設け、そこから直下の砂浜まで来場者に降りてもらおうというのだ。かなりの急角度で海へと近接するこの道は、鴻池によって「逃走階段（エスケープルート）」と名づけられ、秋会期からツアー形式で公開された。

多くの芸術祭を見てきた経験から言うと、芸術祭には数多くの作品の中でもヘソにあたる意味を持つものが必ず存在する。芸術祭は通常の展覧会とは違って一カ所を見て回ればそれで済むというわけにはいかない。参加する作家の数も見て回る展示の数も、会場が広域であればそれだけ増えるし時間もかかる。芸術祭はただの展示の集まりではないから、

kaleidoscope. The ocean seemed to be lifeless; yet when I looked underwater it was a melting pot of every form of being. It was so different from the mountains I knew that I flinched, and was lost for words.

The Setouchi Triennale uses this open sea as the backdrop to the festival – that is a bold decision. I often hear that Japanese work contains fine detail but lacks an impression of grand scale, but I have never seen an international contemporary art festival like this anywhere else in the world. The festival with the longest history is the Biennale, held in Venice, Italy, where the canals interlock the whole town and boats facilitate the movement of goods and people around, living up to its moniker: the "city of water". I took a *vaporetto* (water bus) to the festival venue there for the first time, and it was a fresh experience, but it cannot hold a candle to the Setouchi. And now, the Triennale is aiming to restore the ocean: we need to keep that fact in our minds.

I have been fortunate enough to attend the Setouchi Triennale every year since its first edition in 2010 without exception, and while I cannot say I have seen every single piece of work (how much time would one need?), I have been a continuous observer. Even for myself, there has been no occasion that has made me reflect upon the meaning of holding a festival around the sea more than this year, as the sea has the characteristic of both separating people and connecting them at the same time. On land, by contrast, all you need in order to close a road is a physical wall. Yet the ocean remains fluid, with no solid ground, so shutting it is extremely difficult. As news footage of Syrian refugees fleeing across the Mediterranean Sea on rubber boats aiming for Greece shows, while the ocean divides land and cannot be crossed on foot, it cannot physically be closed, so can also be seen as being endlessly open. If you cannot walk across it freely, you cannot patrol and inspect it, and thus it creates a gap for survival – that is the sea.

The reason I write this is because of one of the artworks that made the strongest impression on me at the Setouchi Triennale 2022 was the new element "Escape Route", added to Tomoko Konoike's *Ringwanderung* in Oshima.

My engagement with Oshima goes back to the first edition of the Setouchi Triennale. During my stay in Setouchi, I was encouraged to visit Oshima by Fram Kitagawa, the director of the festival. Following that encouragement, I was able to delve into the history of how sufferers and people recovering from leprosy were isolated and enclosed on this small island by the national government. At the same time, I learned that the origin of Kitagawa's development of the Setouchi Triennale was based on the principle of "opening" the "negative legacy" left on Oshima and the neighboring Teshima.

My relationship with Oshima continued, and I was involved in the proposal of artists for commissions by Kagawa Prefecture for the 2016 and 2019 editions of the Setouchi Triennale. Two artists I wholeheartedly recommended were Fuyuki Yamakawa, and Tomoko Konoike, who I mentioned earlier. In *Ringwanderung* Konoike recreated walking paths that spread through a section of woodland on a hill, established for the institutionalized residents who were forbidden from leaving the island.

In the summer of the Setouchi Triennale 2022, Konoike expanded a new route in these walking paths. She paved a route that runs down the slope – so precipitous that a path there could hardly be imagined – enabling visitors to descend to the sandy beach below. The path approaches the sea at quite an angle and was named "Escape Route" by Konoike. It was opened for the public in the autumn period as a tour.

From my experience of seeing the work of many artists, I can confidently say that art festivals always contain a navel, or central point. Unlike a normal

必ず主題（テーマ）が設定されているけれども、規模が大きく傑作が多ければそのぶん、皮肉なことに体験の豊かさのほうが前面に出て、主題は後景に引いてしまいがちだ。瀬戸芸ほどの規模の企画となればなおさらだろう。けれども、注意深く見て歩いていると、そのなかから芸術祭の全体を見るときの起点となる展示というのが必ず見つかるものだ。それは人によっても違うし、展示の規模とも関係がないから、ガイドブックで手引きされるような代物ではない。また、出会わなければならない、というものでもない。しかし、「海の復権」に立ち返ることを求められた今回の瀬戸芸について考えるうえで、少なくともわたしにとって、それは必須のものだった。そして今回はそれが鴻池の「逃走階段（エスケープルート）」であったのだ。

それにしても、いったいなにからの逃走（エスケープ）なのか。大島という特別な意味を持つ会場から考えれば、即座に思い浮かぶのは、隔離された入園者たちが閉じ込められた島から海という「閉ざされていると同時に開かれた」場所へと逃げ延びるための秘密のルートを追体験する、ということになるのかもしれない。だが、この逃走路の意味はそれに留まらない。なによりもそれは、コロナによって「陸」に封鎖されたわたしたちが、ありうる明日に向けて新しいルートを切り開くための困難な希望の提示なのだ。いま困難と書いたのは、決して比喩ではなく、このルートが急斜面であるためにひとつ間違えれば下まで転落してしまう危険があるからだ。しかしそれだけではない。仮に無事、下の浜まで降りることができたとしても、その先にあるのは立ち入ることを妨げるように広がる海にほかならない。「逃走階段」であるにもかかわらず、そう簡単には逃走させてはくれないのだ。あるいはこの心境は、新型コロナが収束する一歩手前にいながら、その先が見通せずに茫然と「いま」に立ち尽くすわたしたち一人ひとりの姿かもしれない。もしくは、いっそ瀬戸芸そのものの自画像とも言えなくはない。おそらく次の瀬戸芸は、パンデミックという陸路の感染経路を避けて逃走階段を降りた先に見つけた砂浜を、果たして行き止まりと見るか、それとも新たな「海への通路」と見るかによって大きく変わってくる。そして、それが大島青松園という、かつて国がハンセン病の感染症対策のために設けた隔離施設という大きな過ちの島で作られたということに、コロナ禍での芸術祭での公開という偶然とは思えない一致を見る。

かつてバックミンスター・フラーは、海には歴史がない、という意味のことを言った。いや、海にも大航海時代のように歴史は存在する、と言うかもしれない。けれども、大航海時代こそ植民地獲得競争という陣地争奪戦のための陸地史の一貫なのではなかったか。海には国境線を引くことができない。武力による海上封鎖はあっても、それは海を陸に見立てているにすぎない。海には歴史とは異なる別種の持続力があり、それを権力の交替とそのためのあくなき戦争、はてしなく細分化された領土の奪い合いに終始する世界史に還元することはできない。もし真の意味で海の復権があるなら、それは世界史とは別の枠組みが必要となる。そして、それは地球の資源を有限のものとして考えざるをえなくなったわたしたちにとって火急の課題だろう。だからこそフラーは地球を人類の根城としてではなく「宇宙船地球号」というかたちで船に例えた。そういえば、今回の「瀬戸芸 22」では、随所に宇宙や宇宙飛行士のイメージが散りばめられていた。思えば、地球そのものが宇宙という海に浮かぶ島なのだ。あるいは、領土と国ではなく、島と船からなる人類の歩みを辿り直す必要があるかもしれない。おそらく今後、海の復権があるとしたら、それはこの次元を常にどこかで想起し続けなければならない。もしかしたら、もはや芸術祭ではなく、わたしたちは「芸術船」地球号に乗り合わせているのかもしれない。困難な今回の「瀬戸芸 22」を通じて、わたしはずっとそのことを考えていた。（2023 年 1 月 23 日 記・文中敬称略）

exhibition, an art festival is more than just moving around one space. If the venue spreads through a wider area, the number of participating artists and exhibits increases, and so does the time it takes to view them. An art festival is not just a collective exhibition, and there is always a theme, but in a large-scale festival with wonderful pieces, the fulfillment of the viewing experience becomes more striking than the theme, which sits in the background. And with a festival on the scale of the Setouchi Triennale this holds even more true. However, when you look closely, you will always find a piece that is a prism through which you can view the entire the festival. This differs according to the viewer, and is unrelated to the size of the work, so cannot be expressed in a guide book. And it does not have to be encountered in all instances. Thinking about this edition of the Setouchi Triennale, though, which necessitated a return to the "restoration of the sea", it was – at least for me – essential. This time, the navel was Konoike's "Escape Route".

What is it an "Escape Route" from, anyway? Considering the location, Oshima, which has a special significance, one can perhaps immediately picture visitors experiencing a secret route for the isolated residents fleeing their imprisonment on the island to the "closed yet open" space of the sea. However, the escape is not limited to this reading. More than anything, it is a proposal of hope for everyone, imprisoned on "land" by coronavirus, to pioneer a new route to the tomorrow we may see. The "difficulty" here is not simply a metaphor: the route is so steep that one false step could result in a fall to its foot. And not only that. Even if you make it to the beach safely, what lies beyond is the sea, spreading like a barrier to entry. Contrary to the name "Escape Route", escape is not an easy process. What we find is each one of us, one step from exiting the pandemic yet unable to see what lies ahead, standing still in the "present", vacantly. This could be seen as a self-portrait of the festival itself. The next edition of the Triennale will be quite different, depending on the way it sees the sandy beach at the end of the "Escape Route" from the overland path of infection we know as the pandemic – as a dead end or as a route to the sea. It is no coincidence that this work is exhibited to the public in an art festival on an island that was the site of a great error: an isolation facility named Oshima Seishoen that the nation created to deal with leprosy.

Buckminster Fuller once said something to the effect that there is no history to the sea. One might also counter that there is a history at sea, such as the Age of Exploration, but that is nothing but an extension of the history of land, based around territorial warfare and the race to obtain new colonies. We cannot draw borders in the sea. The idea of a sea closure through military power is merely likening the ocean to land. The sea has its own sustainability and history that cannot be reduced to the transition of power and endless war, nor the ceaselessly subdivided world history that begins and ends with the division of land. If there were such a thing as a restoration of the sea in its true sense, it would require a different framework to world history. This is an urgent agenda for humanity, newly impelled to think about the resources of the planet as finite. This is the very reason that Fuller imagined the world as "Spaceship Earth", rather than a castle for mankind. In hindsight, I recall many images of the universe and astronauts cropping up across the Setouchi Triennale 2022. Now I come to think of it, the earth itself is an island floating in the universe. We may have to reconsider the history of mankind as one of islands and ships rather than territories and nations. Should there be a restoration of the sea in the future, it will certainly evoke this dimension somewhere. Perhaps we are part of "Artship Earth", not simply an art festival. Through the challenges of the Setouchi Triennale 2022, these thoughts played on my mind.

(23rd January 2023, Honorific titles are omitted.)

[YIn]

食の取り組み、地域のおもてなし

「食」はその土地の特徴や生活を最もよく表し伝える。瀬戸内国際芸術祭はスタート当初から「食とアート」「地域の食」に力を入れ、様々な取り組みを行ってきた。過去の来場者アンケートでは「島や地域の食事を食べられたことが良かった」という来場者の声が多い。今回も「食」の充実と強化を進めた。島や地域の食材を使用した料理や住民によるお接待は、多くの人を魅了した。

Food Initiatives & Regional Hospitality

“Food” is the best window into the characteristics and life of a region. Since its inception, the Setouchi Triennale has always been motivated to work with “food and art” and “local dining” in various approaches. In the questionnaires distributed to visitors in the past, many people have expressed their enjoyment of dining on the islands and trying local foods. In this edition, too, the variety and quality of “food” progressed. The cuisine using the resources of the islands and their regions, along with the warm hospitality of local residents, charmed many visitors.

島キッチン　豊島

島のお母さんたちが畑で作る新鮮な野菜や果物、近海でとれた魚を使って「豊かな島」を伝える料理を提供している。メニューは旬の食材によって変わり、リピーターが多い。島でとれる玉ねぎは、その甘さを活かして自家製ドレッシングにして提供。商品化され人気のお土産になった。お母さんたちも次々と新しい野菜育成にチャレンジして、コリンキーやスイスチャードがメニューに登場した。島産の柑橘類や、イチゴを使った自家製ドリンクやシャーベットも人気だ。

Shima Kitchen

Shima Kitchen provides cuisine that exemplifies the “resourceful island”, using fresh vegetables and fruits grown by the women of the islands in their fields, and fish caught in local waters. The menu changes with the seasonal ingredients, and it welcomes back many return customers. Onions harvested on the island were used for homemade dressing, making the most of their sweet flavor. Later, it was made into a product, and became a popular souvenir. The women experimented with growing new kinds of vegetables, adding colinkey and Swiss chard to the menu. Homemade drinks and sherbet made with the island’s citrus fruits and strawberries are very popular.

作品については p.69 を参照 | For details of Artwork, see p. 69.

3点とも [TM]

葺田の森テラス　小豆島

島の食材を使った山と海2種類の創作弁当が人気に。近海で取れた鱧のちらし寿司やお豆腐屋さんで作られたお揚げのちまきなど、お弁当箱も間伐材で作られていて再利用ができる。農園やカフェ等と協力し、コーヒーや手作りのシロップ、お菓子やジェラートも島で作られたものが揃い、味わいながらも島の食資源への目を養うことができる。木漏れ日の中、福武ハウスに新たに登場したテラスは、ゆったりお弁当を食べる人やひと休みする人など、住民や来場者の憩いの場所となった。

FUKITA NO MORI TERRACE

Lunchbox food served in two variations, using ingredients from the island, are very popular. The "*Chirashizushi* of daggertooth pike conger" and "Deep fried tofu in *chimaki*", made with tofu from a specialist shop, are presented in a recyclable lunch box made of timber from tree thinning. Cooperating with farms and cafés, lots of things on the menu are made on the island, such as coffee, home-made syrup, sweets, and gelato, allowing visitors to savor the taste while also learning more about the island's food resources. A new terrace was built onto Fukutake House, in the sun glittering through the trees, and it welcomed people enjoying their lunchboxes or just taking a break. It is a relaxing place for local people and guests.

作品については p.109 を参照 | For details of Artwork, see p.109.

海のテラス　高見島

2013 年から続く建築家 野村正人のプロジェクト。前回に引き続き、高見島の東斜面にある集落にレストランがオープンした。木製のオープンデッキには大きなテーブルやカウンターが配置され、来場者は思い思いの場所で海を眺めながらイタリア料理を楽しむことができた。瀬戸内の食材を使った2種のパスタ「瀬戸内の鯛とフレッシュトマトのマリナーラ」と「鶏肉とスパイス風味のトマトソース」は人気に。

Terrace of Inland Sea

A project by architect Masahito Nomura that has been continuing since 2013. Like last time, a restaurant was opened in a village on the east slope of Takamijima. Large tables and a counter were placed on an open wooden deck, enabling guests to take in the view of the sea in front of them while enjoying Italian food. Two kinds of pasta, made with food from Setouchi – "Setouchi sea bream and fresh tomato marinara" and "Chicken in spicy tomato sauce" – are popular dishes.

作品については p.183 を参照 | For details of Artwork, see p.183.

[SM]

汐まち玉野食プロジェクト たまのの塩　宇野

宇野港周辺にかつて広がっていた塩田に着目し、地元食材を用いてUNO HOTELの瀬戸内レストランBLUNOシェフ、KEIRIN HOTEL10のレストランFORQシェフがオリジナルのお弁当を提案。「白桃を食べて育った桃鯛と瀬戸内パエリア 穴子蒲焼『玉野塩』ふりかけ付」「桜海老と瀬戸内海苔の2色のしおさい弁当」は、今も、玉野市内で作り続けている塩を印象的に味わえる。アドバイザーにEAT&ART TAROを迎え、玉野の歴史や魅力がぎゅっと詰まったランチボックスとなった。

SHIOMACHI TAMANO project - Salt of TAMANO

Focusing on the salt farms that used to spread around Uno Port, and using local ingredients, the chefs of BLUNO in UNO HOTEL and FORQ in KEIRIN HOTEL10 created original boxed food. "Momodai peach-fed sea bream and Setouchi paella with grilled conger eel and Tamano salt furikake seasoning" and "Two-tone sea breeze lunch box with sakura shrimp and Setouchi nori seaweed" are dishes that enhance the impression of the salt that continues to be produced in Tamano City. EAT&ART TARO acted as advisors for the creation of the lunchboxes, which are packed with the history and charm of Tamano.

ドリーム・カフェ　男木島

川島猛とドリームフレンズ作品に併設したカフェ。作家デザインの包み紙が人気の「めおんバーガー」や"おいり"が乗った「讃岐ドリームパフェ」などを提供している。海を望むオープン席では気持ち良い風に吹かれながら休憩する人も。

Dream Café

A café opened alongside a piece by Takeshi Kawashima and Dream Friends. In wrapping designed by an artist, the "Meon burger" and "Sanuki dream parfait topped with *oiri*" are on sale. People could take a refreshing break here, feeling the cool breeze in the open seats.

作品については p.99 を参照 | For details of Artwork, see p. 99.

カフェ・シヨル　大島

社会交流会館の中にあるカフェでは、入所者の方が代々受け継いできた木から収穫した甘夏や梅を使ったお菓子を販売した。6月には梅ワークショップを開催し、サポーターたちが梅のジャムを作った。「大島を味わう」がテーマで、来場者がお菓子を通じて大島を体験した。

Café SHIYORU

In the café in the Oshima Memorial Museum, sweets made with citrus fruits and plums harvested from trees that have been handed down through generations of sanatorium residents are sold. In June, a plum workshop was held, and visitors were encouraged to collect plums and make jam. The theme of the menu was "Taste Oshima", experienced by visitors through sweets.

作品については p.140 を参照 | For details of Artwork, see p.140.

高松港 食のテラス　高松

春に登場した港のオープンテラスには、海に向かって椅子や机が配置され、市民や来場者にとって船が行き交う風景をゆったりと楽しめる場所となった。隣のテントやキッチンカーでは県産食材を使ったお弁当やテイクアウトの料理を販売し、人々で賑わう港の新名所に。夜はキャンドルが灯り雰囲気もよく、待ち合わせや休憩に使う人も多かった。高松港の新しい在り方を提示したプロジェクトとなった。

Takamatsu Port Food Terrace

An open terrace on the port, which appeared in spring, was filled with tables and chairs as a place for local people and visitors to enjoy the sight of boats passing by in a relaxing environment. At the tent and kitchen car nearby, lunchboxes and takeout food made with ingredients from Kagawa were sold, and it became a new tourist spot for the harbor, bustling with people. At night, candles created a wonderful atmosphere, making the spot perfect for meeting up and taking a break. It is a project that introduced a new side to Takamatsu Port.

犬島お母さん市　犬島

毎回好評の「犬島元気市」は、島のお母さんたちによる温かいおもてなしが人気。手作りの総菜やまつり寿司などで来場者を楽しませた。お母さんたちの気さくな人柄は楽しい会話につながり、来場者は住民との交流を深めた。

Inujima Okasan Ichi (Genki Ichi)

Inujima *Genki Ichi* Market is always popular, and is known far and wide for the warm welcome of the women of the island. Their homemade dishes and festival sushi are fun for visitors. The frank personalities of the women engage visitors in lively chat, so they can exchange conversation with the local people.

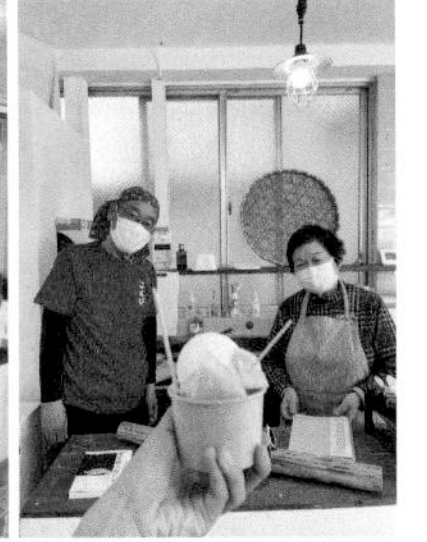

女木島名店街　女木島

寿荘内にあるヴェロニク・ジュマール《カフェ・ドゥ・ラ・プラージュ》は、熱や光によって色が変わる壁や机が設置された作品。来場者はそこで時間を気にせず飲み物やデザートを楽しむことができる。手作りドーナツやメロンクリームソーダが人気に。フードマーケット内には楽しいジェラート屋さんが登場した。

Megijima Meitengai Mall

Café de la Plage, in Kotobukiso, created by artist Véronique Joumard is a work in which the walls and tables change color depending on the heat and light on them. Customers can relax with their drinks and desserts without feeling rushed. Homemade donuts and melon crème soda are popular choices. A bright gelato shop also opened in the food market.

作品については p.74 を参照 | For details of Artwork, see p. 74.

島娘　本島

近海でとれたタコを使った美味しい“たこ飯”が毎回好評の食事処。店内には島のお母さんたち手作りの弁当や総菜が並び、お昼時は島内外の人で賑わう。テイクアウトが可能で、防波堤や港のベンチなど思い思いの場所で母の味を楽しんだ。

Shimamusume

In this restaurant, octopus rice made with fresh ingredients from the nearby ocean is always a popular choice. Inside, the women of the island sell their handmade lunch boxes and small dishes, and it attracts many local people and tourists at lunch time. It offers takeout, so the "taste of home-cooking" can be enjoyed wherever you choose to sit, be it the pier or on a bench in the port.

うららの台所　伊吹島

2016年から続く島のお母さんたちによるお弁当提供は3回目を迎えた。会期外も笠田高校と連携した調理実習を行いメニューを開拓。毎回評判の“釜揚げいりこの天ぷら”や“いりこ飯”に加えて、今回は、いりこ出汁とはたき餅だけで作る島のお雑煮が登場した。うららとは「私たち」という意味。

Urara's Kitchen

Continuing since the 3rd edition in 2016, this restaurant provides lunchboxes made by the women of the island. Even outside of the festival periods they worked together with Kasada High School, carrying out cooking classes and developing their menu. In addition to the popular specialties of *iriko* (small sardine), "*Iriko* Tempura", and "*Iriko* Rice" this time they offered the island's *ozouni*, made with *iriko* stock and *hataki-mochi* rice cakes. *Urara* means "us" in Ibukijima dialect.

さざえ隊のお接待　高見島

元島民やサポーターたちが、今回も元気に来場者をもてなした。2013年に結成した“さざえ隊”は、会期前から島内の整備や花壇づくりなどに励み、秋は島内2カ所で休憩所を開設。オリジナルグッズや飲み物の販売を行った。島内には自動販売機がないことから、休憩所での飲み物の提供は来場者から好評だった。

Sazae-tai's Osettai

Former islanders and supporters offered guests a hearty welcome to Takamijima. Sazae-tai worked on maintaining the island and preparing flowerbeds before the festival periods, and in autumn opened two rest houses, which sold original goods and drinks. Providing drinks at the rest houses was greatly appreciated, as there are no vending machines on the island.

オフィシャルツアーの食事

瀬戸内の食材や芸術祭の食を参加者に楽しんでもらおうと、オフィシャルツアーの昼食は、各店舗と一緒に工夫を凝らした。多くのツアー参加者からもご意見をいただき、会期を追うごとに食事はレベルアップしていった。

Official Tour Lunch

In order to offer the best food at the festival, and showcase the resources of Setouchi, the lunch for the official tour was carefully planned with each restaurant. With input from many tour participants, the food available was updated as the festival periods progressed.

- 島キッチン「豊島や瀬戸内でとれる旬の食材を使った特製弁当」
- 創作郷土料理 暦「小豆島の創作郷土料理の定食」
- 創作料理 野の花「オフィシャルツアー特製弁当」
- 葺田の森テラス「福田の潮風弁当」
「小豆島の食材を使った韓国風混ぜご飯弁当」
- こまめ食堂「棚田のおにぎり弁当」
- カフェ はまひるがお「オフィシャルツアー特製弁当」
- 海のテラス「オリーブ豚の白ワイン煮込み」
- うららの台所「うららの伊吹島弁当」
- 料亭 二蝶「オフィシャルツアー特製弁当」
- 料亭 公楽「オフィシャルツアー特製弁当」
- 畔家「オフィシャルツアー特製弁当」
- 汐まち玉野食プロジェクト たまのの塩
「桜海老と瀬戸内海苔の 2 色のしおさい弁当」「白桃を食べて育った桃鯛と瀬戸内パエリア 穴子蒲焼『玉野塩』 ふりかけ付」

[SM]

瀬戸内アジアフォーラム 2022
～海でつながる世界の「今」をどう考えるか～

Setouchi Asia Forum 2022 – Think of Today's World Connected by the Sea –

瀬戸内アジアフォーラムは 2016 年に始動し、フォーラムの開催、芸術祭視察ツアーの実施、書籍の発行などを通じて、アジアを中心にアートや文化による地域づくりに関わる人々の交流を生み出してきた。

コロナ禍による渡航制限を経て、2022 の公開フォーラムにはオンラインを含め 18 の国と地域から 29 名が登壇。世界的彫刻家アントニー・ゴームリーやウクライナで避難生活を続けるジャンナ・カディロワをはじめ、川俣正、池澤夏樹、北川フラム、福武總一郎ほか各国からのアーティスト・文化芸術関係者がプレゼンテーションを行った。

Since 2016, Setouchi Asia Forum has spurred interaction between people engaged in local revitalization through art and culture, with activities including organizing international conferences, planning art festival tours, and issuing books.

In the open forum in 2022 – the first after the relaxation of travel restrictions due to the coronavirus pandemic – 29 people from 18 countries and regions participated, including those who joined online. Presentations were made by people connected to the issue, such as internationally renowned sculptor Antony Gormley, evacuated Ukrainian artist Zhanna Kadyrova, Tadashi Kawamata, Natsuki Ikezawa, Fram Kitagawa, and Soichiro Fukutake.

4点とも[SM]

プログラム　Program

公開フォーラム　10月16日（日）15:00～18:00

Open Forum October 16th (Sun) 15:00 – 18:00

会場＝レクザムホール多目的大会議室「玉藻」（香川県高松市）
Venues: Rexxam Hall conference room, Takamatsu, Kagawa

共同司会＝北川フラム、リノ・ヴース、前田礼（アートフロントギャラリー）
Co-hosts: Fram Kitagawa, Vuth Lyno, Rei Maeda (Art Front Gallery)

ごあいさつ　Welcome Address

池田豊人（瀬戸内国際芸術祭実行委員会会長）
Toyohito Ikeda (Chairman of Setouchi Triennale Executive Committee)

関口芳史（大地の芸術祭実行委員長）
Yoshifumi Sekiguchi
(Chairman of Echigo-Tsumari Art Triennale Executive Committee)

福武總一郎（総合プロデューサー）
Soichiro Fukutake (General Producer)

基調講演　Keynote Address

北川フラム（総合ディレクター）
Fram Kitagawa (General Director)

Part 1　アジアから世界へ　From Asia to the World

リノ・ヴース　Vuth Lyno
ロ・カーイン　Lo Ka Yin
パウィーナ・ネカマヌラク　Paweena Nekamanurak
アナン・サプトト　Anang Saptoto
アリン・ルンジャーン　Arin Rungjang
徐震　Xu Zhen
リン・クンイン（豪華朗機工）　Lin Kun Ying (LuxuryLogico)
藪本雄登　Yuto Yabumoto
ビクター・ムラス　Victor Mulas
林洋子　Yoko Hayashi
福武ハウス「アジア・アート・プラットフォーム」
Fukutake House: Asia Art Platform

Part 2　ヨーロッパから世界へ　From Europe to the World

ケンデル・ギール　Kendell Geers
マッシモ・バルトリーニ　Massimo Bartolini
アイシャ・エルクメン　Ayşe Erkmen
エカテリーナ・ケニグスベルク　Ekaterina Kenigsberg
タマーラ・ガレーエワ　Tamara Galeyeva
ジャンナ・カディロワ　Zhanna Kadyrova
巻上公一　Koichi Makigami
鴻野わか菜　Wakana Kono

Part 3　激動する世界で　In the Midst of the Turbulent World

田島征三　Seizo Tashima
ジャン＝ミシェル・アルベローラ　Jean-Michel Alberola
クリスティアン・バスティアンス　Christiaan Bastiaans
ムニール・ファトゥミ　Mounir Fatmi
川俣正　Tadashi Kawamata
池澤夏樹　Natsuki Ikezawa
アントニー・ゴームリー　Antony Gormley

芸術祭視察ツアー

Day 1　越後妻有

■　越後妻有 大地の芸術祭 2022（新潟県十日町市・津南町）

作品鑑賞
- 香港ハウス
- 越後妻有「上郷クローブ座」
- リン・シュンロン《国境を越えて・山》
- クリスチャン・ボルタンスキー＋ジャン・カルマン《最後の教室》
- クリスチャン・ボルタンスキー《森の精》
- まつだい雪国農耕文化村センター「農舞台」

昼食　越後まつだい里山食堂
- ジャン・リュック＝ヴィルムート《カフェ・ルフレ》

作品鑑賞
- イリヤ＆エミリア・カバコフ《カバコフの夢》《棚田》
- 河口龍夫《関係―黒板の教室／引き出しアート》
- イリヤ＆エミリア・カバコフ
《人生のアーチ》、《手をたずさえる塔》《手をたずさえる船》
- ナウィン・ラワンチャイクン＋ナウィンプロダクション
《赤倉の学堂》

懇親会　越後妻有里山現代美術館 MonET・サロン MonET 喫茶
- 総合ディレクターによるレクチャー「大地の芸術祭」
- 十日町市長による歓迎の挨拶

Day 2　越後妻有・瀬戸内

作品鑑賞
- 内海昭子《たくさんの失われた窓のために》
- カサグランデ&リンターラ建築事務所《ポチョムキン》
- 鉢＆田島征三「絵本と木の実の美術館」

移動　越後湯沢駅〜東京駅〜羽田空港〜高松空港

■　瀬戸内国際芸術祭 2022

作品鑑賞
- 高松市屋島山上交流拠点施設「やしまーる」
- 保科豊巳《屋島での夜の夢》
- 渡辺篤（アイムヒア プロジェクト）
《プロジェクト「同じ月を見た日」》

Day 3　瀬戸内

作品鑑賞　小豆島
- ワン・ウェンチー《ゼロ》
- 青木野枝《空の玉／寒霞渓》
- 福武ハウス
「アジアギャラリー『時代の風景・時代の肖像＋＋＋』」
「アジア・アート・プラットフォーム協同展 2022『共に在る力』」
《葺田の森テラス》

昼食　《葺田の森テラス》お弁当

作品鑑賞　直島
- 下道基行《瀬戸内「　　　」資料館》
- 三分一博志《The Naoshima Plan「水」》
- 地中美術館

作品鑑賞　宇野港
- ムニール・ファトゥミ《実話に基づく》
- 長谷川仁《時間屋》
- 片岡純也＋岩竹理恵《赤い家は通信を求む》
- 金氏徹平《S.F. (Seaside Friction)》

Day 4　瀬戸内

作品鑑賞　本島
- アレクサンドル・ポノマリョフ《水の下の空》
- アリン・ルンジャーン
《石が視力を失っていないように、盲人も視力を失っていない。》
- 川島大幸《SETOUCHI STONE LAB》
- 藤原史江《無二の視点から》
- アリシア・クヴァーデ《レボリューション／ワールドラインズ》
- ツェ・スーメイ《Moony Tunes》
- 古郡弘《産屋から、殯屋から》
- DDMY STUDIO《遠くからの音》

昼食　「島娘」お弁当

公開フォーラム　レクザムホール 多目的大会議室「玉藻」

[SM]

[SM]

Art Festivals Inspection Tour

Day 1 Echigo-Tsumari

■ Echigo-Tsumari Art Triennale 2022
(Tokamachi City and Tsunan Town, Niigata Prefecture)

Guided Tour
- Hong Kong House
- Echigo-Tsumari Kamigo Clove Theatre
- Lin Shuen Long *Beyond the Borders*
- Christian Boltanski + Jean Kalman *The Last Class*
- Christian Boltanski *Les Regards*
- Matsudai NOHBUTAI

Lunch:Echigo-Matsudai Satoyama Shokudo
- Jean-Luc Vilmouth *Café Reflet*

Guided Tour
- Ilya & Emilia Kabakov *Kabakov's Dream, The Rice Fields*
- Tatsuo Kawaguchi *Relation—Blackboard Classroom*
- Ilya & Emilia Kabakov *The Arch of Life,*
  The Monument of Tolerance, The Ship of Tolerance
- Navin Rawanchaikul + Navin Production *The School of Akakura*

Social Gathering at Museum on Echigo-Tsumari, MonET
- Lecture by General Director about the Echigo-Tsumari Art Triennale
- Welcome speech by Mayer of Tokamachi City

Day 2 Echigo-Tsumari / Setouchi

Guided Tour
- Akiko Utsumi *For Lots of Lost Windows*
- Architectural Office Casagrande & Rintala *POTEMKIN*
- Hachi & Seizo Tashima Museum of Picture Book Art

Travel to Setouchi (Echigo Yuzawa - Tokyo - Haneda - Takamatsu)

■ Setouchi Triennale 2022

Guided Tour
- Yashima Mountaintop Park "Yashimāru"
- Toyomi Hoshina *One night's dream in Yashima*
- Watanabe Atsushi (I'm here project)
  Project "The Day We Saw the Same Moon"

Day 3 Setouchi

Guided Tour on Shodoshima
- Wang Wen Chih *Zero*
- Noe Aoki *Soranotama / Kankakei*
- Fukutake House
  Asia Gallery "The Sceneries and Portraits of the Eras+++"
  Asia Art Platform 2022 "Communal Spirits"
  FUKITA NO MORI TERRACE

Lunch: *FUKITA NO MORI TERRACE*

Guided Tour on Naoshima
- Motoyuki Shitamichi *Setouchi "　　　" Archive*
- Hiroshi Sambuichi *The Naoshima Plan "The Water"*
- Chichu Art Museum

Guided Tour on Uno Port
- Mounir Fatmi *Based on True Story*
- Jin Hasegawa *Time Shop*
- Junya Kataoka + Rie Iwatake *The Red House wants communication*
- Teppei Kaneuji *S.F. (Seaside Friction)*

Day 4 Setouchi

Guided Tour on Honjima
- Alexander Ponomarev *Bottom Sky*
- Arin Rungjang
  The blindman is not missing sightedness just as the stone is not missing sightedness
- Hiroyuki Kawashima *SETOUCHI STONE LAB*
- Fumie Fujiwara *The World from one and only Perspective*
- Alicja Kwade *Revolution / WorldLines*
- Tse Su-Mei *Moony Tunes*
- Hiroshi Furugori *From Birthing Hut to Mourning Rites*
- DDMY STUDIO *The Sound from Distance*

Lunch: lunchbox from Shimamusume

Open Forum at the Rexxam Hall conference room

瀬戸内アジアフォーラム 2022 開催概要

日程	10 月 13 日（木）～ 16 日（日）
主催	瀬戸内国際芸術祭実行委員会
共催	公益財団法人 福武財団 大地の芸術祭実行委員会
助成	文化庁、企業メセナ協議会
協力	NPO 法人 瀬戸内こえびネットワーク
事務局	瀬戸内国際芸術祭実行委員会 公益財団法人 福武財団 株式会社アートフロントギャラリー

Setouchi Asia Forum 2022 Outline

Dates	October 13th (Thu) - October 16th (Sun)
Organization	Setouchi Triennale Executive Committee
Co-Organization	Fukutake Foundation Echigo-Tsumari Art Triennale Executive Committee
Funding	Agency for Cultural Affairs Association for Corporate Support of the Arts
Cooperation	Setouchi Koebi Network
Secretariat	Setouchi Triennale Executive Committee Fukutake Foundation Art Front Gallery Co., Ltd.

SETOUCHI 企業フォーラム 2022

SETOUCHI Corporation Forum 2022

SETOUCHI 企業フォーラムは、文化・芸術による地域振興の先進モデルである瀬戸内国際芸術祭を通して、芸術祭の目指すものや負の遺産、社会課題を抱えた島々の視察などを交えて、持続可能な社会における企業の役割について考察、共有し、企業間のネットワークを構築することを目的として 2019 年から開催している。

現代社会では、コロナ禍やロシアのウクライナ侵攻などの出来事があり、閉塞感が強まっている。このような中で、持続可能な社会の実現に向けて、企業が社会の公益性への貢献をどのように果たしていくか、また官民の連携による地域づくりをどのように進めるかについて議論された。

２回目の開催となる 2022 年には、瀬戸内国際芸術祭の背景の１つでもあるハンセン病の療養所のある大島や近代化産業遺構の跡地である犬島への視察、現代アートを介した対話型鑑賞体験、企業経営者や有識者によるセッションなどを行った。

Setouchi Corporation Forum, which began in 2019, aims to learn the background and goals of the Setouchi Triennale, a pioneering model for regional development through culture and the arts. Its purpose is to consider the roles of companies in sustainable society, and to establish a network between companies through the observation of islands that retain negative heritage and social issues brought about by modernization.

In the contemporary moment, characterized by a strong sense of despair due to the COVID-19 pandemic and the Russian invasion of Ukraine, a longing for peace and a distrust of conventional social schemes is growing. Along with that, the role of corporations is changing significantly. In order to realize a sustainable society, how will corporate entities contribute to the public good, and how will they work with public and private administrations to build communities at a different level than the existing model?

This second edition of the forum included inspections of Oshima with its Hansen's disease sanatorium – which is part of the background of how the art festival came about – and of Inujima with its relics of industrial modernization. It featured conversational viewing experiences where participants could learn different perspectives through contemporary art, as well as discussion sessions with corporate executives and experts.

プログラム

10月7日（金）「瀬戸内国際芸術祭の本質を学ぶ」

- 大島視察・ハンセン病の歴史を学ぶ
- 犬島視察・近代化産業遺構と循環型社会について考える
- セッション① 企業SDGsと瀬戸内国際芸術祭

10月8日（土）「文化と企業の関係を学ぶ」

- 講演「アートによる地域再生」
  福武總一郎（瀬戸内国際芸術祭総合プロデューサー）
- 直島視察・島の文化と地域振興を考える
- 岡山大学×株式会社ベネッセホールディングス
  「瀬戸内サステナビリティ＆ウェルビーイング研究プロジェクト」最終報告会
- セッション② 宇沢弘文と瀬戸内国際芸術祭

10月9日（日）「持続可能な社会の実現に向けて」

- 講演「瀬戸内国際芸術祭の目指すもの」
  北川フラム（瀬戸内国際芸術祭総合ディレクター）
- セッション③「新しい時代における企業の存在意義を問う」
  渋澤健（シブサワ・アンド・カンパニー株式会社代表取締役）
- クロストーク

Program

October 7th (Fri) *"Learning the Essence of the Setouchi Triennale"*

- *Viewing in Oshima: Learning the History of Hansen's Disease*
- *Viewing in Inujima: Examining the Heritage of Industrial Modernization and Recycling in Society*
- Session (1): *Corporate SDGs and the Setouchi Triennale*

October 8th (Sat) *"Learning About Culture and Corporate Relations"*

- Lecture: *Local Regeneration through Art,*
  Soichiro Fukutake (Setouchi Triennale General Producer)
- *Viewing in Naoshima: Examining the Island Culture and Regional Development*
- *Setouchi Suitability & Well-Being Research Project Final Report Session,*
  Okayama University x Benesse Holdings
- Session (2): *Hirofumi Uzawa and the Setouchi Triennale*

October 9th (Sun) *"Towards the Realization of a Sustainable Society"*

- Lecture: *What the Setouchi Triennale is Aspiring To,*
  Fram Kitagawa (Setouchi Triennale General Director)
- Session (3): *Questioning the Meaning of Corporations in the New Era,*
  Ken Shibusawa (Shibusawa and Company CEO)
- Cross Talk

参加者からは、「日本トップクラスの学識経験者や企業経営者と、社会や企業が抱える本質的な課題を真剣勝負で議論することができ、大変有意義な時間を過ごすことができた」「瀬戸内の美しい自然と現代アート、その裏側にある市場資本主義の爪痕を拝見し、我々企業人は何ができるか継続して考え、行動していきたいと感じた」等のコメントが寄せられた。

The participants provided many comments, such as, "we had a very fulfilling experience, discussing an essential agenda shared by society and corporations with leading academic experts and enterprise managers", and "viewing the beauty of nature and contemporary art alongside the scars of market capitalism made me think that I will continue to examine what we can do as business people, and pursue concrete actions".

宇沢弘文と瀬戸内国際芸術祭

「重要なものはお金にかえてはいけない」。経済学者の宇沢弘文は、誰もが必要とする大切なものを社会的共通資本として国や地域で守っていくことが成長につながるとしている。新自由主義では、自然や教育など〝価格〟がつかないものは軽視されていくが、価格のつかないものこそが社会の豊かさを支えている。経済は人間の心があってはじめて動き出す。自然の豊かさと地域の人々がアートによって融合している芸術祭を通じて、我々は未来に向けて何をなすべきなのかを問いつづけていきたい。

Hirofumi Uzawa and the Setouchi Triennale

"You cannot exchange something important for money" – the economist Hirofumi Uzawa argued that, for nation and regions, protecting things that are important and necessary for individuals as "socially common capital" will lead to growth. In neoliberalist thought, things that have no price, such as nature and education, tend to be regarded as inconsequential, but it is those things that the richness of a society rests upon. The economy only moves where there is a human heart. Through the Setouchi Triennale, where nature and local people are merged by art, we will continue to question what we must do for the future.

こえび３年日記

Koebi Diary from 2020 – 2022

こえび隊は芸術祭を支えるボランティアサポーター。作品の管理・清掃、作品制作のお手伝い、芸術祭のPR活動、芸術祭期間中の作品受付、島での催しのお手伝いなどをしている。2009年10月に発足して以来、国内外から延べ４万人以上が参加している。

＊文章と写真は、ボランティアサポーターこえび隊の公式HP（https://www.koebi.jp/）内「活動報告」の一部を抜粋編集しています。

2020

3月25日　女木島

木村崇人作品《カモメの駐車場》設置作業

今日は雲ひとつない良いお天気。久しぶりの活動ということもあり、ウキウキしながら女木島に向かいました。まずは保管している倉庫から港までカモメを移動します。港にカモメが集合したので、いよいよ作業開始です。みんなで手分けをして手作業で設置していきます。無事にカモメが並んだ風景を見ると、気持ちも引き締まる気がします。冬が終わり、春がくるのを感じますね。この日、女木島の桜は一分咲き程度でした。これから島を散策するのにぴったりの季節がやってきますね。

7月11日　豊島

作品開館がはじまりました！

コロナウイルス感染症拡大防止のため、作品開館を長らくお休みしていました。こんなに長い間休館するのははじめてのこと。スタッフも島に通うことを控えていたため、作品の周辺や屋内はかなり汚れていました。再開直前はスタッフ総動員の大掃除。２日間みっちり行いました。待ちに待った開館日初日は、土砂降りの雨。お客さんは普段より少なめでしたが、作品鑑賞や島キッチンでの食事を待ち遠しく思ってくれていた様子に、私たちも元気をもらいました。今は事務局スタッフだけで、感染症対策やこえびさんの活動内容を再確認しながら運営をしています。こえび隊の活動募集をするのは、状況を見ながら。まだ少し先になりそうです。

9月5日　直島

演劇って楽しい！ 1DAY 直島ワークショップ

コロナ禍の中で色々制限はあるけれど、それも逆手に取って演劇を体験して楽しもう！ということで、直島から15人、男木島から２人の子ども達が直島ホールに集まり、越智良江さんによる演劇ワークショップが行われました。子ども達は、創作ゲームや、言葉遊びを通して演劇の基礎を体験しました。午後は成果発表会に向けて練習開始。「直島と男木島は遠い？近い？」「お隣の島？」など、子ども達に質問しながらテキストを作り、動きをつけていきます。発表場所は、宮浦港近くの海岸。短い時間の中で発表まで仕上げた子どもたちの集中力と団結力に駆けつけた保護者も拍手喝采。発表会後はご褒美のスイカ割り。割ったスイカを食べながら種をプッと海に飛ばしたら、ハイ、笑顔で解散。

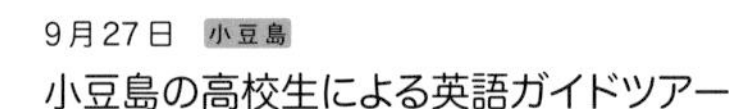

9月27日　小豆島

小豆島の高校生による英語ガイドツアー

久しぶりに生徒のみなさんに会ってみると、みんな緊張した面持ち。生徒さんの手元を見ると、ノートに手書きの英語がビッシリ。１カ月前から自分たちでコースも考え、練習を重ねてきたそうです。バスの中では小豆島のクイズタイムで盛り上がりました。「小豆島の人口は何人ぐらい？」「オリーブの花の色は何色？」と次々に質問が出て、車内は英語が行ったり来たり。また、生徒のみなさんがそれぞれ小豆島の自分の好きな場所を話すコーナーもあり、島の生徒のみなさんならではの場所を聞くことができました。2022年の芸術祭では海外のゲストさんたちを地元の元気なパワーでご案内してほしいと思います。

10月3日、4日　高松

SETOUCHI ART BOOK FAIR 2020

SETOUCHI ART BOOK FAIRは、アートブックやZINEに焦点を当て、瀬戸内国際芸術祭2019にはじまりました。マルチメディアが普及する現代、直接手に取れて、生活の側にある身近な「アートな本」に触れてみようという催しです。こえび隊の活動も数カ月ぶり。朝礼ではひさびさのエイエイオーで、気合をいれます。今回の一番の目玉は、ZINE AWARD。国内外からZINEを公募し、順位を決めるというもの。ズラリと並んだ約150作品のZINEは圧巻でした。また、入場制限で人数が限られるため、トークイベントもオンライン配信を実施。もちろんブックフェアも開催。顔を合わせて、本について、作り手と来場者が話せるのもこのイベントの良さ。みなさん趣のある建物と緑に囲まれて、和やかな時間を過ごしていました。

10月11日　豊島

8カ月ぶりの「島のお誕生会」

島キッチンのテラスに着いて、さっそくテラスの飾り付けです。久しぶりだったのでちょっと手間取るかな？と思いましたが、たった8カ月で忘れるようなこえびさん達ではありません。サクサク準備して、あっという間にいつもの会場に。さぁ14時からのお誕生会！と意気込んだものの、島の方や来島者の方は来てくれるかしら？ドキドキしながら待っていると、親子連れがぞろぞろと来てくれました。テラスでのヨガはお天気もよくて、リラックスして吸ったり吐いたり。お誕生月の方は８名。デザートは豊島で獲れたサツマイモの甘露煮をマフィンにイン。これから安全に開催できたらと思っているので、お誕生月の方も、そうでない方も、ご参加くださいね。

10月17日、11月7日 宇野

たまのスチューデントガイドのお手伝い!

今回の取り組みは、岡山県玉野市の中高生が国際理解・地方創生等に関心を持ち、コミュニケーション力や国際性など、これからの社会で求められる力を身に付けることができる環境を充実させることを目的としたもの。例年は、港で観光客と交流したり、島々でアートや旅の魅力に触れる体験型のプログラムですが、今年度は、リモート開催。宇野港を中心とした瀬戸内の魅力を教えてくれるのは、たまの観光ボランティアガイドの会(つつじの会)の方々。英語の指導もしてくれるので、こえび隊も宇野港のアート作品の紹介をしながら一緒に学ばせていただきます!次回の芸術祭の会場でも、中高校生のみんなと一緒に作品紹介や会場案内ができたらいいなぁ。こえびも英語学習意欲に目覚めた2日間でした。

11月28日〜12月9日 小豆島

王文志《小豆島の恋》の撤去

瀬戸内国際芸術祭2019で大人気だったワン・ウェンチー[王文志]さんの《小豆島の恋》の解体・撤去の活動がはじまっています。人力や重機で解体した竹からねじや針金を取る作業がこえび隊の担当。まずはひたすら竹を運び、そして運びます。ねじねじした部分はまるで知恵の輪みたいです。1本ずつほぐして取っていきます。竹は機械を使ってチップにし、その後、畑の肥料になるそうです。思わず立ち尽くすような果てしない作業に思えますが、終わりました!すっかり何もなくなった中山の棚田の風景。次回も王さんの作品ができるといいなぁ。

12月7日 高松

リン・シュンロン作品《国境を越えて・海》大草刈り大会!

動くと暑くなるくらいの良い天気のなか、こえび隊事務局スタッフと、芸術祭実行委員会の方と一緒に作品周りの大草刈り大会をしました。作業はほとんどがカマやハサミを使った手作業です。普段使わない筋肉を使っているのか、だんだん力が入らなくなる人続出!休憩をはさみながら、少しずつ作業を進めました。すべての草を刈り終えると、想像以上の草の量!いつもこえび隊事務局の窓から作品を眺めては「草刈りしたいなぁ」と思っていましたが、今回きれいにすることができて気持ちもスッキリです。

2021

2月8日 豊島

こえび活動2021 冬の陣!

最近、島キッチンのお手伝いがなんだかちょっとおもしろいことになっています。今年の冬は、少ない募集枠ながら、はじめて活動に参加してくれる方が意外に多いです。特に高校生。島キッチンのデザートにする、みかんジャムのパウンドケーキ作りに挑戦したり、週末の営業時間を利用して、島の方向けの油淋鶏弁当づくりを手伝ったり、大根を島キッチンの軒先に吊るし、割り干し大根を作ったりしました。島の食材を活かし、島や人とのつながりを大切にする島キッチンの取組みを、より深く、より身近に体感できたかな?さて、次回の活動では何が起こるのでしょうか!?

2月17日 男木島

男木小学校の社会科の授業でお話

授業のテーマは「地域の暮らしを守る」。男木小学校は今、3人の生徒が通い、3年生は1人です。瀬戸内国際芸術祭について話をした後は、こえび隊について。「こえび隊は芸術祭に関わるいろいろなお手伝いをしているよ。作品の受付もやるんだよ」と話すと、「僕もやってみたいんだよね」と嬉しい反応。男木島でも、島民のみなさんと運動会や防災MAP作りをしてきました。島に通っているこえび隊が、島行事に参加し、芸術祭を支え、そして島が元気になっていくお手伝いをしていることを知ってもらえたと思います。子どもたちと、島の将来について語り合える日が来るのが待ち遠しいです。

2月28日 高松

初代「めおん」お別れ式 & 新造船「めおん」就航披露式に参列

高松港で開かれた式典には、多くの参列者とファンが駆け付けました。赤と白のツートンでおなじみの初代めおんは、34年間、多くの人を運びました。初代めおんは、高松発12時便が最終便で、14時便が新めおんの初便です。お別れ式では、男木島島民から船長と機関長に花束の贈呈があり、銅鑼の音とともに初代めおんは最後の出航となりました。入れ違うように、新造船めおんが高松港へやってくる様子に、感激の声があがりました。外装の縞々は、「瀬戸内海の小さな島々(シマジマ)の間を、小さな縞々(シマシマ)の船が進んでいく。」そんなイメージで作られたそうです。芸術祭に向けてこえび隊もお世話になります!と心の中で挨拶しました。

[SM]

3月11日 高松

ありがとう!種の船

瀬戸内国際芸術祭2013夏会期、豊島の甲生地区の浜辺にやって来たのは、リン・シュンロン作品《国境を越えて・海》。通称「種の船」。ゴバンノアシという木の実の形で、まるで船のようだからです。2013年芸術祭終了後、一度豊島から台湾へ戻った種の船は2016年、高松港へ戻ってきました。それから約5年間、こえび隊の事務局から見る海の景色には、必ずこの作品がありました。作品の周りに草が生えたら、みんなで汗をかきながら草刈りをした思い出の作品です。そして、この度、種の船は再び台湾に戻ることになりました。見慣れた風景とも、ついにお別れ。種の船は、台湾へ向けて旅立ちました。ありがとう!種の船!

3月17日、24日、31日 男木島

道路補修や草刈りのお手伝い

芸術祭実行委員会のみなさんとこえび隊スタッフで男木島に向かいました。1日目は、コンクリートを使った道路の補修作業と清掃。2日目は、簡易材を使って、アスファルトの補修作業。3日目は草刈り。桜の花が満開の旧男木島保育所周辺。作業をしていても見上げてしまうほどきれいでした。3時間ほどですっかりきれいな公園に。お昼は桜の下でお弁当♪もちろん静かにいただきました。昨年はコロナウイルス感染症拡大のため、なかなか島の方と一緒に作業をする機会がなかったのですが、今年はこうして顔を合わせ、一緒に汗をかきながら島をきれいにすることができ、本当に楽しかったです！

7月11日 豊島

こえび隊による手づくりお誕生会

今回は、「豊島の景色を切り取ってオリジナルエコバッグを作ろう！」の巻♪島のお母さんや子どもたちが続々と集まってくれました。用意していた30セットのエコバッグは子どもたちには行き渡りましたが、大人のみなさんにまでは行き渡らず。それでも、作る人も、見ている人も、みんながわくわくするような楽しい会になりました。こえび隊のみんなも作り方の説明をしたり、みんなが切り抜いた模様をバッグに転写するためのアイロンがけをしたりと大忙し。お誕生月のお祝いも、5月、6月、7月と3カ月分！たくさんの人のお祝いができました。

7月24日 豊島

オンライン配信【せとうちばなし 2021】第1話「豊島〜島キッチンの10年〜」

第1話は「島キッチンの10年」です。島キッチンに野菜を提供してくれている島のお母さんからは、愛情をこめて育てている野菜について、建築を手掛けた建築家安部良さんからは、作品に託した思いを、そして、丸ノ内ホテル総料理長山口仁八郎さんからは、はじめて豊島に来た日や島のお母さんたちとの出会い、厨房で過ごす日々のことなど、それぞれお話しいただきました。

今回はじめてのオンライン配信ということで、本番直前まで、動画編集や画像準備が整わず、台本もちぐはぐ……本当に成立するのだろうか！？というほどの混乱ぶり。本番直前のこえび隊事務局には張りつめた空気が漂っていましたが、スタッフ全員が一丸となって、なんとか1時間の配信を完成させました。

7月31日 大島

大島に行こう！アートと自然を楽しむ子どもサマーキャンプ

今年は形を変えてオンラインで開催。香川県内外の小学6年生から中学3年生までの7名が参加しました。大島と中継し、入所者の森和男さんと野村宏さんが参加してくださいました。お二人は、「偏見や差別、隔離」という観点から、ハンセン病をコロナウィルス感染症と重ねてお話してくださいました。その他に、大島名物のろっぽうやきを味わったり、ロバの音楽座の松本雅隆さんと家にある音が出るものを使いながら大島の歌をつくったりしました。今年もこうして子ども達が入所者さんとつながることができました。これからもなにができるか考え、大島のことを少しでも知ってもらえるきっかけや場面をつくり続けていきたいと思います。

8月14日 女木島 男木島

【せとうちばなし 2021】第2話「女木島・男木島のいま」

まずは、女木島・男木島。ここ数年間、変化し続けている男木島から、「ダモンテ商会」と「象と太陽社」の紹介。また、新しくコワーキングスペースとしてオープンした「鍬と本」と生中継しました。次は女木島。海水浴場や、鷲ヶ峰展望台からの瀬戸内の景色を配信。また中止となった大祭について、祭りの総責任者でもある頭取を務めた方々にお話をお聞きしました。今後、祭りを若い世代に伝えていくために、今までできなかったことをしていきたいと熱く語ってくださいました。最後に、事前にお送りしていたお楽しみ変身グッズのオリジナル顔ハメで記念撮影！

9月25日 大島

【せとうちばなし 2021】第3話「ひとつのお菓子が地域を開く〜カフェ・シヨル10年の軌跡〜」

大島のカフェ・シヨルを立ち上げた、やさしい美術プロジェクトの高橋伸行さんと泉麻衣子さんのインタビューを中心に展開しました。「ひとつのお菓子」とは、こしあんが入った立方体の饅頭、ろっぽうやきのことです。大島でしばらく作られていなかったろっぽうやきは、芸術祭2010にやさしい美術プロジェクトが復刻しました。これがシヨルのオープンへとつながり、大島が開いていくきっかけになりました。

3回のシリーズでお届けしたせとうちばなし。いろいろな切り口で配信することができ、私たちにとっても良い機会になりました。今後も芸術祭や瀬戸内海をテーマにお届けしていきたいと思います。

10月9日、10日、23日、24日 女木島 男木島

2年ぶりの作品公開

芸術祭2019が閉幕してから約2年、ついに作品を開館しました。女木島の港では検温スポットを設置し、作品鑑賞するお客さんに検温と問診票の記入をしてもらいました。その後、お客さんにリストバンドを渡し、手首に着けて作品を鑑賞します。新しい作品受付の作業もありましたが、こえび隊は久しぶりの作品受付で元気にお客さんを案内しました。男木島も同じく港に検温スポットを設置。今回はこえび隊が案内するガイドツアー形式での開館です。男木島の5作品を約90分かけて、ゆっくりと作品や男木島のお話をしながら案内しました。島の子どもたちが友達を連れて参加してくれたのも嬉しかったです。

10月29日 女木島

女木島名画座上映会

今回の上映会は、ハンセン病の元患者を描いた映画「あん」。私たちが「あん」を観てどうしても想い起こしてしまうのが「大島」のことです。映画の中だけではなく、こんなに近くにも残酷な現実があったのだと、その中にも温かな楽しみがあったのだと、感じていただきたいと思いました。映画鑑賞後、案内人の北川ディレクターから、主演の樹木希林さんにまつわるお話があり、今まで聞いたことのないお話がたくさん聞けました。そして、来年の芸術祭の女木島での展開のお話まで！まだ食事付きのツアーは難しいけれど、少しずつ以前の「女木島名画座上映会」にしていければと思っています。

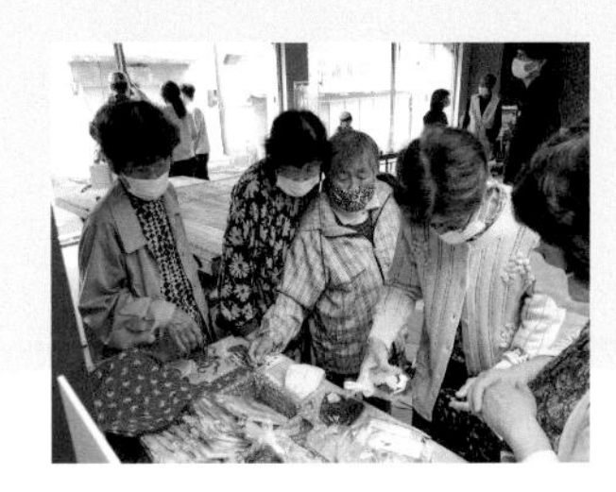

10月31日 女木島

島の中の小さなお店プロジェクト「なんやかんや持ちより市場」

2019年の芸術祭、女木島に「島の中の小さなお店プロジェクト」が登場しました。次回の芸術祭に向けて、より良い作品ができるよう、島の方にお話を聞きながら何ができるか考えました。女木島の文化祭はバザーが人気。そこからヒントを得て、バザーをやってみようということになり、「なんやかんや持ちより市場」を開きました。当日は、野菜やパン、焼き菓子、お惣菜、雑貨などを販売。作品鑑賞ミニツアーも開催しました。「こんな作品あったんやな」「これはおもしろいなぁ」と話されていて嬉しかったです。バザーを通して、島のみなさんに作品について知ってもらうことができました。次回の芸術祭では、どんなお店が登場するでしょうか？

12月10日 大島

こえび、えび餅をつくる！

毎年お餅を楽しみにしてくださっている大島のみなさんに、お餅をお届けしました。今年は、つぶあんが入った白餅とえび餅です。今回は、豊島の方から餅つきの機械を借りて、島キッチンでつくりました。蒸す、こねる、切るまでの一連の作業が全て機械化されています。一緒に手伝ってくれたお母さんも「うちにも機械があるけん、全部私一人でしよるんで」と言っていました。機械は便利ですが、石臼と杵を使って、みんなでぺったんぺったんとお餅つきをしたいものです。お餅をパックにつめて、のしをつけたら完成。コロナが落ち着いて、大島のみなさんと一緒にお餅つきができる日が早く来ますように。

12月5日 豊島

ストーム・ハウス感謝会

2010年の芸術祭で生まれた《ストーム・ハウス》の公開が、11月28日に終了しました。その後、唐櫃公堂に豊島のみなさんをお招きして「あらしの後で〜ストーム・ハウス感謝会〜」が開催されました。感謝会は島のみなさんだけでなく、作家さんや作品に関わった方々へ感謝する会でもあります。オンラインでジャネットさんとジョージさんも参加してくれて、作品制作にまつわるエピソードなどもお話いただきました！会場には、こえび隊の「作品のてびき」や作品公開時の日報も展示して、作家さんや島のみなさんに、こえび隊が楽しく受付していたことをお伝えできました。ひとまず嵐は過ぎ去りましたが、嵐はまたいつどこで起きるかわかりません。次はいつ、どこで嵐が起きるのか！？楽しみにしていましょうね。

2022

1月29日 高松 岡山

今年の芸術祭に向けてこえびミーティング開催！

高松と岡山にサテライト会場を設置し、オンライン開催しました。東京の北川ディレクターともオンラインでつながり、今年の芸術祭の概要をお話いただきました。ディレクターからは、日本と海のつながりの歴史から瀬戸内海が衰退していった経緯、芸術祭開催に向けての動き、そして今年の芸術祭では、どんなアート作品が発表されるのか、たっぷりお話いただきました。全国のみなさんがうずうずして早く瀬戸内に行きたい！という気持ちと期待に応え、みなさんとお会いできるよう準備をしていきます。コロナ対策でアート作品の受付での活動もこれまでとは異なる点も多くなりそうですので、みなさんと一緒に確認したいと思っています。

[SM]

2月24日〜26日 沙弥島

南条嘉毅さんの作品設置会場の掃除大作戦！

午前中は、空き家の荷物の分別整理と運び出し、庭に散らばり何層にも堆積しているプラごみ拾いの作業。午後は、一階部分の床板を剥がし材木を二階に運ぶ作業と、庭での作業を、ふた手に分かれて行いました。休憩時間に南条さんが作品のドローイングを私達にも見せてくださり、作品のことをお話してくださいました。素敵な作品の完成イメージを見て、俄然やる気が湧いてきました。終わりのない作業のように思えた庭のプラごみ拾いも、ずいぶん綺麗になっていることに驚き、みんなと喜び合いました。ふと耳をすますと波の音が聞こえる、とても雰囲気のある素敵なこのお家でどんな作品に仕上がっていくのかな。開幕が今から楽しみです♪（文：こえび隊　佐藤伸子）

4月16日

瀬戸内国際芸術祭 2022 開幕！

今日は3日目。最初の週末を迎えます。高松港や宇野港では毎朝こえび隊のミーティングがはじまっています。今日は北川ディレクターから「こえび隊はお客さんと作品をつなぐ大切な役割を持っている、担当する作品のことや周りにどんな作品があるのか把握し、丁寧にお客さんへご案内すること。」と、お話がありました。今年は、デジタルパスポートや来場カード、紙用とデジパス用のスキャナーなどのアイテムや受付で行うことも新たに増えています。はじまったばかりの芸術祭。毎日たくさんのこえびさんたちのお手伝いが必要です。芸術祭の最前線に立ち、一緒に芸術祭をつくりましょう！

5月18日 大島

「夢がかなった！」家族ではじめてのこえび活動

今回、田島征三さんの作品受付を担当しました。5歳の娘は、パスポートにスタンプはおてのもの。ときどき人魚のこぼした涙のビー玉も拾いに行き、しっかりとこえびの役割を果たすことができました。この日、娘は大島の案内をしていたこえびの鈴木茜さんに付いていき、「生まれてくることのできなかった子どもたちの碑」の説明を聞くことができました。娘はその説明を聞いて、「お友達になりたかった」と思ったそうです。子どもらしい純粋な感性に、胸が詰まる想いです。私たち家族は、沢山の方に支えられながら最後までこえび活動をすることができました。とても貴重で、素敵な思い出になりました。（文：こえび隊 冨永隼史）

5月22日 豊島

島キッチン体験記

私は、大学1年生だった2019年、はじめての一人旅の場所として瀬戸内国際芸術祭を選びました。美術館という建物ではなく島を巡りながらアート作品に浸る、全てが新鮮な経験でした。今年は、休学期間を使って3週間程こえび隊に参加。豊島の「島キッチン」は、一番思い出深い活動です。一言で言えば飲食店のホールですが、島のお母さんやスタッフのみなさんと一緒に「島キッチン」という作品を作り上げているような気持ちでした。こえび隊に参加することで、お客さんとしてでは見えてこない芸術祭の面白さや新しい側面、そして何よりも人に出会えると思います。1日からでも参加できるので、アートや人に出合えます。瀬戸内海が大好きな人にぜひ参加してほしいです。（文：こえび隊 田名麻衣子）

7月2日 小豆島

進行中！ワン・ウェンチー作品制作と虫送り

2月までに島内各地で竹を4000本切り出して保管していましたが、いよいよ、その竹を4～5本に割いて、作品として組付けていきます。こえび隊は、その丸い竹を割いて、節をとって、ワンさんチームに渡していく役割です。ワンさんからデッサン図を見せてもらうたびに、僕らの気持ちも燃え上がり、サポートできるのは嬉しいことです。ワンさんのお手伝いのあとは、3年ぶりに開催された中山地区の伝統行事「虫送り」に参加しました。「と一もせ、ともせ」と声をあげながら、田んぼ道を下っていきます。ちょうど、暗くなってきたタイミングで、たいまつの火が田んぼの水や空に幻想的にうつります。もう1回はワンさんに会いに行くぜっ！と誓った1日でした。（文：こえび隊 白石幸一）

9月4日 高松

浜田知事への感謝＆お疲れ様会！

浜田知事は、1回目の芸術祭である2010年の9月からこの日まで瀬戸内国際芸術祭を牽引してくださいました。夏会期最終日が知事の任期の最終日と重なり、12年の感謝の気持ちを込めてお見送りしたいと、こえび隊有志で企画。こえび隊事務局の大垣里花さんから12年間のエピソードと感謝の言葉を送りました。2013年に行われた現代源平屋島合戦絵巻では、源氏の大将として口上合戦に登場。2019年の開会式では、獅子舞から登場し開会宣言をしました。今年5歳にして大島こえびデビューを果たしたキッズこえびの冨永七帆ちゃんから花束の贈呈がありました。浜田知事も嬉しそうに受け取ってくださり、グーでタッチ！ご挨拶をいただき、音楽が鳴ります。曲は、こえび隊のテーマソング「ひょっこりひょうたん島」。サプライズでCome and Goのダンスチームや瀬戸内少女歌劇団も登場し、知事をお見送りします。ダンスチームが赤絨毯を準備して、拍手喝采の中、知事は公用車へ。最後の最後まで拍手が鳴り止みませんでした。浜田知事、12年間芸術祭を続けてくださり、本当にありがとうございました！

9月4日

暑い夏会期おつかれさまでした！

今年の夏会期は、高校生や大学生が夏休みを利用してたくさん参加してくれました。また、2013年のときに豊島担当だったスタッフが9年ぶりに帰ってきて、豊島の遊撃を担当しました。こえび隊のインスタグラムも毎日のように更新してくれていました。そんな彼女が、最終日の朝礼で言っていた言葉。「こえび活動をしていて、一番嬉しい瞬間があります。それは、こえびのみなさんや島の方に、『おかえり』と言っていただけることです。夏会期は今日で終わりですが、秋になったらみなさん『ただいま』と言って帰ってきてください。」秋会期もこえびさんたちの「ただいま」が聞けること、そしてまたたくさんのこえびさんたちと出会えることを楽しみにしています。秋会期はもうすぐそこです。こえび隊の活動はまだまだ続きます！

9月19日 高見島・多度津 本島

秋会期に向けて西の島の制作、佳境！

秋会期に向けて各会場の作品制作も大詰めです。高見島の《海のテラス》では、同じ場所に展示されるケンデル・ギールさんの《FLOW》の周辺を整備しました。高見島の山の上にある家から程度の良い瓦を運んで、敷き詰めていきました。本島では、アリン・ルンジャーンさんの新作のお手伝い。みんなで大きな石を運び、家の中に設置していきました。多度津の商店街には、築100年以上の旧塩田家の土蔵に尾花賢一さんの作品が設置されます。500枚もの板を二階に運び込みました。今日は多度津町にお住まいのお2人がこえび隊として参加。こえび隊もフルスロットルで頑張ってます。（文：こえび隊 白石幸一）

10月12日 男木島 大島 宇野

秋会期真っ最中！子こえび大活躍

瀬戸内は、一気に涼しくなり、肌寒い日もあるほど。連休2日目は、3つの会場で小さなこえびさんたちが大活躍。男木島では、男木島に住む子どもたちが受付をしてくれました。デジパスのスキャンも慣れた手つき！続いて、大島。小学6年生の子が1人で受付。時々サポートに入りながらもほとんど1人で対応しました。最後は、宇野港。小学4年生のこえびさんです。お客さんから「何年生？」「がんばってね」と声をかけてくれていたようです。今年の芸術祭も、子どもから80代の方まで、幅広い年齢層が活動してくれ、みんなで芸術祭を支えています。一緒にラストの秋会期を盛り上げましょう！えいえいおー！

10月22日 男木島

「ありがとう、また来てね」

秋会期は西の島が会場として加わり、フェリーや高速艇が港を出るたびに、旗を振り、手を振り、大声でお見送りしている風景が印象的です。今年、こえび隊は男木島に行き来する方法が、チャーター船に切り替わりました。男木島発の最終便よりも後にチャーター船に乗るため、お客さんを全力でお見送りしています。題して「ありがとう、また来てね」セレモニーです。作品を閉館した後、フェリー乗り場に駆け付け、《タコツボル》に飾られているTEAM男気の旗を借りてお見送りしています。学校帰りの島の子どもたちも加わって、にぎやかなお見送りになるときも。お客さんもこえび隊も、フェリーが港外に出ても、手を振り続けます。海に沈む夕日が、より旅情を誘うワンシーンです。（文：こえび隊 白石幸一）

11月6日

瀬戸内国際芸術祭2022終了しました

105日間のお祭りが終了しました。今年の芸術祭はコロナ禍での開催となり、思うように活動に参加できなかった方もたくさんいたと思います。作品制作や毎日の運営では、こえび隊、企業ボランティアや県庁OB、県や市の職員さんたち、地元の方々、本当にたくさんの方々に支えられました。春・夏会期に参加してくれた方が、また秋会期に参加してくれたり、企業ボランティアの方がこえび隊に登録して活動に参加してくれた事も！ 秋会期の中旬以降は海外のこえびさんも来てくれるようになりました。105日間、日々のバトンを最後までつないでくれたみなさん、本当にありがとうございました。こえび隊の活動は、また次の芸術祭に向けて、走りはじめます。

11月10日

作品の撤収作業がはじまっています！

閉会式の次の日からは早速、撤収作業。名残惜しくもありますが、作品を撤去し、お借りしていた居宅等を清掃してお返しすることで「終わり」となります。女木島では、あきびんごさんの《瀬戸内カーニバル》の作品会場の撤収を行いました。撤収作業ではじめて作品をじっくり見ることができ、作業を進めるうちに「この作品の裏側はこうだったのか」「鬼の絵は196枚もあったのか」「受付時、お客さんの反応が面白かった」「本が売れた」など、それぞれの思い出話を語り合いながら、作品の撤去を惜しみました。最後に清掃して、作業は完了。撤収作業は、ただいま全島で応募受付中。ぜひ、作品を懐かしみながら、次回開催へのステップを踏んでいきましょう。（文：こえび隊 白石幸一）

できごと 2020－2022
Events 2020－2022

2020年

1月
1月12日　島のお誕生会　豊島

2月
2月 2日　祭第25回女木地区節分文化祭　女木島　★1
　瀬戸芸スタート時の2010年から毎年こえび隊がお手伝いに参加し、2020年は10年目の参加となった
2月 8日　Ⓚかんきつ収穫ワークショップ（～2/9）　大島
2月 9日　島のお誕生会　豊島
2月23日　塩田千春《遠い記憶》お別れ会　豊島
2月29日　新型コロナウィルス感染症拡大を受け、6月まで作品公開、イベントが中止となる

3月
3月　宇野港「連絡船の町」プロジェクト「たまののおとvol.4」完成　宇野港
3月 8日　祭粟島百々手　粟島
3月31日　実行委員会第26回総会

4月
4月 2日　Ⓚこえび新聞18号発行

5月
5月 3日　祭犬島天満宮春季例祭　犬島
5月25日　瀬戸芸2022作品公募要領公表

7月
7月10日　祭犬島天満宮夏越の祓　犬島
7月11日　新型コロナウィルス感染症対策を行いながら、豊島のピピロッティ・リストのアート作品、島キッチンが再開する　豊島
7月28日　実行委員会第27回総会

8月
8月11日　瀬戸内国際芸術祭2019公式記録集発売

9月
9月 5日　演劇って楽しい！1DAY直島ワークショップ　直島
9月15日　瀬戸芸2022作品公募受付開始（～30日）

10月
10月 3日　SETOUCHI ART BOOK FAIR 2020（～10/4）　高松　★2
　Ⓚこえびミーティング（オンライン、会場：高松）
10月 4日　祭沙弥島秋祭り　沙弥島
10月11日　島のお誕生会　豊島
10月17日　祭犬島伊勢大神楽　犬島
　祭粟島秋季大祭　粟島

11月
11月 3日　祭犬島天満宮秋季例祭　犬島
11月 8日　島のお誕生会　豊島
11月13日　祭男木島文化祭　男木島

12月
12月 6日　島のお誕生会　豊島
12月12日　高校生鍛造ワークショップと作品の増殖（～12/17）　宇野港　★3
12月13日　《舟底の記憶》ワークショップ　宇野港

2021年

1月
1月15日　Ⓚこえび新聞19号発行　★4

2月
2月　瀬戸内少女歌劇団公演（Youtubeで配信）
2月14日　島のお誕生会　豊島

3月
3月 7日　島のお誕生会　豊島
　祭粟島百々手　粟島
3月19日　オフィシャルツアー 日帰り伊吹島ツアー（3/20）　伊吹島　★5
3月30日　実行委員会第28回総会

4月
4月11日　島のお誕生会　豊島
4月22日　SETOUCHI企業フォーラム　直島
4月27日　瀬戸芸メインビジュアル撮影　男木島　★6

7月
7月11日　島のお誕生会　豊島
7月24日　Ⓚせとうちばなし第1話ー豊島編ー（オンライン開催、会場：高松、豊島）
7月31日　大島アーティスト・イン・レジデンス事業（主催:高松市、オンライン開催、会場：高松）

8月
8月 8日　島のお誕生会　豊島
8月14日　Ⓚせとうちばなし第2話ー女木島・男木島ー（オンライン開催、会場：高松）

9月
9月25日　Ⓚせとうちばなし第3話ー大島ー（オンライン開催、会場：高松）
9月29日　瀬戸芸2022メインビジュアル発表会

10月
10月 3日　祭沙弥島秋祭り　沙弥島
10月 9日　2年ぶりの作品公開（10/10,23,24）　女木島　男木島
10月16日　祭粟島秋季大祭　粟島
10月17日　瀬戸内アジアフォーラム2021Artists' Breath Live（オンライン開催、会場：高松・十日町）
　祭犬島伊勢大神楽　犬島
　島のお誕生会　豊島
10月18日　祭犬島秋まつり（犬島盆踊り延期の代替）　犬島
10月29日　実行委員会第29回総会
　女木島名画座上映会映画「あん」　女木島

11月
11月 3日　祭犬島天満宮秋季例祭　犬島
11月 9日　瀬戸芸2022企画発表会
　・東京日本橋ホールにて開催
　瀬戸芸公式ウェブサイトリニューアル
11月12日　祭男木島文化祭　男木島
11月14日　島のお誕生会　豊島
11月16日　作品鑑賞パスポート（瀬戸芸デジパス/3シーズン券）発売開始
11月23日　瀬戸内少女歌劇団 男木島出張　公演「豊玉姫のおはなし」　男木島
　・男木島島民に限定して、瀬戸内少女歌劇団による演劇や、島民の方々も参加しての手旗パフォーマンスを行った
11月27日　女木島名画座上映会　ドキュメンタリー映像「日本の詩情」　女木島

★1

★2 [TK]

★3

こえび新聞
愛されて十年
瀬戸内のアート作品
★4

★5

★6

★7

★8 [SM]

★9 [SM]

★10

★11

★12 [SM]

12月

12月12日　島のお誕生会　豊島
12月28日　男木島もちつき　男木島

2022年

1月

1月16日　島のお誕生会　豊島
1月29日　K こえびミーティング（オンライン開催、会場：高松・岡山・東京）
香川県・岡山県以外の在住の方の関心も高く、全体で 100 人近くの参加があった

2月

2月 9日　瀬戸芸 2022 参加作家追加発表

3月

3月 3日　実行委員会「新型コロナウイルス感染症対策の指針」策定
3月 4日　《宇野のチヌ》《宇野コチヌ》お色直し（～ 3/14）　宇野港
祭 第 26 回女木地区文化祭　女木島
規模を縮小して実施
3月 6日　祭 粟島百々手　粟島
3月18日　直島住民説明会　直島
3月20日　宇野港住民説明会　宇野港
3月22日　小豆島町住民説明会　小豆島
3月25日　土庄町住民説明会　小豆島
3月26日　豊島住民説明会　豊島
沙弥島住民説明会　沙弥島 ★7
3月29日　実行委員会第 30 回総会
3月30日　大島住民説明会（オンライン開催）大島
3月31日　瀬戸芸 2022 公式アプリ配信開始

★12 [SM]

★12 [SM]

4月

4月 2日　K こえび新聞 20 号発行
K こえびミーティング（オンライン開催、会場：高松・岡山）
4月 3日　女木島住民説明会　女木島
男木島住民説明会　男木島
瀬戸内少女歌劇団 2 期生　オーディション
4月 5日　瀬戸芸 2022 開幕直前発表会
渋谷ヒカリエ（8 階ギャラリー）にて、瀬戸芸 2022 参加作家の最終発表、作品・プロジェクトの発表
K こえびミーティング（オンライン開催、会場：東京）
4月12日　プレスツアー実施
4月14日　瀬戸芸 2022 春会期開幕、開会式　高松港 ★8
瀬戸芸 2022 公式ガイドブック発売開始
4月16日　安藤忠雄講演会　直島
オープニングセレモニー　沙弥島 ★9　宇野港
切腹ピストルズ「切腹ぴすとるず瀬戸内神出鬼没」（女木島、男木島、沙弥島、高松港）（～ 4/17）
近代化の歴史にふれる—直島・犬島の鍰煉瓦を訪ねて—　直島　犬島
4月17日　市民煎茶グループ曙
「万葉茶会と講演～香を楽しむ～」　沙弥島
坂出親子おてつ隊によるちびっ子ガイド（5/1,3,8,15）　沙弥島
島のお誕生会　豊島
4月18日　直島建築ツアー（4/24、5/16）　直島
4月23日　直島女文楽「麗春の舞」　直島

5月

5月 3日　祭 大島天満宮春季例祭　大島
5月 7日　女木島名画座上映会「命みじかし、恋せよ乙女」　女木島　案内人：北川フラム　食事：味どころ 撰
5月 8日　島のお誕生会　豊島
5月11日　近代化の歴史にふれる—直島・犬島の鍰煉瓦を訪ねて—　直島　犬島
5月14日　木ノ下歌舞伎「竜宮鱗屑譚（せとうちうろくずものがたり）～ GYOTS ～」（～ 5/15）　小豆島
5月15日　香川大学×瀬戸内の伝統生活文化･芸術発信プロジェクトチーム「瀬戸内仕事歌＆四国民話オペラ『二人奥方』」高松
5月16日　オーストラリア大使が豊島、直島を訪問（～ 5/17）
2010 年の瀬戸芸以降、オーストラリアのアーティストと交流が続く豊島の甲生地区のみなさんと温かな交流が行われた　豊島　直島 ★10
5月18日　総合ディレクター北川フラムとめぐるスペシャルツアー第 1 弾 春の新作ツアー　沙弥島　与島　直島
瀬戸芸 2022 春会期閉幕
5月21日　祭 男木地区運動会　男木島 ★11
2 年ぶりにこえび隊もお手伝いに参加。こえび隊考案の競技「なんちゃって瀬戸芸ポスター撮影リレー」で盛り上がった
5月28日　「フラワーフェアリー誕生祭」（6/5）　大島

6月

6月 1日　粟島芸術家村入村式　粟島
6月12日　島のお誕生会　豊島
6月17日　海外アーティスト第 1 号　ワン・ウェンチー［王文志］が来日！夏会期の作品制作がはじまる（～ 8/4）★12
6月25日　K こえびミーティング
（オンライン開催、会場：高松・岡山）
特別ゲストのワン・ウェンチーから新作の紹介があり、こえび隊も制作への参加にさらに気合いが入った

できごと 2020 - 2022
Events 2020 - 2022

7月

7月 2日　祭虫送り（肥土山・中山） 小豆島 ★13
　　ワン・ウェンチー、シャン・ヤン［向阳］も一緒に参加
7月10日　祭大島天満宮夏越の祓 大島
　　島のお誕生会 豊島
7月11日　Ⓚ遠方から参加するこえび隊が宿泊可能な拠点施設 WeBase 高松で、こえび隊特別割引プランを開始（～11/20）
7月12日　TIME 誌「World's Greatest Places 2022」に「Setouchi Islands」が選出される
7月15日　プレスツアー実施（～7/16）
7月17日　祭伊吹島港祭り 伊吹島
7月23日　本島住民説明会 本島
　　高見島住民説明会 高見島
　　粟島住民説明会 粟島
　　Ⓚこえびミーティング（会場：大阪）
7月24日　多度津町住民説明会 多度津
7月29日　瀬戸芸 2022 オリジナルフレーム切手販売開始
7月30日　ワン・ウェンチー《ゼロ》お披露目会 小豆島

8月

8月 3日　プレスツアー実施（～8/4）
8月 5日　瀬戸芸 2022 夏会期開幕
　　高松市屋島山上交流拠点施設「やしまーる」がオープン 高松
　　祭男木島大祭 男木島 ★14
8月 6日　総合ディレクター北川フラムとめぐるスペシャルツアー第2弾 夏の新作ツアー 小豆島
　　シャン・ヤン《辿り着く向こう岸》お披露目会 小豆島
8月 7日　祭小豆島まつり（土庄町） 小豆島
　　島のお誕生会 豊島
8月11日　ひびのこづえ「MAMMOTH」 高松
　　第 104 回全国高等学校野球選手権大会に出場した高松商業高等学校の学校紹介で瀬戸芸が紹介され、全国の高校野球ファンに知られる
8月14日　祭大島盆祭り 大島
8月15日　大島が 10 日間会期を延期して開幕 大島
　　祭小豆島まつり（小豆島町） 小豆島
8月20日　Ⓚこえびミーティング（会場：観音寺）
　　祭直島の火まつり 直島
8月24日　総合ディレクター北川フラムとめぐるスペシャルツアー第３弾 豊島 大島
　　瀬戸芸はなぜはじまったのか、原点とも言える豊島と大島を巡り、瀬戸芸誕生のルーツをたどった
8月27日　女木島名画座上映会「アイスと雨音」 女木島
　　案内人：北川フラム案内人と松居大悟監督のトーク、食事：民宿「umiyado 鬼旬」

9月

9月 4日　葺田夜祭 小豆島
　　総合ディレクター北川フラムとめぐるスペシャルツアー第４弾 福武ハウスと影絵のゲネプロ見学ツアー 小豆島
　　瀬戸芸 2022 夏会期閉幕
　　Ⓚ浜田知事退任お疲れ様会を開催
　　こえび隊有志によって 12 年の任期を終える浜田知事の感謝 & お疲れ様会が開催された
9月 5日　池田豊人知事が実行委員会会長に就任
9月11日　島のお誕生会 豊島
9月17日　Ⓚこえびミーティング（会場：三豊、丸亀、多度津）
9月25日　伊吹島住民説明会 伊吹島
9月27日　プレスツアー実施（～9/28）
9月29日　瀬戸芸 2022 秋会期開幕
　　瀬戸芸公式インスタグラムのフォロワー数、6万人超える
9月30日　オープニングセレモニー 伊吹島

10月

10月 1日　オープニングセレモニー 本島 高見島 粟島
　　送り太鼓（10/16,23,11/6） 本島
10月 2日　祭沙弥島秋祭り 沙弥島
10月 3日　直島建築ツアー（10/19,24） 直島
10月 4日　草間彌生の黄色い《南瓜》が復元制作、展示された 直島
10月 7日　SETOUCHI 企業フォーラム 2022（～10/9）
10月 8日　ひびのこづえ「Come and Go」（～10/10,15,16） 男木島
10月 9日　護王神社遷座 20 周年記念「杉本雅楽　直島御神楽」 直島
　　バシライ「瀬戸内土のレストラン」 高見島
10月10日　島のお誕生会 豊島
10月13日　瀬戸内アジアフォーラム 2022（～10/16） 高松
10月15日　学ぶ！楽しむ！オータムスクール（～10/16） 大島
　　秋会期後半、海外の観光客が少しずつ戻ってくる ★15
　　祭粟島秋季大祭 粟島
10月21日　総合ディレクター北川フラムとめぐるスペシャルツアー第５弾 秋の新作ツアー 本島 高見島 多度津 ★16
10月22日　GREEN SPACE「オーチャード王越」 沙弥島
　　瀬戸内少女歌劇団「瀬戸内物語一塩飽編一」（10/23,29,30） 本島
　　女木島名画座上映会「アートなんかいらない！」 女木島
　　案内人：北川フラム　食事：民宿「umiyado 鬼旬」
10月25日　台風 14 号によりアイシャ・エルクメン《本州から見た四国》が破損 宇野港
10月28日　よるしるべ 2022（～10/30,11/3 ～ 5）観音寺
　　秋会期中、イギリスの人気歌手デュア・リパが直島、豊島、犬島を訪問し、インスタグラム（フォロワー 8000 万人）やツイッター（フォロワー 1000 万人）にその様子が発信された

11月

11月 3日　島のお誕生会 豊島
　　ままごと「あゆみ（短編）」 小豆島
　　ネオン・ダンス「身体と物体を超えて」 多度津
　　祭大島天満宮秋季例祭 大島
　　祭塩飽本島合同文化祭 本島
11月 5日　ままごと「反復かつ連続」 豊島
11月 6日　総合ディレクター北川フラムとめぐるスペシャルツアー第６弾 豊島 大島
　　クロージングセレモニー 本島 伊吹島
　　瀬戸芸 2022 秋会期閉幕、閉会式 高松 ★17
11月15日　祭男木島文化祭 男木島
11月16日　祭地域交流会 女木島

12月

各島、宇野港で住民意見交換会が行われる
12月11日　島のお誕生会 豊島
12月28日　男木島もちつき 男木島 ★18

2023年

1月

1月15日　島のお誕生会 豊島

2月

2月11日　祭第 27 回女木地区文化祭 女木島
2月12日　島のお誕生会 豊島
2月26日　祭伊吹島百手祭り 伊吹島

3月

3月 5日　祭粟島百々手 粟島
3月12日　島のお誕生会 豊島

★13

★14 [SM]

★15 [SM]

★16

★17 [SM]

★18

公式デザイン
Official Design

瀬戸内国際芸術祭 2022 のメインビジュアルのテーマは、「島のお年寄り」。初回からメインビジュアルを手がけているグラフィックデザイナーの原研哉（写真：上田義彦）が制作し、2021 年 9 月 29 日に発表した。ポスターやチラシなどの印刷物、作品鑑賞パスポート、公式ウェブサイト、公式アプリなどに展開し、芸術祭の魅力を伝える重要なコミュニケーションツールとなった。

The theme for main visuals of the Setouchi Triennale 2022 was "the Elderly on the Islands". The visuals were revealed to the public on September 29th in 2021. They were created by graphic designer, Kenya Hara, who has been in charge of the main visuals since the first Setouchi Triennale, and the photographs were taken by Yoshihiko Ueda. Adapted for various media including print materials such as posters and flyers, the Triennale passport, the official website, and the official app, the visuals played a key role in communicating the appeal of the Triennale.

島のお年寄りたちに二つの魔法をかけます。
ひとつは「サングラス」。
思いっきりド派手で、ロックンロールで、グラマラスで、ピカピカに光っている、
パワフルで非日常な黒いサングラスを、じいちゃん、ばあちゃんにかけてもらいました。
サングラスはアートのメタファ。
照れてもいい、ピースをしてもいい。ともかく明るければいい。
ふたつ目の魔法は写真。上田義彦さんの「ポートレートの魔術」。
これは、そこにある素晴らしいものを「生け捕りにする」技術です。
直島のプロジェクトをはじめた福武さんの「直島は老人がいい」という言葉が記憶に残っています。
確かに、瀬戸内国際芸術祭で島々を訪れた際に、じいちゃん、ばあちゃんたちの存在感は眩しかった。
この素晴らしさを、海を背景に、生け捕りにします。
老人大国日本から世界へ、とびきり明るいメッセージ。
2022 のポスターは人をアートにするコミュニケーションでいきます。

原研哉（瀬戸内国際芸術祭 コミュニケーションディレクター）

I brought out the enchantment of the elderly who live on the islands in two ways.
The first way was with sunglasses.
I asked them to wear powerful and extraordinary sunglasses with black lenses that shone brilliantly.
They were flashy and glamorous, with a rock 'n' roll feel.
The sunglasses were a metaphor for art.
The models might have a shy look. They could make a peace sign if they wanted.
Anything goes as long as they are cheerful.
The second way was with the photographs, or "the magic of portraits" by Yoshihiko Ueda.
His magic "captures alive" the natural splendor of what's in front of the lens.
I remember that Mr. Fukutake who started the Naoshima project said, "the elderly people on Naoshima are great".
Indeed, when I visited the islands for the Setouchi Triennale, the elderly had a radiant presence.
The main visuals perfectly capture this brilliance, against the background of the ocean.
This is an exceptionally bright message from Japan, a nation with a large elderly population.
The poster for the 2022 Triennale turns people into art.

Kenya Hara (Communication Director of the Setouchi Triennale)

公式ガイドブック Official Guidebook

作品、イベント、地図、食、交通情報などを掲載した公式ガイドブックを発行した。
本体価格＝税込 1,320 円、発行部数＝ 36,000 部

An official guidebook was published with information about artworks, events, maps, food, transportation, and more. (Sold at 1,320 yen. A total of 36,000 copies were printed.)

公式アプリ Official app

経路検索機能を備えたスマートフォン用公式アプリケーションを無料公開し、来場者の周遊をサポートした。
ダウンロード数＝ iOS 版 28,219 件、Android 版 9,206 件

An official smartphone app with route navigation was provided for free to make it easier for visitors on their trips. (Downloaded 28,219 times on iOS and 9,206 times on Android.)

原研哉

デザイナー。1958 年生まれ。無印良品、蔦屋書店、GINZA SIX 等のアートディレクションで知られる。日本を未来資源としてとらえ直す視点から、様々なプロジェクトの立案を行ってきた。2019 年にはウェブサイト「低空飛行」を開始、「高解像度の旅」をテーマに観光分野への新たなアプローチを試みている。日本デザインセンター代表。武蔵野美術大学教授。

Kenya Hara

A designer. Born in 1958, he is known for his art direction for Muji, Tsutaya Books, GINZA SIX, and more. Reassessing Japan as a future resource, he has proposed ideas for various projects. On "Teikuhiko", a website he launched in 2019, he explores new approaches to tourism with the theme of "High Resolution Tours". President of the Nippon Design Center Inc. and Professor at Musashino Art University.

着地広告物　Advertisement

ポスターやリーフレット等の印刷物の他に、のぼりや横断幕等の広告物、公式ピンバッジ等のノベルティグッズを制作した。また、新たにデジタルサイネージの制作を行い、高松空港・民間鉄道会社などの交通機関、都内などの民間商業施設で配信を行った。

We created printed materials such as posters and leaflets, advertisements such as flags and banners, and promotional items such as official pins. New digital signage content was also created, and it was displayed at Takamatsu Airport and other transportation facilities including those of private railway companies, and at private commercial facilities including ones inside commercial buildings in Tokyo.

グッズ Goods

芸術祭の公式ロゴや今回のメインビジュアルのテーマである「島のお年寄り」をモチーフに公式グッズを制作し、高松港と直島の公式ショップ等で販売した。

Official goods were created and sold at several locations including official shops at Takamatsu Port and Naoshima. The goods incorporated the official logo of the Triennale as well as motifs with the theme of the main visuals, “the Elderly on the Islands”.

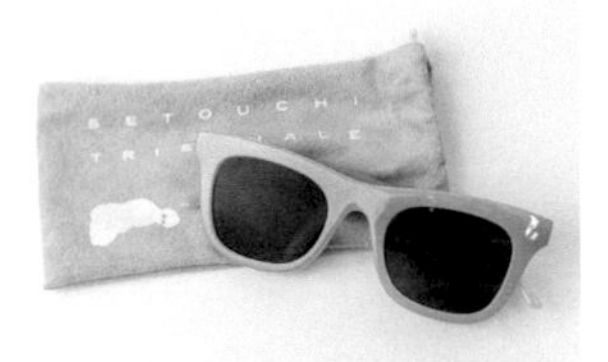

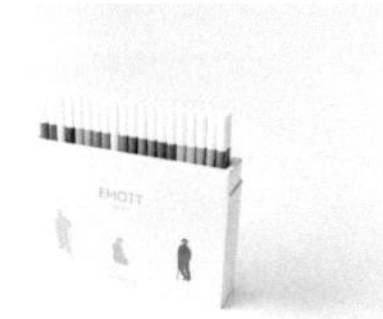

データでふりかえる瀬戸内国際芸術祭 2022
Setouchi Triennale 2022 Data

来場者数 Number of Visitors

総来場者 Number of Visitors by Venue

723,316 人

会期別内訳 Number of visitors by season

春会期 Spring	228,133
夏会期 Summer	187,483
秋会期 Autumn	307,700

会場別内訳 Breakdown of sites

直 島 Naoshima	166,737
豊 島 Teshima	97,391
女木島 Megijima	44,553
男木島 Ogijima	40,228
小豆島 Shodoshima	123,382
大 島 Oshima	6,517
犬 島 Inujima	34,503
沙弥島 Shamijima	44,790
本 島 Honjima	17,679
高見島 Takamijima	21,596
粟 島 Awashima	15,163
伊吹島 Ibukijima	13,167
高松港周辺 Takamatsu Port	62,131
宇野港周辺 Uno Port	35,479

注釈）各島において、作品の配置状況や来場者の鑑賞ルートなどを考慮し、春会期27カ所、夏会期29カ所、秋会期36カ所の基準施設を設け、その来場者数を集計して算出した。

Note: The number of visitors was estimated by gathering data from 27 data collection sites during the spring session, 29 data collection sites during the summer session, and 36 data collection sites during the Autumn session. The location of these sites was determined on the basis of the distribution of artworks and the viewing routes on each island.

公式アートイベント来場者数 Official Art Event Attendance

8,125 人／19 イベント

注釈）個別の来場者数は各イベントページに掲載
Note: See each event page for attendance at each event.

公式ウェブサイトアクセス数 Number of Visitors to Official Website

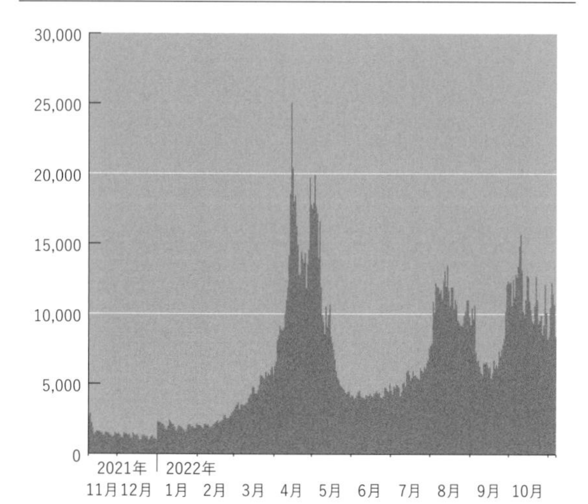

注釈）ページビューは閲覧されたページの合計数、ユニークユーザーはサイトを訪れた人数
Note: Page view indicates the total number of pages viewed, and unique users refers to the number of people who accessed the site.

チケット販売実績 Ticket Sales

作品鑑賞チケット販売数
Number of Tickets Sold

59,177枚

内訳 Breakdown

作品鑑賞パスポート
一般＝39,395枚
（3シーズン前売18,289枚、当日8,795枚｜1シーズン当日 春1,472枚、夏3,517枚、秋7,322枚）
ユース（16～18歳）＝530枚
島民＝1,144枚
1デイチケット＝16,273枚
2デイチケット＝1,835枚

フェリー乗り放題３日間乗船券 3-Day Triennale Ferry Pass

7,848枚

広報実績 Publicity

主な掲載メディア Major Instances of Media Coverage

新聞 Newspapers

朝日新聞、読売新聞、毎日新聞、産経新聞、日本経済新聞、四国新聞、山陽新聞、中国新聞、高知新聞、西日本新聞、熊本日日新聞、The Japan Times など

雑誌 Magazines

FRaU、男の隠れ家、ELLE、GA JAPAN、地球の歩き方 瀬戸内の島々②、XD MAGAZINE、ノジュール、日経アーキテクチュア、エンターテイメントビジネス、婦人画報、ことりっぷマガジン、FIGARO、Harper's BAZAR、BRUTUS、文芸春秋、Discover Japan、Casa BRUTUS、コトノネ、新建築 住宅特集、Fino、Residence Club MAGAZINE、タウン情報まつやま、オセラ、NICE TOWN、月刊タウン情報おかやま、愛媛Komachi、一番日本語（中国）、TIME（USA）、Forbes（USA）、SRTマガジン（韓国）、Jeux Nature（フランス）、Ming Pao Weekly(香港)など

テレビ TV

BS日テレ「絶景！瀬戸内アート旅 北川景子の感動島めぐり」、毎日放送「ANNニュースよんちゃんTV」、テレビ大阪「絶景！できたてアートに出会う旅『瀬戸内国際芸術祭2022』」、テレビ東京「新美の巨人たち『瀬戸内アート旅』」、NHK総合「あさイチ『愛でたいNippon』」、テレビ朝日「朝だ！生です　旅サラダ」、BSテレ東「中村獅童の灯台見聞録 瀬戸内編」、ABCテレビ「相席食堂」、関西テレビ「ちまたのジョーシキちゃん」、NHK BS-1「街角ピアノ 小豆島」、RSK「メッセージ　今こそアートの力で」、NHK高松「瀬戸芸とわたし ～のんがめぐる 早春アート旅～」、NHK岡山「瀬戸芸を旅して」、NHK高松「さぬきドキッ！現代アートのススメ！～こども×瀬戸芸」、NHK高松「瀬戸芸とわたし ～のんがめぐる 新緑アート旅～」、RNC「瀬戸芸ノススメ2022」、RNC「news every 報道特別番組『小さな島の美容室』」、NHK高松「あなたと感じる。アートと瀬戸内」など

ラジオ Radio

TOKYO FM「SUNDAY'S POST」、J-WAVE「TOKYO MORNING RADIO」、RNC/RSKラジオ「島島ラジオ」、FM香川「Letter from 瀬戸内」10/3～27、NHK WORLD インドネシア語放送（インドネシア）

ウェブ Web

SPICE、タイムアウト東京、Tokyo Art Beat、TOKYO Numero、FASHION PRESS、Casa BRUTUS、インターネットミュージアムアイエム、25Ans、Yahoo!Japan SDGs、coLocal コロカル婦人画報デジタル、サンテレビNEWS、Tokyo Weekender、FIGARO、ダイヤモンド・オンライン、美術手帖、Discover Japan、R100 Tokyo、デジタル朝鮮日報（韓国）、National Geographic Traveller（イギリス）、Go Japan、Japan Walker HK（香港）、Nippon Sensor（香港）、Maison（韓国）、Conde Nast Traveler（イギリス）、Lonely Planet（USA）、Global TRAVEL MEDIA『Japan's Best Inland Sea Travel 2022』（オーストラリア）など

SNS

フェイスブックアカウント数 Number of Likes on Facebook

「いいね！」件数＝60,216件（2022年11月6日時点）

ツイッターアカウントフォロワー数 Number of Twitter Followers

フォロワー数＝38,507人（2022年11月6日時点）

インスタグラムアカウントフォロワー数 Number of Instagram Followers

フォロワー数＝61,424人（2022年11月6日時点）

交通整備状況 Transportation Improvements

■海上交通の整備

(1)東の7島（直島、豊島、女木島、男木島、小豆島、大島、犬島）

【臨時航路】

運航区間	便数／日	運航事業者
小豆島(土庄)⇔直島(宮浦)	2	小豆島急行フェリー
小豆島(土庄)⇔犬島	3	
小豆島(坂手)⇔土庄東⇔直島(本村)⇔男木島	1※1	ジャンボフェリー
男木島⇔大島	2※1	
京橋⇔犬島⇔豊島(唐櫃)【新】	1※2	岡山京橋クルーズ

※1 土日祝及びお盆等のみ運航。※2 犬島⇔豊島(唐櫃)間は2便／日、土日祝のみ運航。

【既存定期航路の増便】

運航区間	会期中の便数／日	通常時の便数／日	運航事業者
高松⇔直島(宮浦)	11※1	10	四国汽船
直島(本村)⇔豊島(家浦)※2	1	－	豊島フェリー
宇野⇔豊島(家浦)⇔豊島(唐櫃)⇔小豆島(土庄)	10※3	9	小豆島豊島フェリー

※1 地中美術館の休館日を除く。
※2 高松⇔直島(本村)⇔豊島(家浦)航路の増便。
※3 宇野・豊島(家浦)間を増便(土日月祝及びお盆のみ)。

(2)西の5島（沙弥島、本島、高見島、粟島、伊吹島）

【臨時航路】

運航区間	便数／日	運航事業者
本島⇔高見島⇔粟島	6※	にじ観光

※　平日5便／日、土日祝6便／日、土日祝のみ臨時便を3便運航(定期便と合わせて最大9便／日)。

【既存定期航路の増便】

運航区間	会期中の便数／日	通常時の便数／日	運航事業者
丸亀⇔本島	10	8	本島汽船
児島⇔本島	6	4	六口丸海運
多度津⇔高見島	5	4	たどつ汽船
観音寺⇔伊吹島	8	5	真鍋海運

■島内交通の整備

【新設・増便】

	運行区間	会期中の便数／日	通常時の便数／日	運行事業者
新設	直島｜宮浦⇔地中美術館など	最大15便	－	大川バス
	豊島｜家浦⇔唐櫃、家浦⇔甲生	最大21便	(別に町営バスが計11便)	小豆島交通
	小豆島｜池田港ターミナル⇔草壁港、映画村など	3便	－	小豆島町
	小豆島｜福武ハウス⇔寒霞渓頂(※)	5便	－	
	本島｜本島泊港⇔屋釜浜	10便	－	琴参バス

※　最終便は福田港まで運行。

■本土側港付近の交通整備

【シャトルバスの運行等】

運行区間	便数／1日	運行事業者名
沙弥島｜坂出駅⇔沙弥島など	13便	琴参バス
与島｜坂出駅⇔与島など	5便※1	琴参バス
高見島｜多度津駅⇔多度津港	概ね30分毎	多度津町
粟島｜詫間駅⇔須田港	概ね60分毎	三豊市
粟島｜経面駐車場⇔須田港	随時	
伊吹島｜まちなか交流駐車場⇔観音寺港	13便	観音寺市
伊吹島｜有明グラウンド駐車場⇔観音寺港	13便※2	
犬島｜岡山駅⇔宝伝港(直行バス)	最大2便	両備ホールディングス
犬島｜西大寺駅⇔宝伝港(直行バス)	最大2便	西大寺活性化協議会

※1 復路は6便運行。※2　土日祝のみ

■駐車場

【3シーズンパスポート購入者専用無料駐車場】

会場	駐車場名	台数
高松港	高松港キャッスルプロムナード	100

【その他臨時無料駐車場】

会場	駐車場名	台数
沙弥島	瀬戸大橋記念公園西駐車場	258
	瀬戸大橋記念公園東駐車場	122
	瀬戸大橋記念公園北駐車場	50
本島（丸亀港）	丸亀市蓬莱町臨時駐車場	90
	丸亀港臨時駐車場	40
本島（児島観光港）	児島観光港駐車場	38
高見島（多度津港）	多度津港臨時駐車場	100
	多度津町総合スポーツセンター ※平日のみ	100
	多度津町大通り駐車場	100
	東港町臨時駐車場	130
粟島（須田港）	経面臨時駐車場	350
伊吹島（観音寺港）	ハイスタッフホール(まちなか交流駐車場)※平日のみ	168
	有明グラウンド駐車場 ※土日祝のみ	200

こえび隊参加状況 Koebi-tai Participation

実働人員数 Actual Number (Approximate Sum Total)　延べ3,842人

内訳 Breakdown

作品制作 Artwork Production　1,135人
作品受付 Art Site Desk　2,442人
各種ガイド Guides　101人
イベント運営 Events　164人

2点とも [SM]

企業・団体サポーター
Corporate & Organization Volunteer Supporters groups

総数(社／団体数) Total Number of Groups　52社／団体
総数(参加者数) Total Number of Participants　1,575人

アーティストと地域をつなぎ、作品と来場者を結ぶ役割を果たす瀬戸内国際芸術祭のサポーターには、「こえび隊」と「企業・団体ボランティアサポーター」がある。国内外の個人が参加する前者が中心となりながら、香川県・岡山県内の企業を中心とした団体が参加する後者にも多くの人が携わり、参加者の総数は延べ5,417人となった。コロナ禍での開催となったが、地元を中心とした高校生を含むボランティアサポーターが積極的に芸術祭に関わる姿も見られた。

The Setouchi Triennale, an event which connects artists with local communities, and artworks with visitors, is supported by the koebi-tai as well as by the Corporate & Organization Volunteer Supporters groups. The former is comprised primarily of individuals from inside and outside Japan, while the latter is comprised primarily of companies and organizations in Kagawa and Okayama Prefectures. The total number of people who volunteered was 5,417.

Although the Setouchi Triennale 2022 was held during the COVID-19 pandemic, many volunteers, mainly local people including high school students, were actively involved in the festival.

来場者アンケート結果
Result of the Questionnaire for Visitors

来場者の属性 Visitor Characteristics

■性　別 Gender

女性が64.0%、男性が34.6%であった。

64.0% of visitors were female and 34.6% were male.

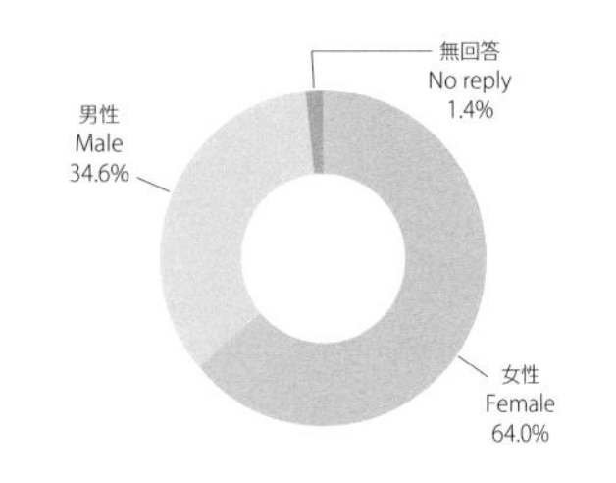

■グループ関係 Group Relationship

「家族と来た」が42.0%、「友人と来た」が34.3%、「ひとりで来た」が21.1%であった。

42% of visitors responded that they came with family, while 34.3% came with friends and 21.1% came alone.

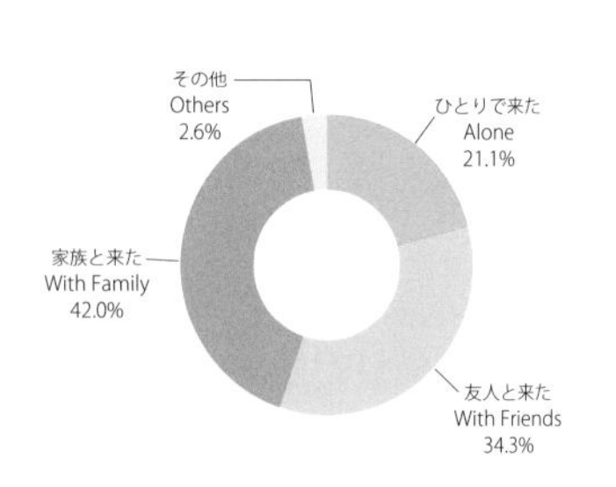

■年齢層 Age Group

20代が最も多く23.0%、次いで50代の20.0%、40代が19.0%であった。

Ages: 23.0% were in their 20s, 20.0% were in their 50s, and 19.0% were in their 40s.

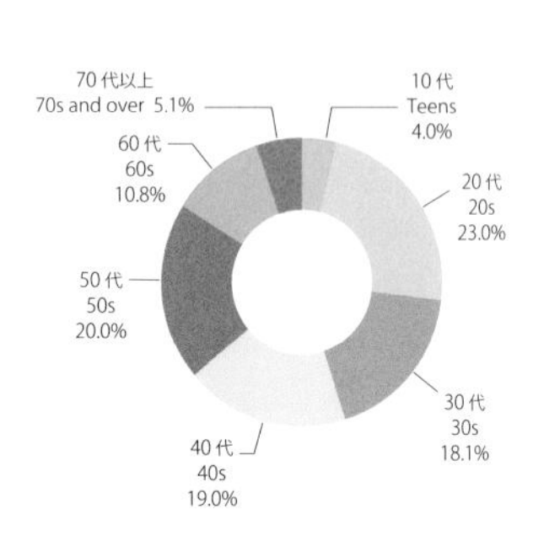

■居住地 Residence

居住地は、香川・岡山両県が43.0%、両県以外の国内が55.7%、国外が1.3%であった。

Of the total number of visitors, 43.0% were from Kagawa and Okayama prefectures while 55.7% were from other prefectures in Japan and 1.3% were from other countries.

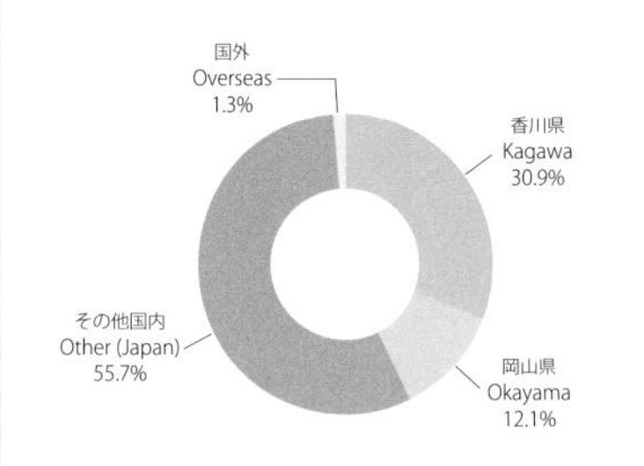

■地　域 From other Prefectures

国内来場者の地域別では、四国地方が36.3%、次いで関東地方が23.2%、近畿地方が16.1%、中国地方が16.0%であった。

By region of domestic visitors, 36.3% were from Shikoku Region, followed by 23.2% from the Kanto Region, 23.3% from the Kanto Region, and 16% from the Chugoku Region.

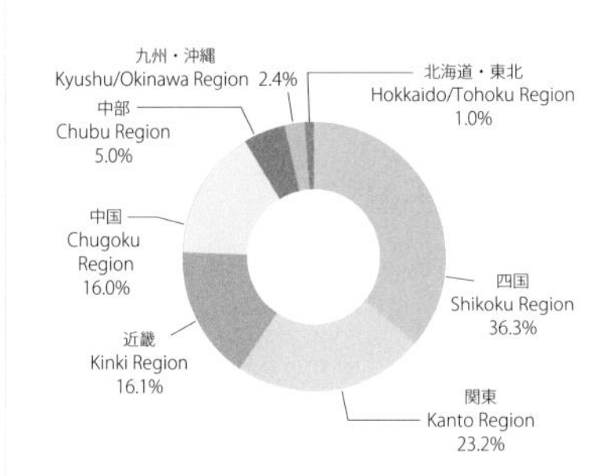

■海　外 Overseas

国外は、中国、台湾、香港が多く、国外来場者の半数を占めている。

The highest number of overseas visitors came from China, Taiwan and Hong Kong.

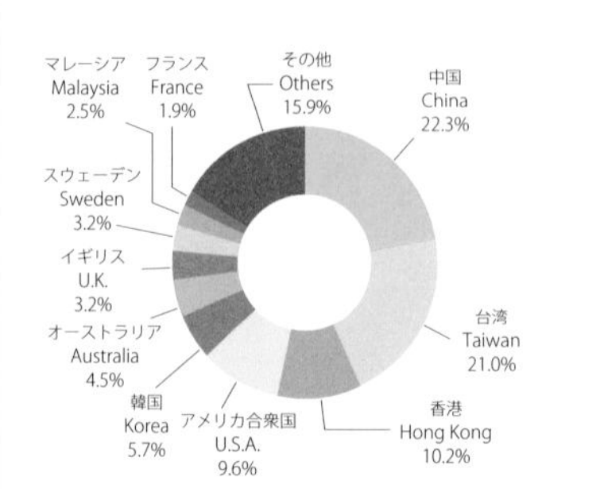

■過去の芸術祭への来場

Previous Visits to Setouchi Triennale

過去の芸術祭にも来場した、いわゆるリピーターは55.0%であった。

Of the total number of visitors, 55.0% were repeaters from previous Triennales.

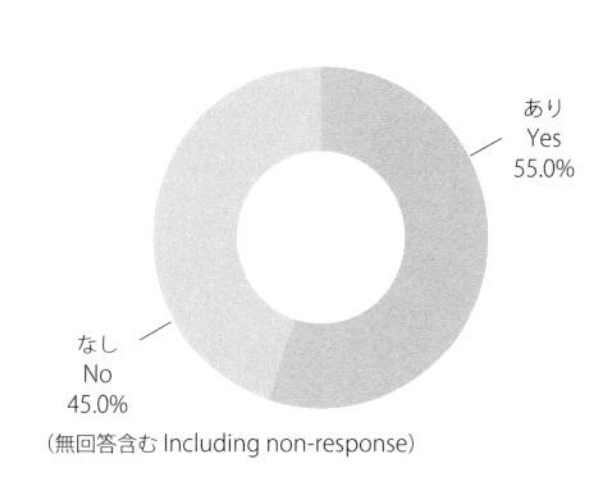

来場者の滞在状況 Visitors' Length of Stay

■滞在状況 Length of Visitor Stays

香川・岡山県以外からの来場者の平均滞在日数は2.85日(芸術祭2019:3.05日)であり、宿泊者の平均宿泊数は2.24泊であった。

The average length of stay for non-local visitors was 2.85 days (2019: 3.05), and the average number of nights spent in the area was 2.24.

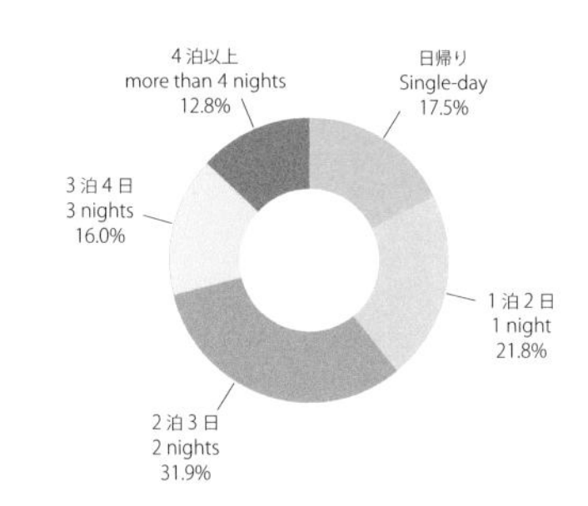

■宿泊地 Location of Accommodation

香川・岡山県以外からの来場者の宿泊地は、高松市内が48.2%、次いで直島が14.4%、小豆島が14.0%であった。

Concerning accommodation, 48.2% of visitors who stayed overnight were accommodated in Takamatsu, followed by Naoshima and Shodoshima.

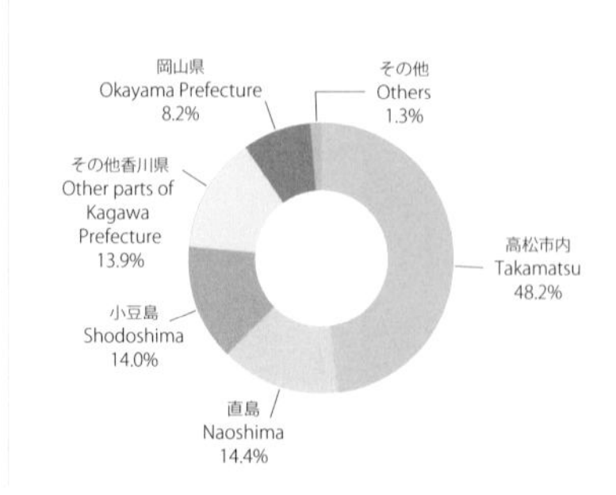

観光地への訪問
Visits to Sightseeing Spots

■芸術祭以外への観光地訪問 Other Sightseeing
約2.4人に1人が香川県内の芸術祭以外の観光地を訪問している。
About 1 in 2.4 also visited local non-Triennale sightseeing spots during their stay.

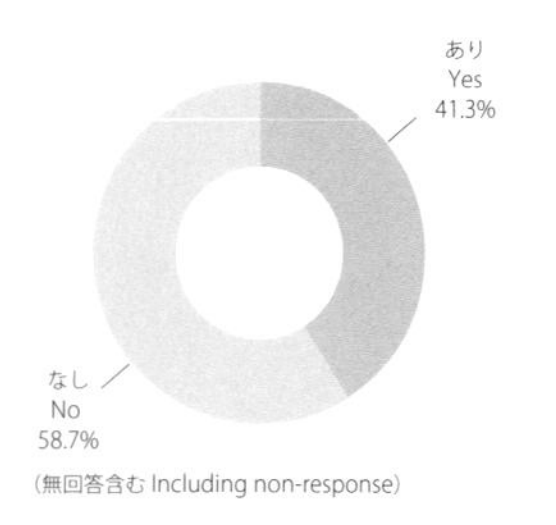

(無回答含む Including non-response)

芸術祭に対する評価 Evaluation of the Triennale

■評価 Evaluation
96.2%が「非常によかった」「よかった」と評価している。
96.2% of visitors responded that the Triennale was "very good" or "good".

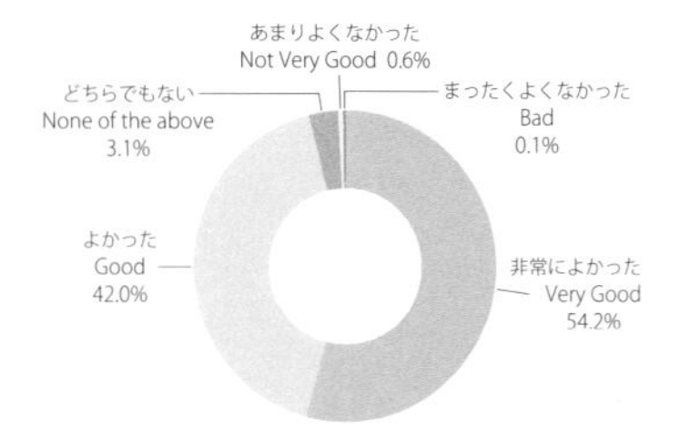

■次回の来場 Return Plans
次回芸術祭が開催された場合、91.6%が「是非来たい」「来たい」と回答している。
When asked if they wished to come to the next Triennale, 91.6% responded "definitely want to" or "want to".

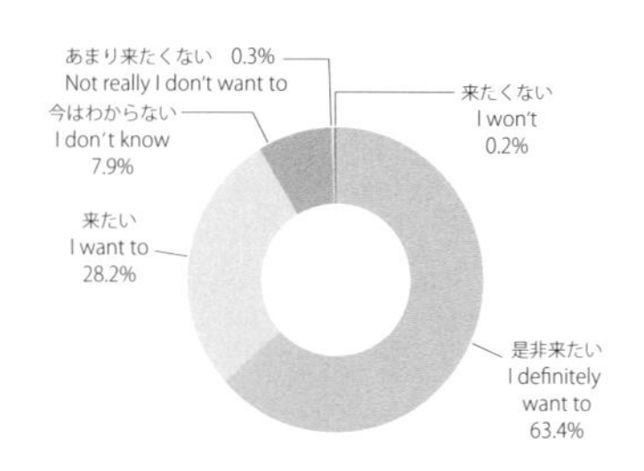

住民アンケート結果
Result of the Questionnaire for Islanders

■地域活性化 Local Revitalization
芸術祭2022が地域の活性化に「大いに役立った」、「少しは役立った」と回答した住民は73.0%であった。
Concerning the impact of the Triennale on revitalization, 73% of residents said that holding the Triennale contributed to revitalization of the local community.

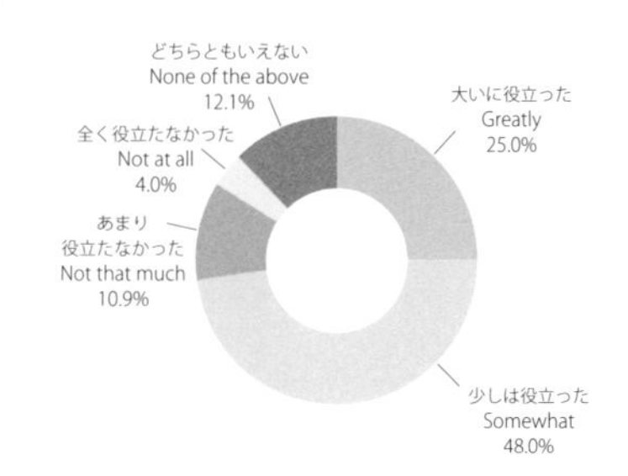

■地域への作品設置 Installation Placement
自分が住む地域に芸術祭の作品が設置されたことについて、「大変よかった」、「まあまあよかった」と回答した住民は70.9%であった。
In addition, 70.9% of residents responded that it was "very good" or "moderately good" to have artworks installed in the area where they live.

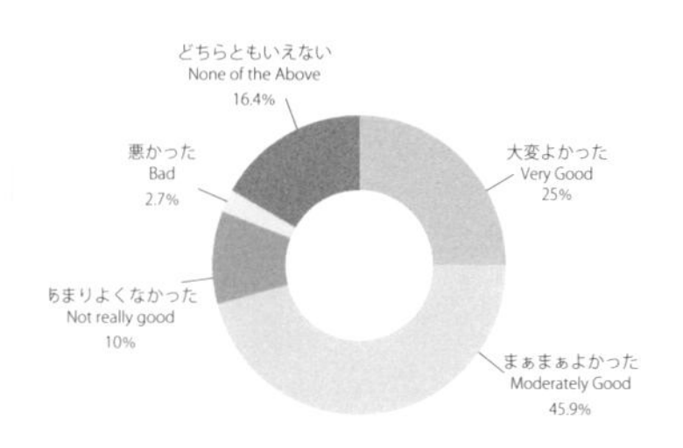

■開催への期待 Future Editions
今後も芸術祭を「ぜひ開催してほしい」「どちらかといえば開催してほしい」と回答した住民が65.8%であった。
Concerning the next Triennale, 65.8% of residents said that they would like it to be held again.

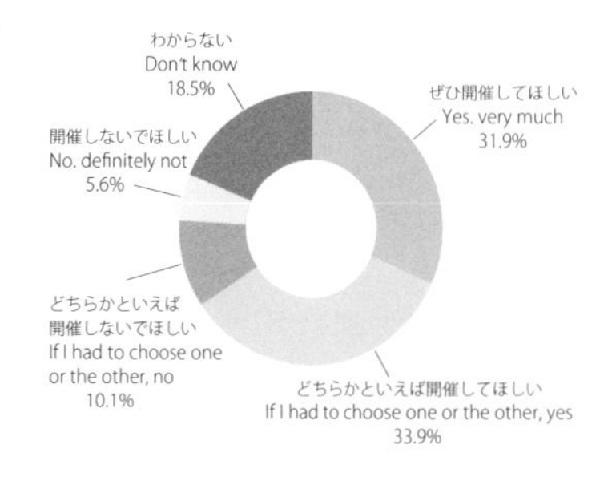

ベーシックツアー参加者アンケート結果
Result of the Questionnaire for Basic Tour Participants

■印象に残った経験 Strongest Impressions
一番印象に残ったこととして40%が「景色」、次いで36%が「アート」と回答している。
40% answered "scenery" and 36% answered "art" as the most impressive thing.

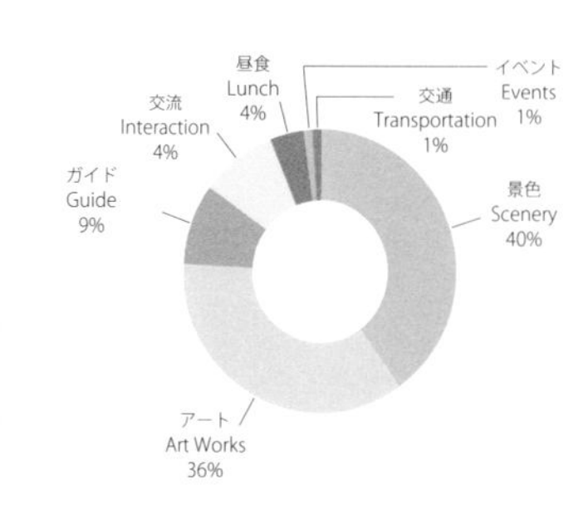

[SM]

学校連携事業

Collaborations with Schools

学校連携事業

未来の瀬戸内を担う子どもたちを育成することを目的として、香川県教育委員会や地元の高等学校等と連携し、会場となっている島々の独自性や県内外からの来場者が多い芸術祭ならではの特性を生かしたさまざまな課外活動等を実施した。芸術祭の開催趣旨や継続的な取り組みを学ぶとともに、島での作品鑑賞、作家や住民との交流、こえび隊の活動参加などを通して、地域や自分たちの将来について考える機会を創出した。

Collaborations with Schools

With the aim of helping to cultivate children who would play a central role in future Setouchi events, we conducted various activities in cooperation with Kagawa Prefectural Board of Education, local high schools, and others. The activities included participating in a tour in which they explained about artworks in Japanese and English as guides, joining koebi-tai guide activities, and helping artwork creation and food services.

実績

●香川県立小豆島中央高等学校との連携

実施日＝2020年8月2日｜内容＝「英語で楽しむ"瀬戸内国際芸術祭"作品鑑賞ツアー」を実施｜参加者数＝9人
実施日＝2020年9月27日｜内容＝作品ガイド体験ツアーを実施｜参加者数＝11
実施日＝2021年10月25日～11月20日｜内容＝日本語及び英語による作品のガイド体験を実施｜参加者数＝7人
実施日＝2022年7月30日｜内容＝作品見学及び作家との交流を実施｜参加者数＝6
実施日＝2022年9月11日｜内容＝瀬戸内国際芸術祭の学習とこえび隊のガイドツアーを実施｜参加者数＝3人
実施日＝2022年10月2日｜内容＝こえび隊活動への参加と作品ガイドの体験を実施｜参加者数＝6人

● 香川県立坂出商業高等学校との連携

実施日＝2021年10月9日｜内容＝櫃石島の住民との交流活動を実施｜参加者数＝12人

● 香川県立多度津高等学校との連携

実施日＝2022年5月29日～11月6日｜内容＝高見島の作家との協働や生徒撮影の写真展示、住民が利用する実用品（テーブル、ベンチ）の制作を実施｜参加者数＝延べ90人

●香川県立笠田高等学校との連携

実施日＝2022年7月19日～11月6日｜内容＝伊吹島の「うららの台所」で提供する弁当のレシピの提案や提供の補助を実施｜参加者数＝延べ26人

● 香川県立観音寺総合高等学校との連携

実施日＝2020年10月24日｜内容＝伊吹島で芸術祭公式カメラマンによるフォト研修やアートツアーを実施｜参加者数＝25人
実施日＝2021年4月25日～2022年1月21日｜内容＝伊吹島の住民が利用する実用品（ベンチ）や芸術祭の来場者への提供を想定した弁当の試作のほか、伊吹島の魅力を伝えるツアー等の企画立案を実施｜参加者数＝89人
実施日＝2022年4月29日～9月24日｜内容＝伊吹島の作家と連携しながら住民が利用する実用品（ベンチ）を製作するなどの課外活動を実施｜参加者数＝延べ79人

● 高校生のための瀬戸内アートサマープログラム（香川県教育委員会生涯学習・文化財課との連携）

実施日＝2020年8月8日～29日｜内容＝「地域を深く知ろう！」をテーマに課題解決に取り組むプログラムを実施（講演、フィールドワーク、プレゼン等）｜参加者数＝49人（12校）
実施日＝2021年7月17日～8月4日｜内容＝「瀬戸内と深く関わろう！」をテーマに課題解決に取り組むプログラムを実施（講演、フィールドワーク、プレゼン等）｜参加者数＝50人（17校）
実施日＝2022年7月18日～8月26日｜内容＝「島へ行こう！芸術祭を伝えよう」をテーマに課題解決に取り組むプログラムを実施（講演、フィールドワーク、プレゼン等）｜参加者数＝49人（12校）

オフィシャルツアー

Official Tours

ベーシックツアー・カスタマイズツアー

2022年の新規作品などを中心とした作品鑑賞とともに、芸術祭の開催趣旨やこれまでの取り組みの成果について理解し、より深く芸術祭の魅力や瀬戸内の食を楽しめる、ツアーガイド付きのオフィシャルツアーを実施した。今回は、香川県発着のコースに加え岡山県発着のコースを新設した計11コースのツアーを催行し、アンケート調査では、95％以上の参加者が「満足した」と回答した。また、公式イベントに参加するツアーやテーマ別のスペシャルツアーを12回実施したほか、旅行者の要望に応じた旅の企画や提案、施設等の手配、ガイド等を行うカスタマイズツアーを実施した。

Basic Tour / Customizd Tour

Several guided official tours were organized. Participants could enjoy artworks, especially those newly installed for the 2022 Triennale, and understand the Triennale's concept while learning about past projects and their achievements. The tours helped visitors fully savor the art festival's atmosphere as well as Setouchi's local food. For the 2022 Triennale, a total of 11 different tour courses were prepared, including those leaving and arriving in Kagawa prefecture and newly added ones leaving and arriving in Okayama prefecture. According to the questionnaire, 95% or more of the participants answered that they were satisfied with the tours. Also, a total of 12 special tours were held, some of which took the participants to official events while some were based on different themes. There were also customized tours, which were offered according to the tourists' requests. For the customized tours, itineraries were proposed, facilities and other arrangements were made, and other services including tour guides were offered.

【ツアーコース】

香川県発着

Aコース：会場＝豊島・犬島｜料金＝15,800円
Bコース：会場＝大島・女木島・男木島｜料金＝12,800円
Cコース：会場＝小豆島｜料金＝12,800円～13,800円
Dコース：会場＝沙弥島｜料金＝8,900円
Eコース（秋会期のみ）：会場＝本島・高見島｜料金＝16,300円
Fコース（秋会期のみ）：会場＝粟島・伊吹島｜料金＝16,800円
Yコース（秋会期のみ）：会場＝屋島｜料金＝3,000円

岡山県発着

Gコース：会場＝豊島・犬島｜料金＝16,000円
Hコース：会場＝女木島・男木島・宇野港｜料金＝13,000円
Iコース：会場＝本島・高見島｜料金＝13,000円
Jコース：会場＝小豆島｜料金＝12,000～13,000円

【参加者数】

春会期	ツアー本数＝50本	定員＝1,675人	参加者＝948人	参加率＝57%
夏会期	ツアー本数＝40本	定員＝1,268人	参加者＝794人	参加率＝63%
秋会期	ツアー本数＝77本	定員＝2,731人	参加者＝1,813人	参加率＝66%
合 計	ツアー本数＝167本	定員＝5,674人	参加者＝3,555人	参加率＝63%

全点とも[SM]

県内連携事業

Collaborations within Kagawa Prefecture

県内連携事業

芸術祭の来場者が、芸術祭開催エリア以外の見どころも楽しめるきっかけ作りとして、香川県内の市町や団体が実施する文化芸術イベントや観光スポットと連携して相互PRを行った。またInstagramを活用した「県内周遊事業(ハッシュタグキャンペーン)」を実施し、特定のハッシュタグをつけて投稿された観光スポットの写真などから特に魅力的な投稿を選出し、撮影者に香川県産品や瀬戸内国際芸術祭2022公式グッズ等の懸賞品を提供した。

Collaborations within Kagawa Prefecture

To encourage visitors to enjoy local attractions other than the Triennale venues, we cooperated in 100 events organized by cities, towns, and organizations in Kagawa prefecture and with organizations or facilities including parks, shopping arcades, art museums, markets, local festivals, and scenic spots, all promoting each other. Also, a hashtag campaign was run on Instagram, and some users whose posts promoted events and sightseeing spots received prizes.

広域

1 かがわ・山なみ芸術祭2022
2 ①香川県内高校生部活動応援企画「青春応援プロジェクト」アート大作戦②海の不思議な生き物展＆ワークショップ③せとうち夏の回廊
3 高松琴平電気鉄道株式会社

高松市

4 あじ竜王山公園
5 うみまち商店街
6 おいでまい祝祭2022 〜みんなでつなぐ、まちとアート〜
7 香川県障害者芸術祭2022 〜キラリ☆と光る芸術祭〜
8 讃岐おもちゃ美術館
9 SANUKI ReMIX(讃岐リミックス)
10 四国村ミウゼアム
11 獅子舞王国さぬき2022
12 史跡高松城跡 玉藻公園
13 SETOUCHI BOOK MARKS
14 第11回うどん県書道パフォーマンス大会 inサンポート
15 高松空港
16 たかまつ工芸ウィーク
17 高松シンボルタワー
18 旅の守り神「SHIP'S CAT」コミュニティダイニング
19 丸亀町グリーン×瀬戸内アートコレクティブ
20 むれ源平石あかりロード
21 屋島山上

丸亀市

22 おしろのまちの秋の月 瀬戸内のイイモノをあつめたマルシェ
23 中津万象園・丸亀美術館
24 広島
25 ボートレースまるがめ
26 丸亀城周辺
27 丸亀市猪熊弦一郎現代美術館
28 レオマリゾート(NEWレオマワールド)

坂出市

29 鎌田ミュージアムスタンプラリー
30 シャッターアートプロジェクト
31 瀬居島アートプロジェクト2022 by神戸芸術工科大学
32 ひついし・福王寺・夢・アート・スタジオ
33 「ヨタの漂う鬼の家　島に渡る」

善通寺市

34 おしゃべり広場
35 旧善通寺偕行社
36 五ヶ寺・七カ所まいり
37 捨身ヶ嶽禅定(しゃしんがたけぜんじょう)
38 JR善通寺駅
39 まちなか黒板アート
40 ゆうゆうロード

観音寺市

41 一の宮公園
42 寛永通宝(通称:銭型砂絵)
43 高屋神社
44 ちょうさ祭り
45 豊稔池堰堤

さぬき市

46 大窪寺の紅葉
47 さぬき市野外音楽広場(テアトロン)
48 津田の松原(県立琴林公園)
49 さぬき市天体望遠鏡博物館
50 門入ブリッジ・椿の城

東かがわ市

51 ジオサイトクルーズ (プレジャーボートで一億年のタイムトラベル!)
52 女郎島
53 手袋(①東かがわ手袋ギャラリー、②手袋神社、③香川のてぶくろ資料館・手袋アウトレット店)
54 ナイトZOO(しろとり動物園)
55 人形劇場とらまる座30周年記念行事 とらまる人形劇カーニバル2022
56 東かがわ市とらまるパペットランド とらまる人形劇ミュージアム
57 ベッセルおおち
58 山田海岸
59 湾岸アートプロジェクト

三豊市

60 志々島の大楠
61 父母ヶ浜
62 津嶋神社
63 戸川ダム
64 漂流郵便局
65 ぶいぶいガーデン
66 三豊鶴 酒蔵 Art Restaurant 〜時空と五感の蔵開き〜

土庄町

67 urara days!
68 オリーヴの大樹
69 宗教法人 小豆島大観音
70 屋形崎夕陽の丘
71 妖怪美術館〜ナイトミュージアム2022〜

小豆島町

72 小豆島町の秋祭り
73 こううん駅(紅雲亭)
74 小豆島手延べそうめん学校
75 橘漁船アート
76 二十四の瞳映画村(Gallery KUROgO)
77 道の駅小豆島オリーブ公園
78 道の駅小豆島ふるさと村

三木町

79 池戸公民館
80 太古の森
81 渡邉邸

直島町

82 ヌーヴォー・シルク・ジャポン2022　in　直島

宇多津町

83 青ノ山山頂展望台
84 宇多津「古街」エリア
85 ゴールドタワー"天空のアクアリウム ソラキン"
86 四国水族館

綾川町

87 うどんといちごの郷　道の駅　滝宮
88 柏原渓谷
89 滝宮の念仏踊り

琴平町

90 一之橋公園
91 旧金毘羅大芝居「金丸座」
92 県立琴平公園展望台
93 金刀比羅宮
94 中野うどん学校琴平校

多度津町

95 県立桃陵公園
96 金剛禅総本山少林寺
97 本通の町並み

まんのう町

98 国営讃岐まんのう公園
99 まんのうひまわり
100 名勝 満濃池

広域連携事業

Collaborations with Other Areas of Japan

広域連携事業

芸術祭の機運醸成や文化的発信を拡大していくため、日本各地で開催されている芸術祭と連携し相互広報を実施し、双方の公式ウェブサイトへの情報掲載や芸術祭会場でのパンフレット配布などを行った。国内で最も伝統ある現代日本彫刻展を開催している山口県宇部市とは連携協定を締結し、第28回UBEビエンナーレにおいて大賞を受賞した三宅之功氏を芸術祭の参加作家として招待。小豆島屋形崎において作品の展示(sd43)を行った。

Collaborations with Other Areas of Japan

The Triennale cooperated with other art festivals held all over Japan, publicizing information about each other on websites and distributing pamphlets about each other at the venues. We concluded a partnership agreement with Ube City in Yamaguchi prefecture, and invited Shiko Miyake, who won the Grand Prize at the 28th UBE Biennale, to participate in the Setouchi Triennale 2022 as an artist.

連携した事業

芸術祭の開催年だけではなく、早い時期から、日本各地で開催されている芸術祭と相互に連携した取り組みを行った。
Not only in the year of the festival, but also from an early stage, efforts were made in mutual cooperation with art festivals across Japan.

せとうち美術館ネットワーク
Setouchi Museum Network

第29回UBEビエンナーレ(現代日本彫刻展)
The 29th UBE Biennale International Sculpture Competition
2022/10/2〜11/27

岡山芸術交流2022 Okayama Art Summit 2022
2022/9/30〜11/27

越後妻有 大地の芸術祭 2022 Echigo-Tsumari Art Triennale 2022
2022/4/29〜11/13

国際芸術祭「あいち2022」Aichi Triennale 2022
2022/7/30〜10/10

Reborn Art Festival 2021-22
[前期]2021/8/11〜9/26
[後期]2022/8/20〜10/2

房総里山芸術祭 いちはらアート×ミックス2020+
Ichihara Art x Mix 2020+
2021/11/19〜12/26

北アルプス国際芸術祭 2020-2021
Northern Alps Art Festival 2020-2021
2021/8/21〜11/21

奥能登国際芸術祭2020+ Oku-Noto Triennale 2020+
2021/9/4〜10/24

第29回UBEビエンナーレ(現代日本彫刻展)ポスター
The 29th UBE Biennale International Sculpture Competition poster

岡山芸術交流2022 フライヤー
Okayama Art Summit 2022 flyer

越後妻有 大地の芸術祭 2022 メインビジュアル
Echigo-Tsumari Art Triennale 2022 main visual

国際芸術祭「あいち2022」ポスター
Aichi Triennale 2022 poster

Reborn Art Festival 2021-22 [後期]フライヤー
[Second Term] flyer

パートナー Partners

瀬戸内国際芸術祭の趣旨に賛同していただき、自社のメセナやCSR活動に位置付けるなど、瀬戸内国際芸術祭の活動を継続して支援する意向を有し、瀬戸内国際芸術祭2022に一定金額以上の協賛をしていただいた企業・団体様を「瀬戸内国際芸術祭パートナー」として、緊密な関係を構築させていただいています。

100年をつくる会社
鹿島

協賛 Sponsors

JR四国

JR西日本

ひとのときを、想う。 JT

NOMURA

株式会社 Life-do.Plus

DNP 大日本印刷

RICE FORCE

大和証券 Daiwa Securities

百十四銀行

UTE.CO.,LTD

アオイ電子株式会社
http://www.aoi-electronics.co.jp/

あなたと世界を変えていく。
NTT docomo

Orientalmotor

香川県建設業協会
高松支部

香川県信用金庫協会
観音寺信用金庫　高松信用金庫

香川證券

ごまで、世界をしあわせに。
かどや

木下製粉株式会社

Kubota
クボタ／クボタ環境エンジニアリング

SAMSOLUTION
For a sustainable future of energy and food
株式会社サムソン

SHISEIDO CREATIVE

NIPPON MARU

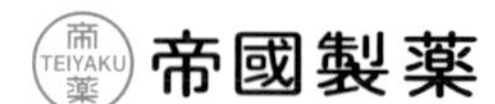

公益財団法人
南海育英会

·HAKUHODO·

ひとりを守る みんなを守る
BIKEN

本四高速

公益財団法人
松平公益会

TOSHIBA

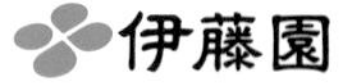

HOTSOX

agnès b.

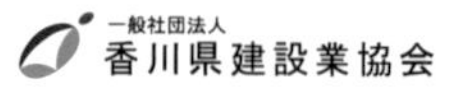

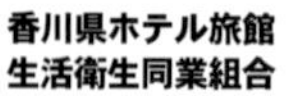

研精堂印刷株式会社

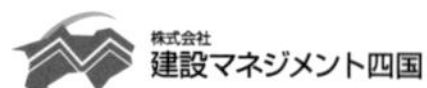

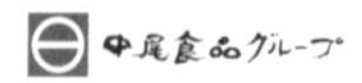

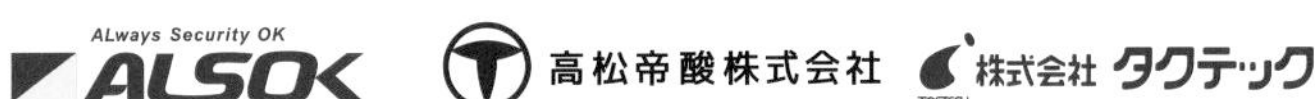

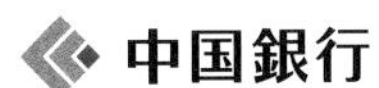

東京美術

TOPPAN

トヨタレンタリース岡山

西崎組

日宝綜合製本

K'sケーズデンキ

株式会社福本ボデー

FUJITSU 富士通Japan

株式会社 マキタ MAKITA CORPORATION

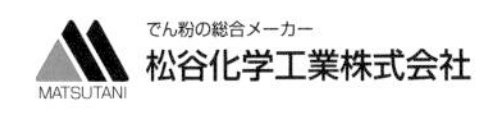

SMBC 三井住友銀行

三菱マテリアル

サカケン株式会社　香川県建設業協会中讃支部　四國団扇株式会社　キリンビバレッジ株式会社
富士建設株式会社　アイプリックス株式会社　株式会社STNet　香川県漁業協同組合連合会
住友商事株式会社　勇心酒造株式会社　株式会社おもちゃ王国　一般社団法人香川県トラック協会
セトラスホールディングス株式会社　株式会社Coaマネジメント　コーホク印刷株式会社
コカ・コーラボトラーズジャパン株式会社　後藤設備工業株式会社　株式会社サニーエイト
一般社団法人四国クリエイト協会　小豆島醤油協同組合　小豆島調理食品工業協同組合
損害保険ジャパン株式会社　第一生命保険株式会社東四国支社　株式会社トロンマネージメント
ピープルソフトウェア株式会社　フジガード株式会社　富士産業株式会社　株式会社松本光春商店
株式会社ムレコミュニケーションズ　レオマリゾート

株式会社NSメッシュ　株式会社日栄建設　谷口建設興業株式会社　株式会社ヒカリ　株式会社フューチャー・デザイン・ラボ
四国計測工業株式会社　四電ビジネス株式会社　eBASE株式会社　株式会社小竹組　高松商運株式会社　第二建築株式会社
株式会社藤田工務店　株式会社高岸工務店　葵機工株式会社　有限会社エイトヒルズ・コーポレーション　有限会社エイファーマ
香川県建設業協会小豆支部　香川県建設業協会西讃支部　香川県建設業協会長尾支部　香川県舗装協会　カンコーマナボネクト株式会社
北浜alley株式会社　株式会社香西鉄工所　琴平バス株式会社　四国塗装株式会社　株式会社七星食品　シンボルタワー開発株式会社
セーラー広告株式会社　株式会社総合開発　大同ゴム株式会社　大和板紙株式会社　高松キワニスクラブ　宝田電産株式会社
株式会社多丸組　有限会社手ぬぐい工房ポスター堂　西日本ビル管理株式会社　ばいこう堂株式会社　株式会社フードテック
丸八商工株式会社　三豊運送株式会社　安田技研株式会社　和田精密歯研株式会社　森永乳業株式会社　株式会社ゴーフィールド
株式会社フクシン　石丸製麺株式会社　ANAクラウンプラザホテル岡山　株式会社ADF・アヤベ　株式会社岡山京橋クルーズ
岡山トヨタ自動車株式会社　株式会社オリコ　有限会社川北縫製　株式会社きんでん四国支社　株式会社グリーンフィールドグラーフィク
株式会社廣榮堂　堺屋醤油株式会社　株式会社サピエント　株式会社サンテック　株式会社CO2資源化研究所　株式会社ジェイアール四国企画
株式会社 JR四国ホテルズ　株式会社ジェイテクト四国工場　株式会社四国総合研究所　四国鉄道機械株式会社　四国塗装工業株式会社
セキ株式会社　ダイヤモンド瀬戸内マリンホテル　株式会社デンショク　東洋オリーブ株式会社　東洋工業株式会社　徳寿工業株式会社
豊田通商株式会社　合同会社直島アートユニット　株式会社長峰製作所　株式会社ネクストインターナショナル　ビジネスホテルプリンス
平井法律事務所　株式会社富士クリーン　株式会社FUJIDAN　株式会社伏見製薬所　株式会社フジワラテクノアート　丸善工業株式会社
株式会社宮地サルベージ　株式会社明電舎四国支店　株式会社名物かまど　矢崎総業四国販売株式会社　株式会社ユーミック
株式会社夢菓房たから　株式会社リプリ　税理士法人六条

助成 Funding

瀬戸内国際芸術祭2022を支えた人びと

Collaborators

瀬戸内国際芸術祭実行委員会（構成団体はP.3参照）

特定非営利活動法人瀬戸内こえびネットワーク

ボランティアサポーター｜こえび隊

2022年1月1日～2022年11月30日の間に、こえび隊として登録し、3回以上活動に参加した方を掲載しています。

団体

坂出第一高等学校（笠井優羽、久保田優亜、和氣結花）

個人（50音順）

青木悟、赤木友子・美緒、赤澤裕子、秋本麻帆、秋山玄、秋山玲美、浅野幸代、浅野麻利江、東歩美、穴吹香織、穴吹誠、阿部慶子、甘利喜雄・すみい、安藤宏子、飯尾俊之、池北美智代、池田学・美代子、池田萌咲、石井笑実里、石井乃々華、石井由紀、石垣樹来、石川英恵、石川裕介、石崎一歩、石崎里美、石田陽子、石谷優我、石原宗祐、石丸恵、泉佳那、磯崎明子、板野洋子、伊丹隆二、市橋福雄、伊津千恵美、井戸隼太、井上雅代、井野川千代子、猪熊展子・さら、猪原早紀子、今栄ゆり子、今西嘉子・由樹・亜衣、岩徹、岩瀬永三可、植田明美、植田朋子・智咲、植松陽子、請川瑞枝、牛込麻依、内海洋子、及川浩奈、大井大三、大浦悠、大賀康恵、大西理奈、大林めぐみ、大平崇代、大前裕、大美瑠莉夏、大山真美子、岡直子、岡萌、小笠原克文、岡本利恵、岡本礼奈、岡山佐千子、岡山創一、奥谷照榮、小河亮平、織田航、小野哲生・玉貴、尾之内嚴博、海沼知里、香川真生、掛川浩之、柏木優里奈、片山光穂、葛西七海、葛石真士・悠史、加藤千佳、金澤輝弥、鹿野桃香、加村晴美、川崎公美子、川西徳大、川畑博子、河原田啓史、神原知江、菊池佐紀子、菊池ナオコ、北賀美代子、北窓隆子、北村喬、木村晃子、木村佳子、木村荘太、木村哲夫、木村万友美、木村美葵、邱亭瑜、櫛田麻衣、国本史絵、窪保彦、久保田雄一郎、黒川雅代、黒田ただよし、小岩綾、香西正惠、合田大輔、合田なぎさ、神山広美、小門直美、小迫遼、児島那奈、小菅杏樹、小関美和、後藤順子、後藤健、後藤努・基伸、小橋広夢、小林花菜、小林隼也、小林洋平、小溝朱里、斉藤節二、齋藤智恵、佐伯南美、坂田圭司、坂元佐知枝、坂本文子、佐々木康介、佐々木公平、佐々木勇仁、笹谷敏恵、佐藤亜沙美、佐藤恵子、佐藤伸子・瑞姫、佐藤百恵、澤村遥、塩山晶子、篠原淳、篠原幸喜、島崎裕崇、島田和雄、島田聡、嶋田幹、島村真子、清水達也、志村みづえ、下山琴羽、朱麗、白井みなみ、白石幸一、城田鎮男、進藤睦子、神内勇樹、新名祐子、神余実加、末岡聖史、須賀聡子、杉村ひばり、杉山春佳、資延宏紀、鈴木茜、鈴木泉、鈴木伸男、鈴木理恵子、砂川秀男、関獅音、関良子、瀬戸優之、千田真美、高井菜緒、高木健二、高木里子、高木楓夏、高木睦美、高嶋利枝、高田英樹・紀久美、高橋暢茂、髙橋遥、高橋正勝、高畠芳枝、高村朋美、竹内恵実、武智麻衣子、多田羅琴梨、橘有紀、田名麻衣子、田中禎雄、田中典子、谷川紀子、田宮誠、田村賢二郎、為平浩一、チェンペイチュ、中條珠代、塚田明広、辻万莉子、津嶋和宏、槌田佳与杏、常久弘美、坪倉英夫、津村咲妃、土居大記、土井猛之、土居優香、東海明寛、時田桃々子、冨重雅也、冨永隼史・公未佳・七帆・湊太、友永浩司、豊田量子、豊田真由、長井佐知子、中井隆徳、中内星子、長尾さゆり、仲里真琉、仲田憲一、中谷篤子、中野行雄、中村彩、長屋耕太、中山享子、中山真理子、中山美樹、新美佳奈、西まち、西岡篤志・知里、西田有里、西谷隆一、西山長、二宮琉音、野崎香菜子、長谷川祐子、畠山弘美、波多野宏美、八田由美、林一馬、林直子、林真琴、林実紀、春田佳子・彩寧・悠妃、坂東美香、板東悠希、土方智恵美、肥田和典、日名川中・奈津子、平岩めぐみ・恋季、平田優里菜、平林徹典、廣瀬彩夏、廣瀬美知子、廣瀬由佳、FENGSHI、吹田桂子・陽、福井光一、福井渚大、福田秀秋、福田真大、福本茂樹、藤井昌子、藤井佳之、藤岡美佐保、藤沢隆弘、藤平佳史、藤村加代、古川京司、星川智子・紫緒里、細谷孝代、細野道恵、堀井大介、堀上麻有、堀上宏、堀川菜穂子、堀川洸輔、堀籠葉子、前田勝則、前田友紀子、増田敬一、増田卓美、増田直樹、松井祥子、松枝純子、松尾絵美子、松川香里、松川幸誠、松永千春、松村綾香、松本香里、マツモトカヨコ、松本由美子、松本陽子・梨歩、眞鍋伊代、間部俊一、三浦美子、三木真菜、光畑典子、三野雅仁、三村加代子、宮崎佑貴、宮本雅大、三好ひさこ、六車武志、村川いくこ、メイン展子、籾田心、森順司、森國真帆、柳生笑子、安井千晶、保田卓也、矢野航士郎、矢野隼也、矢野真二、矢原直、矢吹佳菜、山内彩葉、山岸敏子、山口順子、山口真理、山﨑香織、山崎健悟、山地涼子、山下ルリコ、山田華、山田麻由佳、山田瑞枝、山地桃加、山中佳代、山根孝規、山本あずさ、山本佳奈、山本沙織、山本紗希、山本聡、山本太一、山本哲也、山本直子、横田泰男、吉岡哲司、吉岡春菜、吉川健司、吉村弘、米山敏生、廖詩屏、リンケイホウ、脇清美、和田佳祐、渡邊永理、渡辺翔真、Cha Wong、CHEN YU CHEN、Chih Hsuan Chu、Josée Vaillancourt、LEI JIALU、Wang Cai Ci、WONG TSZ CHUN、ほか約800名の仲間が一緒に活動しました！

ボランティアサポーター｜企業・団体

高松大学
高松短期大学

香川県職員退職者会

百十四銀行

四国電力グループ
四国計測工業

観音寺市
ボランティア
連絡協議会

地域と歩む 新たな未来
観音寺信用金庫

海ほたる隊、岡山県立岡山東商業高等学校、高松信用金庫、三豊広域行政組合、株式会社ＩＨＩ、四国東芝グループ、
四国化成ホールディングス株式会社、香川高等専門学校、社会福祉法人 多度津町社会福祉協議会、
ＮＴＴ西日本 香川支店、株式会社北四国グラビア印刷、四国電力送配電株式会社、株式会社ジップ、
第一生命保険株式会社東四国支社、大手前丸亀中学・高等学校、香川県立高瀬高等学校、
ライフデザイン・カバヤ株式会社、大阪産業大学校友会 香川県支部、香川県立観音寺第一高等学校

穴吹エンタープライズ株式会社、高松帝酸株式会社、多度津町議会、三菱電機株式会社四国支社、西讃観光株式会社、四変テック株式会社、
三菱重工業株式会社四国支社、社会福祉法人 多度津福祉会 特別養護老人ホーム桃陵苑、観音寺市職員有志・元職員有志、
公益社団法人多度津町シルバー人材センター、マックスバリュ西日本株式会社、金剛禅総本山少林寺、株式会社イトーキ、
観音寺市消費者友の会、香川県立観音寺総合高等学校、大倉工業株式会社、香川西高等学校、一般社団法人少林寺拳法連盟、
合田邸ファンクラブ、高松空港株式会社、ほか1団体

個人寄付 池田哲史、川岸さおり、金山和紀、西立野公平、笠井聖也、五十嵐美枝、塚原美穂、その他有志の皆様

会場別協働者

個人、団体の順にそれぞれ50音順（日本・海外）で掲載しています。敬称略。

全域

カミイケタクヤ、本間大悟｜あけぼの丸、粟島汽船株式会社、大川バス、株式会社岡山京橋クルーズ、株式会社鬼ヶ島観光自動車、株式会社 Office Toyofuku、有限会社からこと丸、株式会社かんかけタクシー、国際両備フェリー株式会社、琴参バス株式会社、四国汽船株式会社、四国フェリー株式会社、しましまゴミゼロプロジェクトのみなさん、ジャンボフェリー株式会社、小豆島オリーブバス株式会社、小豆島急行フェリー株式会社、小豆島交通株式会社、小豆島豊島フェリー株式会社、瀬戸内観光汽船株式会社、株式会社豊島フェリー、雌雄島海運株式会社、小豆島フェリー株式会社、西讃観光株式会社、たどつ汽船株式会社、にじ観光有限会社、本島汽船株式会社、株式会社真鍋海運、マルイ観光、両備バス、六口丸海運株式会社｜取材協力・素材や場所の提供、制作やワークショップ・運営に参加いただいたみなさん

直島

赤井重子、安部淳一、阿部成吾、大島恵理子、大舘祐右、大塚剛、大塚美喜子、岡本雄大、片柳木ノ実、玉井和樹、津田愛子、中村信平、中村政太郎、中村田鶴子、名合彩、名合美和子、西瑞子、早野佳恵、三田和弘、村尾三郎、村尾由紀子、山西利恵、四ツ目圭吾、邱資郡、アンドリュー・マコーミック、ほか直島のみなさん｜護王神社氏子総代会、瀬戸内国際芸術祭直島町実行委員会（三菱マテリアル株式会社直島製錬所、四国汽船株式会社、NPO 法人直島町観光協会、直島町商工会、直島漁業協同組合、直島町連合自治会、直島町老人クラブ連合会、うぃ・らぶ・なおしま、直島町文化協会、直島塾）、本村自治会

豊島

植松武義、清水里子、三井恵子、宮路雅行、山坂誠、ほか豊島のみなさん｜家浦自治会、上口石材、唐櫃漁業協同組合、唐櫃自治会、唐櫃棚田保存会、甲生自治会、十輪寺、NPO 法人豊島観光協会、豊島「食」プロジェクト推進協議会、土庄中央漁業協同組合家浦支所、土庄中央漁業協同組合甲生支所、ドンドロ浜商店、株式会社野村組、民宿カラフル

女木島

礒崎裕生、萩原安雄、川井美帆、久米慶子、鈴木豪、高岸朝子、高橋光穂、谷キミ子、為壮真吾、中小路光子、西岡藤八、藤井佳之、星野聡子、増田卓美・民恵、松内卓司、三島恵子、湊健雄、宮脇ケイ子、目加田怜美、横山成子、吉本優子、ほか女木島のみなさん｜鬼ヶ島観光協会、鬼の畠、鬼旬（松内日出男・千帆）、株式会社デザインセンター、東瀬戸漁業協同組合、女木校区連合自治会、女木地区コミュニティ協議会

男木島

河西範幸、中野達樹、ほか男木島のみなさん｜男木島観光協会、高松市立男木小学校、男木地区コミュニティ協議会、男木地区連合自治会、高松市立男木中学校、慶應義塾大学 SFC 坂茂研究室、東瀬戸漁業協同組合、みまや工房

小豆島

井上和也、江森健人、笠井一咲、笠井友香子、門口利正（ひよこ食堂）、金近強氏、金近洋子、鎌田久司（靴のカマダ）、河西範幸、酒井徹、清水里子、炭山幹雄、高橋彰、名和研二、橋本美家子、蓮井秀平、藤本徹、松村英明、松本武夫、三浦尚志、宮下晃、宮下直子、宮下晴渡、宮本忠利、森本秀男、柳生好彦、山下輝人、山本英樹、橄欖、ほか小豆島のみなさん｜池田漁業協同組合、池田港フェリーターミナル、池田地区老人会のみなさん、馬木自治会、馬木ひしお会、オリビアン小豆島夕陽ヶ丘ホテル、オリーブペイント株式会社、有限会社笠井石材加工販売、片城自治会、亀山八幡宮、神懸通自治会、京都芸術大学、京都工芸繊維大学、KYOTO Design Lab、神浦自治会、草壁本町自治会、草壁本町南自治会、国民宿舎小豆島、西光寺、坂手自治会、小豆島内海Ｂ＆Ｇ海洋センター、小豆島オリーブユースホステル、一般社団法人小豆島観光協会、小豆島町観光協議会、小豆島町地域おこし協力隊、小豆島町農村環境改善センター、小豆島ふるさと村、昭和自治会、親交自治会、株式会社制作美術研究所、一般社団法人 setouchi とのしょう、有限会社高橋建設、田中電気工事株式会社、ツジカワ株式会社、肥土山自治会、テーテンス事務所、寺東自治会、天神自治会、土庄港観光センター、土庄町商工会女性部、土庄本町自治会連合会、西中自治会、日進自治会、本町一丁目自治会、本町二丁目自治会、中山イベント推進会、中山自治会、南蒲野自治会、株式会社西崎組、ハフニアムアーキテクツ、浜条老人会、肥土山自治会、肥土山農村歌舞伎保存会、葺田八幡神社、福田影絵団、福田漁業協同組合、福田地区自治連合会、有限会社マル喜井上工務店、三都半島アートプロジェクト実行委員会、MeiPAM、迷路のまちづくり委員会、迷路のまちボランティアガイド協会、屋形崎自治会、屋形崎夕陽の丘継承会、小豆島町立 安田小学校、株式会社矢田建設、山口芸術情報センター［YCAM］、王文志スタッフ、んごんごクラブ

大島

青田ヒロミ、イワモトジロウ、酒井今日子、藏座江美、十河圭一、内藤光穂、森田州、弓指寛治、ほか大島のみなさん｜おかしのはなし、お菓子野山、小木曽庭苑、菓子屋 ten.ten.、国立療養所大島青松園社会交流会館、国立療養所大島青松園入所者自治会、国立療養所菊池恵楓園入所者自治会、一般社団法人金陽会、（株）造園あら井、ハンズクラフト秋田

犬島

犬島のみなさん｜あけぼの丸、犬島町内会、犬島婦人会、岡山市立犬島自然の家、岡山市立山南学園、岡山県備前県民局、岡山市、宝伝連合町内会、宝伝老人クラブ

沙弥島・坂出

濱本敏広、溝淵純、Alexandros Miaris、Mikhail Khodarevsky、ほか与島５島のみなさん、王越地区のみなさん｜王越地区連合自治会、香川県中讃土木事務所、国際ソロプチミスト坂出、坂出親子おてつ隊、坂出海上保安署、坂出警察署、坂出交通安全協会、坂出市観光協会、坂出市漁業連絡協議会、坂出市建設業協会、坂出市国際交流協会、坂出市子ども会育成連絡協議会、坂出商工会議所、坂出市商店街連合会、坂出市ＰＴＡ連絡協議会、坂出市婦人団体連絡協議会、坂出市文化協会、坂出シニアライオンズクラブ、坂出市連合自治会、坂出商業開発協同組合、坂出白峰ライオンズクラブ、坂出青年会議所、坂出東ロータリークラブ、坂出ライオンズクラブ、坂出旅館組合、坂出ロータリークラブ、四国旅客鉄道株式会社坂出駅、沙弥自治会、瀬戸内オリーブ園株式会社、瀬戸内国際芸術祭坂出市実行委員会、瀬戸大橋記念館、高松海上保安部、番の州６社会、東山魁夷せとうち美術館、与島地区連合自治会

本島・丸亀

岡田忠行、善生直樹、谷川政子、豊島正治、信原清、浜脇義弘、原健太、冨木田誠、藤井由美子、三宅邦夫、森中澄子、森中恒夫、安田典子、吉田勉、レアーレ砂本、ほか本島・丸亀のみなさん｜青木

石材協同組合、生ノ浜自治会、笑くぼ、大浦自治会、大倉邸、海鮮亭、笠島自治会、笠島まち並保存センター、gallery&cafe 吾亦紅、甲生自治会、小浦自治会、小阪自治会、コーヒーショップフイム、里浦自治会、茶房伊達、史跡塩飽勤番所顕彰保存会、島そだち、島のたこ焼き屋さん、島まんま、島娘、尻浜自治会、塩飽漁業協同組合連合会、塩飽建設株式会社、瀬戸内国際芸術祭本島実行委員会、DAIFUKU、太陽の家、天理教本島大教会、泊自治会、有限会社冨木田電気商会、福田自治会、久福ブルーイング本島、本島漁業協同組合、本島校区連合自治会、本島コミュニティ、丸亀市立本島小学校、本島スタンド、本島駐在所、特定非営利活動法人本島町笠島まち並保存協力会、塩飽勤番所跡、honjima bakery、丸亀市立本島保育所、丸亀市猪熊弦一郎現代美術館、一般財団法人丸亀市観光協会、丸亀市市民交流活動センターマルタス、公益社団法人丸亀市シルバー人材センター、丸亀市立本島中学校、宮ノ浜自治会、モッコク亭、やかた船、屋釜自治会、山根自治会、山根児童館、山根文化センター

高見島・多度津

阿江天規、池田慎之介、池田亮太、石川久光、石田史郎、石村智彦、太田泰友、岡地幸子、岡山富男、掛札かの子、片岡正文、門和則、亀田ひなた、河西範幸、神田凛、木田光重、木原庸造、久玉勝惠、葛本康彰、隅田保代、倉本博史、坂本直輝、坂本勝、白川洋二、菅原優子、高嶋利枝、武智奏子、田中恵子、中島智靖、中塚幹人、中村二二男、野村友美、林伸光、日向満雄、藤田秀夫、布藤喜帆、古米邦夫、松井千夏、松浦豊、松尾和美、水原涼、村井信之、森田豊美、安井雪乃、山崎直哉、山野清子、山野雅道、山野松子、吉田恭大、吉村聡浩、ほか高見島のみなさん|えがおの会、N's DINNING、海食処笑門家、香川県立ミュージアム、喫茶あい、合田邸ファンクラブ、瀬戸内国際芸術祭多度津町支援協議会、瀬戸内国際芸術祭多度津町実行委員会、多度津町議会、高見浦1区自治会、高見島応援団「さざえ隊」、高見浜1区自治会、高見浜2区自治会、たどつ汽船株式会社、多度津町教育委員会、多度津商工会議所、多度津町高見漁業協同組合、多度津町立資料館、公益財団法人 多度津町文化体育振興事業団、多度津文化財保存会事務局長、香川県立多度津高等学校、まことプラザ、丸亀警察署、民宿森田、株式会社山下建設、六区自治会

粟島・三豊

岩崎環、竹内英裕、ほか粟島のみなさん|粟島ふる里劇団、粟島ぽ～い&が～るの会、粟島連合自治会、海ほたる隊、海上タクシーいせや、香川県漁業協同組合連合会、香川県立善通寺第一高等学校、佐藤建築、四国学院大学香川西高等学校、四国明治株式会社、瀬戸内国際芸術祭三豊市実行委員会、須田自治会、詫間漁業協同組合、詫間町吹奏楽団、まちづくり推進隊詫間、三豊市観光交流局、三豊市漁業協同組合、三豊市商工会、三豊市ホテル・旅館・民宿同業組合、有限会社山田材木店、ル・ポール粟島

伊吹島・観音寺

伊勢妃鶴、伊勢弘隆、岩中博和、篠原幸喜、真鍋正、真鍋信隆、三好兼光、三好正一、三好大地(太鼓 Artist)、三好廣子、三好洋市、ほか伊吹島のみなさん|アオハタ鮮魚店、伊吹漁業協同組合、伊吹島北地区自治会、伊吹公民館、伊吹島元気隊、伊吹商店、観音寺市立伊吹小・中学校、伊吹地区自治協議会、観音寺市立伊吹保育所、伊吹島民族資料館、伊吹八幡神社、うららの台所のみなさん、香川県立笠田高等学校、河童屋、観音寺伊吹郵便局、観音寺漁業協同組合、観音寺市建設業協会、観音寺市ボランティア協議会、観音寺市商店街連合会、観音寺市民会館(ハイスタッフホール)、香川県立観音寺総合高等学校、香川県立観音寺第一高等学校、株式会社久保電機、瀬戸内国際芸術祭伊吹島実行委員会、瀬戸内国際芸術祭観音寺市実行委員会、合同会社銭形マルシェ、トーヨースギウエ株式会社、光工業株式会社、有限会社丸山防災、港町自治会、株式会社山一水産、有限会社山下建設、株式会社 RINGUE デザイン事務所

高松港

庵治石開発協同組合、讃岐石材加工協同組合、四国二期会、香川大学合唱団、香川大学教育学部音楽領域、香川大学経済学部学生チャレンジプロジェクト「TERASU」、高松シンボルタワー管理協議会、高松空港株式会社、認定 NPO 法人・農村歌舞伎祇園座保存会、学校法人のぞみ学園のぞみ幼稚園、原和裁専門学院、屋島山上観光協会、れいがん茶屋

宇野港

宇野港のハルさん、大前裕、糟谷健三、加藤兆可、金川倫子、中野公子、玉野の食を愛する有志(金川洋一、上月慧、小林未歩、武田万実、中山公人、畑明子)、二宮章、三宅泉、山川美佐、ほか築港商店のみなさん| UNO HOTEL、岡山県宇野港管理事務所、岡山県環境文化部文化振興課、国指定重要文化財旧野崎家住宅、成興鋼業株式会社、セイコー堂宇野本店、瀬戸内国際芸術祭たまの☆おもてなし推進委員会、KEIRIN HOTEL 10、玉野市立図書館・中央公民館、玉野海上保安部、たまの観光ボランティアガイドの会「つつじの会」、岡山県立玉野高等学校、岡山県立玉野光南高等学校、一般社団法人玉野コミュニティ・デザイン、一般社団法人玉野産業振興公社、公益社団法人玉野市観光協会、玉野市立玉野商工高等学校、玉野市文化財保護委員会、たまのスチューデントガイドのみなさん、玉野市立玉野備南高等学校、たまの湯、玉野市立築港小学校、築港西コミュニティ協議会、築港東コミュニティ協議会、築港南老人会/婦人会、ナイカイ塩業株式会社、中山靴店、西日本旅客鉄道株式会社岡山支社、野崎家塩業歴史館、株式会社ベネルート、道の駅みやま公園、無天茶坊

株式社社アートフロントギャラリー

瀬戸内国際芸術祭実行委員会事務局/自治体主管

香川県文化芸術局瀬戸内国際芸術祭推進課、高松市創造都市推進局文化・観光・スポーツ部文化芸術振興課、丸亀市産業文化部文化課、坂出市建設経済部産業観光課、観音寺市経済部商工観光課、三豊市政策部産業政策課、土庄町商工観光課、小豆島町企画振興部企画財政課、直島町まちづくり観光課、多度津町政策観光課、玉野市産業振興部商工観光課

[凡例]

- 瀬戸内国際芸術祭 2022 において新たに作品を発表した作家、および既存作品を再制作・新展開した作家について、アルファベット順に記載した。
- ユニットの場合は 1 人目の氏名を基準とし、それぞれの作家情報を記載した。
- 生年、出身地については、作家の意志に従い掲載を省略したものもある。
- 略歴は、2022 年 12 月時点での活動とし、主に編集部で作成した。
- 作品名は《》、建築物・パフォーミングアーツ・展覧会名は「」で示し、書籍・映画のタイトルは『』で示した（一部例外あり）。
- 展覧会やプロジェクトなどの開催地は（）内に「会場名、都市名、国・地域名」の順で示し、複数にわたる場合は「、」で列挙した。また、開催地が首都の場合は国・地域名の表記を省略し、展覧会名や会場名に都市名、国・地域名、開催年が含まれる場合や、文中に同じ都市名などが連続する場合は、表記を省略した（一部例外あり）。
- 過去の瀬戸内国際芸術祭に出展した作家は、参加年を［瀬戸内］の後に記載した。

[Biographical Notes]

- -The listed profiles are only for the artists whose artworks were newly created or developed for the Setouchi Triennale 2022. Artist / Group names are listed in alphabetical order.
- -For units, the name of the first person was used for categorization.
- Depending on the artist's preference, his or her date of birth or place of birth may not be provided.
- Personal biographies were mainly written by editorial staff, and are current as of December 2022.
- Titles of works, books, magazines, and collections, etc. are displayed in italics. (Please note that there are some exceptions.)
- For exhibitions or projects held in multiple venues, cities, or countries, the respective venues are linked with a forward comma (,). In the case of the capital city, the country and region name is omitted, as in cases where the name of the city or country and region is included in the exhibition name or the venue, or where the same venue and city are already known within the same artist or group. (Please note that there are some exceptions.)
- For artists who participated the previous editions of the Triennale, years are mentioned following [Setouchi].

A

アデル・アブデスメッド
Adel Abdessemed

1971 年アルジェリア生まれ、フランス在住。ドローイング、映像作品、彫刻からインスタレーションまで、表現方法は多岐に及び、MoMA PS1、ヴェネチア・ビエンナーレ、サンパウロ・ビエンナーレ、ポンピドゥー・センターなど、国際的に評価の高い展覧会で作品を発表している。

Born in Algeria in 1971, and lives and works in France. His artworks often use video, sculpture, and drawings as a medium and have been presented internationally-acclaimed art festivals and institutions including MoMA PS1 (New York), the Venice Biennale (Italy), The São Paulo Art Biennial (Brazil), and Centre Pompidou (Paris).

あきびんご
Akibingo

1948 年広島県尾道市生まれ。日本画を制作しながら幼児教育に深く関わり、教材の開発や絵画教室に取り組む。還暦を機に絵本制作を始め、デビュー作『したのどうぶつえん』（くもん出版）で第 14 回日本絵本賞を受賞。その他の代表作に『あいうえおん』『でてくるぞでてくるぞ』（くもん出版）など。

Born in Onomichi, Hiroshima in 1948. While producing Japanese paintings, he also committed to education for pre-schoolers, developing teaching materials and running painting classes. At 60, he began creating picture books, and his first, *Shitano Dobustuen (Zoo Below)*, won the 14th Japan Picture Book Award. His other major works include *Aiueo-n* and *Detekuruzo Detekuruzo (Here They Are, Here They Are)* (all Kumon Publishing).

マナル・アルドワイヤン
Manal AlDowayan

1973 年サウジアラビア生まれ。サウジアラビアの今を見つめる女性アーティスト。中東文化圏における女性の表現を中心に、公共とプライベート、伝統と現代、地域と世界、見えるものと見えないものをテーマに活動している。主な展示にヴェネチア・ビエンナーレ（2009・2011）など。

Born in Saudi Arabia in 1973. A female artist examining contemporary Saudi Arabia. Focusing on attitudes towards women in the culture of the Middle East, she is actively interested in the themes of public and private, tradition and modernity, region and world, and visible and invisible. Her major exhibitions include the Venice Biennale (2009, 2011).

安藤忠雄
Tadao Ando

1941 年大阪府生まれ。1969 年安藤忠雄建築研究所設立。プリツカー賞（1995）、UIA（国際建築家連合）ゴールドメダル（2005）、文化勲章（2010）、芸術文化勲章コマンドゥール（2013）ほか受賞多数。ベネッセアートサイト直島では「ベネッセハウスミュージアム」（1992）、「地中美術館」（2004）、「ANDO MUSEUM」（2013）など 8 施設の建築設計を手がける。［瀬戸内］2010、2013、2016、2019

Born in 1941 in Osaka. Established Tadao Ando & Associates in 1969. Recipient of numerous Japanese and foreign awards, including the Pritzker Prize (1995) and the UIA (International Union of Architects) Gold Medal (2005). Ando was also named Commandeur de l'Ordre des Arts et des Lettres (2013). For Benesse Art Site Naoshima, he built eight structures on Naoshima, including Benesse House Museum (1992), Chichu Art Museum (2004), and ANDO MUSEUM (2013). [Setouchi] 2010, 2013, 2016, 2019

青木野枝
Noe Aoki

1958 年東京都生まれ。活動初期より、工業用の鉄板を円などの基本となるかたちに切り出し、それらをつなぎ合わせるように溶接した彫刻作品を手がける。近年は石膏、ガラスなど異素材の作品も発表。主な受賞歴に、芸術選奨文部大臣賞、毎日芸術賞、中原悌二郎賞。［瀬戸内］2010、2013、2016、2019

Born in Tokyo in 1958. From the early stages of her career as an artist, Aoki has been working with basic shapes, such as rings and circles, cut from industrial steel plates and welded into sculptures. In recent years, she has begun branching out to work with diverse materials, including plaster and glass. Major awards include the Minister of Education New Artist Prize, the Mainichi Arts Award, and the Teijiro Nakahara Award. [Setouchi] 2010, 2013, 2016, 2019

コラクリット・アルナーノンチャイ&アレックス・グヴォジック
Korakrit Arunanondchai & Alex Gvojic

コラクリット・アルナーノンチャイ
Korakrit Arunanondchai

1986 年タイ・バンコク生まれ、ニューヨークを拠点に活動。政治的な出来事や歴史、個人的な経験などを、音と映像で収集する。ヨコハマトリエンナーレ（2020）、ヴェネチア・ビエンナーレ（2019）、シドニー・ビエンナーレ（2016）など多数の国際展に参加。

Born in Bangkok, Thailand in 1986, and based in New York. He collects political events, history, and personal experiences in the form of sound and film. He has participated in the Yokohama Triennale (2020), the Venice Biennale (2019), and Biennale of Sydney (2016), as well as other international exhibitions.

アレックス・グヴォジック
Alex Gvojic

1984年アメリカ生まれ。アート、ファッション、音楽など多分野を横断する作品を手がける。近年の展示にベルリン・ビエンナーレ（2016）、パレ・ド・トーキョー（2015）、MoMA PS1（2014）など。

Born in the US in 1984. He specializes in the interdisciplinary fusion of art, fashion, and music. His recent exhibitions include the Berlin Biennale (2016), Palais de Tokyo (2015), and MoMA PS1 (2014).

B

bacilli
土・人々・食にフォーカスし、我々とそれらを繋ぐ役割として空間・環境を創造するアーティストコレクティブ。2014年より、南条嘉毅・James Jack・吉野祥太郎で「世界土協会」として活動してきたアーティストコレクティブが、2022年よりbacilliに改名。bacilli（バシライ）とは土に繁殖する生物の分類の一つ。菌や藍藻などの一般的な細菌、バクテリアを指す。

Artists James Jack, Yoshitaka Nanjo, Shotaro Yoshino form bacilli as care takers nurturing active spaces for living with dirt, people, food, microbes and spirits. Commencing in 2014 as "World Dirt Association", the artist collective has evolved into the form of "bacilli" (Bacillus genus of bacteria) growing exponentially from 2022. As their evolutionary path expands, symbiosis is diversified through interesting mutants discovered in the collaborative creative process.

マッシモ・バルトリーニ
Massimo Bartolini

1962年イタリア・チェチーナ生まれ、在住。1993年以降イタリア国内外で数多くの展覧会に参加している。 日本での主な展覧会にヨコハマトリエンナーレ（2011）、大地の芸術祭（新潟、2012）などがある。

Born in Cecina, Italy in 1962, and lives and works there. Since 1993, he has participated in numerous exhibitions in Italy and shows in other countries. In Japan, he has participated in the Yokohama Triennale 2011 and the Echigo-Tsumari Art Triennale (Niigata, 2012).

D

ニコラ・ダロ
Nicolas Darrot

1972年フランス生まれ、パリを拠点に活動。彫刻、インスタレーション、自動で動くオブジェなど幅広く制作している。科学、歴史、神話、文学などを参照し、科学者とも協働。近年の日本での展示に、大地の芸術祭（2018・2022）、北アルプス国際芸術祭（長野、2021）など。

Born in France in 1972. Currently based in Paris. Darrot's works cover a broad range, including sculptures, installations, and moving objects. Some of his works are collaborations with scientists that reference science, history, mythology, and literature. In Japan, his works have been exhibited at the Echigo-Tsumari Art Triennale (2018, 2022), and at the Northern Alps Art Festival 2020-2021 (Nagano, 2021).

DDMY STUDIO
2010年 にNakarin Rodput（1981〜） とAraya Suwan（1987〜）、Terdpong Pongjinda（1990〜）で設立したアートユニット。人々に新たな認識を与えることに焦点をあて、インタラクティブに作品へ参加する方法を模索している。

An art unit established in 2010 by Nakarin Rodput (1981-), Araya Suwan (1987-), and Terdpong Pongjinda (1990-). With the aim of providing people with a new perception, they search for ways to facilitate interactive participation in their work.

土井健史
Takefumi Doi

1974年滋賀県生まれ。2000年に大成建設株式会社に入社し、現在まで大型公共施設等の建築設計に携わる。代表作に神戸ポートミュージアム（2021）、金沢大学付属図書館（2005）など。2020年からアート制作を開始し、これまでに六甲ミーツ・アート 芸術散歩（2022）、中央線芸術祭（2022）で作品を発表。

Born in Shiga in 1974. He joined Taisei Corporation in 2000, and has been working on architectural planning for large-scale public facilities. His major works include Kobe Port Museum (2021) and Kanazawa University Library (2005). He began creating his own artwork in 2020, which he has exhibited at Rokko Meets Art (2022) and the Center Line Art Festival Tokyo (2022).

E

スタシス・エイドリゲヴィチウス
Stasys Eidrigevičius

1949年リトアニア生まれ、ポーランド·ワルシャワ在住。絵画、版画、挿絵、彫刻、写真、インスタレーションなど、多方面に活動を展開。2001年にリトアニア国民芸術賞、2019年にポーランド共和国功労勲章コマンダー十字章を受賞。

Born in the Republic of Lithuania, 1949. Currently based in Warsaw, Poland. He is active in many fields, including painting, printmaking, illustration, sculpture, photography, and installation. He received the Lithuanian National Prize for Culture and Arts in 2001, and the Commander's Cross of the Order of Merit of the Republic of Poland in 2019.

アイシャ・エルクメン
Ayşe Erkmen

1949年トルコ・イスタンブール生まれ、ベルリンとイスタンブールに在住。その土地の社会的・物理的な環境をもとに既存の状況に介入し、新たな解釈を与え、現実世界に働きかけるような作品を制作する。近年の恒久設置作品にイスタンブール・ビエンナーレでの《Golden Horn in Golden Horn》（2022）など。

Born in Istanbul, Turkey in 1949, and currently resides in Berlin and Istanbul. Based on the local social and physical environment, she enters into existing situations and establishes a new interpretation, creating work that approaches the real world. A recent permanent installation was *Golden Horn in Golden Horn* at the Istanbul Biennale (2022).

F

ムニール・ファトゥミ
Mounir Fatmi

1970年モロッコ・タンジール生まれ、タンジールとパリに在住。機能しなくなったメディアや消費社会崩壊の影響を受け、アーカイブと考古学の間に位置するような作品を多様な表現方法によって展開している。世界各地での個展・国際芸術祭・コレクション等多数。[瀬戸内] 2016、2019

Born in 1970 in Tangier, Morocco. Currently lives in Tangier and Paris. Influenced by the idea of dead media and the collapse of consumerist society, he develops artwork located somewhere between archive and archeology through various methods of expression. Not only has has held solo exhibitions all over the world, but he has also taken part in many international art festivals, and his work has been acquired by numerous collections. [Setouchi] 2016, 2019

フィオナ・ウォン・ライ・チンと香港アートセンターチーム（香港アートスクールの講師と卒業生）

Fiona Wong Lai Ching and HKAC team
(Teachers and alumni of Hong Kong Art School)

香港アートスクールの現・元講師と学生45名がアーティストとして参加。プロジェクトの発案者であるフィオナ・ウォン・ライ・チンは香港アートスクールの講師を務め、2015年に大地の芸術祭に参加したほか、2017年に香港芸術発展賞アーティスト・オブ・ザ・イヤーに選出された。

An artist group consisting of 45 current and former teachers and students of the Hong Kong Art School. Project initiator Fiona Wong Lai Ching is currently a Senior Lecturer at the Hong Kong Art School. She was an invited artist at the Echigo-Tsumari Art Triennale 2015, and was named Hong Kong Arts Development Award Artist of the Year in 2017.

藤野裕美子

Yumiko Fujino

1988年滋賀県生まれ。空家や廃村でのリサーチをもとに作品を構想。岩絵具や麻紙、箔などの日本画材を用い、絵画をベースとした作品を会場での展示形態も含めて構成している。[瀬戸内] 2019

Born in Shiga in 1988. She designs works based on research in vacant houses and abandoned villages. Using Japanese painting materials such as rock paint, hemp paper, and foil, her work, which is primarily painting, is composed in conjunction with the way it will be displayed at the venue. [Setouchi] 2019

藤原史江

Fumie Fujiwara

1976年愛知県生まれ。2000年名古屋芸術大学大学院美術研究科修了。主な展覧会に国際芸術コンペティション「アートオリンピア」(起雲閣、静岡、2022)、あいちトリエンナーレ関連企画「情の深みと浅さ」展（ヤマザキマザック美術館、愛知、2019)、「岡本太郎 現代芸術賞展」(川崎市岡本太郎美術館、神奈川、2019）など。

Born in Aichi in 1976. Graduated from Nagoya University of the Arts with a MFA in 2000. She has appeared in major exhibitions including, the *International Open Art Competition "Art Olympia"* (Kiunkaku, Shizuoka, 2022), the Aichi Triennale-related event *Depth and Shallowness of Emotion, Information, and Compassion* (The Yamazaki Mazak Museum of Art, Aichi, 2019) and *The Exhibition of the Taro Okamoto Award for Contemporary Art* (Taro Okamoto Museum of Art, Kawasaki, Kanagawa, 2019).

G

ケンデル・ギール

Kendell Geers

1968年南アフリカ生まれ、ベルギー在住。反アパルトヘイト運動での経験をもとに、物、材料、イメージ、サイン、シンボルを用いて、ミニマリストの規範をテロリアリズムと呼ぶものへと変化させ、インスタレーションやパフォーマンス、写真、彫刻作品を発表。日本での展覧会に大地の芸術祭（2000）など。

Born in South Africa in 1968, and lives in Belgium. Using objects, materials, images, signs and symbols from his experience in the anti-apartheid movement he created charged installations, performances, photographs and sculptures that shifted the Minimalist canon into what he termed TerroRealism. Mainly exhibitions in Japan includes the Echigo-Tsumari Art Triennale 2000.

ゲゲルボヨ

Gegerboyo

2017年に結成されたジャカルタ・インドネシアを拠点にするアーティストグループ。社会的、政治的な現象を日常的な主題を用いて批判する作品が多く、同時に、ジャワの文化や伝統、現代の都市空間を反映した作品も多く発表している。近年の展示にビエンナーレ・ジョグジャ（2022）など。

Formed in 2017, this artist unit is based in Jakarta, Indonesia. Their work criticizes social and political phenomena with everyday themes, and at the same time draws from Javanese culture, tradition, and contemporary urban spaces. Recent exhibitions include the Biennale Jogja (2022).

五所純子

Junko Gosho

1979年生まれ。文筆家。単著に『薬を食う女たち』(河出書房新社)、共著に『虐殺ソングブック remix』(河出書房新社)、『心が疲れたときに見る映画』(立東舎）など、映画・文芸を中心に多数執筆。

Born in 1979. This writer is the author of many books, primarily about movies and literature, including *Kusuri wo kuu onna-tachi* ("Women Who Eat Medicine", Kawade Shobo Shinsha), and is co-author of *Gyakusatsu Song Book Remix* ("Genocide Song Book Remix", Kawade Shobo Shinsha), and *Kokoro ga tsukareta toki ni miru eiga* ("Movie to Watch When Your Mind Is Tired", Rittorsha).

フリオ・ゴヤ

Julio Goya

1953年アルゼンチン・ブエノスアイレス生まれ。1985年に来日して以来、1988年のロダン大賞展 美ヶ原高原美術館賞をはじめ、多数の彫刻展で受賞。美術館や大学、市町庁舎など公共施設のパブリックコレクションを多数制作。[瀬戸内] 2019

Born in Buenos Aires, Argentina in 1953. Since his first visit to Japan in 1985 he has won many sculpture awards, including the 1988 Rodin Grand Prize and the Utsukushigahara Open Air Museum Prize, amongst others. He has produced many artworks that have been added to public collections, such as those of museums, universities, and official buildings. [Setouchi] 2019

GREEN SPACE

辰己耕造・辰己二朗の兄弟を中心に、大阪で活動する庭づくり集団。代々続く植木屋としての技術やイデオロギーに、現代のアートやファッション、音楽、ストリート、食などのカルチャーを融合させ、時代に合った「庭」を探求する。近年の庭のプロデュースに淺沼組名古屋支店改修プロジェクト（2021)、アゴーラ東京銀座（2020）など。

A group of gardeners based in Osaka, with brothers Kozo and Jiro Tatsumi at the center. In addition to the skills and ideology of plant retailers, they merge contemporary culture such as art, fashion, music, street culture, and food to pursue a garden that fits the time. Gardens they have recently produced include the Asanuma-gumi Branch Renovation Project (2021) and the Hotel Agora Tokyo Ginza (2020).

H

原倫太郎＋原游

Rintaro Hara + Yu Hara

インスタレーション作家の原倫太郎と画家の原游によるアーティスト・ユニット。子どもから大人まで遊べる体験型の作品を多く制作。近年の活動に北アルプス国際芸術祭（2017、2021)、大地の芸術祭（2022）など。[瀬戸内] 2019

The artist unit of installation artist Hara Rintaro and painter Hara Yu. They create artworks that can be enjoyed and experienced by all age groups. Their recent activities include the Northern Alps Art Festival (2017, 2021) and the Echigo-Tsunari Art Triennale (2022). [Setouchi] 2019

長谷川仁

Jin Hasegawa

1972年北海道生まれ。社会学やプロダクトデザインを学んだ後、社会とのつながり、自然とのつながりを皆で分かち合いたいとの想いで活動している。大地の芸術祭、いちはらアート × ミックス（千葉）などの芸術祭に参加。［瀬戸内］2016、2019

Born in Hokkaido in 1972. After studying sociology and industrial design, he began to create art with the desire to share connections with society and with nature. He has participated in the Echigo-Tsumari Art Triennale and Ichihara Art × Mix (Chiba). [Setouchi] 2016, 2019

Eri Hayashi

1990年鳥取県生まれ。現代のユートピアについて考えている。主な展覧会にGlass Works. European Glass Lives in Craft, Art and Industry（Chamber of Crafts、ミュンヘン、ドイツ、2021）、「glassjam」（Galerie erstererster、ベルリン、2021）など。

Born in Tottori in 1990. With a focus on a modern utopia, her major exhibitions include *Glass Works: European Glass Lives in Craft, Art, and Industry* (Chamber of Crafts, Munich, Germany, 2021) and *Glassjam* (Galerie Erstererster, Berlin, 2021)

日比野克彦

Katsuhiko Hibino

1958年岐阜県生まれ。国内外で個展・グループ展を多数開催するほか、パブリックアートや舞台美術などの多岐にわたる分野で活動。主なアートプロジェクトに「明後日朝顔プロジェクト」「the ASIA DAIHYO Project」「TURN」など。［瀬戸内］2010、2013、2016、2019

Born in Gifu in 1958. Hibino has had numerous group and individual exhibitions in Japan and abroad and participated in extensive projects including public arts and performing arts. Major art projects include the *Day After Tomorrow Morning Glory Project*, *The ASIA DAIHYO Project* and *TURN*. [Setouchi] 2010, 2013, 2016, 2019

ひびのこづえ

Kodue Hibino

静岡県生まれ。東京芸術大学美術学部デザイン科卒業。コスチューム・アーティストとして広告、演劇、ダンス、バレエ、映画、テレビ、展覧会など、多岐にわたる場で発表。1997年に作家名を内藤こづえより改める。NHK Eテレ「にほんごであそぼ」のセット衣装を担当中。野田秀樹作・演出の舞台衣装多数。［瀬戸内］2019

Born in Shizuoka. Graduated from Tokyo University of the Arts, Faculty of Fine Arts, Department of Design. A costume artist, active in a wide variety of fields, including advertising, theater, dance, ballet, film, television, and exhibitions. The artist changed name from Kodue Naito in 1997. Currently in charge of set costumes for a NHK E-television program *Let's play in Japanese*. Designed many costumes for stage productions written and directed by Hideki Noda. [Setouchi] 2019

保科豊巳

Toyomi Hoshina

1953年長野県生まれ。東京藝術大学美術学部絵画科教授、美術学部長、副学長を歴任し、現在東京藝術大学名誉教授、京都芸術大学特任教授。パリ・ビエンナーレ（1982）に出品をはじめ、スイス、ギリシア、台湾、フランス等の国際展に参加。［瀬戸内］2019

Born in Nagano in 1953. He has served as Professor in the painting course of the Department of Fine Arts at the Tokyo University of the Arts, as Director at the Department of Fine Arts, and as Vice President of the university, and is currently Professor Emeritus there, and a Specially Appointed Professor at the Kyoto University of the Arts. He submitted work to the Paris Biennale (1982), and has participated in many international exhibitions in Switzerland, Greece, Taiwan and France. [Setouchi] 2019

サマー・ファン&ツァイ・ジアイン

Summer Huang & Tsai, JiaYin

台湾のアーティスト・ユニット。地域社会に根ざしたテーマで制作に取り組み、地域の独自性を探求し、多様な素材を積極的に使ってその物語を作品にすることを実践してきた。地域に由来する作品を作る一方、住民たちにもその制作過程に参加してもらうことで、参加行為自体も作品の中に盛り込み、社会や環境に対しての関心を高めている。

An artist duo from Taiwan who work together on community-based projects. They enjoy working with local communities to explore their uniqueness, and turn their stories into artworks in many kinds of material. Their artwork is grounded in community, and they invite local people to join in the production process. The production itself is part of the work, and functions to raise interest in the community and the local environment they inhabit.

I

伊東敏光

Toshimitsu Ito

1959年千葉県生まれ。広島市立大学芸術学部教授。近年の主な展示にアートフェア東京（2016）、「伊東敏光展」（ギャラリーなつか、東京、2016）、KIAF SEOUL（ソウル、2015）など。［瀬戸内］2016、2019

Born in Chiba in 1959. Currently a professor in the Department of Fine Arts at Hiroshima City University. Recent exhibitions include Art Fair Tokyo 2016, *Toshimitsu Ito Exhibition* (Gallery Natsuka, Tokyo, 2016), and the KIAF SEOUL (COEX Hall, Seoul, 2015) and others. [Setouchi] 2016, 2019

岩沢兄弟

IWASAWA KYODAI

「モノ・コト・ヒトのおもしろたのしい関係」を合言葉に、人や組織の活動の足場となる拠点づくりを手がける兄弟クリエイターユニット。主な展覧会に「つくりかけラボ 06 岩沢兄弟 | キメラ遊物園」（千葉市美術館、2022）など。

This sibling creative unit takes “cool and fun connections between things, actions, and people” as their motto, and seeks to create footholds for the activities of people and organizations. Major exhibitions include *Tsukurikake Labo 06: Iwasawa Brothers / Chimera Playground* (Chiba City Museum of Art, 2022).

K

香川大学 × 瀬戸内の伝統生活文化・芸術発信プロジェクトチーム

Kagawa University × Setouchi Traditional Life Culture and Art Project

香川大学教育学部教授・若井健司を代表とする香川大学のプロジェクトチーム。代表の若井は地域の国際交流・文化事業に取り組み、2008〜2014年にニューヨークのオーケストラとの新説落語風オペラ（三遊亭好楽ほか出演）で演出・構成を担当。2018年四国初のオペラ海外公演（ブルガリア）に公演監督・演出・主演として貢献。

A project team from Kagawa University, represented by Kenji Wakai, a professor in the Faculty of Education. Wakai works on international exchange and cultural development of local communities, including directing and composing a new *rakugo*-style opera with an orchestra, which played in New York from 2008-2014 (starring *rakugo* comic storyteller, Sanyutei Koraku and others), and organizing overseas performances of Japanese opera in Bulgaria in 2018 – a first for a Shikoku-based company – contributing as performance director, stage director, and main actor.

金氏徹平
Teppei Kaneuji

1978年京都府生まれ。日常の素材をコラージュ的手法によって変容させ、新たなイメージを創出する作品を制作する。近年の個展に「金氏徹平 S.F. (Something Falling / Floating)」(市原湖畔美術館、千葉、2022)、「物!物!物!」(Click Ten Art Space、北京、2021)など。[瀬戸内] 2019

Born in Kyoto in 1978. He transforms everyday objects with collage-like techniques to create new images in his work. His recent exhibitions include *Teppei Kaneuji S.F. (Something Falling/Floating)* (Ichihara Lakeside Museum, Chiba, 2022) and *Mono! Mono! Mono!* (Click Ten Art Space, Beijing, 2021). [Setouchi] 2019

アレクサンドラ・コヴァレヴァ&佐藤敬/ KASA
Alexandra Kovaleva and Kei Sato / KASA

アレクサンドラ・コヴァレヴァと佐藤敬によって2019年にKASAを設立。東京とモスクワを拠点に活動する日露建築家ユニット。2021年にヴェネチア・ビエンナーレ国際建築展で特別表彰、2022年にU-35 建築家展で伊東豊雄賞を受賞。

Founded in 2019 by Alexandra Kovaleva and Kei Sato. This Japanese-Russian architect duo are based in Moscow and Tokyo respectively. They received a Special Mention at the International Architecture Exhibition of the Venice Biennale in 2021, and won the Toyo Ito Prize at the *Under 35 Architects Exhibition* in 2022.

片岡純也+岩竹理恵
Junya Kataoka + Rie Iwatake

キネティック作品と平面作品を組み合わせた空間構成が特徴的で、素材や図案の出会いに物語を生み個々の作品の題材がゆるやかに響きあう。近年の展覧会に「MOTアニュアル2020 透明な力たち」(東京都現代美術館、2020)、「BankART Under35」(BankART Studio NYK、神奈川、2017)など。

Their work is characterized by spatial structures combining kinetic installations and two-dimensional pieces, and encounters with materials and pattern design creating narratives. The themes of individual works gently echo one another. Recent exhibitions include *MOT Annual 2020: Transparent Powers* (Museum of Contemporary Art Tokyo, 2020), *BankART Under35* (BankART Studio NYK, Kanagawa, 2017).

川村亘平斎+石田多朗
Koheysai Kawamura + Taro Ishida

川村亘平斎
Koheysai Kawamura

インドネシア共和国・バリ島に2年間滞在し、影絵人形芝居「ワヤン・クリット」と伝統打楽器「ガムラン」を学ぶ。アジアを中心に世界各国で影絵と音楽のパフォーマンスを発表。日本各地でフィールドワークやワークショップを通じて、土地に残る物語を影絵作品として再生させる活動も高く評価されている。ガムランを使った音楽ユニット「滞空時間」主宰。

While living in Bali in Indonesia, he learned *wayang kulit* ("shadow puppetry") and *gamelan* (a traditional Indonesian percussion instrument), and he has performed with shadows and music in the countries of Asia and the world. His work regenerating the stories of local areas through fieldwork and workshops all over Japan and presenting them as shadow picture pieces has won a lot of plaudits. He also organized Taiku Jikan, a music group that uses *gamelan*.

石田多朗
Taro Ishida

東京藝術大学音楽学部在学中より森美術館、ポンピドゥーセンター、伊東豊雄建築ミュージアム、東京都美術館での展覧会、またユニクロをはじめとした企業広告等、環境や映像のための音楽を制作。2019年株式会社Drifterを設立。2020年よりアーティスト活動を開始。

While studying in the Music Department of the Tokyo University of the Arts, he created ambient sound (music) for exhibitions held in the Mori Museum, Centre Pompidou, Toyo Ito Museum of Architecture, Ehime, and Tokyo Metropolis Art Gallery, as well as working on the film music for advertisements of companies such as UNIQLO. In 2019 he set up the company Drifter, and he began his artistic activities in 2020.

川島大幸
Hiroyuki Kawashima

1987年静岡県浜松市生まれ。2016年に東京藝術大学大学院美術研究科博士後期課程美術専攻彫刻研究領域を修了。映像表現と彫刻を横断しながら、様々な素材を用いてヒトの視覚や知覚、光の現象に焦点を当てた作品を発表している。

Born in Hamamatsu, Shizuoka in 1987. Graduated from Tokyo University of the Arts with a PhD in 2016. His artworks focus on human vision, perception, and light phenomena using various materials while crossing the boundaries between visual expression used in film and sculpture that deals with materials.

川島猛とドリームフレンズ
Takeshi Kawashima + Dream Friends

1930年香川県高松市生まれ。1963年に渡米し、米国で53年間の作家活動を経て2016年に帰国。2017年に財団法人川島猛アートファクトリーを設立。ニューヨーク近代美術館、クライスラー美術館、大原美術館、東京国立近代美術館などに作品が収蔵されている。[瀬戸内] 2010、2013、2016、2019

Born in Kagawa in 1930. He moved to the USA in 1963, and after 53 years of artistic activity there, returned to Japan in 2016. He set up the Takeshi Kawashima Art Factory in 2017. His work is held in the collections of MoMA (New York), the Chrysler Museum of Art (Virginia, USA), the Ohara Museum of Art (Okayama), and The National Museum of Modern Art, Tokyo. [Setouchi] 2010, 2013, 2016, 2019

川添善行
Yoshiyuki Kawazoe

1979年神奈川県生まれ。東京大学生産技術研究所准教授。代表作に「東京大学総合図書館別館」、「変なホテル」、著書に『空間にこめられた意思をたどる』(幻冬舎)、『このまちに生きる』(彰国社)など。東京建築賞最優秀賞(2019)ほか受賞多数。

Born in Kanagawa in 1979. He is an Associate Professor in the Institute of Industrial Science at the University of Tokyo. His major architectural works include the University of Tokyo General Library Annex, and Hen na Hotel, and he has also written books such as *Tracing Back the Will in Space* (Gentosha), and *Living in this Town* (SHOKOKUSHA Publishing). He has received many awards, including The Tokyo Architecture Award Grand Prix (2019).

木ノ下歌舞伎
Kinoshita Kabuki

歴史的な文脈を踏まえつつ、現代における歌舞伎演目上演の可能性を発信する団体。あらゆる視点から歌舞伎にアプローチするため、主宰である木ノ下裕一が指針を示しながら、さまざまな演出家による作品を上演するというスタイルで京都を中心に2006年より活動を展開している。

An organization aiming to communicate the possibilities of *kabuki* theater performance in the contemporary era, based on its historical contexts. In order to approach *kabuki* from every possible angle, it retains the style of pieces led by different directors, while Yuichi Kinoshita sets its principles as the organizer. It has developed activities primarily from its base in Kyoto since 2006.

鴻池朋子

Tomoko Konoike

1960年秋田県生まれ。彫刻、手芸、声など様々なメディアを用いて動物との言語の境界を表現。地形や気候なども巻き込むサイトスペシフィックな展示も行い、芸術の根源的な問い直しを試みている。［瀬戸内］2019

Born in Akita in 1960. Using sculpture, hand-made craft art, and various other media, Konoike expresses the border of language between animals and people. She also creates site-specific exhibitions working with the geography and climate, fundamentally questioning the nature of art. [Setouchi] 2019

コシノジュンコ

Junko Koshino

大阪府岸和田市生まれ。ファッションデザイナーとして活躍し、世界各地でショーを開催。近年の活動に個展「コシノジュンコ　原点から現点」（大分県立美術館、2022）や、総合芸術舞台「NOH＋FASHION コシノジュンコと二十六世観世宗家 観世清和の世界」（観世能楽堂、東京、2020）など。［瀬戸内］2016、2019

Born in Kishiwada in Osaka. She became a famous fashion designer, holding shows across the globe. In recent years she has held *JUNKO KOSHINO "From the Origin to the Present"* (Oita Prefectural Art Museum, 2022) and a total art theater performance *NOH+FASHION – The World of Junko Koshino and the 26th Kanze Soke, Kiyokazu Kanze* (Kanze Noh Theater, Tokyo, 2020). [Setouchi] 2016, 2019

草間彌生

Yayoi Kusama

1929年長野県松本市生まれ。1957年に渡米、ネットペインティング、ソフトスカルプチャー、鏡や電飾を使ったインスタレーションやハプニングなど多様な展開を見せ、前衛芸術家としての地位を確立。2016年に文化勲章を受章。2017年、東京に草間彌生美術館開館。［瀬戸内］2010、2013、2016、2019

Born in Matsumoto, Nagano in 1929. After moving to the U.S. in 1957 she developed various forms of art such as net paintings and soft sculptures, as well as organizing happenings and developing installations that made use of mirrors and lights, establishing herself as an avant-garde artist. In 2016, she received Japan's Order of Culture. In 2017, the Yayoi Kusama Museum opened in Tokyo. [Setouchi] 2010, 2013, 2016, 2019

M

眞壁陸二

Rikuji Makabe

1971年石川県生まれ。壁画の手法を使ったサイトスペシフィックアートとキャンバスペインティングを並行して制作し国内外にて活動。断片状の樹や自然をモチーフに生と死、無と無限、混沌と秩序をテーマに制作を行う。［瀬戸内］2010、2013、2016、2019

Born in Ishikawa in 1971. Makabe began creating site-specific works employing mural painting techniques both in Japan and abroad, as well as producing paintings on canvas. Using fragmented motifs of trees and scenes from nature, he creates work that focuses on themes such as life and death, emptiness and eternity, chaos and order. [Setouchi] 2010, 2013, 2016, 2019

ままごと

mamagoto

2009年に劇作家・演出家の柴幸男を中心に旗揚げされた劇団。地域や場所に寄り添った作品を多数手掛け、近年は劇団員それぞれがプロジェクトを立ち上げるなど、団体や活動のあり方について常に模索を続けている。主な作品に「わが星」「わたしの星」「あゆみ」「朝がある」「ツアー」など。［瀬戸内］2013、2016、2019

A theater company set up around the playwright and director Yukio Shiba in 2009. They perform pieces that work alongside local areas and places, and continue to explore the way of being as a group activity – evident in the movement in recent years towards individual members of the company setting up their own projects. Major works include *Waga Hoshi* (My Star), *Watashi no Hoshi* (Star of Mine), *Ayumi*, *Asa ga Aru* (There is a Morning), and *Tour*. [Setouchi] 2013, 2016, 2019

三田村光土里

Midori Mitamura

1964年愛知県生まれ。フィールドワークから得られる自身と世界との接点を手がかりに、空間を「人が足を踏み入れられるドラマ」に見立て、文化的差異を越えて共感する私小説的な追憶や感傷を表現している。近年の主な展覧会に恵比寿映像祭（東京写真美術館、2022）など。

Born in Aichi in 1964. With the connection of self and world fostered through fieldwork as a starting point, she likens space to "a drama people can step into", and expresses memories and sentiments in a form of "I-novel", establishing an empathy that transcends cultural difference. She recently exhibited at the Yebisu Film Festival (Tokyo Metropolitan Museum of Photography, 2022).

三宅之功

Shiko Miyake

1976年大阪府生まれ、兵庫県在住。生命の「存在」を大きなテーマとし、多角的な表現から自然と人間の関係性を問う。 近年は植物を作品素材として組み込み、四季とともに変化する作品を制作。UBEビエンナーレ（現代日本彫刻展）（山口、2019）大賞受賞。

Born in Osaka in 1976, and lives in Hyogo. Miyake deals with the theme of "existence", questioning the relationship between nature and humans, with expression from multiple perspectives. Recently he has been incorporating plants into his work, creating art that changes with the seasons. He received the Grand Prize of the 28th UBE Biennale International Sculpture Competition (Yamaguchi, 2019).

森ナナ

Nana Mori

1990年福岡県生まれ。2016年東京藝術大学大学院美術研究科先端芸術表現専攻修了。書家の家庭に生まれ、幼少の頃より書に親しむ。以後、作品制作に並行し、ワークショップ、ライブパフォーマンス、講義などの活動も展開している。

Born in Fukuoka in 1990. Graduated from Tokyo University of the Arts with a MFA in 2016. Mori was born into the family of a calligrapher, and is familiar with the art along with her own creation. She also develops production activities, such as workshops, live performances, and lectures.

本山ひろ子

Hiroko Motoyama

1975年千葉県生まれ。鋳金技法「蝋型鋳造」という方法で身近な動物や植物をモチーフに立体作品を制作。堆肥舎を改装したアトリエでの制作の傍ら、養蜂により育てたツバチから採れる蜜蝋を精製し、作品作りに取り入れている。

Born in Chiba in 1975. Using the method of wax-mold casting, she creates three-dimensional work with familiar animal and plant motifs. While working in her atelier, a renovated compost depot, she also refines beewax from the bees she keeps, and incorporates it into her work.

村田のぞみ
Nozomi Murata

1994年奈良県生まれ。2019年京都精華大学大学院博士前期課程芸術専攻修了。細いステンレス線やドローイングの線を用いて、場や人の中に宿る時間・記憶を、空間・絵画の中に展開している。[瀬戸内] 2019

Born in Nara in 1994. Graduated from Kyoto Seika University with a MFA in 2019. Using thin stainless steel wires and drawing lines, she expresses the time and memories that reside within places and people through the space of her works and her painting. [Setouchi] 2019

村山悟郎
Goro Murayama

1983年東京都生まれ。博士（美術）。自己組織的なプロセスやパターンを、絵画やドローイングを通して表現。近年はAIのパターン認識／生成の感性的理解を探るなど、表現領域を拡張している。2010年にshiseido art egg 賞受賞。2015-17年、文化庁新進芸術家海外研修員としてウィーンにて滞在制作。[瀬戸内] 2019

Born in Tokyo in 1983. He has a PhD in Fine Arts. He expresses self-organizing processes and patterns through drawing and painting. In recent years he has expanded his field of expression by exploring AI's sensory understanding of pattern recognition and generation. He won the Shiseido Art Egg Award in 2010. Between 2015 and 2017, he stayed in Vienna to produce work through the Agency for Cultural Affairs Program of Overseas Study for Upcoming Artists. [Setouchi] 2019

エカテリーナ・ムロムツェワ
Ekaterina Muromtseva

1990年ロシア・モスクワ生まれ、アメリカ在住。哲学と舞台美術の背景を持ち、叙情的、コンセプチュアルな方法で個人的・集団的記憶を探る作品を制作。2020年にイノベーション賞を受賞した他、Forbes Russia主催の「次世代を担う30名の1人」に選ばれた。

Born in Moscow, Russia in 1990. Currently based in USA. She has a background in philosophy and set design and creates work that explores private and collective memory in lyrical and conceptual ways. She received a nomination for the Innovation Art Prize "New Generation", and was listed on *Forbes Russia: 30 under 30, Art.*

N

中里繪魯洲
Eros Nakazato

1954年東京都生まれ。金属を主な素材にした独創的な空間アートで、見るものを圧倒する作品を旺盛に制作。市川猿之助スーパー歌舞伎美術小道具や、吉田勘緑人形浄瑠璃舞台美術など、日本を代表する芸能文化の裏方としても活躍している。[瀬戸内] 2019

Born in Tokyo in 1954. Using metal as his main material, Nakazato actively creates unique spatial art that overwhelms the audience. He is also known for creative work for major Japanese performance artists, such as prop creation for *Ichikawa Ennosuke Super Kabuki*, and set design for *Yoshida Kanroku Ningyo Joruri*. [Setouchi] 2019

南条嘉毅
Yoshitaka Nanjo

1977年香川県生まれ。土地の風景や歴史を主題とした作品を多く展開し、2021年の奥能登国際芸術祭に際してオープンした劇場型民俗博物館「スズ・シアター・ミュージアム」では、アーティストとしての参加に加えキュレーション・演出を担当した。2022年度香川県文化芸術選奨受賞。[瀬戸内] 2019

Born in Kagawa in 1977. He has developed many pieces that deal with the landscape and history of certain locations, and theatrical folk museum *Suzu Theater Museum* opened at the Oku-Noto Triennale (Ishikawa, 2021), where he was not only a participating artist but was also involved in curation and direction. He received the 2022 Kagawa Prefecture Culture and Art Encouragement Prize. [Setouchi] 2019

直島女文楽
Naoshima Onna Bunraku

江戸時代から芸能が盛んだった天領・直島で、一度は下火になっていた文楽を女性3人が再興。1955年、香川県無形文化財に指定。現在も香川県無形民俗文化財として受け継がれている。[瀬戸内] 2010、2013、2016、2019

The performing arts have flourished on the island of Naoshima since the 17th century. Although Naoshima Onna Bunraku, a local form of puppetry performed by an all-female cast of puppeteers, almost died out at one point, it was revived by three women in the mid-20th century. In 1955, it was designated by the prefecture Intangible Cultural Asset and continues to be performed to this day. [Setouchi] 2010, 2013, 2016, 2019

西本喜美子
Kimiko Nishimoto

両親が農業指導のために渡ったブラジルで生まれる。女学校・美容学校を卒業後に美容院を始めるが、競輪選手となった2人の弟に憧れて22歳で女子競輪選手に転向し、数多くのレースを経験したのち27歳で引退。アートディレクターの長男・和民が主宰する写真講座「遊美塾」をきっかけに72歳からカメラを始め、その作品群は独特の個性を持つ。

Born in Brazil, where her parents had traveled to advice on agriculture. After graduating from a girl's school and a beauty college she opened her own hair salon. Inspired by two brothers who were professional *keirin* cyclists, she became a *keirin* racer herself, until retiring at the age of 27 after many races. Through the opportunity of the Yu-bi Juku photography class organized by her eldest son, Kazutami, she began photography at 72. Her work shows her unique personality.

西山美なコ
Minako Nishiyama

1965年兵庫県生まれ。1990年代より日本の消費社会の表層にひそむ「カワイイ」や「ピンク」、「装飾」といったテーマに着目し作品を制作。砂糖を使って王冠を作り時間の経過を観察する。主な展覧会に「フェミニズムズ／FEMINISMS」（金沢21世紀美術館、石川、2021）など。[瀬戸内] 2013

Born in Hyogo in 1965. Since the 1990s she has been focusing on themes such as "kawaii", "pink", and "decoration", which lie under the surface of Japanese consumerism. She makes crowns of sugar and observes the effect of time passing. Her major exhibitions include *FEMINISMS* (21st Century Museum of Contemporary Art, Kanazawa, Ishikawa, 2021). [Setouchi] 2013

ネオン・ダンス
Neon Dance

2003年にイギリス、ロンドンにて結成され、国際的に活動するダンスカンパニー。エイドリアン・ハートが芸術監督を務める。映像や音楽など、多様なコラボレーションをともなう作品を制作。小さな劇場空間から祝祭的空間までさまざまなサイズの空間でパフォーマンスを行っていることも特徴的である。[瀬戸内] 2019

Neon Dance is an internationally renowned company that embraces a diverse and digital population; a place where artists, partners and people can engage in experiences that are experimental and original, yet accessible to all. [Setouchi] 2019

O

尾花賢一
Kenichi Obana

1981 年群馬県生まれ。人々の営みや、伝承、土地の風景や歴史から生成したドローイングや彫刻を制作。虚構と現実を往来しながら物語を体感していく作品を探求している。2021 年 VOCA 賞受賞。

Born in Gunma in 1981. He creates drawings and sculptures formed out the life, traditions, landscapes, and history of locations. In his work he explores the experience of narrative, while moving back and forth between fiction and reality. He received VOCA Art Prize(2021).

Asaki Oda

神奈川県生まれ。幼少時代をブラジルのサンパウロで過ごす。舞台美術を学んだのち、アメリカのセレクトブランド Anthropologie にディスプレイアーティストとして参加。素材を深く学び、その新しい可能性を探求している。

Born in Kanagawa, and grew up in São Paulo, Brazil. After studying stage design, Asaki joined the US clothing brand Anthropologie as a display artist. Having worked deeply with material, he is pursuing its new potentials.

小谷元彦
Motohiko Odani

1972 年京都府生まれ、東京都在住。日本の仏像彫刻、近代彫刻の系譜への関心と意識を持ち、彫刻の新たな可能性を追求し続けている。ヴェネチア・ビエンナーレ日本館（2003）をはじめ、数多くの国際展に出品。近年の展示に Reborn Art Festival（宮城、2021-2022）など。

Born in Kyoto in 1972, and lives in Tokyo. With an interest in Japanese Buddhist sculpture and the history of modern sculpture, he continues to explore new potentials in the medium. He has participated in many international exhibitions including the Japan Pavilion at the Venice Biennale (2003). Recent exhibitions include Reborn Art Festival (Miyagi, 2021-2022).

大岩オスカール＋坂 茂
Oscar Oiwa + Shigeru Ban

大岩オスカール
Oscar Oiwa

1965 年ブラジル生まれ。日本人の両親のもとにサンパウロで生まれ育つ。物語性と社会風刺に満ちた世界観を、力強く表現するアーティスト。独特のユーモアと想像力で、サンパウロ、東京、ニューヨークと居を移しながら制作を続けている。[瀬戸内] 2010、2013、2016、2019

Born in Brazil in 1965, and grew up in São Paolo with his Japanese parents. He is an artist who powerfully expresses his way of viewing of the world, which is filled with narrative and social satire. With his distinctive sense of humor, he continues to produce while splitting his time between São Paolo, Tokyo, and New York. [Setouchi] 2010, 2013, 2016, 2019

坂 茂
Shigeru Ban

1957 年東京都生まれ。1995 年から国連難民高等弁務官事務所（UNHCR）コンサルタントを務め、同時に災害支援活動団体ボランタリー・アーキテクツ・ネットワーク (VAN) 設立。これまでに、プリツカー建築賞 (2014)、紫綬褒章 (2017)、マザー・テレサ社会正義賞（2017）など受賞。

Born in Tokyo in 1957. Ban has worked as a consultant for the United Nations High Commissioner for Refugees (UNHCR) since 1995, and also set up the Voluntary Architects' Network. He has received the Pritzker Architecture Prize (2014), the Purple Ribbon Medal (2017), and the Mother Teresa Memorial Award for Social Justice (2017).

大川友希
Yuki Okawa

1987 年千葉県生まれ。物に残る記憶や時間、思い出の断片を掘り下げ、繋げて、新たな時間のかたちとして再構成した立体作品やインスタレーション作品を制作。2021 年の奥能登国際芸術祭 では、スズ・シアター・ミュージアムにて地元市民とともに制作した作品を出展。

Born in Chiba in 1987. Okawa creates her sculptures and installations through examining and connecting memories retained by objects, time, and memory fragments, reconstructing them as a new form of time. She participated in the Oku-Noto Triennale in 2021, and created a work with local residents at the Suzu Theater Museum.

尾身大輔
Daisuke Omi

1992 年香川県生まれ。木彫を主な表現とし、小豆島の三都半島アートプロジェクトに継続して参加。近年の展示に「広島市立大学彫刻専攻教員作品展【彫刻の輪郭】」(2018)、「広島–対馬」展（2017）など。[瀬戸内] 2016

Born in Kagawa in 1992. His main mode of expression is wooden sculpture, and he has been a participant in the Mito Peninsular Art Project in Shodoshima for several years. His recent exhibitions include *Contours of Sculpture: Exhibition by Tutors of the Department of Sculpture at Hiroshima City University* (2018) and *Hiroshima-Tsushima* (2017). [Setouchi] 2016

大宮エリー
Ellie Omiya

1975 年大阪府生まれ。東京大学薬学部卒業。2012 年から絵画制作を始め、2016 年には個展「シンシアリー・ユアーズ―親愛なるあなたの大宮エリーより」（十和田市現代美術館、青森）を開催。2019 年に TICOLAT TAMURA（香港）、2022 年に Galerie Boulakia（ロンドン）の個展でも評価を受ける。

Born in Osaka in 1975. Graduated from Tokyo University's Faculty of Pharmaceutical Sciences. Began creating paintings in 2012 and held her first museum-based solo exhibition, *"Sincerely Yours"* (Towada Art Center, Aomori), in 2016. Her work has also gained recognition in solo exhibitions at Ticolat Tamura in Hong Kong, and Galerie Boulakia in London.

小沢剛
Tsuyoshi Ozawa

1965 年東京都生まれ・埼玉県在住。東京芸術大学先端芸術表現科教授。芸術選奨文部科学大臣賞受賞（2019）。近年の個展に「小沢剛展　オールリターン―百年たったら帰っておいで 百年たてばその意味わかる」（弘前れんが倉庫美術館、青森、2020）。[瀬戸内] 2013、2016

Born in Tokyo in 1965, and lives in Saitama. A professor in the department of Intermedia Arts at the Tokyo University of the Arts. He received the Minister of Education Award for Fine Arts in 2019. Held the recent solo exhibition *Tsuyoshi Ozawa All Return: Come back in a hundred years' time. After a hundred years you'll understand.* (Hirosaki Museum of Contemporary Art, Aomori, 2020). [Setouchi] 2013, 2016

P

ソピアップ・ピッチ
Sopheap Pich

1971 年カンボジア・バッタンバン生まれ。カンボジアを代表するアーティストで、国際展にも多数参加。近年の個展に「Sopheap Pich: Walking the Woods」（Tina Keng Gallery、台湾、2022）、「RECLAIM - 再生」（小山登美夫ギャラリー、東京、2019）など。

Born in Battambang, Cambodia in 1971. As a standout artist from

Cambodia, she has participated in many international exhibitions. Recent shows include *Sopheap Pich: Walking the Woods* (Tina Keng Gallery, Taipei, Taiwan, 2022) and *RECLAIM* (Tomio Koyama Gallery, Tokyo, 2019).

R

アリン・ルンジャーン
Arin Rungjang

1975年タイ・バンコク生まれ、在住。東南アジアの歴史、象徴、記憶と深く関わり、複数の時代、場所、言語にわたって、主要な物語とマイナーな物語を重ね合わせる作品で知られている。主な展覧会にドクメンタ（2017）、ヴェネチア・ビエンナーレ（2013）など。

Born in Bangkok, Thailand in 1975, and lives and works there. Known for work in which major and minor narratives overlap across multiple eras, locations, and languages. He is deeply connected with the history, symbols and memories of Southeast Asia. His major exhibitions include the Documenta (Kassel, Germany, 2017) and the Venice Biennale (2013).

S

三分一博志
Hiroshi Sambuichi

1968年山口県生まれ。故郷である瀬戸内を中心に建築が地球の一部となることをテーマに建築に取り組む。「犬島精錬所美術館」で日本建築大賞・日本建築学会賞作品賞を受賞。「直島ホール」で日本建築学会賞作品賞・村野藤吾賞を受賞。その他主な作品に「宮島弥山展望台」、「おりづるタワー」、システアナ美術館「The Water 展」（デンマーク）など。[瀬戸内] 2010、2013、2016、2019

Born in Yamaguchi in 1968. Based in his home region of the Setouchi. Sambuichi strives to create architecture that becomes part of the earth. He was awarded the Architectural Institute of Japan Design Prize and the Murano Togo Prize for Naoshima Hall, and both the Japan Institute of Architects Grand Prix and the Architectural Institute of Japan Design Prize for the Inujima Seirensho Art Museum. [Setouchi] 2010, 2013, 2016, 2019

クヴァイ・サムナン
Khvay Samnang

1982年カンボジア・スヴァイリエン州生まれ。プノンペン在住。ユーモラスで象徴的なジェスチャーを使い、伝統的文化儀式、歴史や現在の出来事について、新しい視点を提示する。近年の展示にバンコク・アート・ビエンナーレ（2020）、ドクメンタ（2017）など。

Born in Svay Rieng in 1982, Cambodia. Lives and works in Phnom Penh. His multidisciplinary practice offers new views on historical and current events and traditional cultural rituals using humorous, symbolic gestures. Recent major exhibitions include Bangkok Art Biennial (2020), Documenta (2017).

アナン・サプトト
Anang Saptoto

1982年インドネシア・ジョグジャカルタ生まれ。エコロジーと社会変革に焦点を当て、アートをツールとして問いかけ、新たな可能性を切り開くプロジェクトを展開。子どもや学校、障害者コミュニティ、社会組織とのコラボレーションも多数行う。2021年にSEED Awards from the Prince Claus Fund, Amsterdamを受賞。

Born in Yogyakarta, Indonesia in 1982. He focuses on ecology and social transformation, which he questions through art, developing projects that pioneer new potentials. He often collaborates with children, schools, disabled communities, and social organizations. In 2021, he was a SEED Awards recipient from The Prince Claus Fund, Amsterdam.

佐藤悠
Yu Sato

1985年三重県生まれ。祝祭、パフォーマンス、語り・話し、ワークショップ、鑑賞プログラム、レクチャー、絵画など、多様な表現方法を用いて、一見何もないところから、誰かが関わることで表現が紡がれてゆく現場を作る。

Born in Mie in 1985. Using diverse methods such as festivals, performances, talks, workshops, viewing programs, lectures, and paintings, he creates spaces where, from nothing at first glance, expressions are woven by participants.

切腹ピストルズ
Seppuku Pistols

「日本を江戸にせよ！」を合言葉に、野良着を身にまとい、和楽器を演奏し、地方探索と研究、映画、職人、農、寺子屋など、隊員それぞれの活動も展開する。1999年大晦日に東京で始動、現在日本各地に隊員10名程度で編成。太鼓や三味線、鉦、篠笛での演奏を披露し、港から集落を練り歩くなどのパフォーマンスを行う和楽器チーム。[瀬戸内] 2016、2019

With the slogan “Let’s recreate the Edo period in Japan!” and wearing old Japanese-style farm clothes, Seppuku Pistols play musical instruments around the nation. Each member plays a role in individual activities such as local exploration and research, movies, crafts, agriculture, and *terakoya* (private elementary schools). They perform on drums, *shamisen*, handbells and *shinobue* flutes, parading from the port to the village. [Setouchi] 2016, 2019

瀬戸内少女歌劇団
Setouchi Girl’s Theater

瀬戸内国際芸術祭2019の秋会期に「せとうち物語 —粟島編— 」と題し、粟島でツアー型演劇を開催。海員学校を中心に展開される物語を上演。芸術祭終了後も瀬戸内の物語を演劇化して上演する活動を継続している。[瀬戸内] 2019

In the autumn period of the Setouchi Triennale 2019, they held a tour-form performance entitled *The Story of Setouchi – Awashima ed. –* , and performed a story about the marine school. Even outside of the festival, the project continues, perform the narratives of Setouchi converted to theater. [Setouchi] 2019

新建築社 ＋ SUNAKI
Shinkenchiku-Sha + SUNAKI

新建築社
Shinkenchiku-Sha Co., Ltd.

1925年創業の建築専門の出版社。雑誌『新建築』や『a+u』などで国内外の建築を取り上げつつ、近年ではオンライン上で誌面アーカイブを検索・閲覧できる「新建築データ」や、場をメディアとして捉えた「新建築ハウスプロジェクト」などを行う。

Founded in 1925, Shinkenchiku-Sha is a publisher that specializes in architecture. In recent years, the company launched Shinkenchiku Data, which allows users to search and browse the magazine’s archives online, and the Shinkenchiku House Project, which views “place” as a form of media.

SUNAKI
建築家の砂山太一と木内俊克が主宰する共同体。2021年にヴェネチア・ビエンナーレ国際建築展の日本館展示に参加。

A community led by architects Taichi Sunayama and Toshikatsu Kiuchi. Participated in such projects as the Japan Pavilion for the International Architecture Exhibition at the Venice Biennale in 2021.

下道基行

Motoyuki Shitamichi

1978 年岡山県生まれ。フィールドワークをベースに、生活の中に埋没し忘却されかけている物事を、写真やインタビューなどの手法により編集することで視覚化する。作家活動と並行して「旅するリサーチラボラトリー」（2015 〜）などの様々な人々と協働するプロジェクトも多数実施。［瀬戸内］2019

Born in Okayama in 1978. Building on fieldwork, he composes elements that have sunk into oblivion in everyday life, using methods such as photography, events, and interviews to visualize their stories. Parallel to his artistic activities, he conducts many projects in collaboration with others, such as *Traveling Research Laboratory* (since 2015). [Setouchi] 2019

杉本博司

Hiroshi Sugimoto

1948年東京都生まれ。1974年よりニューヨーク在住。活動分野は、写真、彫刻、インスタレーション、演劇、建築、造園、執筆、料理と多岐に渡る。主な収蔵先にメトロポリタン美術館やポンピドゥー・センターなど。代表作に「海景」、「劇場」、「建築」シリーズがある。［瀬戸内］2010、2013、2016、2019

Born in Tokyo in 1948, and has lived in New York since 1974. His field of work encompasses photography, sculpture, installation, theater performance, and architecture, as well as garden design, writing and cooking. His work has been acquired by the Metropolitan Museum of Art (New York), and the Centre Pompidou, as well as many other famous museums. Sugimoto's major series include *Seascapes*, *Theaters*, and *Architecture*. [Setouchi] 2010, 2013, 2016, 2019

周防貴之

Takashi Suo

1980 年滋賀県生まれ。SANAA での勤務を経て 2015 年に SUO を設立。代表作に「S-House Museum」（岡山、2016）など。Chim↑Pom「ハッピースプリング」展（森美術館、東京、2022）をはじめ、現代アートの展覧会の展示構成等も手がける。

Born in Shiga in 1980. After working at SANAA (Sejima and Nishizawa and Associates), he established his own firm, SUO in 2015. His major works include S-House Museum (Okayama, 2016) and others. He also works on exhibition design for contemporary art shows such as *Chim↑Pom's Happy Spring* (Mori Art Museum, Tokyo, 2022).

鈴木健太郎

Kentaro Suzuki

1996 年京都府生まれ。対象となるものと、そのものを形づくる環境との関係に焦点を当てて作品を展開。近年は寺社に貼られた千社札をモチーフに「全く違う地域、時代を生きた人々の、存在や記憶の繋がり」をテーマに、サイアノタイプの技法を取り入れた独自の制作方法で表現を探求している。

Born in Kyoto in 1996. Suzuki focuses on the relationships between subjects and the environment that forms them, and develops them in his work. He has recently been using the motif of *senjafuda* found in temples and shrines to explore the theme of "connections of presence and memory between people living in completely different places and times", with his unique mode of production incorporating cyanotype.

ヘザー・B・スワン + ノンダ・カサリディス

Heather B. Swann + Nonda Katsalidis

1961 年オーストラリア生まれのアーティストであるヘザー・B・スワンと、1951 年ギリシャ生まれ・オーストラリア在住の建築家ノンダ・カサリディスによるユニット。これまでの共同プロジェクトに《Man Barrow Forkers》（2001 〜 2003）、《Gates of Hell》（2007）など。

An artist unit of Heather B. Swann, born in Australia in 1961, and architect Nonda Katsalidis, born in Greece in 1951 and lives in Australia. Their collaborative works to date include *Man Barrow Forkers* (2001-2003) and *Gates of Hell* (2007).

T

竹腰耕平

Kohei Takekoshi

1992 年岐阜県生まれ。主に木を扱い、自然との関わりを考えながら、制作活動を行う。2015 年に UBE ビエンナーレ（現代日本彫刻展）大賞受賞。［瀬戸内］2016、2019

Born in Gifu in 1992. Primarily uses wood, and creates artwork that considers relationships with nature. He won the Grand Prize of the UBE Biennale International Sculpture Competition in 2015. [Setouchi] 2016, 2019

田中圭介

Keisuke Tanaka

1976 年千葉県生まれ。木を主な素材とし、人間と自然の関係をテーマに制作。主な展示に「福島現代美術ビエンナーレ 2014 〜氣 Circulate 〜」、「CURRENTS」（The James Christie Room、香港、2014）など。［瀬戸内］2019

Born in Chiba in 1976. Tanaka uses wood as his primary medium and works with the theme of the relationship between humans and nature. His major exhibitions include the Fukushima Contemporary Art Biennale (2014), and *CURRENTS* (The James Christie Room, Hong Kong, 2014). [Setouchi] 2019

市民煎茶グループ 曙

Tea Ceremony Group Akebono

1985 年に香川県坂出市で結成（代表=大塚律子）。瀬戸内国際芸術祭では 2013 年から継続して茶会のイベントを開催してきた。2018 年にアメリカのサウサリートの小学生に煎茶パフォーマンスとワークショップ、2017 年にミャンマーのヤンゴンで交流茶会を開催するなど、海外での活動も行う。［瀬戸内］2013、2016、2019

Formed in 1985 in Sakaide, Kagawa under the leadership of Ritsuko Otsuka. It has held tea ceremony performances at every edition of the Setouchi Triennale since 2013. It is active overseas as well, demonstrated by a green tea ceremony and workshop with elementary school children in Sausalito, USA in 2018, and a ceremony conducted in Yangon, Myanmar in 2017. [Setouchi] 2013, 2016, 2019

鐵羅佑

Yuu Tetsura

1998 年愛知県生まれ。溶接を主な制作手法とし、本来金属同士を接着する際に生まれるビード（溶接痕）を鉄の新しい表情として展開。また、自身が行う舞台表現の経験から、劇的な作品展開を研究している。

Born in Aichi in 1998. Metal bonding is his main mode of production, and he uses the weld beads created in the combination of metals as a new expression in iron. From the experience of his own theater performances, he explores the development of drama in his work.

レオニート・チシコフ

Leonid Tishkov

1953 年旧ソ連生まれ。世界各国で展開するプロジェクト「僕の月」や、絵本『かぜをひいたおつきさま』（徳間書店、2014）など、月をテーマにした作品に継続して取り組む。医学・文学など多分野に見識を持ち、瀬戸内国際芸術祭では沙弥島にゆかりある柿本人麻呂の和歌を2019年から作品に引用してきた。［瀬戸内］2019

Born in the former Soviet Union in 1953. He has continuously worked with the theme of the moon, including the world-wide project *Private Moon*, and the picture book *Moon with Catching a Cold* (Tokuma Shoten Publishing). He has deep knowledge in medicine, literature, and other fields, as seen at the Setouchi Triennale in his quote of a *waka* poem by Kakinomoto no Hitomaro, who is known to be related to Shamijima. [Setouchi] 2019

冨安由真
Yuma Tomiyasu

1983 年広島県生まれ。不可視のものや現実と非現実の狭間を、没入型のインスタレーションや絵画、立体など多様なメディアによって表現する。近年は金沢 21 世紀美術館（2021 ～ 2022）、KAAT 神奈川芸術劇場（2021）で個展を開催したほか、いちはらアート × ミックス（2021）などグループ展にも多数参加。

Born in Hiroshima in 1983. She expresses the invisible, or the gap between reality and unreality, via various media including immersive installations, paintings, and three-dimensional pieces. In recent years she has held solo exhibitions in the 21st Century Museum of Contemporary Art, Kanazawa (2021-2022), and KAAT Kanagawa Arts Theatre (2021), as well as participating in many group shows, such as Ichihara Art x Mix (2021).

内田晴之
Haruyuki Uchida

1952 年静岡県生まれ、京都府在住。金属と磁石を主な素材とし、重力と浮遊感の共存する彫刻を多く手がける。近年は、土地の歴史に根ざした継続的な作品により、表現の幅を広げる。1984 年の日本国際美術展、1997 年の現代日本彫刻展で大賞を受賞。［瀬戸内］2010、2013、2016、2019

Born in Shizuoka in 1952. Focuses on metals and magnets as primary materials, and creates many sculptures with coexisting elements of gravity and buoyancy. Broadened his range of expression in recent years through continuous works rooted in the history of the land. He received the Grand Prize at The Japan International Art Exhibition (1984) and the Grand Prize at Contemporary Japanese Sculpture Exhibition (1997). [Setouchi] 2010, 2013, 2016, 2019

ワン・テユ［王德瑜］
Wang Te-yu

1970 年台湾生まれ。シンプルなメディアで空間の存在感を探り、その空間における人間の存在形態や状況を考察する作家。身体感覚を視覚体験に置き換えながら、空間をテーマに研究し続けている。主な展覧会に「No.101 Wang Te-Yu Solo Exhibition」（台東美術館、台湾、2020）など。

Born in Taiwan in 1970. She explores presence in a space though simple media, and theorizes the existence, form, and status of the human. She has continuously worked on the theme of space, letting the body's sensory experience take precedence over visual experience. Her major exhibitions include *No.101 Wang Te-Yu Solo Exhibition* (Taitung Art Museum, Taiwan, 2020).

ワン・ウェンチー［王文志］
Wang Wen Chih

1959 年台湾生まれ。竹を使った巨大な建築物をつくることで知られ、瀬戸内国際芸術祭第 1 回から関わりの深いアーティスト。近年の展示に Taoyuan Land Art Festival（桃園、台湾、2020）、Woodford Art Festival（オーストラリア、2016）など。［瀬戸内］2010、2013、2016、2019

Born in Taiwan in 1959. Wang is known for his huge bamboo structures and has been closely associated with the Setouchi Triennale since its inception. Recent exhibitions include Taoyuan Land Art Festival (Taiwan, 2020), and Woodford Art Festival (Australia, 2016). [Setouchi] 2010, 2013, 2016, 2019

渡辺篤（アイムヒア プロジェクト）
Watanabe Atsushi (I'm here project)

1978 年神奈川県生まれ。近年は、自身も経験者である「ひきこもり」にまつわる関係性の課題について、当事者との協働企画を多数実施。近年のプロジェクト展に「修復のモニュメント」（BankART SILK、神奈川、2020）など。

Born in Kanagawa in 1978. In recent years, he has worked on numerous projects that used the internet to get the cooperation of emotionally scarred people, in order to investigate hidden social issues, as well as his own experiences as a *hikikomori*. Recent project exhibitions include *Monument of Recovery* (BankART SILK, Kanagawa, 2020).

チャールズ・ウォーゼン
Charles Worthen

1958 年アメリカ・ボストン生まれ。広島市立大学芸術学部教授。現代の新しい素材を用いたユーモラスなオブジェを発表。近年の展示に「チャールズ・ウォーゼン みて さわって つくって beyond my fingertips」（アートギャラリーミヤウチ、広島、2022）など。［瀬戸内］2016

Born in Boston, USA in 1958. Currently a professor in the Department of Fine Arts at Hiroshima City University. He creates humorous objects with new materials. His recent exhibitions include *Beyond My Fingertips* (Art Gallery Miyauchi, Hiroshima, 2022). [Setouchi] 2016

シャン・ヤン［向阳］
Xiang Yang

1967 年中国生まれ、中国とアメリカを拠点に活動。中国の伝統である哲学や宗教思想、美術、工芸を、西洋で出会った新しい素材、形態、批判的思考と合成した作品を制作する。近年の展示に個展「Encounter」（WF セントラル、北京、2021）、Art at Fuliang（浮梁県寒渓村、中国、2021）など。［瀬戸内］2019

Born in China in 1967, and based in China and the USA. He creates work that combines traditional Chinese philosophy, religious theory, and arts and crafts with new materials, forms, and critical thinking that she encountered in the West. Recent exhibitions include *Encounter* (WF Central, Beijing, 2021), Art at Fuliang (Fuliang County, China, 2021). [Setouchi] 2019

山田悠
Haruka Yamada

1986 年神奈川県生まれ。変動する都市環境の中で自らの行為をどのように作品として成立させることが出来るかについて関心を持ち、都市、自然、人間という要素を相対的に捉え、ものごとの関係を測り直す。そのプロセスを鑑賞者が再体験出来る方法を模索している。

Born in Kanagawa in 1986. Yamada is interested in how she can establish her own actions as artwork within urban environments that are always in flux, and in the attempt to grasp elements such as urban spaces, nature, and humans in relativity, and re-evaluate the relationships between things. She explores the ways that the audience re-experiences her process.

山田紗子
Suzuko Yamada

1984 年東京都生まれ。藤本壮介建築設計事務所の勤務を経て、2013 年に山田紗子建築設計事務所を設立。主な受賞に Under 35 Architects exhibition 2020 Gold Medal、2022 年日本建築学会作品選集新人賞など。[瀬戸内] 2013、2016、2019

Born in Tokyo in 1984. After Working at Sou Fujimoto Architects, she established own practice in 2013. Major awards include Under 35 Architects exhibition 2020 Gold Medal, and AIJ Young Architect Award for Selected Architectural Designs 2022. [Setouchi] 2013, 2016, 2019

山川冬樹
Fuyuki Yamakawa

1973 年イギリス生まれ。身体や声と社会や環境の関わりを探求しながら、美術、音楽、舞台芸術の境界を超えて活動。代表作として個とマスメディアの記憶を巡るインスタレーション《The Voice-over》(2008、東京都現代美術館蔵) など。己の身体や声を駆使したサウンド・パフォーマンスを得意とし、これまでに 16 カ国で公演を行う。[瀬戸内] 2016、2019

Born in the UK in 1973. While exploring how physicality and voices form relationships with society and environment, he conducts activities that transcend the borders between art, music, and theater performance. He is known for the installation work *The Voice-over* (2008, the collection of the Museum of Contemporary Art, Tokyo), which deals with the memory of individuals and mass media. He favors sound performance using his own body and voice, and has performed in 16 countries. [Setouchi] 2016, 2019

山下茜里
Akari Yamashita

1997 年大阪府生まれ。自分が「人間」であるということへの執着、生き物としての「ヒト」への強い興味から、「人間」そのものの表現を試みている。

Born in Osaka in 1997. With the feeling of attachment from being "human" and a strong interest in "mankind" as a creature, she attempts to express what a "human" is.

柳建太郎
Kentaro Yanagi

1969 年東京都生まれ。ガラス造形作家、漁師。2005 年に個人工房「アトリエ炎」を構え作家活動を始める。思わず笑ってしまうような作品が多いが、社会性や、愛、夢などのメッセージが、精度の高い技術で表現されている。

Born in Tokyo in 1969. Glass artist and fisherman. In 2005, he set up a private atelier, Atelier *Honoo* (Flame), and began his creative career. Many of his pieces make people smile, yet his social consciousness, message of love, and dreams are all expressed with a high degree of precision.

やさしい美術プロジェクト
Art for the Hospital Project, Yasashii Bijutsu

2002 年から病院とアーティストとの協働で「安らぎのある医療環境」「地域に開かれた病院」を創出するやさしい美術プロジェクト。国立療養所大島青松園での取り組み〔つながりの家〕で、2013 年度グッドデザイン賞を受賞。ディレクターは髙橋伸行。[瀬戸内] 2010、2013、2016、2019

Began as a hospital project undertaken by a cooperative work group consisting of hospital staff, artists, and designers to create a medical environment where people can feel at ease in a community-based open hospital. *Tsunagari no Ie* at the National Sanatorium Oshima Seishoen won a 2013 Good Design Award. The Director is Nobuyuki Takahashi. [Setouchi] 2010, 2013, 2016, 2019

イ・スーキュン [李秀京]
Yeesookyung

1963 年韓国・ソウル生まれ。近年の個展に「I am not the only one but many」(Massimo De Carlo、ロンドン、2020) がある。ヴェネチア・ビエンナーレ (2017)、シドニー・ビエンナーレ (2012)、大地の芸術祭 (2006) などの国際展に多数参加。

Born in Seoul, Korea in 1963. Recent solo exhibitions include *I am not the only one but many* (Massimo De Carlo, London, 2020). She has participated in the Venice Biennale (2017), Biennale of Sydney (2012), and the Echigo-Tsumari Art Triennale (2006) amongst other international exhibitions.

よるしるべ
Yorushirube

2004 年から香川県観音寺市の柳町通り商店街を中心にアートを通した場づくりを展開。2005 年から「ドピカーン観音寺 〜 創ろう！街のアートステーション」を開始。アーティストインレジデンスや交流イベントのほか、2011 年からは新たな街歩きコンテンツとして「よるしるべ」を実施し、2013 年には瀬戸内国際芸術祭の公式イベントとして秋会期に展開した。[瀬戸内] 2013、2016

Since 2004, it has developed place-defining art in the town around the Yanagimachi shopping street near Kan-onji, Kagawa. In 2005, it began *Dropika-n Kan-onji – Let's Make an Art Station in Town*, conducting artist in residence programs and other exchange events. In 2011, it introduced Yorushirube as a new town walking event, and in 2013, this was developed in the autumn period as an official event of the Setouchi Triennale. [Setouchi] 2013, 2016

作家索引

SETOUCHI TRIENNALE 2022

瀬戸内国際芸術祭 2022

2023 年 5 月 19 日発行

[監修]
北川フラム／瀬戸内国際芸術祭実行委員会

[編集・アートディレクション]
佐藤壮生［裸足出版］

[編集]
岡本濃、野村翠［株式会社アートフロントギャラリー］
甘利彩子［NPO 法人瀬戸内こえびネットワーク］
江口奈緒［現代企画室］

[執筆・編集協力]
株式会社アートフロントギャラリー
NPO 法人瀬戸内こえびネットワーク
公益財団法人 福武財団
株式会社ベネッセホールディングス

[表紙デザイン監修]
原研哉［日本デザインセンター］

[DTP]
山猫屋

[英訳]
トライベクトル株式会社
ギレットサイモン、ギレット麻由子

[印刷・製本]
藤原印刷株式会社

[発行]
株式会社現代企画室
〒 150-0033　東京都渋谷区猿楽町 29-18
ヒルサイドテラス A-8
tel. 03-3461-5082 fax. 03-3461-5083
http://www.jca.apc.org/gendai/

Publication: May 19th, 2023

Supervisor:
Fram Kitagawa
Setouchi Triennale Executive Committee

Art Director:
Sosei Sato (Hadashibooks)

Editors:
Koi Okamoto, Midori Nomura (Art Front Gallery Co., Ltd.)
Ayako Amari (Setouchi Koebi Network)
Nao Eguchi (Gendaikikakushitsu Publishers)

Art Front Gallery Co., Ltd.
Setouchi Koebi Network
Fukutake Foundation
Benesse Holdings, Inc.

Cover Design Supervisor:
Kenya Hara (Nippon Design Center, Inc.)

DTP:
Yamanekoya

Translation:
Trivector Co., Ltd.
Simon and Mayuko Gillett

Printer:
Fujiwara Printing Co., Ltd.

Publisher:
Gendaikikakushitsu Publishers
Hillside Terrace A-8, 29-18 Sarugaku-cho
Shibuya-ku, Tokyo, 150-0033 Japan
tel. 03-3461-5082 fax. 03-3461-5083
http://www.jca.apc.org/gendai/

ISBN 978-4-7738-2303-5 C0070 ¥3000E
Printed in Japan

©2023 Setouchi Triennale Executive Committee /
Gendaikikakushitsu Publishers